FROM SELMA TO APPOMATTOX:
THE HISTORY OF THE JEFF DAVIS ARTILLERY

by

LAWRENCE R. LABODA

WHITE MANE PUBLISHING COMPANY, INC.

This White Mane Publishing Company, Inc. publication
was printed by
Beidel Printing House, Inc.
63 West Burd Street
Shippensburg, PA 17257 USA

In respect for the scholarship contained herein, the acid-free paper used in this book meets the guidelines for permanence and durability of the Committee on Production Guidelines for Book Longevity of the Council on Library Resources.

For a complete list of available publications
please write
White Mane Publishing Company, Inc.
P.O. Box 152
Shippensburg, PA 17257 USA

Library of Congress Cataloging-in-Publication Data

Laboda, Lawrence R.
    From Selma to Appomattox : the history of the Jeff Davis Artillery
  / by Lawrence R. Laboda.
        p.   cm.
    Includes bibliographical references and index.
    ISBN 0-942597-80-X (alk. Paper) : $30.00
    1. Confederate States of America. Army of Northern Virginia.
    Jeff Davis Artillery. 2. United States--History--Civil War,
    1861-1865--Regimental histories. 3. United States--History--Civil
    War, 1861-1865--Artillery operations. I. Title.
    E547.J4L33   1994
    973.7'455--dc20   94-41925
                                                                CIP

PRINTED IN THE UNITED STATES OF AMERICA

DEDICATED
TO THE MEMORY OF MY BROTHER, RON,
AND TO THOSE GALLANT MEN WHO FOUGHT
FOR THE CONFEDERACY AS MEMBERS OF THE
JEFF DAVIS MOUNTED ARTILLERY

LIST OF PHOTOGRAPHS

PAGE

Private John Purifoy 3

Lieutenant Robert F. Beckham 7

Lieutenant General Daniel H. Hill 18

Colonel James W. Bondurant 19

Brigadier General Samuel Garland, Jr. 25

Mechanicsville Road Bridge 30

Bondurant's Position at Cold Harbor (June 27, 1862) 37

Bondurant's First Position at Sharpsburg (1:00 P.M.) 60

Bondurant's Second Position at Sharpsburg (4:00 P.M.) 60

Bondurant's Position at Fredericksburg (December 13, 1862) 71

Colonel Thomas H. Carter 84

Proposed Flag Design 91

Major General Robert E. Rodes 103

Chancellorsville – Jackson's Flank March (May 2, 1863) 109

Chancellorsville – Fairview 115

Lieutenant General Richard S. Ewell 122

Gettysburg – House of Samuel Cobean 134

Gettysburg – Cobean farm 135

Gettysburg – Oak Hill 139

Brigadier General Armistead Lindsay Long 165

Private Matthew Tucker 213

Fort Delaware Prison 223

Lieutenant Colonel Robert A. Hardaway 230

Lieutenant Colonel Wilfred E. Cutshaw 233

Elmira Prison, Elmira, New York 266

Sergeant John Fox Maull 268

Private Washington B. Traweek 271

Private John P. Putegnat 272

Elmira Prison Escapees 274

Reese's Oath of Allegiance 315

LIST OF MAPS

PAGE

Centreville, Virginia – 1861 10

Campsites of the Jeff Davis Artillery near Centreville, Va. 11

Route followed by Jeff Davis Artillery from Yorktown 21

Attack at Seven Pines – May 31, 1862 24

Route followed by Jeff Davis Artillery – June 27, 1862 34

Advance at Cold Harbor; position of Jeff Davis Artillery – June 27, 1862 . 36

Battle of Fox's Gap – September 14, 1862 48

Position occupied by Jeff Davis Artillery at 12:00 noon; Antietam 55

Alabama Battery's Position at 4:00 p.m.; Antietam 59

Afternoon Action, December 13, 1862; Fredericksburg 72

Battery's Winter Quarters – 1862-1863 81

Positions Occupied by Jeff Davis Artillery – May 2-3, 1863 117

Position of Alabama Battery – July 2, 1863 – 9:00 a.m. 142

Jeff Davis Artillery at Gettysburg; William J. Reese 147

Confederate Retreat From Gettysburg – July 4-14, 1863 153

Positions Occupied by Jeff Davis Artillery – October-November 1863 174

Movements of Jeff Davis Artillery – December 1863-April 1864 182

Battle of the Wilderness – Movements of May 4, 1864 194

Spotsylvania – May 10, 1864 – Page's Battalion in Reserve 208

Spotsylvania – Page is Ordered Forward – Morning of May 12, 1864 212

Positions (approximate) to be Occupied by Page's Battalion on the

    Morning of May 12, 1864 216

Patrolling the James River 240

Battle of Cedar Creek – October 19, 1864 258

Withdrawal of Fry's Battery – October 19, 1864 262

Fort Clifton and Vicinity 282

Sailor's Creek – April 6, 1865 300

Morning of April 9, 1865 – Prior to Attack 309

TABLE OF CONTENTS

CHAPTER   PAGE

LIST OF PHOTOGRAPHS   iv

LIST OF MAPS   v

INTRODUCTION   xi

I   AN ARTILLERY COMPANY IS BORN   1

II   A DIFFICULT WINTER   9

III   FINALLY, THE BATTERY MEETS THE YANKEES   17

IV   A NEW COMMANDER, A NEW ARMY,
A TASTE OF HELL!   28

V   CRISIS IN MARYLAND
     PART I –
     A Close Call On The Mountain   41
     PART II –
     Another Desperate Fight For Bondurant's Men   53

VI   GUNBOATS AND ARTILLERY   63

VII   A WINTER OF CHANGE   80

VIII   THE CHANCELLORSVILLE CAMPAIGN
     PART I –
     Maneuvering Along The Rappahannock   95
     PART II –
     The Battle Nears And The Artillery Moves North   99
     PART III –
     The Confederates Take To The Offensive   105

CHAPTER   PAGE

IX   ONCE AGAIN, THE SOUTHERN ARMY PUSHES NORTH
          PART I -
          Reorganization And The Start Of A New Campaign   121
          PART II -
          The Opposing Forces Collide   132
          PART III -
          Two More Days of Battle:
              The Alabamians Wait...Then Fight   141
          PART IV -
          The Retreat   152

X   ATTEMPTING TO BEAT THE ODDS   163

XI   MORE CHANGES WITHIN THE ORGANIZATION   181

XII   TWO MAJOR BATTLES; TWO DIFFERENT ROLES
          PART I -
          Much Waiting In The Wilderness   193
          PART II -
          An Urgent Appeal, Then Catastrophe And Nearly
              The End Of An Organization   203

XIII   ANOTHER TRANSFER AS THE BATTLE LINES
          MOVE SOUTH   224

XIV   FROM ONE THEATER OF OPERATIONS TO ANOTHER
          PART I -
          Much Action On The Northside   238
          PART II -
          A Month Spent Protecting 'The Valley'   247
          PART III -
          Yet Another Transfer Following More Action
              In The East And To The West   251

XV   NEWS, BOTH BAD AND GOOD
          PART I -
          A Bold Design, Fine Execution, But Then...Catastrophe   256
          PART II -
          The Grand Exodus From Elmira   266

CHAPTER		PAGE

XVI	THE FINAL CAMPAIGNS OF 1864 AND NEW ATTEMPTS AT REORGANIZATION *PART I –* Continuing to Combat The Enemy On Two Fronts	275
	PART II – A Most Difficult And Frustrating Winter	280
XVII	THE FINAL CAMPAIGN	292
	APPENDIX A *THE STORY OF "MOLLIE GLASS"*	318
	APPENDIX B *DOCUMENTS, LETTERS, MISC. ARTICLES, ETC.*	320
	APPENDIX C *ROSTER OF THE JEFF DAVIS ALABAMA ARTILLERY*	321
	ENDNOTES	350
	BIBLIOGRAPHY	367
	INDEX	371

INTRODUCTION

This is the story of one of the more illustrious, though not well-publicized, light artillery companies which fought on the side of the Confederacy during the Civil War. The Jeff Davis Artillery had its origins in Dallas County, specifically the Selma, Alabama area, but would only spend a comparatively short time on the soil of its home state. Within two months, the battery was on its way to Virginia in order to join General Joseph E. Johnston's Army of the Potomac. Then, during the more than three and a half years that followed, the Alabamians engaged the enemy on the far-off battlefields of Virginia, Maryland and Pennsylvania. The battery, or at least parts of it, would also be attached to two different armies during the war, most of the time as part of the Artillery Corps of the Army of Northern Virginia.

Though the men of the Jeff Davis Artillery found themselves under many different commanders, it was when First Lieutenant Robert F. Beckham, Captain James W. Bondurant and Captain William J. Reese led, that the battery matured as a military organization, and provided its most efficient service on the field of battle. That is not to say, however, when unfortunate circumstances caused the company to be divided between two commands later in the war, that the fine work of the Alabama battery was not continued in the engagements that followed. A prime example occurred at the battle of Cedar Creek, where the Alabamians showed the same spirit and determination as they had when the battery was at full strength. In the face of adversity, the company, nevertheless, continued to fight on in a courageous manner.

On more than one occasion, the Jeff Davis Artillery received praise from the Confederate high command, including General Robert E. Lee himself. Within the Confederate Army, the reputation of the battery

xi

was no doubt one of the best, but after the fighting was done, the war record of this particular company, except for a rare article or mention in an obituary, never received proper recognition. It is only fitting, therefore, that the entire story of the gallant Alabamians finally be told.

But what of my interest of the Jeff Davis Artillery. Up until the fall of 1983, the existence of this fighting unit was, for all intents and purposes, virtually unknown to me. I may have encountered the name of the battery, or its commander, in books, but those brief mentions held little significance at the time. Then, while at a collector's show in Virginia, a dealer told this writer, who is an avid Civil War enthusiast, of the availability of a Confederate artillery officer's uniform coat. I went to examine the coat the following day, and after learning its complete history, bought it. As it turned out, the coat had been worn by an officer of the Jeff Davis Alabama Artillery. Afterwards, I searched for anything that could be found about the battery. No book had ever been published about that command, but there were invaluable individual and company records in the State of Alabama's Department of Archives and History and the National Archives in Washington, D.C., not to mention various libraries and other institutions. As I gathered that information on the Jeff Davis Artillery, I decided to write a book about that Alabama battery.

After more than ten years of research, it has all come together in the volume that now sits before you. Hopefully, it will provide you, the reader, with both an enjoyable and informative look into the service record of what I feel was one of the more efficient fighting units that took part in the Civil War.

It should be noted that a good deal of the information used in the book was gleaned from the manuscript, entitled *Jeff Davis Artillery, History of,* which was written by Judge John Purifoy and was entered in the records in 1904, but was never published. Mr. Purifoy was a member of the battery, and his writings provided the most complete picture, so far, of the events both on and off the field of battle. He also contributed a number of articles to the *Confederate Veteran* which have proved most helpful.

Moreover, it will quickly become evident as the reader goes through passages and quotes taken from Mr. Purifoy's works, and other sources, that they were reproduced here just as they appear in the original, with no attempt to make note of misspelled words or missing punctuation. This, I believe, makes for easier reading, as opposed to quotes infiltrated by the distracting "*sic.*"

On yet another note, I have also attempted to weave the activities of the Jeff Davis Artillery, where possible, into the various battles and campaigns. There will, however, be times when the Alabama battery receives little mention, and that is because I could not find anything of significance concerning the company's actions during the fighting, or movements of the opposing armies. I felt it was better to continue the narrative so that the reader would not lose sight of what was happening around the battery.

During this project, I have received invaluable assistance from a number of individuals and organizations, and it is only proper that they receive recognition. First of all, I would like to thank Mrs. Marie V. Melchiori, without whose assistance at the National Archives, I would never have been able to make the kind of progress I made. Then there is Mrs. Eleanor Falkenberry, whose record searches in Selma, Alabama turned up important letters and other information about the Jeff Davis Artillery. In addition, I'm grateful to Mrs. Miriam C. Jones, of Montgomery, Alabama for her work at the State Archives.

At the same time, I would be remiss if I did not thank those people connected with the National Park Service for their able assistance. Included among them are Mr. Robert K. Krick, Fredericksburg and Spotsylvania National Military Park; Mr. Christopher W. Calkins, Petersburg National Battlefield; Mrs. Kathleen Georg Harrison, Gettysburg National Military Park; and Mrs. Betty Otto, Antietam National Battlefield. My thanks also go out to Mr. Timothy L. Decker and the Chemung County Historical Society for information about Elmira Prison, as well as to Mr. Steven R. Stotelmyer for his in depth tour of the Fox's Gap Battlefield. The assistance of the Museum of the Confederacy in Richmond, Virginia and the Sturdivant Hall Museum Association in Selma, Alabama are also appreciated.

Special thanks also go out to Mr. Ronald W. Laboda, Dorothy E. Habben and Eric L. Habben, Jr. for their countless hours spent proofreading and critiquing the manuscript. Thanks to Mrs. Doctorow and the staff of the Fine Arts Section of the Adelphi University Library for the assistance they provided during my numerous visits to their study area. In addition, a thank you to Mr. William W. Combes of Wedgewood Studio for the excellent photographic prints he produced; as well as to Dr. Sidney W. Bondurant and Mr. John Michael Priest for the important material they supplied. To Ms. Christine M. Schneider, I'm most appreciative of her work with the computer.

I would also like to express my gratitude to the State of Alabama Department of Archives and History, the National Archives, the Library of Congress, the New York Public Library, the University of Alabama Library, Mr. John Bosco and the reference staff of the Garden City Public Library and the Manuscript Department of the Duke University Library. In addition, I would like to acknowledge the help of my patient editor, Dr. Martin K. Gordon. And finally, a special thank you goes out to Mr. John Bracken, for affording me the opportunity to purchase the frock coat which led to the study of the Jeff Davis Artillery, and to Mr. Maurice B. Andrews, not only for his encouragement, but for the information that he provided about his grandfather who served with that proud battery from Alabama.

(The writer would be most interested in hearing about any new material that may surface having to do with the Jeff Davis Artillery. Please send any correspondence to him c/o the Publisher.)

HAPTER I

AN ARTILLERY COMPANY IS BORN

The inhabitants of Selma, Dallas County, Alabama were filled with the type of emotions that few had probably ever experienced before. On April 12, 1861, their fellow secessionists, as many called them, had fired on the Federal garrison holding Fort Sumter in Charleston Harbor, South Carolina, prompting the start of the conflict soon to be labelled by them the "War for Southern Independence." War fever had spread through the city. In Selma, as well as throughout the rest of the newly formed Confederacy, preparations for the coming military confrontation with the armies of the Union proceeded rapidly, as a steady stream of men enlisted and were formed into companies. By the latter part of June, Selma's residents had witnessed the formation of one company in particular, whose men were destined to bring much glory to that proud Southern city.

The Reverend Joseph T. Montgomery, the head of a school in nearby Summerfield, organized those volunteers, intending to form an independent cavalry unit, which he himself would probably be leading against the enemy. As it turned out, however, his 'Independent Company of Alabama Cavalry' was not destined to serve its country in the form originally intended. Instead, his company would be molded into a light artillery command.[1] The volunteers travelling to Selma in order to enlist in that new formation would be joining the Jeff Davis Flying Artillery from Alabama. Named for the president of the Confederate States of America, the company would also be known as the Jeff Davis Mounted Artillery.

1

The men came from all walks of life, many already with the skills required in an artillery company. They included veterinarians, blacksmiths, and artificers (craftsmen). Most were from nearby Lowndes and Wilcox Counties as well as from Dallas County itself. The majority were under twenty-five years of age and unmarried. One notable exception was a man soon to be known to the others as "Palmetto" Anderson. He entered the ranks at age forty and had been a member of the celebrated Palmetto Regiment that had served in the War with Mexico in 1848. Undoubtedly, that veteran had many tales to tell his fellow soldiers.

That June, the company held its first election of officers. The men elected Joseph Montgomery Captain, and E. M. Holloway and Dr. Sprott, Senior and Junior First Lieutenants, respectively. In addition, J. W. Garrett and John G. Snediker were selected to hold the ranks of Senior and Junior Second Lieutenants. Dr. Sprott and J. W. Garrett, however, refused to accept their new positions.[2] As it turned out, only Joseph Montgomery and John Snediker would remain with the company.[3]

Consequently, it was necessary to hold new elections shortly thereafter. The results were as follows: Joseph Montgomery retained his captaincy, while Alexander K. Shepard, Charles W. Lovelace and William A. Fitts were elected to hold the rank of First, Third and Fourth Lieutenants, respectively. John G. Snediker was made Quartermaster Sergeant of the battery.

As June drew to a close, the camp of the newly organized artillery company was clearly in evidence. Numerous tents could be seen along the east bank of Beech Creek, approximately a mile or two northeast of Selma.[4] While the artillerymen were camped along the creek, they acquired the first horses for use by the battery. At the same time, they hoped that their equipment would soon arrive at the camp. The company, as it turned out, would remain at their first encampment for about three weeks.

The company then broke camp and headed for Montgomery, Alabama, which until May 21 had been the capital of the Confederacy. Missing from the ranks was Private John Purifoy, who had been "...permitted to go to his home, at Snow Hill, in Wilcox County, to solicit horses."[5]

On the way to Montgomery, the artilleryman encountered Matthew Tucker, who was in the process of plowing a field along the side of the road. "They [the members of the company] yelled at him to come join them. He tied his mule to a tree, jumped the fence and marched off to four years of war."[6] He was but seventeen years of age at the time.

PRIVATE JOHN PURIFOY

From Snow Hill, Wilcox County, Alabama; served with battery from July of 1861 to April of 1865.

(*Confederate Veteran* XXIV [May 1916], 223.) Broadfoot Publishing Company, Wedgewood Studio.

The Jeff Davis Artillery reached Montgomery "...about the 22nd of July,..." and set up camp on the Old Fair Grounds near the Montgomery and West Point Railroad station.[7] During rainy weather, however, the campsite flooded, and it moved to Gunter's Warehouse on the south bank of the Alabama River.

Soon thereafter, the camp routine became more like that of a military organization. Guns were now fired to announce the daily roll call. Drilling and the other business of camp life began in earnest. At the same time, the rolls continued to grow as more recruits arrived in the city, intent on joining Captain Montgomery's command. It was also by then that the much needed equipment began to reach the camp. That, however, did not include cannon, the delivery of which was still months away.

In the meantime, the gathering of horses continued. Several had been brought in by Purifoy, who had since rejoined his command. "Through the liberality and patriotism of the citizens of the country from which the men came the company was furnished with horses for an eight gun battery."[8]

On July 27, 1861, the Jeff Davis Artillery was mustered into the Confederate service for three years or the duration of the War. Major James L. Calhoun, the mustering officer, attested to this act when he wrote, "I certify, on honor, that I have carefully examined the men whose names are borne on this Roll, their horses and equipments, and have accepted them into the service of the Confederate States for the term of the War from this 27th day of July 1861."[9]

The company, at that time, already numbered approximately one hundred and fifty-five officers and men, the maximum number of men required to operate a six gun battery. The Jeff Davis Artillery, however, was to be equipped with eight cannon. Therefore, even more men would be adding their names to the company rolls in the weeks ahead.

As of July 27, Captain Montgomery's command, as best could be determined, contained the following:

Captain	1
Lieutenants	3
Quartermaster Sergeant	1
Sergeants	8
(incl.: one First Sergeant and one Sergeant of the Stable Guard)	
Corporals	11
Artificers	6
Surgeons	1
Buglers	2
Engineers	1
Privates	114-124

Having been officially mustered in, the company marched to the state capitol building where it was issued more supplies, namely haversacks and canteens. "The latter were rude affairs, being made of wood, and the haversacks were rough."[10]

The uniforms worn by the men of the newly formed battery no doubt varied greatly in style,[11] with some trimmed in red (for artillery) and others with no special markings at all. At the same time, though, the outfits worn by the members of the battery did contain distinctive unit insignia. As Private Wilber F. Claughton remembered, "We had no buttons [of one particular style], but wore letters on our hats or caps. Our letters were "J.D.M.A.," for Jeff Davis Mounted Artillery."[12]

While at the capitol building, the Governor of Alabama, Andrew B. Moore, spoke to the new soldiers in a grand manner, infusing them with feelings of patriotism. Private John Purifoy recalled, "We were encouraged to go to the front and meet the enemies of our country and in deadly conflict teach them the lessons of independence."[13] Following the events of that memorable day, the Jeff Davis Mounted Artillery was ordered to LaGrange, Georgia.

While the men were waiting for the order to break camp, another company election was held, and William J. Reese was chosen to fill the unoccupied position of Second Lieutenant. At the same time, Montgomery made an effort to find someone qualified to hold the position of commander of the stable guard. By that time, the battery had 120 horses, and it was imperative that Montgomery find the right person to hold that important position. Several men from the company were given the opportunity to fill the post, but all failed to meet the requirements of the job. Thus, inquiries were made elsewhere by Montgomery and his officers in an attempt to find the best suited for that special duty.

Montgomery and his four Lieutenants, Shepard, Reese, Lovelace and Fitts, thought that Private Seth Shepard of the Alabama Mounted Rifles, then stationed near Pensacola, Florida, was highly qualified. On July 29, they all signed a letter written by Montgomery to Major General Braxton Bragg (who commanded the Confederate forces at Pensacola), requesting Shepard's transfer to the Jeff Davis Artillery. Governor Moore endorsed the request, and on August 14, the Secretary of War gave his approval for the transfer. But on September 15, Shepard was discharged from the service.[14]

Before Montgomery's battery left for LaGrange the names of two men were deleted from the company rolls. Privates Louis Luchow and R. A. Ferguson, who had enlisted on June 27 and July 1 respectively, had left camp without permission: Ferguson leaving before being mustered into the service, Luchow just one day after having been mustered in.

Shortly thereafter, the company left for LaGrange. The march to that city proved uneventful, and once there, the artillerymen received kind treatment at the hands of the citizenry. Montgomery had once taught school at LaGrange and had many friends in the area.

The Alabama battery was to spend a few weeks in the city. During that time, however, it soon became evident that all was not well. Disease, attributable in part to the unsanitary conditions in camp began to manifest itself and would haunt the company from that time forward. Diseases such as the measles, mumps, diarrhea and dysentery quickly spread through the encampment.

While at LaGrange, Private John Purifoy contracted the mumps. Privates William Breithaupt and William J. Dennis, as well as Lieutenant William J. Reese also fell ill. Both Breithaupt and Reese, not to mention Purifoy, would have to leave the service temporarily to recuperate. Privates John N. Cowan, John J. S. Crosby, James A. Melton, Charles T. Watts and Francis M. Wootan had also been incapacitated by disease and were either convalescing in camp or in a hospital. Those men were most likely only a small percentage of those that suffered from some sort of malady during the months of July and August.

Meanwhile, three new recruits attempted to join the company. But on August 9, they were arrested and sent back to Montgomery, Alabama under orders from Major James L. Calhoun. The men in question, Privates William A. Bolton, Henry A. DuPriest and William J. Pollard, had deserted from Captain Benjamin Lane Posey's Company of the 1st

Alabama Volunteers. Either their enlisting with the battery was a ploy to avoid discovery by the authorities, or they actually intended to stay with the Jeff Davis Artillery. In any case, Detective August McGibony took charge of the deserters and escorted them back to the capital city.

By the middle of August, the rolls of the Jeff Davis Mounted Artillery showed the following officers. Captain Joseph T. Montgomery commanded the battery. Next in authority was First Lieutenant Alexander K. Shepard. Then came Second Lieutenant William J. Reese, Third Lieutenant Charles W. Lovelace and Fourth Lieutenant William A. Fitts. Following in rank was Abraham Adams, who from August 10 was acting sergeant of the battery. Also, John Billingslea, had been promoted to sergeant on August 10, the same day, as it turned out, that Sergeant William L. Callihan was reduced to the ranks.[15] On or soon to be added to the list of sergeants were the names Dwight Bates, James Bondurant, Euphroneus Carter, Robert Cobb, Columbus McCrary, James Moore, James Norwood, John Snediker, Hugh Thomas, Robert Walker and Robert Yeldell. John Snediker remained the company's quartermaster sergeant. Next were Corporals Alexander Hunter, Brittan Lee, John Maull, James Mundy, Edward Nobles, Augustus Patton, Joseph Soles, Thomas Traylor, Fred Vaughan and William Yeldell. Of those officers listed above, many would eventually receive promotions. Though still without a single cannon, the company certainly did not suffer from a lack of officers.

Now it was time for the Alabamians to move on. From LaGrange, they took the road to Atlanta, Georgia. Those men who were not well enough to make the trip had to be left behind, so that they might recuperate more quickly. The company arrived in Atlanta but stayed there only a short time before moving on to Richmond, Virginia.

It was "...about the 1st of September..."[16] that the battery reached its destination and began what was to be a several week stay at the capital of the Confederacy. While there, another vacancy within the commissioned staff was filled. On September 20, the men elected Robert S. Walker their junior second lieutenant.

Five days later, the Secretary of War issued an order directing Montgomery to Manassas, Virginia. Once there, the Alabamians would join the Confederate Army of the Potomac, commanded by General Joseph E. Johnston.

Montgomery's battery left Richmond and moved northward. Arriving in the vicinity of Fairfax Court House, the Jeff Davis Artillery halted and set up camp on the Warrenton Turnpike. The company remained there until October 15, when they moved to a location about one mile west of Centreville, Virginia, a short distance from Manassas and the site of the famous battle of Bull Run which had been fought the previous July.

Montgomery was conspicuously absent from the encampment near Centreville. He had been sent on recruiting service on October 14.[17]

By the latter part of October, the patience of the men was finally rewarded. They received eight cannon (two twelve pound Howitzers, two- three inch Rifles and four- six pounders), and the related equipment. They would now have the opportunity to master their skills as artillerymen using their own guns.

In order to assist in the training of the company, First Lieutenant Robert F. Beckham, a West Point graduate and proven officer, had been assigned to the unit. He would take charge in Captain Montgomery's absence. Though the men were no doubt anxious to improve their skills as artillerymen, any chance for progress by the battery as a whole would be hampered by a condition becoming more and more prevalent in camp. "The Company is, I regret to say, very inefficient owing to the extensive sickness which prevails amongst the men."[18] The rigors of life in camp near Centreville were not what the men of the battery were accustomed to, and conditions would only worsen, especially with the approach of winter.

While the men of the company were waging a war with disease, another serious problem had finally come to a head. Montgomery, by this time, had proven himself totally unfit as their commander. A dangerous rift had developed within the command structure of the battery. Shepard had, in fact, brought charges against him.[19] The case had then been brought up before General Johnston, who had sent Montgomery on his recruiting mission and had ordered Beckham to take temporary command of the battery.

Wishing to avoid a court-martial proceeding, Johnston had contacted Judah P. Benjamin, the Secretary of

LIEUTENANT ROBERT F. BECKHAM

Shown here as a colonel, took command of the battery in Captain Joseph T. Montgomery's absence, from October 1861 to February 1862.

(The Museum of the Confederacy, Richmond, Virginia. The Long Arm of Lee.) J. P. Bell Co.

War, in hopes that President Jefferson Davis could be persuaded to intercede and dismiss Montgomery. The Secretary of War replied:

> My dear Sir: I have just seen General Wigfall, and find from my conversation with him that you cannot have understood my note in relation to Captain Montgomery. I had no funds in the appropriations from which I could pay for recruiting, and not knowing what to do with him, left him subject to your orders, but no idea of interfering in any way with any arrangement you might make for the command of the battery. I merely suggested (not knowing that there was any charge against him) that it might be well to let him learn how to manage his battery under the command of the officer you had chosen....Wigfall says that the men won't obey Montgomery, and that he is not fit to command, but that you wish to avoid a court-martial, as they are ineffective and troublesome machines with volunteers...I know of no other means of getting rid of an incompetent or unworthy officer. The President has no power to dismiss him. I leave the whole matter to you to do the best you can, and have written these few lines only to remove the impression that I desired at all to interfere with the command of the battery as ordered by you....
>
> Yours, & c., J. P. Benjamin[20]

As indicated by the above letter, Johnston would have to do as he saw fit concerning the battery. Though a final decision would not be made immediately, some definitive motion would, needless to say, have to be taken for the good of the company. The Jeff Davis Artillery could not possibly operate in an efficient manner with a commander whose competency was questionable at best.

CHAPTER II

A DIFFICULT WINTER

With all of Montgomery's shortcomings, the novice artillerymen were indeed fortunate to have another officer teaching them the art of war. Under the able direction of First Lieutenant Robert F. Beckham, the Alabamians developed into a respectable body of cannoneers. Headquarters recognized his accomplishments, as Second Lieutenant William J. Reese acknowledged: "Our company has the honor of defending one of the most advanced positions in our field works. We will man but four pieces as there are only embrasures in the fort for that number of guns."[1] Reese went on to describe the role of his company as far as its disposition with regard to the rest of the artillery of the Army of the Potomac was concerned. He remarked, "...our company is attached to what is known as the 'Reserved Artillery' a corps composed of eight companies and forty pieces of ordnance. And commanded by Col Pendleton."[2]

During November, all had remained quiet in front of the works occupied by the Jeff Davis Artillery. Beckham's gunners waited patiently for their chance to engage the enemy.

The company from Selma, however, was already fully involved in another kind of battle. Disease continued running its course through the Centreville camp, disabling many, and proving fatal to others. For example, Privates Seabron O. Hobby, John A. Mathews, John A. Powers and Whitfield S. Quarles were discharged from the service during November because of physical disabilities brought on by illness. "And our ranks have been somewhat thinned by disease and death,"[3] wrote Reese.

CENTREVILLE,
VIRGINIA
1861

Positions of Artillery,
including Jeff Davis
Artillery (Beckham's
Command), around
Centreville, Virginia.

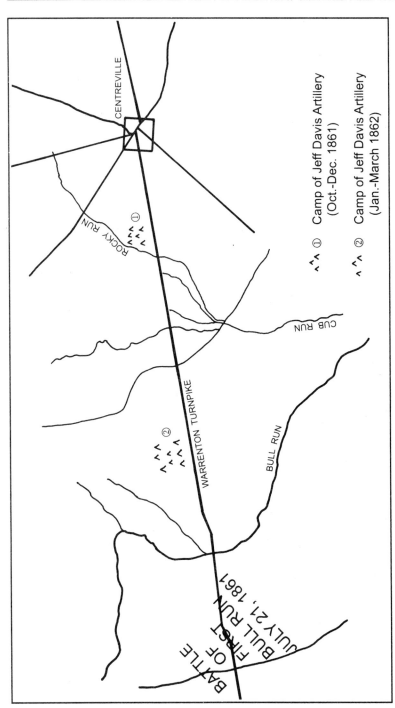

CAMPSITES OF JEFF DAVIS ARTILLERY NEAR CENTREVILLE, VA.

Recreated from Plate III-1 of The Official Military Atlas of the Civil War.

① Camp of Jeff Davis Artillery (Oct.-Dec. 1861)

② Camp of Jeff Davis Artillery (Jan.-March 1862)

Measles and camp fever, a form of malaria, were the most prevalent of the diseases that struck down many of the men of the company.
Unsanitary conditions in camp contributed largely to the spread of those
dreaded illnesses.

Inexperience in properly preparing food only made conditions
worse. The still novice soldiers did not always thoroughly cook their
meals which resulted in even more sickness. Also, in some cases, men
who had been sick were too anxious to return to duty, even though
they had not fully recovered. Once back on active duty, they would
suffer a relapse and find themselves worse off than before. As Private
John Purifoy recalled, "...the exposure was almost sure to follow measles
with pneumonia, which proved fatal in a number of cases."[4] While still
becoming acquainted with correct camp life practices, the men of the
Jeff Davis Artillery were learning some very hard lessons. Privates William Caldwell, Handy Sills and James S. Bentley were just three of the
unfortunate victims who would never cross swords with the enemy.
All died that November.

As sickness and death continued to diminish the company rolls,
trying the entire command, an event occurred that brought with it a
badly needed boost in morale. On December 13, Captain Joseph T.
Montgomery was cashiered by court-martial.

With Montgomery gone, Colonel William N. Pendleton ensured that
Beckham would succeed as battery commander. Though it was in vio-
lation of Army Regulations, Pendleton called a forced election whose
aim was to give Beckham the leadership post. The results were as expected. By month's end, Johnston issued a Special Order which confirmed the election placing Beckham in command of the Jeff Davis
Artillery. The future looked considerably brighter for the battery.

By the time of Beckham's installation as company commander, a
part of the Alabama battery had already participated in its first battle.
It, however, was not the artillerymen themselves who had encountered
the blue-clad foe. Ironically, it was their cannon that had first seen
action.

In the latter part of December, Brigadier General Jeb Stuart had organized a foraging expedition to Dranesville, located between the lines.
Captain Allan S. Cutts' command took along a section of guns (2) from
the Jeff Davis Artillery and used them during a hot confrontation with
the enemy. In that fight at Dranesville, Stuart's force had received rough
treatment from the Federals they had encountered.

When the two borrowed cannon were brought back to the Jeff Davis
Artillery, one of the pieces provided the men with a taste of the war

they had yet to experience. "When returned one gun was bespattered with the brains and blood of an artilleryman who was killed during that engagement. This was an evidence of real war, and afforded something of a sensation for the men."[5] Some of the members of the company regretted that it was not they themselves that had been in the thick of the fighting. No doubt others were shocked into the realities of the conflict by what they saw!

It was not long before the Alabamians received another shock. There had been some irregularity in Captain Montgomery's court-martial, and, as a result, President Davis had revoked Montgomery's sentence. Any feelings of relief within the ranks that had resulted from Montgomery's dismissal were quickly squelched when it was learned that the President had reinstated him as commander of the Jeff Davis Artillery. That action caused a deep resentment among the officers of the company. It wouldn't be too long a time before these men showed their displeasure by taking drastic steps of their own.

As if the restoration of Montgomery to the command of the company was not unsettling enough for the men, the struggle against disease was intensifying, taxing the battery as whole. By January 2, 1862, the artillery company, now in a new location about three miles from Centreville, on the north side of the Warrenton Pike, was only at three-quarters strength.

During December, three more men had been lost by the company. Privates Charles H. Montgomery and John F. Pierce had been discharged because their constitutions had been so weakened by disease. Another sufferer, Private John Callihan, had never been afforded the luxury of returning home. He had died on December 22. It was becoming more and more evident that the harshness of the Virginia winter weather was more than many of the Alabamians were used to or could withstand.

On January 19, Second Lieutenant Robert Walker described the weather in a letter written to his sister.

> ...; on the 15th we went out for inspection. The inspection came off at one. We harnessed up at eleven and spent from that time until half past one atleast in a shower that froze as it fell. Icickles hung from our coats + caps, (I saw them atleast two inches long on some of the men) and our hair was completely matted. The horses mains and tails looked as though they were made of glass instead of hair.[6]

Having to endure such severe conditions did little to improve the health of the battery. Still, such incidents did little to dampen the spirits of the company. As Walker continued, "We are having a gay time all to ourselves here in the pines."[7] Or was he sparing his sister from the other unpleasantries associated with life in winter-quarters? Even if Walker had purposely painted a rosier picture than what actually existed, there was still one aspect of camp life about which he did not have to exaggerate.

The lodgings that the company had constructed at Centreville were, in fact, quite comfortable. "We have a fire place to one of our tents, which we use as a sitting room the other we keep for a bed room. The Capt has a tent to himself. All the men have either fire places to their tents or houses; and we get on very well in that particular,"[8] wrote the Lieutenant. The animals were not so fortunate. "For the horses we have brush sheds, but they do little or no good."[9] This was a situation that would have to be corrected for the good of the horses, if not the battery itself.

While the rest of the company made the best of life in camp near Centreville, the five lieutenants of the Jeff Davis Artillery decided that they had had enough. The return of Montgomery to the post of battery commander could only mean more serious difficulties in days ahead, and that was something none of the aforementioned officers were prepared to accept. It was time to take definitive action.

On January 8, Reese sent his letter of resignation, to the Secretary of War. In it he stated, "Capt. J. T. Montgomery is a person for whom I have no respect either as a gentleman or an officer."[10] By the time another week had passed, Shepard, Walker, Lovelace and Fitts had written letters of resignation or requested a transfer to some other command.[11] Walker echoed Reese's sentiments when he wrote, "Capt. J. T. Montgomery is a man in whom I have no confidence as a commander to whom it is most grinding to pay the respect due a superior officer."[12]

But the latter part of January saw Montgomery once again exercising command over the company. Upon his return, the election that had placed Beckham in command of the battery was declared null and void, whereupon that able officer left the Jeff Davis Artillery. Several days later, Montgomery ordered Sergeant James W. Bondurant reduced to the ranks. That action created a good deal of excitement within the ranks. Shortly thereafter, on January 25, 1862, the company elected Bondurant to one of the existing vacancies for first lieutenant.

Montgomery had obviously lost his already tenuous grasp on the command, and he was left with one choice of action. On or about February 7, he resigned and left the company, that time for good. His departure brought to a close, five months of strife within the ranks of the Jeff Davis Artillery. Looking back, one member of the battery put it thusly, "From the time we reached Richmond until the resignation of Capt Montgomery the Company was involved in a perpetual row."[13]

Not long thereafter, Davis commissioned Montgomery a lieutenant colonel and sent him back to Alabama in order to organize another artillery battalion. That was the work that Montgomery was best suited to perform.

Though a bad situation had finally been resolved, the Jeff Davis Artillery had lost much more than just one officer. The difficulties caused by its former commander had left the battery virtually stripped of its higher ranking officers. Little time was wasted, however, in filling the vacancies and reorganizing the company. Colonel Pendleton assigned Lieutenant Hilary P. Jones to the temporary command of the company. Sergeant Bondurant, previously elected a first lieutenant, was commissioned as such upon Montgomery's resignation. He would eventually take over the Jeff Davis Artillery. To fill other vacancies, Sergeants Robert A. Yeldell and Hugh P. Thomas were elected junior first lieutenants, while Private Edward Knight was elected second lieutenant. Finally, the Jeff Davis Artillery was back in capable hands.

The past five weeks had proven to be unsettling for both the officers and enlisted men of the Alabama battery. Besides the resignation of six officers, including its captain, the company had lost two more enlisted men for different reasons, though not for reasons unfamiliar to the command. The two men in question, Corporals Joseph M. Soles and James J. Mundy, were discharged because their bouts with sickness had made them unfit for further duty. Mundy was over forty-six years of age at the time, which undoubtedly contributed to his difficulties.

Except for the events surrounding Montgomery's resignation, February actually proved to be relatively uneventful. Though the number of men on the sick list was a matter for much concern, the company hoped that the gradually improving weather conditions with the coming of spring would help speed the recovery of many of the unwell.

By that time, the Jeff Davis Artillery had been reduced from an eight to a six gun battery. Presumably, that was a reorganizational move aimed at improving the battery's effectiveness and maneuverability, as well as any other artillery unit of the army in a similar situation. Ironically, that reduction made it possible for the numerically reduced and dis-ease riddled company to more easily serve its field pieces. Its dimin-ished strength would, in all probability, have made it next to impossible for the Jeff Davis Artillery to bring eight guns into battle, and properly serve those cannon. Even so, the company would have its hands full serving the six remaining pieces until the men's health improved and more recruits rejoined the ranks.

As soon as circumstances allowed, the Army of the Potomac would be leaving its camps about Manassas, and begin what would be termed the spring campaigns. There, however, were several men from the ranks of the Jeff Davis Artillery who would not be moving with the army. One of these men, Private James S. Montgomery would probably be well on his way home by the time his company hit the road. He was suffering from a bad case of rheumatism and was discharged on March 6.

Nor would Privates Joseph Bryant or Ira Skinner be marching with Johnston's army. Both were confined to hospitals in Richmond and were destined never to recover from the diseases that had taken hold of them. They would breathe their last during the month of April.

The Jeff Davis Artillery had been left decidedly weakened as a re-sult of its experiences near Centreville. "A reference to the roster will show that the deaths in the company that winter numbered 15, and the discharges from physical disability numbered 16, making 31 loss for the first winter..."[14] No doubt, the survivors would never forget that horrid winter of 1861-62.

CHAPTER III

FINALLY, THE BATTERY MEETS THE YANKEES

By the second week of March, preparations had been completed and orders had been issued for the withdrawal of the Army of the Potomac from Manassas. The immediate destination of General Joseph E. Johnston's forces was to be the south side of the Rappahannock River. There, the Confederates would take up a defensive position against which it was anticipated that the Federals would be moving before too long. A large portion of the enemy's forces, known collectively as the Union Army of the Potomac (then under the command of Major General George B. McClellan), occupied ground on the Maryland side of the Potomac River and was showing signs of unusual activity which indicated that some type of offensive maneuver was about to be undertaken. In order to prevent the Union army from gaining a tactical advantage, and a position from which they could easily threaten Richmond, Johnston had to move his lines further south. Once the Southern forces were below the Rappahannock, it was believed that they could more easily block any advance aimed at the capital.

On March 9, the Confederates began to move south. By the following morning, only cavalry remained in position along the old line about Manassas.

The Alabama battery's progress towards the Rappahannock was slowed by roads turned muddy by recent rains. It was no easy matter for the teams to pull the company's six cannon along the slippery highways. Still, in spite of the trying march, it must have been gratifying for the men of the company to leave the camps near Centreville behind

17

them. Finally, for the men from Alabama, the prospects of their confronting the "blue devils" before long seemed favorable.

Within a few days, Johnston's forces had reached the south side of the Rappahannock. There, he would remain for the next several weeks.

Towards the end of March, the Confederate high command received word that McClellan's army was moving, not by land towards the Rappahannock line, but by transport towards Fort Monroe, located to the east, where an enemy buildup was underway. It, however, would not be until the first week of April before his exact designs could be determined. Johnston, though, had already guessed the enemy's intentions.[1] The Federals planned to push westward along the Peninsula towards Richmond.

Standing in the Union army's way were heavy fortifications, located in the immediate vicinity of Yorktown, as well as an incomplete line of field works along the Warwick River, which were currently being held by a force of less than 15,000 men under Major General John B. Magruder. Those defenders were hardly a match for the numerically superior invading army.[2] At best, they might be able to delay McClellan's advance until help arrived. The need for Johnston to interpose at least part of his army between that of McClellan and the city of Richmond was an urgent and obvious one. On March 27, Johnston received orders from Richmond to transfer 10,000 men from their positions along the Rappahannock, to the Peninsula.

On April 4, McClellan's army began its advance from the vicinity of Fort Monroe. One day later, part of his force arrived opposite the Yorktown defenses.

By that time, three of Johnston's divisions had been transferred to the Yorktown area. Including Major General Daniel H. Hill's Division and the Jeff Davis Mounted Artillery. The Alabama battery, which had been assigned to Brigadier General Jubal A. Early's Brigade since the start of the new year, was part of the artillery

**LIEUTENANT GENERAL
DANIEL H. HILL**

Commanded division to which Jeff Davis Artillery was attached from May to December of 1862.

(National Archives)

branch of Hill's division. Hill would have at his disposal an artillery company still rebuilding after many difficult months at Centreville. (Even by April 30, 1862, the Jeff Davis Artillery would still be under-strength, with only eighty men present for duty.[3])

Once at Yorktown, the antici-pated change in command of the Jeff Davis Artillery took place. First Lieu-tenant Hilary P. Jones, who had di-rected the Alabamians on the marches from Manassas to the Rap-pahannock and then to Yorktown, had left the company. First Lieuten-ant James W. Bondurant had then been promoted to the rank of captain and taken over the command of the battery.

Starting on April 5, McClellan's forces launched several attacks against Southern positions about Yorktown. Those assaults, however, were all repulsed and McClellan be-came convinced that he was facing a much larger force then actually ex-isted behind the Confederate works. Consequently, he felt that he had no choice but to conduct siege opera-tions in order to force the defenders from their position.

COLONEL JAMES W. BONDURANT

Commanded Jeff Davis Artillery from May of 1862 to April of 1863.

(Painting, location unknown; Photograph courtesy of S. W. Bondurant M.D.)

During the next few weeks, while the Federals were constructing works and mounting their heavy guns, more of Johnston's forces were being shifted eastward. By April 12, the divisions of Major Generals James Longstreet and Gustavus W. Smith were on their way to the Pen-insula. Once those troops arrived at their destination, they, and the other forces already at Yorktown, were to be aligned as follows: Hill would occupy the left, including Yorktown itself, while Longstreet took the center, Magruder the right and Smith, a supporting position in the rear.

By May 1, McClellan's preparations were almost completed, mean-ing that he could soon start his bombardment. Johnston, realizing what he was up against, saw himself with only one option. His guns were no match for McClellan's heavy ordnance, and so Johnston decided to withdraw, abandoning his Yorktown defenses.

The night of May 3, Johnston masterfully removed his army from the Yorktown area. Even so, his move was not popular with his government in Richmond, for it meant that Johnston would be placing his army in a defensive position just a few miles from the Capital itself.[4] However, being the tactician that he was, Johnston felt it was the best available move under the circumstances. Unfortunately, as a result of this maneuver, the gray troops were forced to abandon most of the heavy guns in the works around Yorktown, something the Confederacy could ill-afford.

During the retreat from Yorktown, the Jeff Davis Artillery, and the rest of Hill's division, acted as the army's rear guard. On May 5, Early's brigade participated in a rear guard action at Williamsburg and suffered heavy loss. Though not involved in the fighting, Bondurant's battery was held in a reserve position during the battle. That action only delayed McClellan's pursuing army for a short time. Following that engagement, the Jeff Davis Artillery resumed the march with the rest of the army in the direction of Richmond, still confident they would be serving their guns quite soon.

During the campaign, and especially as the Confederate army moved away from Williamsburg, the weather proved itself to be both friend and foe. Heavy rains fell during the retreat which served to delay or at least slow the movements of the Federal army, but the downpours hindered the Confederates as well. "The roads, from numerous vehicles, horses and men passing over them, became loblollys,..."[5] The wagons and artillery pieces sank down to the axles in the muck, and the men had to wade into this quagmire in order to free the vehicles. The elements, as a result, permitted neither of the opposing armies to gain much ground on each other.

As if the torturous march wasn't burden enough for the Alabama battery, not to mention the rest of the army, there was yet another hardship to endure. There was a serious lack of food for the slow moving divisions. That deficiency, combined with the extra exertions needed to keep the army moving, resulted in complete exhaustion for many. The general health of the Jeff Davis Artillery was being threatened once more. Still, however, the company moved steadily on its way.

Three days out of Yorktown, Bondurant's battery lost contact with the rest of the army. On their own at the close of the day's march, the Alabama company made camp near New Kent Court House. After parking the battery and caring for the horses, as well as eating the scant rations available to them, the men prepared for a night's sleep. Under those circumstances, especially without knowing the location of any friendly troops, the company was in grave danger.

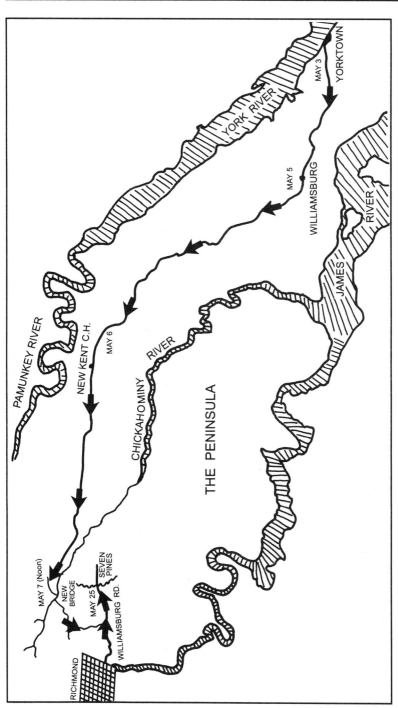

ROUTE FOLLOWED BY JEFF DAVIS ARTILLERY FROM YORKTOWN

Recreated from Plate XVI of The Official Military Atlas of the Civil War.

It wasn't long, however, before a band of Confederate cavalrymen appeared and told Bondurant that it would be unsafe to remain where he was for the night. The northern troops were not far behind, and that cavalry unit, the only force protecting the isolated artillery company, would be themselves moving on that evening. The Jeff Davis Artillery had no choice but to move on as well or risk capture by the Federals.

" 'Boots and Saddles' were sounded and an all night march began."[6] It wasn't until noon of the next day that the company reached its destination, the Chickahominy River at New Bridge. Here they were reunited with the first friendly troops they had seen, excepting the cavalry escort, since the previous day.

Altogether, the march had taken about thirty hours to complete, and, as one might imagine, the men of the company were exhausted by the time they reached New Bridge. Private John Purifoy recalled, "The writer [Purifoy] will never forget that night march....His fatigue was so great that he actually went to sleep while walking along the road....my good friend, Joe Blankinship, with whom I was marching discovered I was asleep and took my hand to guide me, fearing I would fall into a ditch or hole."[7] It was fortunate that the Jeff Davis Artillery had pushed on through the night, for the advancing Yankees did indeed take the campsite that the Alabamians had left behind. Now it was time for Bondurant's men to catch up on their badly needed rest.

After a brief stay at New Bridge, the company travelled to the immediate vicinity of the defenses that had been constructed outside Richmond. Upon its arrival, the company set up camp on the Williamsburg Road, where it would remain for the next few days. There, the men received their first glimpse of President Jefferson Davis, as well as his military advisor, General Robert E. Lee. The presence of those two men near the front indicated that the anticipated battle was not far off. With McClellan's army still moving towards Richmond, there was little doubt in the minds of the Alabamians that they would soon be confronting the enemy. Johnston, in fact, was hoping that he would, by some fortunate occurrence, be given the opportunity to set his army into motion against the Federals.[8]

On May 25, several days after it had set up camp on the Williamsburg Road, Bondurant's battery was sent out on picket duty near Seven Pines. The road the Alabamians had to travel upon to reach the outpost was in such bad shape, because of the rains, that the men had to aid the horses in moving the artillery vehicles. The horses were in no condition for such an undertaking, having been worn down by their earlier marches. At their new post, with guns unlimbered and ready for action, the horses probably stood a fair chance of recovering their strength; that is, as long as the enemy remained quiet.

The position that the battery had been assigned was far advanced. It was actually within the Confederate picket line. Here, the men had to remain ever on the alert, for the enemy's own picket line was but a short distance away.

Except for some skirmishing that took place on May 29 and 30, in which Bondurant's gunners did "...some good execution...,"[9] little of importance was to occur while the battery was out on picket duty.

By those last days of May, however, Johnston had finally been afforded the kind of opportunity to give battle that he had been waiting for. By some tactical blunder, attributable in part to the terrible weather conditions, part of McClellan's army had found itself on the Richmond side of the rain-swollen Chickahominy River and virtually cut off from the rest of the Federal forces. If the Confederates took the offensive, they could catch McClellan off balance and strike a severe blow. The necessary preparations were made, and the attack scheduled for May 30. Torrential rains, however, had forced a one day postponement of the advance. With the weather as bad as it was, there was no chance that McClellan could take advantage of the delay and reunite his army.

Now, finally, in the early morning hours of May 31, Bondurant's men made ready for the attack in which they were to play a part. The battery was to advance, along with Hill's division, down the Williamsburg Road in accordance with Longstreet's orders. The movement was to begin at dawn.

As dawn on the 31st came and went, without the sounds normally associated with the start of a battle, it was obvious something had gone wrong with the planned offensive. Marching orders had somehow became confused, and not until one o'clock that afternoon, was Hill's division in position and ready to advance. Even though many valuable hours had been lost, and a good number of Confederate troops could not, because of the confusion earlier in the day, be brought in time for the assault, the opportunity to damage McClellan's army still existed.

At last the time had come, and the guns of the Jeff Davis Artillery erupted, signalling the start of the Confederate advance. The infantry moved forward. Bondurant's battery moved up the Williamsburg Road in support of the attack.

Almost immediately after they started to advance, the Alabamians were hit by Federal artillery fire from works about one-half mile west of Seven Pines. Private Monroe W. Knight, the driver, and the horses pulling the lead gun were killed instantly. The Alabama battery was

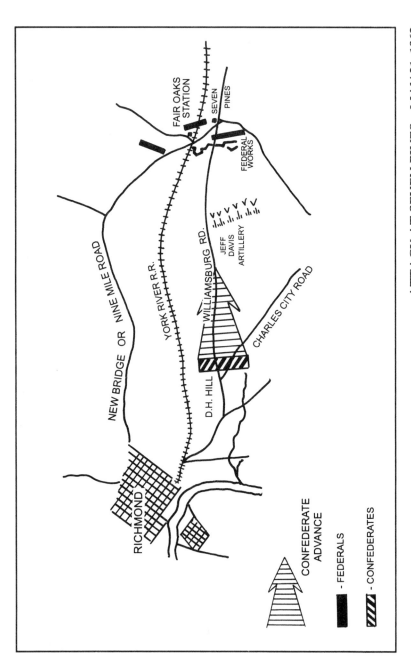

ATTACK AT SEVEN PINES – MAY 31, 1862

Recreated from Plate XX-1 of The Official Military Atlas of the Civil War.

forced to come to a temporary halt in order to get reorganized. While doing so, it was passed by Captain Thomas H. Carter's King William Artillery, which went into position and began firing. Soon thereafter, Bondurant's men advanced once more and added their metal to the bombardment. It was there, according to Brigadier General Samuel Garland, Jr., from "...a position to the right of the road, where Captain Bondurant delivered a telling fire, first with two and then with all six pieces."[10]

The artillery fire helped to dislodge the Federals from their works. "But a short time elapsed before the fugitives from the field in our front began to crowd through our own lines in their retreat,..."[11] reported Colonel Julius W. Adams of the 67th New York Infantry. Soon the Union redoubts were taken, with the cannon therein falling into the hands of the Confederates. The advance continued with the Alabamians remaining where they were for the time being.

Later in the afternoon, Bondurant was ordered forward once again. The Yanks were sending reinforcements

BRIGADIER GENERAL SAMUEL GARLAND, JR.

Commanded brigade to which Jeff Davis Artillery was attached from May to September of 1862. Mortally wounded at South Mountain, Maryland, September 14, 1862.

(Eleanor S. Brockenbrough Library, The Museum of the Confederacy, Richmond, Virginia)

up the Williamsburg Road, probably in an attempt to recapture the works lost some hours earlier. Hurrying to the front, the Jeff Davis Artillery relieved Carter's battery, which had been in action near the captured enemy works, and began firing at the approaching Federals. General Garland reported that Bondurant "...reached that ground in time to render handsome service in playing upon the enemy's reenforcements coming up the road."[12] The battery's fine work, however, had not been achieved without cost.

By this time, both Privates Jacob A. Meek and James Spinner had received serious wounds.[13] Private Meek would eventually die from the effects of his injury. Private Spinner, on the other hand, would recover from his wound but never return to duty with the company. In addition, more horses were killed or disabled, bringing the total lost that day to twelve.[14]

The Federals failed to retake the lost ground, and the fighting on both sides gradually wound down. The battle of May 31 came to a close with results far from what Johnston had hoped for. His attack had been disjointed at best and had met with only limited success. The enemy had been driven back with considerable loss to both sides, but the Confederates had also lost the services of Johnston. Near dusk, he had been seriously wounded and had to be carried from the field. At that critical moment, command of the army had fallen to Major General Gustavus W. Smith.

With the close of the fighting on their front,[15] Bondurant's company was witness to a sight, as described by Private Purifoy, that most of its members had not seen before.

> As the smoke of battle cleared away, and there was a lull in the firing, the picture that presented itself to this writer [Purifoy] was awe inspiring. This field and its carnage were more vividly impressed on his mind than any other he saw during his service,...He had seen pictures on canvas and paper that were intended to present battle fields as they appeared. No picture previously seen by him came near showing what he gazed on here and now. Spread out before him were the bodies of nearly four thousand men, dead, no picture men, but men of real flesh and blood. Several thousand wounded Confederates were being taken from the field. As many as were hobbling away on one foot, the other leg or foot dangling by their side, a gun or stick being used as an improvised crutch. Others were carrying broken arms, tenderly held with the sound hand. And still others, though whole of limb, were making their way to a place of safety and comfort, their palid faces indicating that they received severe wounds in some part of the body. The harrowing picture completed a scene that no language can describe.[16]

Indeed, that first view of what remained after the conclusion of a great battle must have been "awe inspiring", if not a bit of a shock for the Alabamians. Even though the company had received its baptism of fire at the start of the day's fight, and sustained casualties during the course of the battle, such experiences could not have totally prepared the men for the horrors that had unfolded before their eyes when the guns fell silent. And yet all that had come about as a result of the day's fighting was not so terrible. There, in fact, was something very positive that had come out of the events of that day.

The Jeff Davis Artillery had participated in its first battle, and the men of the battery had good reason to feel pleased with their performance at Seven Pines. The Alabamians had fought their guns well. Apparently, all the months of privation and sickness had failed to hinder the battery's effectiveness on the battlefield.

For Privates Monroe W. Knight, Jacob A. Meek and James Spinner, those who had fallen on May 31, there would be no chance to establish a reputation for themselves. Private Knight's life had been snuffed out before his gun had even reached the front. He had the "honorable" distinction of being the first from the company to die on the field of battle.

Though casualties had been suffered, the battery had come out of the intense fighting in comparatively good shape. It now remained to be seen what the morrow would bring.

On June 1, General Smith renewed the attack on the Federals. That day, however, the results would be different. The enemy had been reinforced and were ready for the Confederates. The Yankees drove back the attackers, forcing an eventual withdrawal by the Southern forces later in the afternoon.

For the entire day, the Jeff Davis Artillery had remained positioned near the Williamsburg Road. The battery had taken an active part in the fight but had suffered no losses. From their position, the Alabamians had also witnessed a costly advance made by one Confederate regiment. "...we saw the 3rd Alabama regiment of infantry form and march into a thicket where it run into an ambush and was hurled back, bringing its gallant commander, Col. Tenant Lomax, a corpse."[17] That action typified what had been in store for Smith's army on the 1st of June.

That night, the Jeff Davis Artillery was pulled back to its former position west of Seven Pines. Hours earlier, even before the battery's withdrawal, some important changes had already been made which would effect the future of those brave Alabamians, not to mention every other soldier of the Confederate Army of the Potomac.

C HAPTER IV
A NEW COMMANDER, A NEW ARMY,
A TASTE OF HELL!

Immediately following the Southern withdrawal on June 1, a decision of major importance was made. President Jefferson Davis, who had been witness to the entire affair at Seven Pines, was not pleased with the lack of vigor shown by Johnston's successor in carrying out the assault. Consequently, Davis lost no time replacing Gustavus W. Smith with Robert E. Lee as commander of the Confederate forces. Lee immediately renamed his army the Army of Northern Virginia. Lee set about reorganizing his army, taking whatever measures he deemed necessary.

While McClellan's army remained relatively inactive, Lee went to work preparing for another strike. He used his army, at the outset, to strengthen the works around Richmond. Strong defenses required less men to hold them against attack, which meant that more troops would be available for an offensive thrust. Lee also planned to order General Thomas J. "Stonewall" Jackson's force, then operating in the Shenandoah Valley, to join him, thus increasing the forces defending Richmond.

While Lee's plans were being carried out, life remained quiet for the Jeff Davis Artillery. As previously mentioned, the unit, following the retreat from Seven Pines, had returned to the same place on the Williamsburg Road that it had occupied before the start of the battle. There the Alabamians were to stay for the next several weeks, sharpening their skills for the next campaign. During that time, Sergeant James L. Moore, a member of the battery since the previous July, left the company. On June 10, he was discharged in order that be might be pro-

moted to the rank of captain and join the Army of Tennessee.[1] The sergeant left a company plagued by an all too familiar problem.
The marshy surroundings of the Chickahominy River had proven
to be an unhealthy environment for the Alabamians. Once again, diseases such as dysentery and typhoid thinned the ranks of the company.
Private Martin L. Alexander was just one of many who were sent to
nearby hospitals to recuperate from some ailment. Bondurant's company, an artillery unit supposedly taking advantage of the respite between battles to improve its overall condition, was, in fact, weakened
during those weeks spent near the river.

As June entered its final week, the disease-riddled battery prepared
to join the rest of the Army of Northern Virginia in the campaign to
drive McClellan from the Peninsula. The Jeff Davis Artillery, a company deficient in numbers as it was, would be embarking on an expedition that would provide the most severe test to date of the battery's
effectiveness on the field of battle.

On the night of June 25, Lee was ready to put his army in motion
against McClellan. Acting in accordance with Lee's plans, Major General Daniel H. Hill had his division in column and ready to march at
2:00 a.m. At the appointed hour, it marched off into the early morning
darkness. Carrying with them three days of cooked rations, the men of
the Jeff Davis Artillery knew that serious business was ahead.

D. H. Hill's division travelled through the night and reached its
destination before eight o'clock on the morning of Thursday, June 26.
The command was now situated behind a ridge that overlooked the
point where the Mechanicsville Road Bridge crossed the Chickahominy
River. Private John Purifoy remembered, "On looking back on a straight
stretch of road, one of the grandest sights the writer [Purifoy] ever be-
held presented itself. For several miles, and as far as the eye could reach,
were to be seen marching masses of men, with bright bayonets, glisten-
ing in the early morning sun, interspersed with artillery."[2]

Hill had moved his division from the extreme right to the extreme
left of the Confederate army's position, where they could clearly see
the town of Mechanicsville in the distance. There, as well as in position
guarding nearby roads and river crossings, lay Brigadier General Fitz
John Porter's V Corps and Brigadier General George A. McCall's Division of the Army of the Potomac. The Union force had also established
a formidable line of defense along Beaver Dam Creek, about one mile
east of the town. The remainder of McClellan's army was south of the
Chickahominy River within supporting distance of Porter.

"The Bridge That Stood"

View of Mechanicsville Road Bridge – crossed by Jeff Davis Artillery with D. H. Hill's Division on June 26, 1862 during attack at battle of Mechanicsville.

(Library of Congress)

Lee's plan was for Jackson to turn McClellan's right flank, north of the Chickahominy (the position currently held by Porter's Corps.) Then while the Federals were withdrawing from their defensive positions, Brigadier General Lawrence O'B. Branch's Brigade would move down the left bank of the Chickahominy, clearing the Meadow Bridges of the enemy, thereby allowing Major General Ambrose P. Hill's troops to cross the river and move to Jackson's support. After that, the Mechanicsville Bridge would be cleared, permitting the divisions of D. H. Hill and James Longstreet to also move to the north side of the Chickahominy. With his forces concentrated on the other side of the river,[3] Lee would be in a position to threaten McClellan's supply line which ran north to White House on the Pamunkey River. Under such circumstances, the Federals south of the Chickahominy would have to either pull back or move to the attack. Whatever course the enemy eventually took, Lee hoped that his strategy would ultimately lead to the destruction of McClellan's army.

It was now past eight o'clock, and the rest of the Southern forces waited for word of the arrival of Jackson's command beyond Porter's flank, which was to signal the start of the advance across the Chickahominy. In the meantime, the Alabama battery took advantage of the pre-battle lull to rest in the shade of some nearby trees.[4]

The morning came and went, and still there was no word from Jackson. Finally, at three o'clock in the afternoon, the Southern advance began. A. P. Hill's division, which was to be the first to move, pushed its way across the Chickahominy at the Meadow Bridges. Some three miles downriver, Lee climbed on top of the works along the Mechanicsville Road in order to observe the movement.

As A. P. Hill's division neared Mechanicsville, pushing back any Federals in its way, the Confederates suddenly came under heavy fire from artillery posted along Beaver Dam Creek. Something was wrong! If Jackson was moving as planned, the enemy should have been flanked and would be withdrawing from its position along the Creek rather than contesting Hill's advance. Obviously, Jackson's force was delayed in its approach and had not yet reached the field. A. P. Hill, not willing to wait any longer for Jackson to come up, had, in fact, sent his division forward on his own accord. Lee now set his other divisions in motion and rode to the front.

Bondurant's company, which had been awaiting orders to move with its division, was soon on its way towards the bridge that crossed the Chickahominy River. While enroute to the crossing, the gray-clad troops were passed by Davis, riding to join Lee. However, even before the Jeff Davis Artillery had reached the bridge, the President was seen riding back from the direction of Mechanicsville, having been persuaded to return to a place of safety behind the lines by Lee.

D. H. Hill's division arrived at the Mechanicsville Road Bridge but was unable to cross because the Yankees had wrecked the bridge, and a long delay ensued while repairs were made. While waiting its turn to cross the bridge, the Jeff Davis Artillery unlimbered its guns in the immediate vicinity of Chickahominy Bluff. From that position, the Alabamians, with assistance from Captain Robert A. Hardaway's Battery, fired on the troops that were falling back through Mechanicsville before A. P. Hill's advance.

Finally, with repairs completed, the lead elements of D. H. Hill's division started across the river. Brigadier General Roswell S. Ripley's Brigade led the way, followed by his artillery. Some time later, the Alabama battery fell in behind Garland's brigade and crossed the

Chickahominy. Once north of the river, the Jeff Davis Artillery again went into action.

Bondurant's company advanced rapidly with the other batteries of their division and went into position opposite the Federal artillery which was posted on the near side of Beaver Dam Creek. The Confederate guns opened "...and drove the Yankee artillery off the field."[5] All the while, A. P. Hill's men had been sent forward in fruitless assaults against the Federal defenses along the Creek. Ripley's brigade, thrown into the fight near dusk, was torn apart by the withering fire of Porter's men. With darkness came the end of any offensive movement by the Confederates, though it would still be several hours before the guns of both sides were quiet.

It had been a disappointing day for the Army of Northern Virginia. The Confederates had suffered heavy losses while gaining nothing for their efforts. Jackson had never even reached the battlefield, though his part in the overall plan was crucial to the success or failure of the Southern attack. Worst of all, McClellan's army was still intact.

For Bondurant's command, however, the day had gone relatively well. During the limited action of the 26th, the Jeff Davis Artillery had performed effectively. The fire from their guns had been instrumental in, first, helping to drive McClellan from Mechanicsville,[6] then in forcing the Federal artillery from the field later that same afternoon. Throughout the course of its participation in the battle of Mechanicsville, the battery had suffered but one casualty. Private James K. Smith lost his right arm when the gun he had been serving fired prematurely. He would be discharged from the service in the spring of the following year.

McClellan determined that with Jackson's force in position beyond the Federal right, Porter would find himself in a difficult situation when action resumed the next morning. With Jackson moving around his flank, Porter would soon find himself in a vulnerable position. Rather than risk the action, McClellan decided to withdraw his forces from the vicinity of Beaver Dam Creek. At two hours past midnight, Porter was ordered to pull his troops back from the Creek to a new position beyond Gaines' Mill, about four miles to the east.

The repositioning of Porter's command was done in accordance with a grand plan of McClellan's to change his base of operations. His base at White House, north of the Chickahominy River, was to be abandoned in favor of Harrison's Landing on the James River, on the other side of the Chickahominy. Such a maneuver would be a difficult undertaking, especially in light of the ever increasing pressure from Lee's pursuing army.

With the combined forces of Lee and Jackson moving against him, McClellan was no longer thinking of renewing his drive against Richmond and he ordered a rapid withdrawal to Harrison's Landing. On Friday, June 27, while McClellan removed the bulk of his army towards the safety of his James River base, which was protected by gunboats, the task of resisting the Confederates would, once again, belong to Porter.

The morning of the 27th, Bondurant's company joined the rest of D. H. Hill's division on the road and awaited its marching orders. By this time, A. P. Hill's men were already pressing those Federals who were still in the process of evacuating the Beaver Dam Creek line. Before the waiting column containing the Alabama battery commenced its own march, an incident occurred involving Bondurant and one of the Confederate generals who, up to that point, was not a familiar face to the company commander. Purifoy described the confrontation that took place between the two officers:

> The Jeff Davis Artillery had taken its position in the column, according to the orders of General D H Hill, to whose division it was attached, and shortly there came along an officer whose dress indicated that he was a Major General. On reaching the battery he ordered the Captain, Bondurant, to move his battery to a certain point different to the one occupied by it. The Captain did not know who was giving him orders, hence he said, "General Hill has ordered me to take this position and as I am under his command, I shall hold the place until ordered by him to move." The officer replied, "I am General Longstreet, and repeat to you to move your battery as directed." Captain Bondurant seeing his dilema, but not a whit abashed, being an old Virginia gentleman, replied, "I beg your pardon General, had I known you were General Longstreet I would have readily obeyed." It is needless to say that the order was obeyed and this ended what might have been more serious friction.[7]

It is more than likely that the incident was but one of many similar occurrences that took place at this stage of the war. A short time afterward, D. H. Hill's division stepped off in pursuit of the enemy. The gray column's destination was Old Cold Harbor, a town not far from the new Federal line near Gaines' Mill.

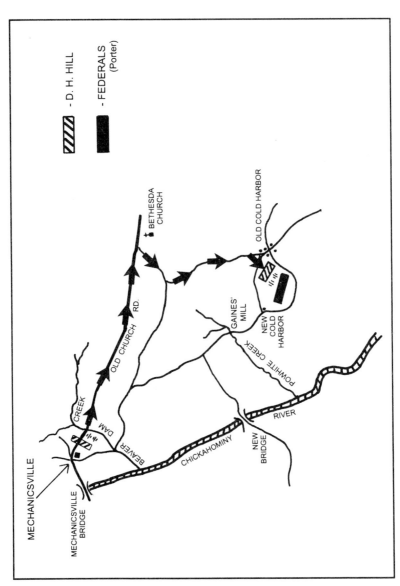

ROUTE FOLLOWED BY JEFF DAVIS ARTILLERY JUNE 27, 1862 (D. H. HILL'S DIVISION)
Recreated from Plate LXIII-8 of The Official Military Atlas of the Civil War.

The division moved along the Old Church Road with Bondurant's Alabamians occupying a position towards the front of the column. Along the route, they passed the troops belonging to Stonewall Jackson's command which had, again, just recently arrived on the Peninsula. Up until that meeting, the consensus among Bondurant's men was that Jackson's presence in the area had been merely a rumor.[8] Moving to the left of Jackson's column, D. H. Hill's division took an indirect route by Bethesda Church, then marched in the direction of Old Cold Harbor. Reaching that place, the column continued on towards New Cold Harbor. It was by now, early Friday afternoon.

Advancing more cautiously, D. H. Hill's command soon arrived at Powhite Swamp, enroute to New Cold Harbor. Here the road needed for the movement of the artillery was found to be covered by twelve of Porter's guns. The Federals were strongly posted to contest any attempt by Hill's men to continue their advance.

Because the Jeff Davis Artillery was already in an advanced position in the column, it was ordered forward. It should be noted that Bondurant was able to bring only four of his six guns into action. Sickness, discharges, and death had so severely reduced the strength of the battery that it was impossible for the Alabamians to properly serve the four pieces of artillery now going into battle. As a result, some of the gunners had to perform the duties usually undertaken by two or more men. The skill of the individual gun crews were tested that day.

Advancing at a gallop, the Jeff Davis Artillery moved into position just to the right of the road, about one quarter of a mile from the town of Old Cold Harbor. Immediately to their front was a line of skirmishers, while the infantry forces commanded by Brigadier Generals George B. Anderson and Samuel Garland, Jr. supported them to the rear. The Alabamians quickly began to unlimber their pieces.

Even before they were able to bring their guns to bear on the Union forces, the Federal gunners spotted the Alabamians. "In a very few moments thereafter the enemy appeared on the height opposite me with artillery. I at once opened fire with evidently good effect; the distance was not over 1,000 yds,"[9] reported Captain Stephen H. Weed of Battery I of the Fifth U.S. Artillery.

The Jeff Davis Artillery was suddenly the recipient of a storm of canistery shrapnel, and shell.[10] Undaunted by their predicament, Bondurant's cannoneers swiftly went to work and began to return the fire in earnest. Because of their close proximity to the lines, the Alabamians were also subjected to small arms fire from the Federal infantry.

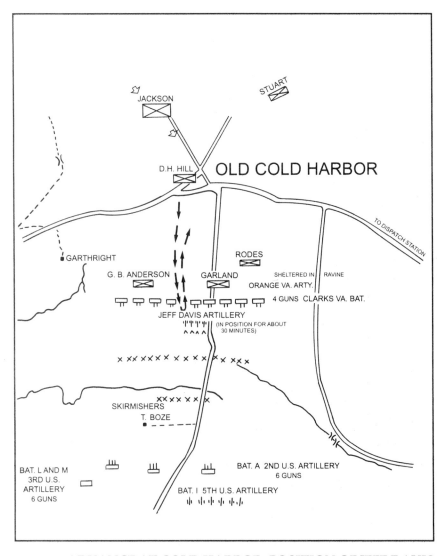

ADVANCE AT COLD HARBOR; POSITION OF JEFF DAVIS ARTILLERY, JUNE 27, 1862

Richmond National Battlefield Park. (Troop Movement Map #4 – Gaines' Mill)

The accuracy of the enemy's gunfire began to tell, as casualties mounted. "In fact the missiles of death were so thick it would seem that no living thing could exist in its range. From this fire men and horses fell in rapid succession."[11] Even the caissons, with their deadly contents, were hit, causing explosions that added to the slaughter.

In hopes of taking at least some of the pressure off of Bondurant's men, Major Hilary P. Jones, in charge of the artillery of D. H. Hill's division, acted accordingly. First, he brought A. Burnett Rhett's battery to the front in order to support the Jeff Davis Artillery by diverting the enemy's fire from them. P. H. Clarke's and C. W. Fry's batteries were also moved up within supporting distance. These moves, unfortunately, could not undo the damage that had been done.

The fire had become so hot for the artillerymen that they could not have held on much longer even with the assistance of the other batteries. The company was literally being cut to pieces. The ammunition of the battery had been just about exhausted, and there was little point in keeping the weakened battery where it was any longer. The Alabam-

Modern View of ground occupied by the Jeff Davis Artillery during battle of Cold Harbor on June 27, 1862.

ians, except for one gun crew which had volunteered to remain at the front, was relieved and sent to the rear.

While their comrades departed from the battlefield, the volunteers manned one remaining piece, but their gun was silent. Sergeant John Fox Maull, who was in charge of this detachment, had been instructed to fire only on advancing infantry. Obviously, the situation had changed dramatically. No longer were the Alabamians the focus of attention for the Yankee gunners. By that time, their fire had either slackened considerably or had been directed elsewhere, allowing Sergeant Maull's men to hold their present position. Otherwise, their remaining where they were for any length of time, would have been suicidal. Even so, Maull's detachment was soon forced to withdraw. The Yankees had been able to advance undetected to within a few yards of the artillerymen, and there was no choice for them but to limber up and move to a safe reserve position.

Except for those volunteers, the Jeff Davis Artillery had only been able to hold its post for about a half an hour in the face of so devastating a fire on the part of the enemy. Those thirty minutes, in the midst of what could have been considered "hell" for an artilleryman, must have seemed like many hours to the men from Alabama.

Following the departure of the remainder of Bondurant's company from the field, there was a temporary lull in the fighting. The opportunity now existed to remove the dead and wounded from the area, and Purifoy was one of those involved in performing that task. Though the air was free of metal for the moment, Purifoy would soon find out that this unpleasant business was not without its dangers.

With the wounded already transported to a place of safety, Purifoy returned to retrieve the bodies of those who had been killed in the terrible fight. Suddenly, the calm was broken as the guns of the opposing sides opened up once again. Purifoy was caught in the crossfire between the Union artillery and a Confederate battery that had been placed just to the rear of the position that the Jeff Davis Artillery had previously held. Purifoy wrote of his predicament, "For some time I was uncertain which battery would hit me first. The missiles of both seem to have a special spite at me. I soon decided to deflect from this line and get out of line with the danger. On reaching the point we had occupied I found that the enemy had possession of it."[12] He eventually made it to safety, most fortunate to have escaped with his life.

While Bondurant's men attempted to regroup after their latest encounter with the enemy, heavy action was already occurring to the west along the opposing lines. From the Confederate center and right, assaults were launched, first by A. P. Hill's then by Longstreet's division, in hopes of dislodging the Federals. Porter's men, however, had the advantage of strong artillery support and a well-established position. They easily repulsed the Confederate attacks, while inflicting heavy casualties upon the gray ranks.

Realizing that things had gone poorly on the right, Jackson set his and D. H. Hill's troops in motion against the blue host. Not about to ease the pressure along the rest of the line, Lee now ordered a general advance. Throughout the late afternoon, the Confederates attacked, only to be beaten back time and time again. As before, enormous losses were sustained by the gray forces with little noticeable gain. The Union position, however, had been weakened by the poundings it had received at the expense of so many Southern lives. There was still time for one more attack.

As dusk approached, the Confederates were successful in their final thrust. They drove the Yankees from their positions and forced them to retreat. With darkness came a halt to what had been the severest test to date for the Army of Northern Virginia. The battle of Gaines' Mill or Cold Harbor was over.

Lee's army had been victorious, but at a considerable cost, including the near destruction of the Jeff Davis Artillery. It had suffered the heaviest casualties of any battery of D. H. Hill's division that had participated in the fighting of June 27. Private Thomas H. McDonald and Corporal John C. Gregory had been killed while Private Joseph W. Carter received a wound from which he would never recover. He would die on July 5, 1862. A total of fourteen men had been wounded including: Privates John D. Campbell, Wilber F. Claughton, James W. Cox, J. M. Jones and William H. Templin. Because of the severity of his wound, Private Claughton would have to be discharged on October 18, 1862. Privates Cox and Jones (wounded in the right leg) would eventually return to active service with the company. In addition to these losses, twenty-eight horses had been killed or disabled.

Obviously, the Jeff Davis Artillery was in no condition to resume an active role in the present campaign. It was ordered to proceed to Richmond so that it might refit. After remaining there for a couple of days, the Alabamians returned to their division.

Porter's stubborn defense at Cold Harbor had given McClellan the time to work out the details of getting his army to the new base on the James River. There would be other battles in the succeeding days as Lee sought to deliver the death blow to the Army of the Potomac. The pursuit culminated in the Federals' final stand at Malvern Hill, where the Confederates made numerous assaults, only to be cut down as they tried desperately to gain the Union position. During that battle, fought on the 1st of July, Bondurant's battery was held in reserve. After the battle, the Alabamians utilized their horses in bringing off captured artillery. With the close of the terribly one-sided affair at Malvern Hill came the end of the Peninsula Campaign. In the end, McClellan was able to successfully withdraw his forces to Harrison's Landing.

To Lee's chagrin, the Army of the Potomac had escaped from his attempt at its destruction. The invaders, however, had been turned back and Richmond was safe. For the Alabamians, there probably would be little thought of celebrating though they had again proven their mettle under adverse conditions. Even so, the battery's performance had not gone unnoticed. Referring to the action at Gaines Mill, Brigadier General Garland reported, "That fine officer, [Bondurant] his men, and officers, behaved well and rendered an effective fire;..."[13]

Now it was time for that artillery unit to recoup the losses that had resulted from the severe punishment it had received on June 27. The battered condition of the Jeff Davis Artillery had forced Major S. F. Pierson, the Chief of Artillery of the 3rd Division, to order that company back to camp in order to recruit more men and to replace the horses lost in the recent campaign. While in camp, many of those who had been disabled by sickness prior to the start of the Peninsula Campaign rejoined the command. Their return helped to restore the battery to more respectable numbers.

All told, the Alabamians would spend the next several weeks refitting themselves for the upcoming campaigns. Not until the end of July would the Jeff Davis Artillery be ready, once again, to resume an active role in the war. With a new army already posing a threat to the Confederate communications near Gordonsville, Virginia, the promise of renewed fighting loomed near.

CHAPTER V

CRISIS IN MARYLAND

PART I - A CLOSE CALL ON THE MOUNTAIN

The movements of the Federal Army of Virginia in the area of Gordonsville concerned General Robert E. Lee. It was commanded by major General John Pope, whose impressive exploits in the western theatre of the war had earned him the leadership position of that newly formed army. The Army of Virginia had been created while the Peninsula Campaign was taking place, to protect Washington and the Shenandoah Valley.

By the second week of July, Pope had advanced towards Gordonsville and posed a threat to the Virginia Central Railroad. If the Federals gained control of that rail line, communications between Richmond and the Shenandoah Valley would be severed. From there, Pope would also have the opportunity to advance on Richmond. Lee could not ignore that threat. Consequently, he sent Jackson to thwart whatever designs Pope might have. That, in turn, reduced some of the pressure on the Army of the Potomac at Harrison's Landing, but, at present, Major General George B. McClellan had no plans to leave his base on the James River.

Lee continued to send troops against Pope's army, and within a couple of weeks, only D.H. Hill's division remained in front of McClellan. Not long thereafter, Hill's division, including the Jeff Davis Artillery, made a reconnaissance and discovered that the Union forces were shrinking. McClellan's army was being evacuated from the Landing to reinforce Pope.

41

Now that McClellan's force was no longer a serious threat, Hill marched northward to rendezvous with the rest of the Confederate army. Marching through Thoroughfare Gap, the division arrived just as the Second Battle of Bull Run or Manassas was coming to a close. In that engagement, fought on August 29 and 30, Pope's army had been soundly defeated, and his force was in full retreat towards Washington.

D. H. Hill's men joined in the pursuit of the Federal army. On September 1, the Confederates attacked the enemy's rear at Ox Hill. However, there was only limited fighting during that encounter, and there was no opportunity for the Jeff Davis Artillery to take part in the fray. Following that action, the Army of Virginia continued to retreat. With Pope out of the way, a new campaign was about to start for Lee's army.

Fresh from victory at Second Bull Run, the Army of Northern Virginia turned its attention northward. Maryland, and then Pennsylvania, were to be the initial targets of the gray-clad troops.

A successful campaign would mean a great deal to the future of the Confederacy. An invasion into Maryland would, it was hoped, result in a substantial number of recruits for the Confederate army. There was also the possibility that a successful campaign would bring foreign recognition of the Confederate States of America.

On September 4, the Army of Northern Virginia began its march towards Maryland. Moving by way of Leesburg, Virginia, D.H. Hill's division continued on its northerly trek until well after dark, when it reached Noel's Ferry on the Potomac River. "As the men approached the water they were instructed to cross quietly. The September of the water, however, was too much for them, and before they had gone into it far, gave several hoops, such as were used in their charges and had come to be known as the 'rebel yell.' "[1] Once across the river, Hill's men halted and rested for the remainder of the night, now on Maryland soil.

The next morning, the Confederates came across a substantial amount of corn in some nearby canal boats. This forage was a most welcome find, for the horses of the division, including those of the Jeff Davis Artillery, were in an emaciated condition.[2] Meanwhile, the men had to subsist on green apples and rotted ears of corn. For an army starting out on an arduous campaign, that was poor fare indeed.

Meanwhile, disease claimed the life of yet another Alabamian. On August 25, 1862, Private William L. Reid had passed from the company rolls forever.

Early on September 5, the division formed into column and marched in the direction of Frederick, Maryland. Upon reaching the point where the Baltimore and Ohio Railroad crossed the Monocacy River, the men rested. Frederick city was just a short distance away from the opposite shore. Thus far, the Army of Northern Virginia had been unopposed on their march into Maryland.

At that point, several of the artillery companies, including Bondurant's, were parked in a broken field near woods that bordered the field on one side.[3] The horses were unhitched and fed. The gunners rested close by, some seeking out the cool of the shade beneath the artillery vehicles. Privates Purifoy and Calvin J. Kirvin decided to lounge under one of the caissons where they would be protected from the September heat. All was quite relaxed, so relaxed in fact, that through someone's neglect, no guards had been posted to watch over the area.

Suddenly, the air was rocked with the sound of a loud explosion! The caisson beneath which Purifoy and Kirvin were resting was immediately struck by flying debris. Hastily the two men raced out into the open, fearing that they might be caught in another explosion. Burning wood and loaded shells were falling together to the ground! A real catastrophe seemed imminent.

Men rushed to try to extinguish the flames before any of their explosive shells were ignited. Fortunately, they quickly doused the fire and prevented further damage. Without spirited action on the part of several men, numerous casualties might have resulted. Bondurant, as well as Private Joe Blankinship, George G. Jackson and others "...faced the danger and by prompt and cool work prevented the explosion of a single shell."[4]

That explosion had originated in the rear ammunition chest of a caisson two vehicles away and to the right of the one occupied by the two privates. Purifoy described what happened to a fellow artilleryman who was reposing in closer proximity to the blast. "A comrade lying under the caison, next the one that exploded, had his clothing ripped along the seams on the exposed side, so that not a stitch held from his shirt collar to the hem of his pants. His hat was torn to fragments. Yet his skin was broken nowhere, and he seemed to suffer no inconvenience except that he was about naked."[5]

Purifoy also spotted a man, who appeared to be a Confederate soldier, running from the scene. It was believed by Purifoy, however, that the individual in question had been in disguise and was actually an enemy saboteur intent on doing as much damage as possible to the artillery battalion. That would explain the suspicious nature of the blast. It is a wonder that more explosions had not been triggered by the first.

Following their stay near the river, the Jeff Davis Artillery moved with Hill's division as it crossed the stream and moved up the turnpike towards Frederick. They stopped and made camp where they would remain for the next few days, a short distance from the city.

On September 10, the march was resumed, and after passing through Frederick, the division continued to move in a northwesterly direction through the state. They crossed South Mountain and finally halted a mile or two west of Boonsboro, staying there until September 13.

While the Confederate troops marched north into Maryland, Pope had resigned, and he had been replaced by McClellan as commander of the Army of the Potomac. Once reappointed, McClellan had wasted little time in reorganizing his army, which was made up in part of Pope's Army of Virginia, in addition to new recruits and the veterans of the Peninsula Campaign.

On September 5, the I and IX Corps, the first of McClellan's troops to be set in motion, headed for the mountains that were between them and the Southern army. The remainder of the army was soon to follow.

In five days' time, the advance units of the Army of the Potomac reached Frederick, and Lee was worried. He had just divided his army in order to eliminate any enemy forces in the area that might pose a threat to his communications. Jackson had been sent with three columns to take care of the garrison at Harpers Ferry. En route, Jackson would also attend to any Yankees still at Martinsburg, Virginia. Also, Longstreet and D. H. Hill had been ordered to march as far as Boonsboro. However, when a Federal force was rumored to be heading for Hagerstown, Longstreet was told to continue his march to that city. D. H. Hill's division remained in the vicinity of Boonsboro.

With McClellan's army now closing in, Lee's detached forces were quite vulnerable to attack. To make matters worse, a copy of the orders detailing Lee's present operations had fallen into Federal hands. McClellan received a golden opportunity to attack the Army of Northern Virginia. Lee would have to delay the enemy's advance at South Mountain while he attempted to reunite his army. At his immediate disposal were D. H. Hill's division and Stuart's cavalry. Also, Major General Lafayette McLaws and his division could be called upon to aid in the defense of South Mountain.

With so few troops at his disposal, Lee would be hard pressed to hold his ground. Still, the South Mountain ridge was cut by several passes or gaps that had to be defended. Turner's Gap was the northernmost pass that could not be lost to the enemy. Through it ran the road leading to Boonsboro and the wagon trains of the Confederate army. One mile down the ridge, and of much strategic importance, was Fox's Gap. If that pass fell, the way to Turner's Gap would be open to the Federals. Finally, there was Crampton's Gap which was four miles further to the south. The loss of that gap would permit McClellan to place his army between the two halves of Lee's army. It was obvious that the loss of any part of South Mountain would spell disaster for the Army of Northern Virginia.

The defense of Crampton's Gap would be the responsibility of McLaw's division. To D. H. Hill's command would fall the task of holding Turner's and Fox's Gaps. Reinforcements would soon be on the way from Longstreet's division.

By nightfall of the 13th, Hill had placed Colonel Alfred H. Colquitt's Brigade in position at Turner's Gap. Later that night, Brigadier General Samuel Garland's Brigade, to which the Jeff Davis Artillery was attached, started up the mountain. They would be defending Fox's Gap.

Early on the morning of September 14, Bondurant's company reached the crest of South Mountain and went into position. The guns were unlimbered in a nearby field that was surrounded by a stone fence.[6] Not far to the rear, along the road the artillerymen had used to reach their present post, their limbers and caissons were parked. Garland's brigade was close at hand, as support for the battery.

As the morning fog lifted, the Alabamians were able to discern Union movements in the distance. At the same time, the battery was hardly hidden from the Federals. "We could be plainly seen from the valley, east of the mountain..."[7] recalled Private Purifoy. Due to some oversight, no pickets from Garland's brigade had been sent out in front of the battery. Unaware of the enemy's proximity to their position, the infantrymen were relaxing with their arms stacked to the rear of the Jeff Davis Artillery.

Within an hour of going into battery, the artillerymen spotted what were soon discerned to be several Federal soldiers at the far end of the same field they now occupied. The thickness of the foliage around the Confederate position had permitted the enemy to move from the valley up the mountain to their present location without being seen. The sudden appearance of the Yankees had to be a source of deep concern for the men of the Jeff Davis Artillery.

After he was apprised of the situation, Bondurant immediately sent back to the infantry support to see if pickets could be sent out to at least delay the enemy's advance. Garland could not be found, however, and none of the officers present would take the authority and give the necessary orders. A second attempt was made for help, but this also failed.

Bondurant now found himself in the middle of a desperate situation. What chance would his battery have without proper support? Finding it was pointless to pursue the matter any further, he prepared to meet the advancing Federals.

Meanwhile, another force, concealed by the heavy underbrush, had been moving up to the right of the Jeff Davis Artillery. Unaware of that new threat, the Alabamians continued to watch the detachment that had been spotted earlier. Suddenly, the Yankees, who had been heretofore hidden from view, appeared "...almost within a stone's throw..."[8] of Bondurant's right. Bugles sounded, and the Federals began a rapid advance towards the unsupported battery. Almost at the same time, "...a storm of bullets from a volley flew into our [the gunners] midst..."[9] The Alabama company had been caught by surprise and would have to act fast in order to avoid disaster.

Garland rode up and gave orders for the battery to open fire, then retire from the field. Bondurant gave the necessary command, and the guns of the Jeff Davis Artillery quickly changed front! Under the circumstances, there would only be time to fire one round from each piece before it was withdrawn to a safer position.

Having completed the difficult maneuver of turning and realigning their guns to oppose the attack on their right flank, the cannoneers opened fire. One after the other, they sent canister into the advancing infantry. The effectiveness of that storm of iron immediately told as the Federals halted and were forced to regroup. They had not expected such a warm reception from the artillerymen. Bondurant's men than hastily withdrew and moved to a new position further up the ridge, near the cabin belonging to Daniel Wise. After taking up a semi-circular position facing south and southeast, the battery resumed their bombardment of the enemy.

Thus far, the Jeff Davis Artillery company had sustained only two or three minor casualties.[10] During that initial confrontation at Fox's Gap, Purifoy lost a piece of his nose to an enemy bullet. After the war, Corporal Francis M. Wootan would correspond with Purifoy and recall the events that led to the memorable wound. Wootan would write:

> Do you reccollect the South Mountain or Boonsbor fight? When we were almost surrounded by the enemy and were getting out a piece at a time; my piece was the next to last, which was yours or Blankinship's and while you were limbering up, I saw two of the enemy near the fence, in the position to shoot, when I fired my gun in their faces, which caused

them to miss their mark, taking off the tip end of your nose and missing Joe Blankinship entirely. Such times we will never see again.[11]

Considering the plight of the Alabama company, Purifoy had been lucky to escape with only a minor wound. In fact, the entire battery had been fortunate to have eluded the advancing Yankees.

That is, except for one private whose fortunes had taken a decidedly evil turn before the adventures on South Mountain had even begun. Two days earlier, Benjamin Ryan had been captured in Frederick by the Federals. It is not known why the Private was in the city on September 12, but by the morning of the 14th, he was in enemy hands and on his way to Fort Delaware prison.

Fortunately, Ryan's confinement at Fort Delaware would be of short duration. Within a few weeks he would be on his way to Aiken's Landing on the James River for exchange. Later, he would rejoin his old company.

Federal pressure on D. H. Hill's and McLaws' commands was intensifying, and it looked like only a matter of time before the defenders would be forced to relinquish their hold on the Gaps to the enemy.

Garland's brigade had also been a victim of the same onslaught that had necessitated the rapid retreat of Bondurant's battery from its first position on the ridge. The infantry had been caught off balance by the sudden attack, and Garland had had his hands full keeping his men in line. During the heat of the struggle, he fell mortally wounded, and it wasn't long thereafter that the weight of the assault began to tell. The gray line began to break up, as many now demoralized Confederates headed for the rear. Except for some resolute defenders who stood firm, the brigade was in a shambles. Hill sent what few reinforcements he could spare to support the artillery and to bolster what was left of the infantry in that sector. Still, the Confederates were in serious trouble. Amazingly, however, the Yankees did not press their advantage any further, and the lull that followed gave Hill time to strengthen his lines even more.

Already, Brigadier General George B. Anderson was bringing his brigade forward to reinforce what was left of Garland's command. While en route to the front, Anderson's brigade had passed by the Jeff Davis Artillery. About this time, the Alabamians also saw General Garland being carried from the field "...with his buck gauntlets across his breast..."[12]

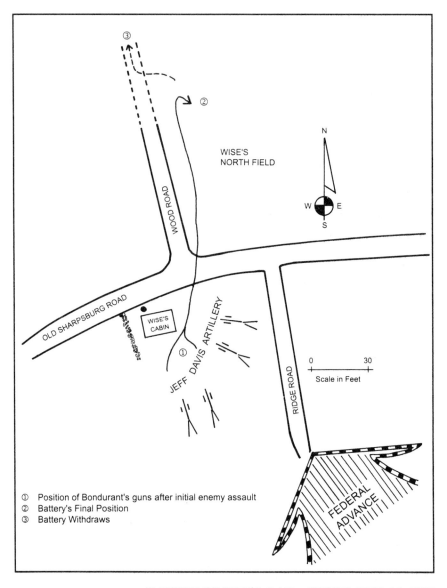

BATTLE OF FOX'S GAP – SEPTEMBER 14, 1862
Based on map by Steven R. Stotelmyer. Sharpsburg, Md.

Bondurant's gunners, as mentioned above, had wasted little time in reaching their new post near the Wise cabin. Once in position, the Alabama battery had opened up upon the enemy and assisted in stopping advance coming from above the road the artillerists had just recently used. The Jeff Davis Artillery kept up a steady fire, until pressure from a Yankee battery made it necessary for Bondurant to shift one section of guns, those located just south of the Wise cabin, to a field further up the ridge. With the repositioning of the guns completed, it wouldn't be long before the Alabamians attention would be drawn to another Federal battery that had just opened to their front.

It had been just about midday when Captain Asa M. Cook, commander of the Eighth Massachusetts Battery, was ordered to position a section of his guns far in advance of the Union army's left. Cook, whose battery was attached to Brigadier General Orlando B. Willcox's 1st Division of the IX Army Corps, placed his two cannon about four hundred yards from the summit of the mountain and commenced firing at a Confederate battery about a mile to the right.[13] After having fired a few rounds, one of Cook's guns became disabled. As a replacement piece was being brought forward, the men of the Eighth Massachusetts Battery were suddenly hit by the canister fire of the unmasked Jeff Davis Artillery, to their left. The Confederate guns were only one hundred and fifty years away. Under fire from such close range, Captain Cook's battery was facing possible annihilation.

Bondurant's gunners had the distinct advantage over their opponents, as they bombarded the Federals with shell and canister. Losses to both men "...1 man having been killed and 4 wounded in one section by the first discharge..."[14] and horses were sustained as the Confederate projectiles hit their mark. So intense was the fire of the Alabama battery, that it "...drove Cook's cannoneers and drivers down the road with their limbers."[15] The remaining artillerymen were forced to seek out cover lest they become casualties as well.

Even the infantry, supporting, and in line to the rear of the Massachusetts battery, was caught in flank by the artillery barrage. "The attack was so sudden, the whole division being under this fire (a flank fire), that a temporary panic occurred..."[16] Though severely rattled, the men in blue were able to adjust their lines so that they faced the Jeff Davis Artillery. Still, the Federals had no choice but to hide as best they could from the terrific gun fire. The Alabamians were holding an entire division at bay.

The guns of Bondurant's battery were continuing to play havoc with the enemy troops, "...killing and wounding at all points..."[17] when

Willcox "...received orders from Generals Reno and McClellan to silence the enemy's battery at all hazards."[18]

While the Federal infantry was preparing for the assault on the Jeff Davis Artillery's position, the brigades of George B. Anderson, Roswell S. Ripley, G. T. "Tige" Anderson and Thomas F. Drayton, emerged from the woods and advanced upon the bluecoats. Reinforcements from Longstreet had arrived, and Hill, now with more men at his disposal than at any other time during the day, had taken to the offensive in hopes of relieving the pressure on his right.

The Union troops were immediately ordered forward to meet the attack, and a serious clash occurred. The Confederate advance, however, had been disjointed, and the men in gray were eventually forced to give ground. Soon, Federal pressure also caused the one section of guns belonging to the Jeff Davis Artillery that had remained in position close to Wise's cabin for most of the day, to abandon its post in favor of one still further up the ridge. At the crucial moment, Brigadier General John B. Hood's troops arrived and stabilized the situation until nightfall when the fighting died down. Fox's Gap had been held.

Thanks to a determined and vigorous defense, Turner's Gap was also secure by the end of the day's fighting. Again, men from Longstreet's division had helped to stem the blue-clad tide at that place.

In the meantime, the news from further down the ridge was not good. Crampton's Gap had fallen. In spite of a gallant fight put up by McLaws' division, Union forces had overwhelmed the Confederate position. Following the debacle, a line was hastily drawn up in the valley beyond the gap in hopes of stalling the Federal advance. The Yankees, however, did not push their advantage. As darkness fell, operations ceased around Crampton's Gap, and McLaws could breathe a sigh of relief.

Back at Fox's Gap, it was well past dusk. The Jeff Davis Artillery had exhausted its ammunition, and the Alabamians were forced to return to the trains in order to replenish their supply. Upon reaching the artillery train, they found that the supply of ammunition was severely diminished. Nevertheless, the cannoneers procured what they could for their four pieces.[19] Bondurant's battery now had the opportunity to catch up on some much needed rest. The exhausted artillerymen quickly dropped off to sleep, surrounded by the wagons of Lee's army.

Even with Longstreet's division at hand, the Confederate position on South Mountain was still precarious at best. Federal reinforcements were already being brought forward, and with the forces under Jackson still some distance away at Harpers Ferry, the rest of the southern army could not remain where it was. A retreat was ordered back to Virginia. However, shortly thereafter, news came of the impending fall of Harpers Ferry. The following morning, Jackson would be on his way to rejoin Lee. Orders were quickly changed, and just before midnight, the defenders of South Mountain began a march that would take them to Sharpsburg, Maryland.

While the men of the Jeff Davis Artillery enjoyed the sleep that they so richly deserved, the situation around them was undergoing a dramatic change. Their army was abandoning its lines on South Mountain. That same night, the enemy moved forward and occupied those positions that had been so stubbornly defended by the Confederates on the 14th. By some oversight, Bondurant's Alabamians, as well as Captain W. P. Lloyd's Battery and Colonel Allen S. Cutts' Battalion of reserve artillery, had not been notified that the rest of the Confederate army was pulling out. Even the noise of the departing wagon train had failed to give warning to the artillerymen that some general movement was underway. The men continued to sleep soundly, unaware that their position was in danger of being swallowed up by the advancing Federals.

The following morning, the picture that presented itself to the eyes of the waking Confederates was not very encouraging. Bondurant, Lloyd, Cutts and their commands were all that remained in the area, and without orders.[20] The trains were gone. The artillerymen were now isolated from the rest of the army. If quick measures were not taken, the artillery units would be trapped.

Small arms fire, as well as an occasional artillery round, was soon heard from the direction of Boonsboro. McClellan was coming too close. Private John Purifoy recalled, "After waiting for some time our Captain, Bondurant, fearing we had been overlooked, rode off in the direction of the firing..."[21] He did so in hopes of finding answers and instructions for his men. Bondurant soon located Brigadier General Fitzhugh Lee, the commander of the cavalry force that was covering the retreat of the infantry. Bondurant learned that the way to the Sharpsburg Road, which had been used during the withdrawal, had been cut off. Another road would have to be found if the Jeff Davis Artillery was to escape capture. Time was running out for the Alabamians.

Fortunately, an alternative route was located, upon which the artillery could probably move and not encounter the enemy. Travelling the selected route in the direction of Sharpsburg, however, proved to be quite an adventure, as the road was uneven at best, with hills and rocks being encountered the entire way. Even so, the horses pulled the artillery vehicles rapidly along the road, in itself, was truly a remarkable feat because of the condition of the horses. They themselves were worn out from the rigors of the campaign. "For days previous our jaded horses could not pull the guns and caisons, except by the help of the canoneers pushing at the wheels,"[22] wrote Purifoy. The horses must have understood that they were in a race for their lives.

Every second counted for Bondurant's battery. The enemy was not very far behind. Every so often, a gun would be halted, unlimbered and used to fire a shot back at the advancing foe. This caused the pursuing Federals to move more cautiously, allowing the Jeff Davis Artillery more time to escape.

The battery continued to move along swiftly, and finally, it reached the safety of the Confederate lines at Sharpsburg just by a hairsbreadth. In fact, it was only a few minutes before the route that had been utilized by the Alabamians was in possession of the enemy, who had extended his lines right across the road. To be sure, it had been a narrow escape for the Jeff Davis Artillery. Now safely within their own lines, the men of Captain Bondurant's command would have plenty of time to prepare themselves for the next encounter with the enemy. The battery would remain in an artillery park for the balance of the day.

PART II - ANOTHER DESPERATE FIGHT FOR BONDURANT'S MEN

While Lee's army concentrated west of Antietam Creek along the ridges that ran north and south of the town of Sharpsburg, McClellan moved into position on the east side of the stream. At that stage, Lee was still at a decided disadvantage. His available force was badly outnumbered, and a massive attack could spell disaster. McClellan, however, failed to take advantage of the opportunity that lay before him on September 15.

The following morning evidenced no change in disposition for the Jeff Davis Artillery. Though an artillery duel did shatter the stillness of the early daylight hours, Bondurant's company was not called upon to participate in the bombardment that raged for some time back and forth across Antietam Creek. Much of the 16th would be spent maneuvering troops in preparation for the approaching battle.

Early that day, Jackson's force arrived from Harpers Ferry and went into position north of Sharpsburg. Upon his arrival, Jackson took command of the Confederate left. Longstreet commanded that part of the line that ran from just north of Sharpsburg to about a mile south of the Maryland town. During the afternoon, the Confederate position below Sharpsburg was bolstered by the arrival of Brigadier General John Walker's Division. Even with those additional troops, Lee would still be hard pressed to present a strong enough front when the north finally moved against him. That same afternoon, the Federals prepared for their first offensive strike west of Antietam Creek.

At 2:00 p.m., Major General Joseph Hooker's I Corps of the Army of the Potomac began a march that would take it across the Antietam to a position north of the Confederate left. The troops moved as far as the Hagerstown Pike, in the immediate vicinity of the North Woods, where they were formed for an attack against Lee's flank.

As the daylight disappeared, the line moved forward. Soon the opposing forces collided, and a sharp, but brief, fight ensued. Artillery from both sides joined in, but darkness put an end to the engagement. Nothing had been gained as a result of this encounter, and the enemy withdrew back to the North Woods. Nevertheless, the stage had been set for what was to occur the following morning.

At first light on September 17, the battle opened as the skirmishers of each army became involved in a heated exchange of gun fire. Soon thereafter, a massive attack was made against the Confederate left by Hooker. During the furious struggle that followed, both sides sustained severe casualties.[1] Men were literally killed in rows on that part of the battlefield later to be referred to as the bloody cornfield. The Union troops forced the gray-clad combatants back, and the intense fighting continued for some time as Lee's men bitterly contested every inch of ground. Not until counterattacks were made by the forces under Hood, McLaws and others, were the Federals driven back enough to relieve the pressure on the defenders in that sector.

As Hooker's men drifted back to the safety of their own lines near the East Woods, Major General Joseph Mansfield renewed the attack with his XII Corps. During the advance, Mansfield was mortally wounded, and his assault met with mixed results. One division was torn apart by the heavy fire of the Confederate troops, while the remaining division was able to advance as far as the Dunker Church, located on the Hagerstown Pike. That force, under Brigadier General George S. Greene, encountered stiff resistance there, and was forced to remain where it was until support arrived. None came and his division would eventually be driven back from its isolated position near the church.

Soon thereafter, came yet another assault aimed at the Confederate left. Major General John Sedgwick's Division, of Major General Edwin V. Sumner's II Corps, advanced into the West Woods, unaware that the Confederates were waiting for them. Sedgwick's men marched right into a trap and were quickly routed. The action now shifted to that portion of the battlefield held by D. H. Hill's division.

While the fight on the Confederate left continued in all its fury, the Jeff Davis Artillery had remained in reserve near the center of the main line. Now with the Federals moving against Hills' Division, the Alabama battery would not remain idle as it had on previous days.

Hill's men were posted along a farm lane known as the Sunken Road, and it was here that they awaited the next onslaught. At about 10:30 a.m., Brigadier General William French's Division of Sumner's Corps advanced on the Confederate defenders. The Federals, however, were hit with a murderous gun fire, and they could make little headway against Hill's men. French's force began to waiver, but reserves were sent in which helped to steady the badly shaken infantrymen. Again the Federals advanced, but a counter-attack by Brigadier General Robert Rodes' Brigade held the enemy in check. Then Major General Israel Richardson's Division arrived on the scene, and the Yankees surged forward once again.

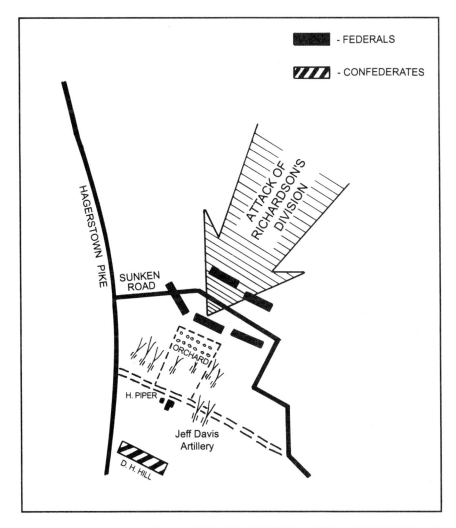

**POSITION OCCUPIED BY JEFF DAVIS ARTILLERY AT
12:00 NOON; ANTIETAM**
Antietam National Battlefield (After Carman and Cope – 1904; Antietam Map #10.)

In order to help relieve the pressure on Hill's men, Major General Richard H. Anderson's reserve brigades were sent forward. However, General Anderson was wounded, and the attack sputtered out. Suddenly, a gap opened within the Confederate line along the Sunken Road. Because of a misinterpreted order, most of Rodes' brigade had withdrawn from their position, and the center began to crumble. A catastrophe seemed imminent! The advance had to be stopped! It was about midday, and the Jeff Davis Artillery was ordered to enter the fray.

Moving on to the field of battle at a gallop, one section of Bondurant's battery was hurriedly unlimbered. The other section of guns had to be left behind, because there was no ammunition for them.

Bondurant placed his two cannon on an elevation approximately 150-200 yards to the rear of the Henry Piper farm house. Looking to their front, or in a northerly direction, the Alabamians could see an apple orchard and beyond that, at a distance of about five hundred yards, was a cornfield. That cornfield extended all the way to the Sunken Road, from which the Confederates were retreating, followed by the men of Richardson's division. In no time at all, the gunners were ready to fire at the advancing Federals.

Already, other artillery units had been positioned, or were being brought forward and posted, not far from the hill upon which the Jeff Davis Artillery was poised for action. Soon all the Confederate batteries were pouring a devastating fire into the ranks of the Union forces. Lieutenant Colonel Nelson A. Miles, of the 61st New York Infantry, reported:

> ...While moving through the corn-field the enemy opened fire with grape and canister from two brass guns on our front, and shell from a battery on our right. It was by this fire that Colonel Barlow fell, dangerously wounded. He was struck by a small piece of shell in the face and a grape-shot in the groin.[2]

In the face of that murderous fire, the Yankees could go no further, and their advance ground to a temporary halt.

By that time, however, the artillerymen were also under heavy fire from the Federal guns. While the Union batteries on the near side of the Creek kept up a steady fire, the heavy ordnance along the east bank of the Antietam enfiladed the area of the Piper farm. Confederate casualties began to mount. Still, in spite of the pounding they were receiving, the southern gunners had to stand firm. The infantry in that sector, though providing a heroic and effective fire, was spread terribly thin and could not hope to hold back the blue tide on its own. The fate of the Army of Northern Virginia rested, to a large degree, upon the shoulders of the artillerymen on Hill's front.

It wasn't long before the situation around the Confederate center, though still extremely critical, began to change as a result of the southern artillery fire. First of all, the guns on the Piper farm succeeded in silencing and forcing the withdrawal of the Federal batteries that had been placed in advanced position opposite D. H. Hill's line. Also, the steady cannonade, plus the determined efforts of the infantry, had proved effective in checking the Federals who had already progressed well beyond the Sunken Road. But they were not content to stay where they were for very long. Soon, the Federals endeavored to, once again, breach the Confederate center. The Yankees moved forward, but the fire of Lee's artillery broke up that advance before it moved far. Shortly thereafter, at about two o'clock, a lull in the fighting occurred. McClellan was satisfied with the situation as it now stood and was unwilling to commit more troops in an attempt to further the gains made on that portion of the battlefield.

For Bondurant's battery, playing a part in the successful defense of the Confederate center had turned out to be a costly endeavor. Private Mitchell W. Day had been killed. At least a half dozen Alabamians had also been wounded, including Private Calvin J. Kirvin who had been shot through both thighs. Private Kirvin would survive his wounds and later be discharged.[3] In addition, the Jeff Davis Artillery had suffered "...the loss of several horses and the explosion of a caisson and limber chest..."[4]

Though severely punished, the Confederate center had held! In fact, Richardson's division had advanced no further than the northern fringe of Piper's apple orchard. But had it not been for the artillery that had been rushed forward, his division may well have delivered the blow that would have led to the ruination of Lee's army. Even so, another of McClellan's corps, in action below Sharpsburg, seemed destined to achieve what all the previous attacks against the Confederate left and center had failed to do.

While the Federal attacks in the vicinity of the Piper farm were being repulsed, another major thrust was being made against the Confederates defending the Lower Bridge that crossed the Antietam to the south. Since about nine o'clock, Major General Ambrose E. Burnside had been endeavoring to move his troops of the IX Corps across the creek. Brigadier General Robert Toombs' Brigade, of Major General

David R. Jones' Division, had been assigned to the defense of the crossing, and they had stubbornly held on to their important position on the
Confederate right for the entire morning. By midday, however, the enemy had located fords above and below the bridge and were already
crossing the Antietam Creek at those points. Also, by that time, Toombs'
brigade was virtually without ammunition, and it pulled back to a new
position on the hill located a short distance to the rear.

At one o'clock, the Federals were finally able to cross the bridge. In
two more hours, Burnside's men were moving up the heights in the
direction of Sharpsburg. The enemy advanced and easily drove the
meager forces of Jones' division that stood in their path, before them.
Another hour passed, and the Yankees were but a half mile from Lee's
only possible avenue of escape across the Potomac.

Confederate batteries could not slow the advance of Burnside's
troops. It wasn't long before the Federals were visible from the town
itself. The enemy appeared unstoppable. Major General Ambrose P.
Hill's "Light Division", which had left Harpers Ferry early on the morning of the 17th[5], had almost reached the battlefield. The only question
was whether that force's arrival would be enough to stave off the disaster that loomed ever closer with the passing of every minute.

At a little past four o'clock, Burnside's IX Corps was within a few
hundred yards of the Confederate line of retreat. Some of the Federals
had even progressed as far as the streets of Sharpsburg. Lee's right
seemed on the verge of collapse, but help had finally come to the hard
pressed defenders. A. P. Hill was already arriving to the south of the
advancing Federal left.

With little hesitation, the exhausted but determined men crashed
into the flank of Burnside's Corps. The shock of the powerful Confederate assault caught it by surprise, causing the Union attack to grind to
a halt. The blue lines swayed, and a general movement back towards
Antietam Creek began. The men of the IX Corps received a deadly fire
from the Confederate artillery as they retreated, not stopping until they
reached the ridges located along the west bank of the creek. A. P. Hill's
attack had preserved the Confederate right and averted an almost certain calamity from befalling Lee's army.

As the shadows lengthened and disappeared, the action gradually
subsided on the Confederate right. Meanwhile, on another part of the
battlefield, the tired Alabamians prepared to leave their post near the
Piper farm for their camp to the rear. They had had a busy afternoon.
During the latter part of the day, the Jeff Davis Artillery had again been
called upon to aid in the defense of the Confederate center. That time,

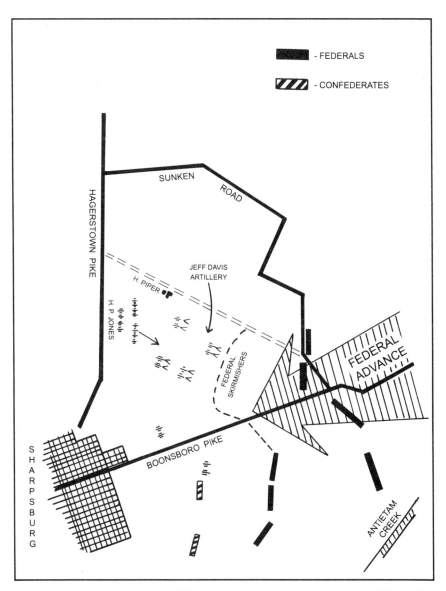

ALABAMA BATTERY'S POSITION AT 4:00 P.M. – ANTIETAM

Antietam National Battlefield (After Carman and Cope – 1904; Antietam Map #13.)

Modern view of hill (in foreground) occupied by Jeff Davis Artillery at battle of Sharpsburg, September 17, 1862 at 1:00 p.m.

(Author's collection) Wedgewood Studio

Modern view of ground occupied by Jeff Davis Artillery at battle of Sharpsburg, September 17, 1862 at 4:00 p.m.

(Author's collection) Wedgewood Studio

however, the Federal attack had originated to the right of the position that the battery had held since about noon.

At about four o'clock, while the desperate fight on the right was nearing a climax, the Alabamians had been shifted from their position on the hill to a spot about three hundred yards southeast of the Piper farm house. Their job was to stop an enemy column that was approaching by way of the Boonsboro Pike. With its guns now facing east, Bondurant's command, several other supporting batteries, as well as a small band of infantry, all readied themselves for the confrontation with the enemy.

The gunners anxiously held their fire as the Federal skirmishers moved towards them, followed by a heavy column of infantry. The men of the Jeff Davis Artillery, whose two guns were closest to the enemy, must have been a bit concerned as they watched the Yankees move within a range of their artillery pieces. The Confederate gunners and the thirty or so men of Lieutenant Colonel W. H. Betts' Thirteenth Alabama Regiment, acting as support for the artillery, silently awaited the order to fire.

Onward the men in blue moved, ever narrowing the gap between themselves and the Confederates, and seemingly unaware of what lay ahead. Suddenly, the air was filled with the shouts of the gray-clad officers, followed by a deafening roar as their men sprang into action and let loose with every available gun. The Federal reeled in the face of the overwhelming fire, and the "...sudden storm of grape and canister drove them back in confusion," routing them.[6] For the remainder of the day, the Yankees were satisfied not to attempt any more assaults against that Southern position.

For the next few hours, sporadic fire continued across the entire battlefield. There would be no more heavy action this day. As night fell, any remaining gunfire came to a halt. By that time, the Jeff Davis Artillery had already arrived back in camp. There, the Alabamians sought "...rest and food such as could be had for both men and horses."[7] During the fighting on the 17th, they had performed admirably in two crisis situations. Their respite was well deserved.

The Army of Northern Virginia had sustained heavy losses on that memorable September day, but Lee was not about to abandon his position. On the morning of the 18th, Bondurant's battery was again sent forward. The company occupied a position "...that to every man seemed a veritable death trap. Every man seemed impressed with the idea that if the battle opened there with us the chances of escape with life were exceedingly slim."[8]

The Jeff Davis Artillery had been placed in the same area they had held until the close of the previous day's action. Their position was opposite the center of McClellan's line, and it is probable that if the Federal forces advanced, they would envelop the very spot upon which the guns of the Alabama company sat. The battery would remain in that hazardous position for the entire day, but the enemy would not take the offensive. All remained quiet on September 18, to the immense relief of all, each of whom "...had determined to sell himself as dearly as possible."[9]

That same afternoon, Lee concluded that there was no longer any advantage to keeping his army on Maryland soil. McClellan was being reinforced, and his position was just too strong to assail. Therefore, the Army of the Northern Virginia would be withdrawn from Sharpsburg.

That night, with Longstreet's men leading the way, the army departed for Virginia. The Jeff Davis Artillery took its place in the column and moved towards the Potomac. By the following morning, the battery had reached and waded across the river. The invasion of the north had come to an end.

C HAPTER VI

GUNBOATS AND ARTILLERY

The Confederate invasion of the North had led to two major battles in which the Jeff Davis Artillery had distinguished itself. In those engagements, the battery's performance had not gone unnoticed. General Robert E. Lee's Chief of Artillery, Brigadier General William N. Pendleton, praised it shortly after the battle of Sharpsburg. In his report, Pendleton referred to Bondurant's command as "...an admirable battery, that has rendered eminent service;...."[1] Nonetheless, how ever admirably the batter had performed during the heat of battle, the rigors of the campaign had still taken their toll on the men of the company and, in particular, Captain James W. Bondurant.

Bondurant had taken ill, and without him the Jeff Davis Artillery could not be expected to operate in its usual excellent manner. As Pendleton remarked, while referring to the Captain's role, in his report of October 2, 1862, "...he is its life; without him it is inefficient..."[2] Consequently, the battery was ordered by Pendleton to remain in the rear while its commander recuperated. The Alabamians could look forward to a well deserved rest.

During the month of October, the Army of Northern Virginia rested and reequipped itself in Virginia's Shenandoah Valley. For the time being, the Confederates did not have to worry about any offensive action on the part of their chief adversary. For about a month, Major General George B. McClellan would be content to stay put and reorganize his army.

Back in the Valley, Lee's army continued to recoup its losses and prepare for the next battle. In spite of the hardships and disappointments of the previous campaign, the morale of the men was remarkably high.[3] "The jest, the practical joke, the ready laugh passed around; and for a time the whole army seemed to be in extravagant spirits, cheering upon the least provocation, like a party of boys, and permitting no occasion for indulging in laughter to escape them."[4]

The wearers of new clothing very often fell victim to the humorous taunts of their fellow soldiers. Here is one soldier's account of what went on:

> A cavalryman comes rejoicing in immense topboots, for which, in fond pride he had invested fully forty dollars of pay; at once the cry from a hundred voices follows him along the line; 'Come up out of them boots!- come out- too soon to go into winter quarters! I know you are in thar- I see your arms sticking out!'[5]

Even the officers were not immune from the quick comments of the men within the ranks:

> A fancy staff officer was horrified at the irreverent reception of his nicely twisted mustache, as he heard from behind innumerable trees: 'Take them mice out o' your mouth!-take 'em out- no use to say they ain't thar: see their tails hanging out! Another sporting immense whiskers, was urged to 'come out of that bunch of har! I know you are in thar!- I see your ears working!'[6]

These brief comical encounters no doubt helped the Confederate soldier to better cope with the realities of war. Meanwhile, the seriously ill Private William H. Smith of the Jeff Davis Artillery died in a Staunton, Virginia hospital on November 3, 1862.

The constant threat of disease was just one of the problems that the army was faced with in the Shenandoah Valley. Throughout the encampment, there was a serious lack of proper protection for the men from the elements. Tents were scarce, and the soldiers had to put to good use any items they thought would be of help in constructing a shelter. As a result, the camps took on an interesting appearance and were described thusly by one soldier, "Hence, although a wall tent or Sibley graces an occasional locality, the most of the men ensconce themselves in bush built shelters of various shapes, in fence corners, under gun-blankets, eked out by cedar boughs, or burrow semi-subteraneously like the Esquimaux."[7]

By the end of October, the organization of the Army of Northern Virginia had changed. The army had been divided into two major fighting units. One part, the First Corps, would be commanded by Lieutenant General James Longstreet, while the other, or Second Corps, was given to Lieutenant General Thomas J. "Stonewall" Jackson. To the Second Corps, in addition to Jackson's own division, were to go the commands belonging to Major Generals Richard S. Ewell, Ambrose P. Hill and Daniel H. Hill. This meant that the Jeff Davis Artillery would be serving under perhaps the most renowned general in the army. With Jackson at the helm, the future certainly showed much promise for Bondurant's command.

Near the end of October, the newly reorganized Army of Northern Virginia prepared to leave its encampment in the Shenandoah Valley. The Army of the Potomac was showing signs of renewed activity and would have to be watched. Because Lee could not yet determine the enemy's plan of operations, he divided his army. On the 28th, Lee sent Longstreet in the direction of Culpeper, while Jackson was directed to proceed with his forces closer to Winchester.

For about three weeks, Jackson's Corps operated independently in the upper portion of the Valley. During that time there was little opportunity for combat, so Jackson destroyed as much of the railroad track in the area as possible. Though the destruction of the railways was necessary to prevent their use by the enemy, that task did not sit well. As one disgruntled soldier wrote, "The only 'useful occupation' of this brigade for some time past has been to destroy all the rail roads in reach; apparently, too, for no better reason than the fellow had for killing the splendid anaconda in the museum, because it was his 'his rule to kill snakes wherever he found them.' "[8]

Meanwhile, the Union army had crossed the Potomac River and had moved in a sluggish fashion towards Warrenton, Virginia. Though McClellan was supposed to be moving after Lee, his lack of aggressiveness had already caused much frustration in Washington. On November 7, Major General Ambrose E. Burnside replaced McClellan as commanding general of the Army of the Potomac.

Shortly after he assumed his new position, Burnside reorganized his forces. The most important of these changes was the dividing of the army into three Grand Divisions, commanded by Major Generals Edwin V. Sumner, Joseph Hooker and William B. Franklin. Burnside did that to reduce the number of generals reporting directly to him.

On November 15, the lead elements of the Army of the Potomac left the Warrenton area on their way to Falmouth, located on the east side of the Rappahannock River. In just four more days, Burnside would have his entire army concentrated there. Across the river was the city of Fredericksburg, and beyond that lay Richmond.

The rapid Federal movement towards Falmouth caught Lee by surprise, and he immediately countered Burnside. He sent Longstreet's Corps to Fredericksburg, and told Jackson to return to the rest of the army.

On November 20, Jackson left Winchester and in five days, moved his forces as far as New Market, Virginia. The Second Corps then turned east and continued on to Orange Court House where the men were given a three-day rest. Jackson then continued towards Fredericksburg.

Since its arrival at Falmouth, the Army of the Potomac had not stirred from its position. That period of inactivity proved invaluable to Lee, as it gave him ample time to gather his forces together and ready them for the anticipated confrontation.

To the west, meanwhile, the bite of winter was already gnawing at the Jeff Davis Artillery, as they moved with D. H. Hill's division on the road to Fredericksburg. Even before they had departed from the Valley, the men had been witness to the first snows of the season.[9] Though they were certainly tougher and more prepared to deal with the rigors of military service, one could not help but wonder if the Alabamians were really ready for the hardships associated with a winter campaign. These artillerists could ill afford a repeat of the horrors of the previous winter, when disease had struck down so many. Foremost in importance, however, was the Federal presence on the far side of the Rappahannock which presented a more serious threat to the battery's existence than any of the other difficulties faced by the Alabama company at that time.

On November 30, Jackson's Corps reached the Fredericksburg area and began to move into position to the right of Longstreet's troops. A few days after his division's arrival near the city, D. H. Hill was ordered to continue his march to Port Royal, which was about twenty miles further down the Rappahannock River. There, the division was to guard against any crossing that the Federals might endeavor to make.

As it turned out, Hill's men would remain at Port Royal for about nine days, during which time they would see comparatively little of the enemy while according to Private John Purifoy, "...almost freezing from the cold."[10] There were, however, two encounters with the Yankees, one of which resulted in action for the Jeff Davis Artillery.

When the Confederates reached Port Royal, they found that the enemy had four gunboats anchored near the town. As a result, part of the division's artillery was brought up and positioned so as to challenge that floating menace. Then on December the 5th, Hill's guns opened on the ships and drove them down the river. "In a few days the pirates returned as high as Port Tobacco with five more of their thievish consorts."[11] On this occasion, all the guns of the division, including Bondurant's joined Colonel John Thompson Brown's First Reserve Artillery Battalion in bombarding the enemy. As Hill reported, "The firing was bad, except from the Whitworth, and it soon drove them under cover of a thick growth of woods, where they lay concealed."[12] This ended for a time, any trouble that the gunboats' presence may have caused the Confederates.

Except for those two incidents, Hill's division had a relatively uneventful stay down the river. They had seen nothing to indicate any Federal desire to attempt a crossing at Port Royal and to resume offensive operations against Lee's army. Them, on one December morning, all heads turned up river to hear the distant sound of artillery fire.[13] The men knew something big was afoot, but where?

It was Thursday, December 11, and the rumble of the guns was coming from the Union artillery on the far side of the Rappahannock River opposite the city of Fredericksburg. "This was no new sound. For a year or more it had been the music we marched to," wrote John Purifoy.[14] Though they were unaware of it at the time, the Confederates at Port Royal were actually hearing the crescendoing sounds of a battle that had already been in progress for hours.

Since first light, Burnside had been trying to complete three pontoon bridges traversing the river in the immediate vicinity of Fredericksburg. However, a determined resistance by the defenders occupying the west bank had forced the Federal engineers to stop their work soon after it had begun. Burnside's force had employed its artillery in support of the bridge builders, but even that had not discouraged the Confederates. The deadly sniping of the Southern marksmen, who were in positions along the river bank and within the city itself, continued to thwart any efforts to finish the task of laying the pontoons.

A frustrated Burnside decided to utilize more of his firepower in hopes of driving the Confederates out of Fredericksburg. At ten o'clock, all of the Federal guns within range of the city opened with a furious roar that reverberated up and down the river for miles. The tremendous storm of iron that followed left much of the town in ruins but failed to achieve its real objective of ending Southern resistance on the west shore.

Then the Union force undertook a new strategy. Volunteers manned a number of the pontoons and rowed across the Rappahannock. Moving with the support of their artillery, the Yankees gained the opposite side of the river with little loss and, soon thereafter, established a firm footing at the landing point. Reinforcements followed, and the struggle for Fredericksburg moved into and through the streets of the city. The Confederates refused to yield and stubbornly fought on until well past dark, when they withdrew to the heights beyond the town. By then, the Federals completed a number of pontoon bridges, at and below the city, and began moving their army across the river. The bulk of Burnside's army would follow on the morning of the 12th.

Meanwhile, after a day of listening to the distant sound of battle from their post at Port Royal, the men of D. H. Hill's division anticipated the order that would start them on their way to their next confrontation with the enemy. Finally, in the decidedly chilly pre-dawn hours of December 12, orders were issued for the men to cook three days' rations. "Before day the rations had been prepared, our scanty camp equipage packed, and before daylight were marched out and put in order to be moved to any point most needed," remembered Purifoy.[15] However, hours passed, and still the column did not move. Up river, Lee was watching the enemy's movements with keen interest, and, as yet, there was no urgent need for Hill's division to rejoin the rest of the army. They would have to wait.

That morning, while they awaited their marching orders, no doubt Hill's men could hear the sound of cannon fire coming from the same direction as on the previous day. Unknown to them, Burnside's army was across the Rappahannock attracting the fire of the Confederate batteries located on the heights beyond Fredericksburg. Even so, the morning passed, and the day wore on, with still no change in disposition for the men of Hill's division. Finally, near sunset, however, the order to move was received from Jackson, and the column started on its way.

At first, they were only aware that they were heading in the direction of the heavy fire that they had heard earlier in the day. They soon learned, however, that the source of the thundering noise, had, in fact, been Fredericksburg itself, and that city was to be their immediate destination. The march was a long one, and not until very late that same night did the column arrive at the end of its journey.

The division had reached the extreme right of the Confederate army's position on the ridge west of Fredericksburg, and it was here, along a nearby road, that the tired soldiers made camp. The night air was bitterly cold, so the men of the Jeff Davis Artillery joined their comrades in gathering and burning "...miles of brush fence to keep from freezing."[16]

The next morning, they awoke to the sound of troops being shifted into position in thick fog that hung over the entire area. Before long, the Alabama company was moved with the rest of the batteries of D. H. Hill's division to an artillery park on the Confederate right in the vicinity of Hamilton's Crossing. For the present, the Jeff Davis Artillery would occupy a reserve position behind the lines, while Hill's infantry would be held in readiness near Jackson's right flank.

Soon the fog burned away, and as Purifoy remembered, "...there was one of the most magnificent sights that ever presented itself to the writer [Purifoy]."[17] Before him was a valley that had virtually been turned blue by the great numbers of men who had been placed there in preparation for the attack against Lee's lines. As expected, the contest was not long in starting. The opposing pickets opened fire on one another, and soon the blast of an occasional cannon joined the rattle of musketry. Then the Federals advanced towards the Confederate right, and the sound of battle increased until a deafening roar filled the air.

Major General George G. Meade's Division, of Major General John F. Reynolds' I Corps, led the attack aimed at Jackson's position. Meade was supported by Brigadier General John Gibbon's Division, and the two moved forward until Confederate artillery fire caused a temporary halt. Resuming their advance, they again had to recoil in the face of even heavier fire from the Southern troops, stopped well short of their objective.

A long delay ensued, but then at about one o'clock, the Yankees were ready to try again. Artillery support was stepped up, and the two divisions moved forward. Once again, the infantrymen were hit by a heavy cannon fire. The blue lines wavered, but this time the hesitation they showed was only temporary. The advance continued.

As chance would have it, directly ahead of the blue-clad soldiers lay an opportunity that, if properly grasped, could only result in a major success for the Federals. Meade's division was fast approaching a section of the Confederate line that had been left undefended because of the swamp nature of the ground. Under normal conditions, the marshlike terrain would have proved to be a serious obstacle for any advancing troops, but such was not the case on this December day. The boggy ground was, in fact, partially frozen and did not delay the attacking foe in the least. It wasn't long before the enemy had entered and was exploiting that gap.

The situation was a serious one for Jackson's men, as Meade's battered, but determined troops swept forward. Several hundred prisoners fell into Federal hands, and casualties continued to mount on the Confederate side. Meanwhile, Gibbon's division became involved in a fierce fire fight with the gray-clad troops occupying the defenses immediately to the right of the break through. There, that Union force was being held in check and could lend little support to their comrades who were then pushing towards the Confederate rear.

Soon, however, the progress of Meade's now unsupported division began to slow, as it ran into increased opposition from the Southern troops. Reaction to the crisis on the right had been swift, and reinforcements from nearby brigades had been moved into the area to bolster the already hard pressed defenders who were stubbornly resisting the Yankee advance. Assistance was also on the way from Major General Jubal A. Early's Division, which was rushing from its reserve position to the breach in Jackson's line.

Suddenly, events took a dramatic turn, as "Old Jube's" men arrived and crashed into the enemy force like a tidal wave! The Federal assault was wrecked, and Meade's division driven back through the gap. The weight of the counterattack also forced Gibbon to give ground, and soon the Confederates were pursuing the retreating Yankees back down the hill to the valley below. The pursuit continued until Federal reinforcements arriving on the field, counterattacked. That, plus a hot fire from the Union artillery, forced the Confederates to withdraw back to their own lines. Though the gray-clad troops were retiring, their spirited counterattack had restored Jackson's broken line and preserved the Confederate right.

The Second Corps position was once more intact, but the repulse of the Federals, and the subsequent withdrawal of the pursuing Confederates, had not reduced the action on Jackson's front. A violent artillery duel had commenced, and the batteries that had inflicted so much damage upon the Yankee infantry were now subjected to a terrible pounding themselves. Soon, some of the guns, which had been in action all day, had to be pulled from the fight. Ammunition was low, and the cannoneers were "...exhausted from working with diminished numbers..."[18] The reserve artillery was brought forward under heavy fire, to fill the vacated spots along the line. Included among those units that were now joining the battle for the first time was the Jeff Davis Artillery.

At about two o'clock, one section of the Alabama battery had received orders to move to the front. Advancing rapidly from the rear,

Bondurant soon had his two pieces in position "...on the hill crowning the valley."[19] The Alabamians wasted no time in engaging the enemy, and, at once, were the recipients of a violent counter fire. "Where the enemy's cannon were directed, in this battle it would seem that no animate object could pass through it and live."[20] Even the one section of the Jeff Davis Artillery that had been held in reserve was not safe from the Federal bombardment. Still, in defiance and without hesitation, Bondurant's battery "...belched forth its share of destruction..."[21] against the Yankees.

The contest waxed warm for some time, with several men falling victim to Union artillery fire. Private John J. S. Crosby, who had been released from a hospital just two months earlier after recuperating from a facial wound, was killed, "...struck by a solid shot."[22] In addition, others were wounded, including Private William J. Dennis and Corporal Edward W. Nobles, both of whom received serious foot wounds. Those losses, however, did not hurt the battery's performance, their places were quickly filled by others, and the Alabamians remained steady in their work. Soon the cannonade began to slacken to sporadic firing which continued throughout the rest of the afternoon.

Meanwhile, on Jackson's left, a portion of Major General William F. Smith's VI Corps was making a threatening demonstration against the

Modern view, near Hamilton's Crossing, of position occupied by Jeff Davis Artillery at battle of Fredericksburg, December 13, 1862 at 2:00 p.m.

(Author's collection) Wedgewood Studio

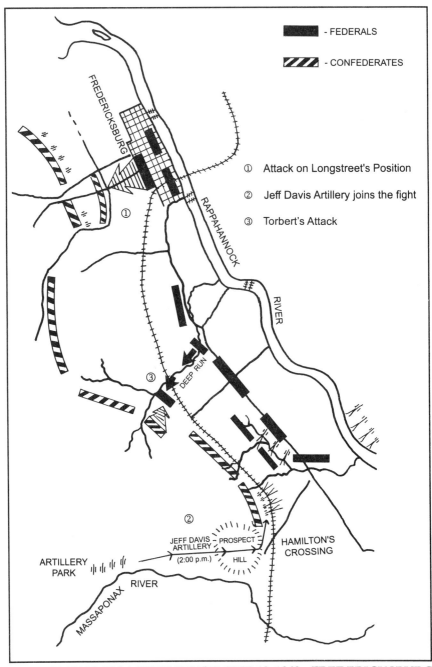

AFTERNOON ACTION DECEMBER 13, 1862 – FREDERICKSBURG
Recreated from Plate XXXIII-1 of The Official Military Atlas of the Civil War.

Confederates who held the railroad cut in the area of Deep Run. There, the Federal advance, which was being made by Colonel Alfred Torbert's Brigade, had already met with some success. Torbert's men had driven back the first gray-clad troops they had encountered and, by now, a number of Confederates were in the hands of the enemy. However, the folly of sending an unsupported brigade against the Southern lines soon became evident when Brigadier General Evander M. Law's Brigade came up, counterattacked, and easily drove the Yankees back to their own lines. With that repulse came the end of any concerted action against the Confederate right.

By late afternoon, firing along Jackson's front had quieted to some degree, but further up the line Longstreet's Corps was fully involved with the enemy. Since about midday, Major General Darius N. Couch's II Corps had been assailing the Confederate defenses on the heights immediately west of Fredericksburg. That Federal attack continued, and each division that was thrown forward suffered horrible losses in their futile attempts to reach the Southern works. Not until twilight would the slaughter finally end on the Confederate left. But even as the skies darkened, there was renewed activity on the Confederate right. Jackson was taking advantage of the twilight to set in motion a plan designed to surprise, and, hopefully, inflict great damage upon Burnside's army.

For several hours, Jackson had been mobilizing his troops in preparation for an attack against the enemy on his front. His plan was to make a rapid strike, near sunset, with every available brigade of his corps. Several batteries were to support the counter-offensive and would go forward shortly before the main advance in order to soften up the Federal position. The fast approaching darkness would offer his infantry some protection, especially if it was forced to retreat. But the artillery that announced the attack would be quite visible and at the mercy of Burnside's guns. The cannoneers would have to act swiftly in order to gain the upper hand on the Yankee artillery. Thus, the element of surprise was crucial to the success of the assault to be made by the Second Corps.

The artillery employed for the operation would have to be in excellent condition and not worn down by the day-long fight. Those batteries that had seen less action, or had been held in reserve during the course of the battle, would furnish the firepower that would pave the way for Jackson's infantry advance. In light of the perilous nature of the duty that the artillerymen were to perform, officers were sought who would be willing to offer the services of their batteries to the Confederate counterattack.

As it turned out, three battery commanders volunteered, including Bondurant. His Alabamians, though exposed to a heavy fire earlier in the day, had not sustained serious enough damage to prevent their participation in another action. Also answering the call were Lieutenants S. H. Pendleton and W. P. Carter who commanded the Morris Artillery and the King William Artillery respectively. They were not strangers to one another. All three were attached to D. H. Hill's division and had fought side by side on numerous occasions.

Time was of the essence, so the cannoneers quickly brought up their pieces and prepared for the upcoming contest. Near dusk, all was ready, and the artillerists awaited the order that would start them on their way.

Soon thereafter, the advance was ordered, and the lead battery emerged from the woods, racing to get into position. The other two companies quickly followed and took their posts well within Federal range. The Yankees quickly spotted the renewed activity on their front, and soon their artillery opened up on the advancing batteries. As Jackson later reported, "The first gun had hardly moved forward from the wood 100 yards when the enemy's artillery reopened..."[23] The Confederates were now subjected to a rapidly intensifying cannon fire. It was obvious that the hoped for element of surprise had been lost.

In spite of that, the gunners remained undaunted and returned the fire. Still, the rapid powerful response of the Federals to the initial phase of his plan left Jackson with no alternative, but to swiftly call off the offensive.[24] His batteries were up against overwhelming odds and could not possibly have achieved the results that were needed for the general advance that was to follow. If his infantry had been sent forward under those conditions, it would have been cut to pieces by the Union artillery. Consequently, the Southern batteries were withdrawn to safety. Gradually the roar of the enemy guns subsided, and the battle of December 13 was over.

That day, the Army of Northern Virginia had achieved an important victory. On the whole, Lee's forces had dealt severely with Burnside's army, while suffering comparatively few casualties themselves. It had been a battle where the Confederate artillery had, once again, played a crucial role from start to finish, but like the Jeff Davis Artillery, not without paying a price for its efforts. The Alabamians, as mentioned, had seen one man from their unit killed, Private John Crosby, and several others wounded during the shellings that had occurred on that memorable afternoon.

Private William J. Dennis' injury had led to the amputation of his foot on the day of the battle. Complications later set in, and in just over a month he was dead. News of the death of Private Dennis came as a complete surprise to his comrades who thought that he would recover following the surgery.[25]

Though unexpected, it seems that the loss of William Dennis, not to mention that of John Crosby, had already been foretold. In a conversation held between Dennis and Purifoy, while awaiting marching orders at Port Royal on December 12, Dennis revealed a terrible premonition. As Purifoy recalled:

> While in this condition, W. J. Dennis, a member of the Jeff Davis Artillery, stopped and was resting with the writer, [Purifoy] who greeted him cheerfully, inquiring after his health, and Dennis replied: 'I am feeling rather sad, Jack. I had a dream last night which impressed me very much. I dreamed I had been in battle and was killed, and in a spirit form was wandering about in space, when I met John Crosby (another member of the company), who also seemed to be in spirit form, having been killed before I was.' ...I tried to impress upon him that dreams had no significance, and to relieve himself of any trouble on that account.[26]

Still considering all that took place on December 13, "Here was an exact foreshadowing of coming events. Who can explain it? There were only two deaths in that battle."[27]

Corporal Edward W. Nobles, on the other hand, was luckier than his battery-mates. He had been wounded in the left foot by an exploding shell, and though he would eventually recover, his days with the Jeff Davis Artillery were over. The list of casualties, however, did not end there.

Even the prized horse "Mollie Glass" had fallen victim to the enemy guns, causing much sadness. The mare, Mollie Glass, had been with the Jeff Davis Artillery almost from the beginning of the company's active service. She had endured the hardships of every campaign and had won a special place in the hearts of the proud artillerymen with whom she served. It is no wonder that her death was so deeply felt. (For the story see Appendix A.)

"Sunday morning (14th) the decisive battle was expected,"[28] reported Brigadier General Pendleton. The morning fog burned off, and there was Burnside's artillery still trained upon the heights occupied by the Confederates. The infantry of the Army of the Potomac was also occupying the same ground as when the previous day's struggle had broken off. The North, however, showed no desire to resume the offensive. In fact, there was surprisingly little activity along the Federal lines.

Occasionally the crack of the skirmishers' rifles broke the silence that hung over the area, and yet, the action that followed would be short-lived and of small consequence. At other times, the Yankee artillery would open, but its fire would only invite a limited response from the Southern batteries. The Confederate gunners were conserving ammunition for the expected Federal push. No such attack, however, took place, and the balance of that day, and all of the next, were marked by little more than desultory fire from both sides.

Then on the rainy night of December 15, the Army of the Potomac stole back across the Rappahannock River, and the battle of Fredericksburg was over. The following morning found the Confederates in possession of the field, but the victory that they had achieved was not complete.

Though the battle of Fredericksburg had concluded, the Confederates still had to be watchful of the events occurring across the Rappahannock. The Army of the Potomac had retreated back to Falmouth, but it was certainly no less of a threat than when its Grand Divisions had first made an appearance along the east bank of the river. The weather had not yet become a deterrent to the moving of troops. Still, for the time being, Burnside was still, and all remained quiet on the far side of the Rappahannock.

For the Alabamians, the lack of enemy activity along the river was no cause for celebration. Several days had passed since the Federal retreat, and so far, the artillerymen had done little more than shiver away the long hours in their camp near Fredericksburg. The battery could not yet move into its permanent winter quarters.

Nevertheless, all was astir within the upper ranks of the company. Once again, the Jeff Davis Artillery was beset by internal problems which, as in the past, would have a significant effect on the entire command.

Specifically, there was unrest among the officers because of Bondurant's demand that First Lieutenants Hugh P. Thomas and Robert A. Yeldell, as well as Second Lieutenant Edward Knight, all submit to an examination by the military board in order to prove their qualifications as officers. This action on Bondurant's part probably came about as a result of two new general orders from Richmond.

On November 1, the Adjutant and Inspector General, General Samuel Cooper, had issued order #81 establishing how many officers and men were to be attached to a four gun battery. A command of that size was to have, "One captain, 1 first lieutenant, 2 second lieutenants, 1 sergeant-major or first sergeant, 1 quartermaster sergeant, 4 sergeants, 8 corporals, 2 buglers, 1 guidon, 2 artificers, 64 to 125 privates."[29]

Then on November 22, an act of Congress (General Orders No. 93) was passed "...to relieve the Army of disqualified, disabled and incompetent officers."[30] This act authorized the commanding general of a department to appoint an examining board "...to examine into the cases of such officers as may be brought to their attention for the purpose of determining their qualifications for the discharge of the duties properly appertaining to their several positions."[31]

It appears that Bondurant was making an effort to conform to army regulations as specified in those general orders. The Jeff Davis Artillery currently had two first lieutenants and one second lieutenant, which had to be changed. This meant possible advancement, demotion or even dismissal from service with the battery for Thomas, Yeldell and Knight.

Regardless of what the outcome of the examinations might have been, events came to a head by the third week of December with Thomas, Yeldell and Knight all handing in their resignations and departing from the company. As a result, the battery suddenly found itself without any lieutenants. A company election would soon have to be held to fill the new vacancy.

On December 24, the Alabamians were finally relieved of their duties at the front. That day, the Jeff Davis Artillery, as well as the majority of the Second Corps Artillery, were led from their camps by Colonel Stapleton Crutchfield, Jackson's Chief of Artillery.

Forage had become scarce in recent days. Because the surrounding countryside could no longer provide enough food for the animals, it was essential that the bulk of the army's artillery be relocated. Lee had directed Crutchfield to move his batteries south of Fredericksburg, where his horses could be more easily provisioned. Thus, a situation that would have proved disastrous to the artillery corps was avoided, even if it did mean that the army would soon be left with but a fraction of its usual artillery support.

But that weakening of the army's potential firepower posed little danger to the Confederate forces remaining along the Rappahannock. Considering the number of guns left behind, plus the strength of the Southern works, and the number of troops available, there was, in reality, little for the defenders to be concerned about. Of course, the enemy's listless state also helped.

On the appointed day, all of the artillery units attached to D. H. Hill's division, except for Captain Robert A. Hardaway's command (which was retained for duty at the front) withdrew from the heights they had defended just days before. Arriving at the nearby railway line, the artillerists boarded a train and were soon rattling south towards Richmond. After travelling about twenty miles, they detrained at Milford Station and moved off a short distance to establish their winter quarters. The Jeff Davis Artillery occupied a wooded area where it went to work building log shelters for protecting against the elements.

Now that the Alabamians were so far from the front lines, the prospects for their participating in any further fighting before the start of the spring campaigns had certainly dimmed. Nevertheless, conditions to the north were to vary little in the days ahead, and December ended on a quiet note for Bondurant's company.

The past year had seen the Jeff Davis Artillery actively participate in all except one of the major campaigns involving the Army of Northern Virginia. The battery had achieved varying degrees of success on the battlefield, but it had had to travel a difficult road to get that far. None of the military maneuvers, nor the idle months leading up to them, had been without their share of deprivations. A lack of proper food and clothing, plus an unhealthy environment, had contributed in many cases to the company's decimation by disease.

That most dreaded of enemies had plagued the command since its inception, but the problems it created peaked during the late spring. At that time, the number of sick men had grown to such a disproportionate level that Bondurant had been forced to temporarily drop one section of guns. Though the general health of the company improved during the summer, the problem of ill health persisted for the balance of the year.

Just as potentially dangerous had been the internal strife caused by disagreeable actions on the part of the officers in command. As previously mentioned, the entire company had been in an uproar over Montgomery's return to the captaincy, especially following his court-martial in December of 1861. Fortunately, though, thanks to the decisive actions taken by the officers and men of the battery, his stay had been brief. Still as a result, the command had been hurt by the resignations of several officers who had already shown much potential.

Life in the artillery company had returned to normalcy shortly after Montgomery's departure, and not until the last two months of the year did problems flare up again among the higher ranking officers. That time, however, the problems which the demands of the Captain caused had not resulted in the degree of disruption that had been witnessed months before. It remained to be seen what the consequences, if any, of this unrest would be in 1863.

Still, even with that and all the other difficulties that had been experienced during the year, the élan of the company had not diminished. This had been abundantly shown by its performance in the field. The battery had come through many critical situations with flying colors and had won the praise of the commanding generals on numerous occasions. Already, the Jeff Davis Artillery had earned distinction within army circles, and now, with the new year upon them, these men from Alabama no doubt wanted to continue where they had left off in mid-December.

How soon it would be before they returned to the battlefield would, for now, be up to the enemy. Whether or not Burnside would move before the storms of winter set in was a question that only he could answer.

CHAPTER VII

A WINTER OF CHANGE

During the early part of January, Major General Ambrose E. Burnside's army had, as in previous weeks, engaged in little more than cavalry reconnaissance while camped near Falmouth. Nevertheless, the Southern forces could not relax their guard. Conditions continued to favor a resumption of operations. Still, it was growing late in the season, and the possibility of renewed fighting before winter hit hard, looked remote. Needless to say, time was working against the Union.

Meanwhile, at their encampment near Milford Station, the men of the Jeff Davis Artillery were also finding an overabundance of time to be a problem. They had only long days in winter quarters to look forward to.

The first of several important reorganizations, however, both at company and division levels, were about to be made. More important though was the fact that each move would have a direct bearing on the future of Captain James W. Bondurant's artillery company.

In fact, exactly two weeks into the new year, on January 14, Major General Daniel H. Hill ordered the Inspector and Adjutant General, General Samuel Cooper, to report to him in Richmond. Hill, as it turned out, was to be given command of the forces in North Carolina. D. H. Hill had been with the Jeff Davis Artillery in every action since the battle of Seven Pines and had proven to be a most conspicuous leader.[1] He, however, would never again assume a leadership role within the Army of Northern Virginia.

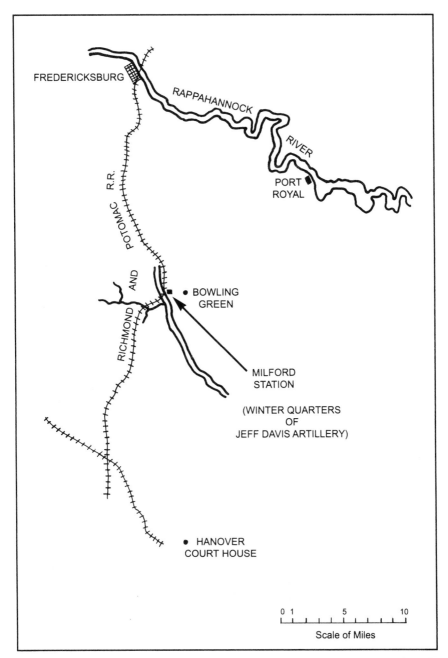

BATTERY'S WINTER QUARTERS – 1862-1863

Recreated from Plate XVI-1 of The Official Military Atlas of the Civil War.

Just one day after Hill was ordered to Richmond, another impor-
tant command decision, though on a totally different scale, was made
about the upper ranks of the Jeff Davis Artillery. On January 15,
Bondurant started to fill the vacancies created by the resignations of
Lieutenants Hugh P. Thomas, Robert A. Yeldell and Edward G. Knight.
He wrote the Chief of Artillery, Brigadier General William N. Pendleton,
recommending that Pendleton commission First Sergeant Dwight E.
Bates a second lieutenant.

Bondurant highly praised his 48 year old sergeant, especially Bates'
achievements early in the war when he "...won from Our much lamented
General Garland on the fields of Seven Pines + Coal Harbor his personal congratulations for his skill at the former + bravery and endurance (on the latter field."[2] With such a glowing endorsement as that of
the late general on his side, Sergeant Bates' advancement seemed certain. However, as the need for company grade officers was urgent,
Bondurant chose not to wait for his request to go through the usual
channels. Taking the initiative, he went ahead and appointed Bates an
acting second lieutenant just five days later, on January 20.

The promotion of Bates was popular among his fellow artillerists.
"The men of the command were personally very fond of Bates, and
when it became known that he had been appointed a lieutenant in the
company, there was a feeling of general relief that the command had an
officer who would not tyrannize over them."[3]

Also important was Bates' potential to help the Alabamians achieve
an even greater efficiency in the field. According to Private John Purifoy,
"He was probably the best qualified man in the company for the position, because of superior education and broad experience."[4] Ironically
though, the Jeff Davis Artillery's location, far to the south of the army's
position near Fredericksburg, was about to nullify what might have
been his first test under fire as an officer.

Even as Bates' first day as an officer was winding down, the situation to the north was changing dramatically. All was again astir along
the Rappahannock. Burnside was moving! By late on the 20th, his divisions had started from their camps, and it was soon apparent that a
major Federal offensive maneuver was under way.

Once again, Burnside was trying to gain the advantage, though he
would be employing a different strategy than he used during the campaigns of the previous December. He was endeavoring to position his
army at crossings up river, in the vicinity of Banks' Ford, for an advance against Lee's left flank. The grand divisions belonging to Major
Generals Joseph Hooker and William B. Franklin (with Major General

Edwin V. Sumner's troops acting as support) were to spearhead the attack, designed to drive the Army of Northern Virginia from its present position. It was a complicated maneuver.

On the night of the 20th, weather conditions took a turn for the worse, and the Yankees suddenly found themselves up against a different foe. A steady rain struck, and before long the ponderous Federal machine literally became stuck in the mud. Though it would try for a day and a half to make headway in the morass, it was a hopeless struggle. The operation was called off, and the now demoralized Union army slogged back to Falmouth.[5] It would be some time before the Army of the Potomac would again do battle. On January 25, Hooker replaced Burnside as commander of the army.

For the Confederates, that meant a period when they would not have to be too concerned about any hostile activity on the enemy's part. While Hooker remolded his army, the Southerners were able to relax and settle into their winter quarters. Moreover, just a few days after the Army of the Potomac had retraced its steps back to Falmouth, another storm had blanketed the area with enough snow to effectively block any chance that either army would soon be moving, let alone returning to the battlefield.

Already, Bondurant, Bates and their company had been subjected to a full month of the tedium and fixed routine that went with life in winters quarters and the season still had a long way to go. But, in spite of that rather dreary outlook, it was not going to be an uneventful winter for the men of Bondurant's command.

The battery's reorganization was still a top priority for Bondurant, and on February 1, 1863 came more internal change. That day, Privates J. M. Jones and Francis M. Wootan were promoted to corporal. Both were combat veterans, and Wootan had been one of the gunners who had shown great skill during the fight for South Mountain.

Two weeks after the promotion of Wooten and Jones, a much larger organizational change took effect. On February 15, all of the artillery attached to D. H. Hill's former division was redistributed into two battalions.

The first, Carter's battalion, included Bondurant's battery, along with Captain William P. Carter's King William Artillery, Captain C. W. Fry's Richmond Orange Artillery and Captain Richard C. M. Page's Louisa Morris Artillery. Though now technically all part of a new fighting unit, those four batteries had nevertheless been in the same division since the Confederates' withdrawal from Maryland, in September 1862. They had first seen action as a team during the arduous Freder-

Colonel Thomas H. Carter

Commander of the battalion to which
the Jeff Davis Artillery was attached
from February of 1863 to May of 1864.

*(Museum of the Confederacy, Richmond,
Virginia. The Long Arm of Lee.) J. P. Bell*

icksburg campaign. Then, they had
made the trip to Milford where they
awaited spring, so they might resume
the real business of war.

The new battalion's commander,
Major Thomas Hill Carter, former`
Captain of the King William Artillery,
was a skilled officer who had conspicuously led his battery since its
first major combat in May of 1862 at
the battle of Seven Pines. He had received numerous accolades because
of his performance in the field. Referring to the artillery's role during
one particular stage of the attack at
Seven Pines, Brigadier General Robert E. Rodes had reported, "It was at
this juncture that Captain Carter and
his men gave a second illustration of
their extraordinary coolness and
courage, the first having been given
in unlimbering his pieces in an open
field and attacking with success the enemy's redoubt, defended by heavier
pieces than his, at the distance of 400 yards."[6] There could be little doubt
that Major Carter was the right man to command the battalion.

With the organization of the four batteries of Carter's battalion now
completed, there was left but one battery from Hill's old division to be
considered. That was Captain Robert A. Hardaway's Alabama battery.
That unit, which had been held for duty along the Rappahannock, was
grouped with three others to form Major David Gregg McIntosh's Battalion of the Second Corps Reserve Artillery. Hardaway, however, was
to be promoted to Major, then assigned to Colonel John Thompson
Brown's battalion, with Captain William P. Hurt taking over the battery.

That innovation was actually just a small part of a full reorganization of the artillery corps of the Army of Northern Virginia as Pendleton
had proposed to Lee on February 11. As Pendleton wrote:

> ...it is respectfully proposed that in each corps the artillery be
> arranged into battalions, to consist for the most part of four
> batteries each, a particular battalion ordinarily to attend to a
> certain division, and to report to, and receive orders from, its

commander, though liable to be divided, detached, etc., as to the commanding general or corps commanders may seem best; past associations to be so consulted in the constitution of these batteries that each shall, as far as practicable, contain batteries that have served together, and with the division which the battalion is still ordinarily to attend....[7]

It should be noted, however, that Lee did not accept Pendleton's recommendations without changing some of his ideas for officers. Also, any promotions could not become official until the required commissions arrived from Richmond, and that, as it turned out, would not occur until April 14. Nevertheless, the first of some very necessary measures, aimed at the betterment of the artillery, had finally been taken, thereby ridding the army of some burdensome and out of date organizational practices.

The practice of attaching a battery to each infantry brigade had long since ceased being effective. In Pendleton's own words,

...Burdened as are brigade and division commanders, they can scarcely extend to batteries thus assigned that minute supervision which they require, and the supply officers, whose chief care lies with considerable bodies of infantry, cannot devote to one or more batteries the time and attention they imperatively need. This is injuriously experienced in time of pressure. The existing arrangement moreover affords insufficient scope for field officers of artillery. Batteries, besides, permanently attached in this way, can scarcely be assigned elsewhere, whatever the emergency, without producing some difficulty, almost as if a vested right were violated. But, most injuriously of all, this system hinders unity and concentration in battle.[8]

The difficulty in rapidly calling up and concentrating artillery, especially when the army was on the move, had been most apparent at the battle of Mechanicsville. There, the crossing of D. H. Hill's artillery at the Mechanicsville Road Bridge had been delayed because each battery had been required to remain with and cross as part of its respective brigade. As a result, valuable time had been wasted at a critical point in the fighting when faster movement of the artillery may have made an important difference.

Another problem involved the proper use of the reserve artillery. Specifically, doctrine required that the general reserve was officially the only source from which reinforcement batteries could be drawn. That practice had precluded the use of the guns of other divisions that might have been more easily accessible. The result had been that the rapid deployment of massed batteries had become nothing less than a monumental task when it need not have been.[9]

After the reorganization of the artillery corps was completed, Lieutenant Edmund P. Dandridge made an inspection tour of the different battalions. On February 20, Dandridge reported,

> Captain Bondurant's Battery – Two 3-inch rifles, one Napoleon, and one 12-pounder brass howitzer, in good order; ammunition good; harness, same as in last report, with the addition of one set of wheel and two of lead; 54 horses and 5 mules in tolerable order and improving; 2 officers and 81 men present; 1 officer and 4 men absent with leave; 4 without leave; 5 men detached; 9 men sick; sends 60 miles for forage, and supply limited, but these batteries will in future get 150 bushels of corn every five days from Hanover Court-House.[10]

As indicated by the above report, the armament of the battery had been changed. In fact, the firepower had been upgraded by the substitution of a Napoleon for one of the howitzers. The effective range of the Napoleon was substantially greater than that of the howitzer, which made the battery more effective at greater distances against the enemy. The report also bears out that the overall health of the company had improved. Though approximately ten percent of the men were afflicted with some ailment, that was still a sharp decline in the number of sick when compared with the same period the previous year. Obviously, the artillerists had been steeled by months of campaigning, and, as a result, were now better prepared to meet whatever discomforts Virginia's winter weather had in store for them.

Also on the positive side, was the fact that the condition of the battery's horses and mules was improving. Forage supplies were being closely monitored by the Second Corps Chief of Artillery, Colonel Stapleton Crutchfield, which combined with the long period of rest afforded the horses, was proving beneficial. The teams and the company they were to transport would both be in excellent condition by the time of the next campaigns.

Even though Dandridge's report contained a number of pluses regarding the status of the Jeff Davis Artillery, it had omitted one important fact. The men were not getting enough to eat. In fact, rations were so inadequate that it was not unusual for a local farmer to find his livestock reduced in number from one day to the next by some soldier attempting to relieve his hunger pains. Even foraging expeditions conducted by a number of men were not uncommon occurrences.

Unfortunately though, the prospects for a quick or even radical improvement in the food situation were slim at best. Without question, foraging was serious business. Even so, the gathering of food could and did lead to some amusing situations for the men of the Jeff Davis Artillery.

T. [Private Matthew Tucker] as brave Confederate soldier as ever faced an enemy, conceived the idea of gathering chickens sufficient to make him a gizzard pie. To those unacquainted with conditions, this would seem wanton waste, not so. Our short rations kept us with sharp appetites all the time. So when T. had his gizzard pie, his messmates willingly compromised on chicken pie. This same forager came in one night and reported that he had killed two nice hogs about a mile and a half from camp, and such a report readily obtained a sufficient number of his messmates as volunteers to bring them in. Two pairs of men went out and strung them on poles between them, and wagged along towards camp. In crossing a broad shallow branch with a sandy bottom, it was necessary to walk some narrow poles to keep out of the water. The first pair with their hog made the trip all right. The next, in their effort to cross, the rear man's foot slipped off and he went down, the pole bearing the weight of the hog falling on his neck, sank his head and face into the sand and water. In the dark his partner could not tell the trouble, but knew there was a fall. After sputtering awhile the unfortunate fallen man, extricated himself, from what proved to have been a dangerous predicament, as he showed that his face was under water and sand. As he came up said "J, god ding you, you would stand there and gigle and let a fellow drown before you would come and help him." These two hogs supplemented the short rations for T's mess for quite awhile.[11]

Surely, the capture of the two hogs must have seemed like a god-send to the hungry artillerymen. Yet, those successful expeditions were still an all too infrequent occurrence for those men encamped at Milford.

No doubt the almost continual food shortages made the men un-witting targets for ills such as smallpox and dysentery. Among those so afflicted were Privates Philip L. Gregory, William B. Marble and David M. Sanders. They all spent at least some portion of the winter in a hos-pital. Sanders for one, had been sick since the previous November but would not be discharged until the first week of May. Both Gregory and Marble would be hospitalized by the end of February. Gregory, as it turned out, would spend two months on the sick list, while Marble was to be incapacitated for the next nine months.

On the other hand, others like Sergeant John Fox Maull, were sent home to recover. In fact, Maull was now finishing a four month fur-lough and soon would be back on duty.

Altogether, a total of eighteen men from the company were ill for extended periods during the winter of 1862-3.[12] It is well worth noting that there were substantially fewer men on the sick rolls that winter than the previous year, when in January, for example, fully one fourth of the men were ill. All things considered, Bondurant's command was actually faring quite well in spite of the trying conditions it was up against.

In addition, during February, five more men had enlisted from Ala-bama, intent on joining the Jeff Davis Artillery.[13] Some were friends or relatives of those who were presently with the battery.

There was one recruit who, unlike the others, had an additional motive, which had prompted his appearance in camp. George A. Jarrett had come to Milford in early February not only to enlist but to serve as a substitute for Private Napoleon B. Merritt.[14] Actually, it had been on February 2 that Merritt had been discharged and replaced by George Jarrett.

Jarrett and the other new enlisted men entered the Confederate ser-vice at a difficult time of the year and had to adjust quickly to a not always friendly environment. Fortunately though, there was also a harmless side to their initiation. A new recruit would often find him-self the object of some practical joke or trial that had been devised by the battery's veterans. C. A. Cobb and George Jarrett were just two of the newcomers duped by the scheme of some veteran.

Cobb's trial came early and was fun:

Young C A Cobb was a recruit, and it entered the mind of the writer [Purifoy] to challenge him for a snow ball contest, during the first snow storm that occurred, after he reached camp. The challenge was accepted and the battle began in earnest, the writer advancing at a rapid run, and pelting him with snow. The battle soon became a hand to hand affair. We soon clinched and snow was freely rubbed into each other's faces and put down the collars and inside of our scant clothing. Finally the work of both ceased, and we grasped each other's hand and were ever afterward good friends, each respecting the courage and endurance of the other. [15]

Jarrett, on the other hand, fell prey to a humorous plot that was planned and acted out by a number of veterans.

Geo W Jarrett had come into the company as an under-age substitute for N B Merritt. Blanks, a veteran who had been among the first to enlist when the company was organized, conceived the idea of getting some rare sport out of the young recruit, the tender boy. He began a series of taunting and jeering at him and continued to become worse and finally pretended that he had been grievously insulted and challenged Jarrett for a dual. The challenge was promptly accepted, the terms arranged, when the seconds chosen, and the place of meeting and the arms to be used, agreed upon. At the time agreed upon each party met at the appointed place, arms, consisting of pistols, properly loaded and positions taken. All but Jarrett, understood that the pistols were to be loaded with blank cartredge. Jarrett really thought they were loaded with ball as well as powder. At the proper time the command was given by the seconds to fire. As the pistols fired, Blanks fell, and Jarrett thinking he had killed him cooly remarked, as his second took him from the field "I have told all these damned fellows to let me alone, that I would hurt some of them. I guess Blanks will not bother me again." On reaching camp Jarrett was charged with neglect of duty, having failed to obey in the performance of some small duty. He was put to work policeing camps as a penalty. He went to work evidently disturbed by the fact that he had killed Blanks, not knowing what might be the final outcome of it. Reflection, of course, caused him to see it in a more grave light than he had, while he was acting under the feeling that carried him into accepting the challenge. In this mood, and steadily raking away in silence, Blanks slipped up behind him silently, and before he was aware of what was taking place, Blanks had seized him, and with a loud guffaw laughed in his face. Jarrett could not have been more surprised if a ghost had clinched him. Explanations followed, and the hand of friendship was extended by each and it was remarked by all that ever afterwards, these two were fast friends until Blanks was killed at the "Bloody Angle," Spotsylvania Court House, May 12, 1864. [16]

Those were just two examples of the mischief that took place during the months in winter quarters. Though other diversions also helped break the monotony of the season. In their spare time, card playing, the organizing of snowball battles and even ice skating provided much amusement for the men. Those activities, along with the necessary foraging, made time pass more quickly, but even so, participation in them did not mean that the business of the battery was left unattended.

The company continued its efforts to find the right people to fill the openings that existed, though so far without much success. By the end of February, Bates was still the only lieutenant, although still without a commission. Earlier on, the company had elected Corporal John Mitchell to fill the post of second lieutenant, but in Bondurant's opinion, he was not an acceptable choice. Hence, he was not commissioned. But, Bondurant's decision left the company even more short of officers.

Then, on February 28, First Lieutenant William J. Reese reached Milford, Virginia and the camp of the Jeff Davis Artillery to assume command of the battery. Bondurant was up for promotion, and would soon be leaving the men he had led since the spring of 1862.

Major General Daniel H. Hill had been impressed by Bondurant's skillful handling of the Alabama battery and had requested his services. Hill wanted Bondurant to be his chief of artillery, which meant a promotion for the captain and yet another vacancy in the company's upper ranks. Fortunately, Reese agreed to return to his old unit.

Reese was undoubtedly a well-liked and respected officer because during the previous month, the Alabamians had in fact elected him first lieutenant, even though he was then serving with the 51st Regiment Alabama Partisan Rangers. [17] Upon his arrival in camp, as one might expect, Reese, in his own words, "...was very kindly received by my old company." [18]

Reese, a dentist by trade, was certainly no stranger to life in the military. He had seen action in the Mexican War at age seventeen and had resumed his career by enlisting in the Jeff Davis Artillery in July of 1861. He had remained with the battery as a second lieutenant, until January 1862 when he submitted his resignation. Like many others, Lieutenant Reese had lost all respect for the battery's incompetent captain, Joseph T. Montgomery.

Following his departure from the artillery company, Reese had served, for a time, under Brigadier General Nathan B. Forrest, in Company H of the 51st Alabama Partisan Rangers. He had stayed with the Rangers until late February 1863 when he began the journey that would bring him back to the Jeff Davis Artillery.

One of the first orders of business for the new commander was to restore the company to its proper strength. As a courtesy to Reese, Bondurant had awaited his arrival before making a nomination for the position of lieutenant. Remembering an acquaintance of his, Reese suggested that Robert S. Walker, formerly an officer with the Jeff Davis Artillery, be considered for one of the openings. Bondurant approved,

Flag design proposed for Jeff Davis Artillery as sketched by Captain William J. Reese. Spring of 1863.

(Sturdivant Hall Museum Association, Selma, Alabama)

and offered Walker a commission with the battery. Whether the ex-lieutenant could be induced to rejoin his old company was still a possibility. Walker no doubt still had a bad taste remaining from his earlier days with the Alabama battery. He had, like Reese, been one of the officers who had been left no choice but to resign from the company in January of 1862. Even so, conditions had changed radically since then, and maybe he could be enticed to return to his former command. Reese solicited the aid of Walker's sister, Margaret, hoping that she could convince her brother to accept the commission. As Reese wrote: "The Company is in better health and spirits now than at any time since its organization, so that everything promises a pleasant time to Robert should he come." [19] However, that and all other efforts failed, and it was a long time before someone else was considered for the position of lieutenant.

During his first days in office, Reese had also shown much interest in another project that had to do with how his battery was to be represented in the field. He early mentioned a design which he wanted used on his company's banner. He spoke of submitting the drawing "...to the 'flag committee' in Congress,"[20] for approval, but that is where the story ends. This topic is not mentioned again in his surviving correspondence, and no such flag has ever been found.

Meanwhile, the routine continued, March offered little excitement. The change of command had unofficially taken place (Bondurant had not yet received his promotion, and until he did, Reese could not receive the rank of captain, and officially be in command.), and everything continued to proceed smoothly for the new commander. Bondurant remained in camp, but Reese exercised control over the company. Moreover, as battery commander, Reese was now more than ever required to keep a vigilant watch over the animals that were expected to move his guns.

In fact, by mid-March, the proper care of the horses had become even more of a priority for this and every battery of the Corps, and for good reason. Though efforts had been made to improve supplies during the winter, it had not been an easy task. Nor had it been totally successful. Because of a lack of food, many horses had taken longer than expected to recover from the hard campaigning done months before. Those particular animals could not be depended on for use in the near future.

Also, the supply of horses available to replace those that had been lost over the winter had begun to dwindle; thus, increasing the value of

the existing stock. On March 19, Colonel Crutchfield reminded his battalion commanders to properly attend to their horses:

> I   The instructions heretofore issued to the com-
> manding officers of Battalions respecting the care of their
> horses in camp, are intended to apply equally on marches +
> during all active operations in the field. When the circum-
> stances of the case do not admit of their adhering to the horses
> they have chosen for stable calls, they will prescribe others
> adjusted to the requirements of the situation, but they will in
> no case admit any failure to have the horses well thoroughly
> groomed twice a day for at least an hour each time.
> They will make it their first care under all contingencies
> to promote the efficiency of their horses, by seeing that they
> receive all possible care and attention in every respect...giving
> the matter their own personal supervision, they are hereby
> specially required to immediately arrest and report to these
> Hd. Qrs. any commanding officer of a battery who may in
> any manner fall short of his own duty in this respect or allow
> those under his command to neglect theirs in any particular.
> II   On the march Commanding officers of Battalions
> will see that no Article whatever except the equipments ap-
> propriate to each are carried on the horses or on the gun car-
> riages or on the caisons of the Batteries. Any Commanding
> officer of a Battery either committing or allowing the Slight-
> est infraction of this order will be at once arrested and re-
> ported to these Hd. Qrs. by his Battalion Commander.[21]

For Reese and his men, that directive only reinforced something
that they had long since learned. To a light artillery command, horse
flesh was nothing less than sacred.

The unit's strength grew through March as men returned to duty
from the sick list. One recruit, John Hartigan, also arrived as a substitute for Private John T. Billingslea. Though Billingslea's reason for leaving the company is not known, Hartigan was found to be an acceptable
substitute. His name was entered upon the rolls on March 29, presumably the same day that Billingslea left Milford. Billingslea later joined a
cavalry unit with the Army of Tennessee.

The latter part of April saw the departure from the Jeff Davis Artillery of the man who had played a major role in helping the battery to
achieve its fine reputation, Captain James W. Bondurant. Also, before

the month was out, Bates would finally receive second lieutenant's commission thanks again to Bondurant's efforts, who on April 14, had put
his signature to a letter endorsing the promotion of the former sergeant.
There were still to be more changes in personnel. On April 20, Corporal William A. Yeldell was discharged.[22] He was replaced by James
Kane, his official substitute. Two days later, however, Kane deserted.
Finally, on April 26, William Breithaupt reenlisted back in Selma, Alabama in order to rejoin the company from which he had been discharged
due to illness during the summer of 1861. He would be reunited with
his comrades a short time later.

    Then, on April 29, 1863, Crutchfield directed his artillery to break
camp. It was at last time for the spring campaigns to commence.

CHAPTER VIII

THE CHANCELLORSVILLE CAMPAIGN

PART I - MANEUVERING ALONG THE RAPPAHANNOCK

The Federal army's movements prompted Lee to direct Brigadier General William N. Pendleton to start his artillery for the front on April 29. That same day, Pendleton had Colonel Stapleton Crutchfield issue marching orders to his different battery commanders, including Lieutenant William J. Reese of the Jeff Davis Artillery. Two days earlier, Major General Joseph Hooker had started endeavoring to outflank the Army of Northern Virginia.

Since the morning of the 27th, Hooker had been conducting operations designed to keep the Confederates off balance and thus, ill-prepared for the crushing blow that he soon hoped to deliver. To do that, he had divided his army into three elements, each with its own critical assignment.

Foremost were Major Generals George Meade's V, Oliver Otis Howard's XI, and Henry Slocum's XII Corps.[1] Hooker's main strike force, they had been the first force to move out on the 27th. That day, those three corps, about 42,000 men, had started up the Rappahannock River on the first leg of a forty mile march designed to bring them around and in behind the Confederate left. Such a journey would take several days to complete, and during that time, it was essential that their movements be concealed from Southern eyes for as long as possible. Only first did the geography of the area shield the Union forces. But, Hooker had worked out other ways of screening his flanking maneuver, using the rest of his army.

On April 28, the remaining four corps of the Union army had begun a series of maneuvers to distract and confuse Lee. Two divisions of
Major General Darius N. Couch's II Corps moved to Banks' Ford, a few
miles up river from Fredericksburg, where they stopped and made an
aggressive show of force. Meanwhile, down the river, Major Generals
John Sedgwick's VI, John Reynolds' I, and Daniel Sickles' III Corps, of
what could be called Hooker's main diversionary force, had marched
to points close to the Rappahannock in preparation for a crossing. Once
across the river, an attack was to be threatened, but not made.

As late as the morning of the 29th, the element of surprise was still
on the side of the Federal army; likewise everything on the flank march
had gone like clockwork. With the bridging of the Rappahannock behind them, the blue columns then turned on to two roads for the march
which was to place them behind the Confederates. Now heading in a
southeasterly direction, the three corps marched towards a strategic
crossroads at a place called Chancellorsville. There, Hooker's main strike
force was to gather its strength, prior to launching the assault to destroy Lee's army.

Meanwhile, Hooker's feint below Fredericksburg had already begun, with blue-clad troops growing in numbers on the near side of the
Rappahannock. Unaware as they were of Hooker's designs, the Confederates spent much of the morning preparing to receive the anticipated attack.

The Yankees' movements below the city had succeeded in distracting the Confederates from the very real and increasing danger to the
west. By late morning, however, Major General Jeb Stuart's cavalry had
discovered the flanking force's movements and notified Lee.

But, by that time, Lee's available forces were already being brought
forward and concentrated along the front. Among those troops was
Major General Daniel H. Hill's old division, now under the direction of
Brigadier General Robert E. Rodes.[2] It took a position on the far right
near Hamilton's Crossing. Meanwhile, back near Milford Station,
Reese's battery, with the Second Corps Artillery, continued to prepare
for the march on Fredericksburg.

In spite of the threats to Lee's army from both front and rear, he still
had no accurate information as to the extent or direction of the Union
force to the west, so he delayed shifting troops in that direction. Then
again, though the immediate threat was below Fredericksburg, an attack on that front would mean exposing the Southern brigades to the
powerful Federal artillery and risking great loss.

As the Confederates took their positions along the line, they strengthened their defenses. Lieutenant General Thomas J. "Stonewall" Jackson had on hand the divisions belonging to Major Generals Jubal Early and Ambrose P. Hill, as well as the troops commanded by Brigadier General Rodes. Another division, led by Brigadier General Raleigh Colston, was on its way from a point downriver, about 12 miles from Fredericksburg, where it had been guarding the crossings at Moss and Skinker's Neck.

To the left of Jackson, and guarding the center was Major General Lafayette McLaws' Division of the First Corps. That same morning, McLaws had ordered up his reserves. Now as it neared twelve noon, those brigades took their place with the rest of the division.

Farther up river and west of Fredericksburg, were located four of the five brigades belonging to Major General Richard H. Anderson's Division, also of the First Corps. Anderson's men held positions opposite Banks' and U. S. Fords[3], two strategic crossings whose far shores were already in enemy hands. Meanwhile, another brigade, that belonging to Brigadier General Ambrose Ransom "Rans" Wright, now moving up from the rear, had been ordered to support Jackson on the Confederate right.

At that point in time, Lee could count on two full divisions of infantry from the First Corps, as well as most of Jackson's Second Corps to deal with the Federal menace. Even so, it was a deceptive kind of strength, for Lee was actually without the services of a major portion of his army, and this at a time when every gun counted.

For example, the bulk of his heavy ordnance was still in winter quarters far to the south. Included again, was the Jeff Davis Artillery which had not yet begun to move forward. As mentioned, orders for that transfer to the main line had already come from Pendleton, but that large a scale movement was going to take considerable time to carry out. Actually, it would be at least another hour (it, again, was near midday) before any of the numerous caissons, wagons, and related equipage belonging to the artillery would be ready to start northward, and that, of course, did not include the many hours to be spent on the road prior to reaching Fredericksburg itself.

For some time then, Lee only had a small portion of his artillery on hand. Fortunately though, Hooker was not applying pressure against his lines, and what artillery he did have was more than adequate for the time being.

Perhaps even more conspicuous for their absence than Pendleton's guns, however, was Lieutenant General James Longstreet and his First

Corps' two full divisions of infantry and two battalions of artillery. Since February 25, Longstreet had been exercising semi-independent command over the newly established Department of Virginia and North Carolina, a military department which actually encompassed the Richmond area and all of the territory as far as the Cape Fear River to the south. With him were the divisions of Major Generals George Pickett and John Hood.

The importance of keeping Longstreet and his men occupied in such detached duties had waned in the face of the renewed Federal activities to the north. Lee was most anxious to get his missing divisions and their commander back to the front, and had in fact advised Longstreet to speed his operations in case it should become necessary to rapidly recall Pickett and Hood. Even so, the return of Longstreet to Lee's front would not be possible until the commissary trains were recalled and his forces disengaged at Suffolk, movements that would take considerable time to carry out.

Circumstances, therefore, denied Lee a substantial part of his army at a time when numbers counted. In fact, without Longstreet's divisions, the Confederates would only be able to muster just over 60,000 effectives, or six men for every eleven or twelve Yankees on the field. Faced with such a serious numerical disadvantage, Lee would have seemingly been well justified in deciding to fall back to another position. The fact remained, however, that he was, as yet, still not fully aware of what he was up against. Certainly, until more facts were known about the enemy, it would be imprudent for him to make any major move. For the present then, the Army of Northern Virginia would stay put and wait.

PART II - THE BATTLE NEARS AND THE ARTILLERY MOVES NORTH

The situation around Fredericksburg demanded extraordinary efforts on Lee's part to halt the Union army. And, as indicated by the orders issued during the morning of the 29th, Lee was preparing to move. At the same time as the men of Anderson's division were keeping track of events up river, there was stirring south of the Confederate lines. There, in the vicinity of Milford Station, the winter camps of the Second Corps artillery had sprung to life.

That forenoon, as already indicated, the order directing "everybody to the front"[1] had reached the battalion commander, Lieutenant Colonel Thomas H. Carter and the batteries under his command. Immediately, there had followed the expected bustle of activity, as each company, including the Jeff Davis Artillery, set about readying itself for the long journey ahead. Rumor had it "...that the enemy were crossing in heavy force at Fredericksburg and above,"[2] and there was little time to lose.

The Jeff Davis Artillery's trip back to the front lines promised to be nothing like the one that had brought the Alabamians south to their winter quarters. Rail transportation was not available at that time, so the arduous task of moving the artillery would have to fall entirely upon the horses and mules. At the same time, there was a limit to how much personal baggage could be brought. Therefore, "Many of the heavy accumulations of the winter had to be thrown aside."[3] Preparations were completed, and the artillery took its leave of the encampments near Milford. It was then one hour past noon.

The artillery column traveled on throughout the balance of the day. Even so, reaching Fredericksburg required a night march, although a number of sizeable detachments were already clogging the roads in the area.

The Federals were now crossing the Rapidan River at both Germanna and Ely's Fords, pushing towards the Confederate rear. Slocum's XII Corps was the first to reach the Rapidan, and, thus far, had little difficulty in gaining the opposite shore. In fact, after brushing aside a hundred or so defenders at Germanna Ford, Slocum's troops had bridged the river and were now moving across it without opposition. Following close was Howard's XI Corps.

As for the rest of the flanking force, Meade's V Corps had recently arrived at Ely's Ford. There, they had also pushed aside a small guard and were starting to wade across the Rapidan. Both that crossing, and the one already in progress at Germanna Ford, would continue well into the night.

Meanwhile, Lee had just learned of the Federal movements along the Rapidan and was taking steps to secure his army's position. First, he ordered McLaws to occupy and maintain the heights beyond Fredericksburg. This meant McLaws had to pull his troops from the city, as well as realign that part of his division which was already in position close to the main line.

Shortly thereafter, Lee told Anderson to move in the direction of Chancellorsville. First, he was to remove William Mahone's and Carnot Posey's brigades from U. S. Ford, a position the Yankee advance had made untenable. They, along with Ambrose "Rans" Wright's brigade, which had originally been sent to support Jackson and had since been moved to the left, were to converge on the crossroads. Near that point, they were to block the Federal advance on Lee's rear.

Meanwhile, Anderson left Cadmus Wilcox's brigade to guard Banks' Ford, while Brigadier General E. A. Perry's Brigade was moved to a point near Stansbury Hill, in order to take up a position on the extreme left of Lee's ever strengthening line of defense.

In addition, Lee asked Stuart to close on the main army, so that his force would not be cut off by any Union advance. Meanwhile, his cavalry was to continue harassing the Federal columns in an effort to slow their progress.

Currently filling the roads leading to Fredericksburg were not only Carter's battalion, and the bulk of the Second Corps artillery, but also most of the remaining batteries of the First Corps. The few battalions that had remained behind would themselves be making the trip north on the morrow.

Heavy rains delayed the batteries making their way back towards the Rappahannock, as conditions continually worsened. Already, the Jeff Davis Artillery, along with the rest of Carter's battalion, was struggling over roads in "...wretched condition...,"[4] the likes of which had not been seen since the Peninsula Campaign, more than one year ago.

Those awful traveling conditions would persist all the way to Fredericksburg and would necessitate "...a night's march of eighteen or twenty miles,..."[5] Not until the following morning would the Alabama battery finally reach the front line.

Upon its arrival, Carter's entire battalion was assigned to Rodes' division on Lee's right. Immediately surveying the situation around him, Reese noted that the rest of the army was already "...drawn up in line of battle,..."[6] and, as he expected, it was not long before he was ordered into position. Moving forward, the Jeff Davis Artillery took up a post in front of the Southern works and to the right of that portion of the line that the battery had been assigned during the battle of Fredericksburg.[7] The Alabamians, according to Purifoy, occupied ground "...near where Pelham had done so much execution..."[8] The company's arrival on the field seemed well timed, for to their immediate front, and not too far away, could be seen the pickets of the enemy.[9]

And yet, the battery was in a quiet place. The Federals were, in fact, showing little inclination to advance and, at present, were not exerting pressure anywhere on the Confederate right. Hence, there was no urgent need for the Alabamians to do anything but prepare for action and await developments.

That changed during the late afternoon, as the cannon of both armies began to fire at one another. The 3 inch rifles from the Jeff Davis Artillery joined the fray and soon were in the middle of a furious artillery duel. From their position in front of the Southern lines, Reese's cannoneers kept up a steady fire against the suddenly aggressive foe. Caught in the Confederate artillery fire was not only a pontoon bridge used by the enemy to cross the Rappahannock, but also Reynolds' I Corps. Soon "...it became necessary to move the Second Division (massed in the ravines where it sustained some loss) to the shelter of the river road,"[10] reported Reynolds. In reference to the accuracy of the Confederate gunners, Colonel Charles S. Wainwright, of the First New York Light Artillery reported, "Their practice was very good,..."[11]

Back on the Southern right, the Alabamians were themselves targets of the Federal artillery. Of the projectiles sent their way, however, Reese remembered that "...many passed over our heads, and the shells burst all around us without doing any harm."[12]

During the course of the duel, the two remaining cannon of the battery were also subject to a shower of projectiles, but those pieces were not returning the hostile fire. They were shorter range guns, and at the distances of that fire-fight, were virtually useless. Therefore, both pieces sat idly by while the bombardment continued.

Meanwhile, farther to the rear, the battery's artillery park was also feeling the effect of the heavy fire. Two shells had found their way to that supposedly protected area, but, fortunately, no injuries or damage had resulted. Certainly, it was beginning to look like nothing was immune from the Yankee barrage.

The fight raged on, but finally, with darkness, came a slackening of the fire and the close of what had, to say the least, been a very heated contest. The two guns of the Jeff Davis Artillery alone had expended seventy-two rounds, while having to endure countless shots in return. Even so, the battery had come out of the difficult action with not a single casualty to man, horse, or mule.

No matter how intense that confrontation of April 30 had been, it in itself had held little consequence except that it marked the first battle-field action that the artillery company had seen under its new com-mander. Beyond that, the whole affair had been inconclusive. Neither side had gained any ground, and no infantry had been committed in order to exploit what gains the artillery might have achieved. That duel could have been nothing more than an attempt by both sides to flex their muscles.

Even so, that action confirmed Lee's belief that the Federals actu-ally had no intention of advancing any further from the lower crossing sites than they already had. In fact, at no time during the day had the Federals even intimated that an advance against the Southern right and center was about to begin.

That the just included artillery duel had been the only fighting on the afternoon of April 30 was most significant. Even though Hooker's main strike force had arrived at its rendezvous point hours before, no unusual pressure had yet been felt on the Southern flank. That, in part, was because Anderson's three brigades had long since taken up a more defensible position a few miles east of Chancellorsville, thereby negat-ing any chance that they would have encountered the enemy on its approach to the crossroads.[13] Additionally, Hooker had not permitted his flanking force to advance any further towards Fredericksburg since its arrival at Chancellorsville. Therefore, any possibility of a fight with Anderson, even in his new position, had been erased as well.

The Federals, however, had not lost their initiative. By postponing the advance, Hooker was in fact allowing time for the reorganization and reinforcing of his main strike force. At that very moment, the bulk of Couch's II Corps, which had previously been held in position near Banks' Ford, was taking up a post near the rendezvous point. Their march had been trouble free and had, again, been facilitated by the Con-federates' evacuation of U. S. Ford, a crossing the II Corps subsequently used as a bridging site on its way to Chancellorsville. To further supple-ment his main force, Hooker moved Sickles' III Corps from opposite Lee's front to the flankers, who were poised to attack. Ultimately, the addition of Sickles' Corps would give Hooker five corps, or more than seventy-five thousand men with which to deliver the blow designed to destroy the Confederate army.

But despite being outflanked, Lee was determined not to relinquish any more ground. Giving up his position under present conditions would necessitate a retreat across the front of the Federal position, making his army a most inviting target. In addition, the evacuation of the Rappahannock line would also leave a critical part of the state, an invaluable source of supply to the Southern forces, open to Federal occupation. Obviously, neither alternative was acceptable, and, therefore, he decided that, if at all possible, the Army of Northern Virginia would fight its way out of its predicament.

But first, Lee had to complete a series of defensive maneuvers. Foremost was the reinforcing of Anderson's three lone brigades to the west.[14] This meant starting columns towards Chancellorsville during the night, so that they would arrive at Anderson's position in time, should Hooker start his assault at an early hour. Timing would play an important part in that operation. Fortunately, there would be little difficulty in getting the necessary forces on the road.

Lee had decided to send three brigades from McLaws' division, followed by Rodes', Hill's and Colston's divisions of the Second Corps. In the meantime, Early's command would remain behind, and it, combined with Brigadier General William Barksdale's Brigade (from McLaws' division), would defend the heights overlooking Fredericksburg against any Federal advance. In this way, the enemy would be held in check in Lee's front, while the bulk of the army was sent on a westward march to clear the more serious threat to the rear.

MAJOR GENERAL ROBERT E. RODES

Commanded division to which Jeff Davis Artillery was attached during Chancellorsville and Gettysburg Campaigns. Killed at Winchester, Virginia, September 19, 1864.

(National Archives)

Still, all that was hours away, and the Confederates rested and prepared for the predawn marches ahead. For the Jeff Davis Artillery, who would be marching with Rodes' division, that meant a most welcome respite, especially following the hot afternoon's fight. However, even as his men were settling back, Reese noted:

Only an occasional shot came from the enemies' batteries. The camp fires began to twinkle through the darkness and fog along our second line of battle. When a noble anthem of praise and thanksgiving to the Almighty swelled out from the stillness, coming from thousands of voices. I thought of the days of Cromwell then, And I felt grateful that the "Great God of Battles" had put it into the hearts of so many of our soldiers to remember their dependence upon Him in that awful hour.[15]

At midnight, defensive maneuvers began as McLaws' three brigades pulled back from their positions along the center. They would be the first troops to reach Anderson, bolstering his comparatively fragile, but still well established line of defense protecting the army's rear. Less than three hours later, Jackson's command began forming for the march that would eventually bring them into a supporting position behind both Anderson and McLaws. The Second Corps' withdrawal from the main line would begin at three o'clock, with Rodes' division leading the way.

Vacating their post near Hamilton's Crossing, the Jeff Davis Artillery joined Rodes' division and marched with it in column along the Military Road. Gradually moving away from the Rappahannock, the artillerymen continued until road's end, where they picked up another route whose northwesterly track took them directly to the Orange Plank Road. After reaching the intersection of the two highways, the entire command swung on to the Plank Road and moved in a westerly direction towards Anderson's works, located about three miles southeast of Chancellorsville.

The Alabamians, though knowing they were on the Orange Plank Road, at first were not sure of their exact destination.[16] Still, according to Purifoy, "We knew, however, that when Jackson moved, it meant business."[17]

About eight o'clock that same morning, Rodes' division, the van of Jackson's force, was fast approaching its destination. Not far ahead was the First Corps, busily strengthening its defenses in anticipation of Hooker's advance. Though the Confederates were well aware of a huge Federal presence to their front, there had, thus far, been no hint that an attack was forthcoming. Consequently, Anderson's and McLaws' brigades, the latter of which had come up before sunrise, were taking advantage of the opportunity to improve further their present position. And yet, unknown to them and the Alabamians whose guns were to lend support along the front, was the fact that all those defensive preparations were to be thrown aside soon in favor of a new and more potent strategy.

PART III - THE CONFEDERATES TAKE TO THE OFFENSIVE

Arriving at the First Corps' position in advance of his troops, Jackson at once decided that it would be better to attack, rather than to sit in an entrenched position and await attack. Therefore, he halted the digging and readied his brigades for an offensive thrust of their own. Jackson even recalled Posey's and Wilcox's brigades from the Rappahannock. Within hours, Jackson's force had completed its preparations, and at precisely eleven o'clock on May 1, his advance began.

Pushing forward along both the Old Turnpike and the Orange Plank Road, the Confederates quickly closed the gap that lay between themselves and the Yankees. However, unknown to Lee, Hooker's grand movement was also starting at about the same time, thereby putting him even closer at hand than might have been expected. In fact, at that moment, two Federal corps were moving east along the exact routes the Confederates were using. Both armies were on a collision course. Within minutes, the opposing pickets made contact, and the battle was joined.

Farther back on the Plank Road, Purifoy remembered that "...we could hear the guns of our friends and enemy in our front."[1] Even so, the Jeff Davis Artillery's march continued, with the company covering another half-mile before they, and the entire division, finally stopped. Little distance now separated Rodes and the heavy fighting going on around him.

At this point, with the entire column stopped along the road, Brigadier General Stephen Dodson Ramseur's Brigade was ordered forward to add its weight to the struggle going on ahead. Not long thereafter; "The rest of the division was moved by the right flank to the top of the ridge near the road, and, after being established in line of battle, was directed by Lieutenant General Jackson to shelter itself and await orders."[2] The position now occupied by the Jeff Davis Artillery was just beyond the right flank of the enemy force then operating on what was known as the "Old Turnpike."

On into the afternoon the battle raged, and still there was no change in the disposition of the Alabama battery. Actually, things were going well for the Confederates, and thus far, there had been no need to send Rodes' remaining troops into the fight. On the Old Turnpike, McLaws had successfully countered the enemy's advance and was now pushing him back. A bit farther to the south, Anderson's brigades had halted the other Federal drive along the Plank Road and were now themselves involved in a sharp fight with the enemy. Jackson's offensive strategy had checked the Federal advance, but even so, it was too early to claim victory.

At that point in the battle, heavy Federal reinforcements were moving up the Old Turnpike, and more troops would soon be coming up the Plank Road. Then, quite suddenly, events took a dramatic turn. Incredibly, at about 2:00 p.m., the enemy began what was soon to become a general withdrawal back towards Chancellorsville. Jackson had caught Hooker by surprise, causing him to lose faith in his own capabilities.

Back on the Confederate side, as news of what looked to be a Federal retreat reached Jackson, he pressed his attack down the two roads. About the same time, A. P. Hill threw three brigades forward to aid in the pursuit. Not long thereafter, Rodes' division joined the attack.

Pickets were soon encountered by Rodes' advance units. Combat followed, during which several Yankee prisoners were taken. However, by the time the Confederate skirmishers had cleared their front, the Union's main force had retreated. Rodes then spent the balance of the afternoon in place, deployed in line of battle, and away from the main action.

Meanwhile, Hill and Anderson continued to press the retiring Yankees; however, resistance quickly mounted as the distance to the crossroads diminished. By later in the day, the pursuers were compelled to stay their own advance because of strong opposition. By then, most of Hooker's five corps were concentrated around Chancellorsville, and any attack on the Federal army's position would have proven ineffectual. As a result, the Confederates had to be content with their gains until circumstances permitted a renewal of their offensive.

By then it was nearly dusk, and battlefield conditions were such that Rodes' division could be moved closer to the lines. Returning to the Orange Plank Road, it marched as far as the Alrich Tavern, about $1^1/4$ miles from Chancellorsville. There, the division halted to bivouac for the night.

For the Jeff Davis Artillery, the arrival at Alrich's must have been welcome for it brought what had been a long, as well as frustrating, day to an end. Since the company's early morning departure from the right at Fredericksburg, no regular rations had been issued to the men. Besides that, the artillerymen, though well within earshot of heavy fighting for many hours, had not been afforded the opportunity to share in any of the day's action. Little could be expected to change at this late hour, and, for now, the men would have to be content, in John Purifoy's own words, in "...taking our rest as best we could, on such improvised beds as could be arranged."[3]

The Federal army's retreat to Chancellorsville, and assumption of a more defensive strategy, had effectively wrecked any tactical advantage that Hooker may have held. He thus surrendered the initiative to the Confederates. That same night, Lee and Jackson planned their counterattack. Recent scouting reports by Brigadier General Fitzhugh Lee, the cavalry commander, had indicated that the Federal right was "up in the air," and Lee and Jackson decided that that would be where they would strike.

During the early morning hours, Jackson received information from the Second Corps' topographical engineer, Major Jedediah Hotchkiss, that a route existed which could bring the Confederates around Hooker's flank to a point safely west of his position along the Orange Plank Road. The entire route covered about eleven miles, and the roads were well-concealed and in good condition. By marching at a good pace, the head of Jackson's column could reach its destination some time before mid-afternoon. Thus, once the flanking movement was completed, there still would be ample time before darkness fell to deploy, launch and carry out the planned attack.

With little hesitation, Lee and Jackson agreed that the entire Second Corps (three divisions totalling about 28,000 men) would be committed to that effort. As it had on the previous day, Rodes would take the lead, to be followed by Colston and Hill, in that order. Additionally, the artillery of each division would take its place behind its infantry for the march. The column would, for the most part, be screened from the enemy by the cavalry and the wooded terrain, but even so, it was still going to be a dangerous maneuver. Not only were the Confederates dividing their forces in the face of the numerically superior foe (in Jackson's absence, 14,000 men belonging to McLaws and Anderson would be left to hold Hooker's entire army at bay), but they were also moving right across Hooker's front. The risks were high, but it was a chance to first roll up the Federal army's vulnerable right, then get in the rear, cutting it off from the river.

Preparations for the movement continued on throughout the first daylight hours. Finally, at about eight o'clock on the morning of Saturday, May 2, the flank march began, with Brigadier General Alfred H. Colquitt's brigade of Rodes' division leading the way. Not long thereafter, Carter's battalion, including the Jeff Davis Artillery, fell in behind the infantry and moved off down the road.

The lead division moved without incident until it reached the area of Lewis's Creek. There, while moving across an exposed piece of ground leading to the stream, it suddenly came under fire. The Confederates had been spotted by Federal artillery who opened their guns on the column. What transpired then is described by Purifoy:

A slight halt followed. Of course we expected to be rushed right into battle, and to become hotly engaged immediately. We did move and in the direction from which these guns of the enemy had shot into our ranks. We had not gone far, however, before we found we were turning from the main road into what seemed a neighborhood road. Our movements were quickened and we were soon travelling at a rapid rate, almost at a double quick. This pace was kept up some time and we seemed to be moving away from the firing. And this proved to be a fact.[4]

Having successfully passed over the exposed section of roadway, the Jeff Davis Artillery had then veered left at the Catharine Furnace, and was now traveling almost due south along the Furnace Road.

Not far to the north, Federal observers had already caught sight of the column moving down the Furnace Road. Before Hooker lay an opportunity. However, he was, for the moment, unwilling to take any aggressive action. As yet, Hooker was unsure what the maneuver meant, and he needed more time to learn what Lee was up to. Though he did estimate that Lee was either retreating or conducting operations aimed at his flank, Hooker still did not want to change his defensive alignment.

Meanwhile, the column continued to push on at a steady pace, and by late morning was already swinging north in the direction of the Orange Plank Road. The men were in exuberant spirits, and "Jackson, moving with the column and passing along its line occasionally, injected his intense energy into it."[5] Still, the combination of steadily increasing temperatures and a shortage of water was, by that time, having a discomforting effect.[6] To make matters worse, many of the men, including those of the Jeff Davis Artillery, were also again marching on empty stomachs. Purifoy would later remark, "I was one of the latter and have an acute recollection of that fourteen-mile march when as hungry as the grave.[7]

Such conditions were too much to endure, and some literally began to drop from the ranks. As Reese recalled:

Never shall I forget that march. The day was oppressively hot and many fell on the roadside from exhaustion. Gen Jackson rode up and down the column telling "the boys" that every moment was a fortune and they rushed forward throwing away blankets, knapsacks everything but their guns and ammunition. I blessed my stars that I had a horse to ride. I passed hundreds on the roadside perfectly unconscious and poured water on the faces of many who never knew where they received assistance. Many must have died from sun stroke.[8]

That journey continued until about 1:30 p.m., when the van of Rodes' command finally arrived at a point near where the Orange Plank Road crossed the Brock Road, which was the route utilized by the flanking column. There, the division halted under arms.

As it turned out, however, that was not a scheduled stop. Just minutes before, Fitzhugh Lee, whose cavalry were covering the advance, had told Jackson that a better opportunity to assault Hooker's flank and rear existed a little farther to the north, along the Old Turnpike. Jackson immediately stopped the lead division of the flanking column, and both generals had then rode off to reconnoiter the Federal right. It was a critical moment, and one that stood out in Purifoy's mind,

Modern day view of portion of road followed by Jeff Davis Artillery during "Stonewall" Jackson's flank march; battle of Chancellorsville, May 2, 1863.

(Author's collection) Wedgewood Studio

"Well do I remember seeing Jackson and Fitzhugh Lee ascend the long red slope to the east of the position then occupied by the troops, preceded by a small squad of cavalry."[9]

After reaching that vantage point and briefly examining the Yankees' position, Jackson quickly realized that they had remained unaware of the force that was moving against them. He also saw the advantage of attacking down the Old Turnpike and, without further delay, moved Rodes' division to the intersection of that route.

The march resumed, with Rodes rapidly covering the mile and a half that existed between the Plank Road and the Turnpike. Arriving at the intersection, the head of the column turned east and marched yet another mile before coming to a final halt behind a low ridge. Shortly thereafter, skirmishers were thrown forward, and the rest of the division began deploying on either side of the road. While the infantry was forming for the attack, the Jeff Davis Artillery, and the rest of Carter's battalion, took up a position to the right of the Turnpike as a precautionary measure.[10] It was at that time a little past three.

Except for the brief encounter near Lewis's Creek, Rodes' division had marched unopposed to within close striking distance of the Federal right.

But behind it, Brigadier General David Birney's Division of Sickles' III Corps had struck the column in the vicinity of Catharine Furnace. During that attack, the 23rd Georgia Infantry Regiment, guarding the trains bringing up the rear, had been surrounded and captured en masse, before reinforcements from both Hill's and Anderson's divisions successfully checked the Federals' advance.

Hooker's now more aggressive strategy towards that force moving across the army's front was primarily due to his belief that Lee was retreating. Reinforcements from Major General Oliver O. Howard's XI Corps, which occupied the vulnerable right flank, were even sent to Sickles in order that he might resume his attack. Unbeknown to him was the fact that Jackson's rear elements had already pushed west, leaving only Anderson's troops opposite his front.

It was already 5:00 p.m., and back up along the Turnpike, Jackson was nearly ready to advance. The brigades of Rodes' division, after fighting their way through the thickets that existed on either side of the road, were now aligned across and perpendicular to the Turnpike. Immediately behind them on the road could be found the Jeff Davis Artillery and Carter's three other batteries.

To the rear of Carter's battalion, and parallel to Rodes, were spread the various parts of Colston's division. Presently aligning themselves behind them were two brigades belonging to A. P. Hill's division. The rest of Hill's command had not yet come up. Farthest away, and by now destined to miss the flank attack, were the brigades of Brigadier Generals James J. Archer and Edward L. Thomas, both of which had been delayed by the action at Catharine Furnace. And yet, the absence of those two commands was not critical, for Jackson still had ten brigades (plus two more in reserve) to attack his unprepared enemy.

Even so, the forming of the numerous brigades for the assault had not gone totally unnoticed. Since earlier in the afternoon, Federal pickets had anxiously reported that the Confederates were massing in the woods to their front. Any warnings of the Southern buildup, however, had and were continuing to fall on deaf ears. Though apprised of the situation, Howard nevertheless remained steadfast in the belief that Lee was fleeing and did nothing to improve his position.

Moreover, both inside Howard's defenses, and on the flank, the men were seemingly very much at ease. Arms were stacked, and many were already eating their supper. Even if the Yankees suspected that something was up, they certainly were not taking it seriously.

At exactly 5:15 p.m., Purifoy remembered "...the shrill bugle call that rang out, which was echoed from the right and left of the line of sharpshooters and sent them forward, the assaulting lines close at their heels."[11] The advance had begun. Pushing through the heavy undergrowth along the Turnpike, Rodes' division led the way towards their vulnerable foe. Preceding them were droves of forest animals which the approaching troops had scared out of hiding.

Farther ahead, the unsuspecting Northerners were initially startled by the sudden activity on the part of the animals, but before long were cheering the frenzy that was taking place; that is, "...until presently something else they heard and saw froze the laughter in their throats. Long lines of men in gray and butternut, their clothes ripped and tattered by the briers and branches, were running toward them..."[12]

Contact was made with the thin enemy line, and as might have been expected, the Federal right began to crumble under the weight of the attack. Attempts to resist the onslaught were pointless, as unit after unit was forced back on one another in what soon appeared to be a general rout.

For the men of the Jeff Davis Artillery there was as yet no opportunity, or need for that matter, to make use of their firepower. The enemy had, for the most part, been taken by surprise, and thus far, there had been little need to support the attack with artillery. For the present then, the Alabamians had to be content to just be a part of the chase. However, even that was not without its rewards. "We followed at a rapid pace, finding provisions and coffee, on the fire, cooking. The rations were acceptable,"[13] recalled Purifoy.

Even so, Purifoy did not partake in the feast just described, but actually had already tapped another source for his share of the rations left behind by the enemy. He had "...spied a well-filled haversack attached to the neck of a dead Federal soldier. Its contents were hardtack, salt pork, and coffee."[14]

This was an irresistible prize for Purifoy had not eaten in over twenty-four hours. Purifoy continued, "Proprieties were banished in favor of the great necessity of the living, and my pocketknife was whipped out, and the strap that held it to the dead owner's neck was cut that I might eat as I trotted along. No food ever tasted sweeter."[15]

The attack continued, with the Yankees fleeing down the Turnpike. Farther to the east, Major General Carl Schurz's Division of the XI Corps became another unwitting victim to the stampede. As Purifoy later reported, "The officers of this division did not have time to give a command before the confused mass of guns, horses, and men broke lengthwise through the regiments. The whole line, deployed on the turnpike and facing toward the south, was rolled up and swept away in short order."[16] By about 7:00 p.m., Howard's entire corps had been driven from the field.

Daylight was fading fast, however, and the cohesion at the start of the Confederate flank attack had all but disappeared in the now darkened woods. Rodes' and Colston's commands had become intertwined, and were halted in order to reorganize. Hill received orders from Jackson to move up and press the attack, while Rodes, then the commander of the Second Corps himself, rode ahead to reconnoiter.

Just prior to this, several guns from Carter's battalion had been posted on both sides of the road (at Melzi Chancellor's house) behind some enemy works which had been come upon during the advance. Though intended to be used "...to repel an attack of the enemy should our lines be driven back at the woods just ahead,...,"[17] these cannon had not fired a shot. In fact, the position had only been occupied a short time, when the guns were removed, and Carter was ordered by Crutchfield to advance them nearer to the lead section, farther up the Turnpike.[18]

Before long, Rodes returned from his survey ahead without finding any Union lines between his present position and Chancellorsville. Crutchfield responded by advancing three guns, a section of Napoleons and a Parrott Rifle from Captain William P. Carter's King William Artillery, which soon opened in the direction of the strategic crossroads.

Within moments, however, the Confederate cannon had attracted a terrible return fire, from a nearby Federal artillery unit, which swept the length of the Turnpike currently occupied by Carter's battalion. The teams became wild, several carriage tongues were broken, and within minutes, both men and horses fell victim to the deadly bombardment.[19] Private Patton McCondichie's leg bone popped as it was struck and crushed by an enemy projectile. John Purifoy heard that noise and went to the aid of McCondichie, his "...army bedfellow, schoolmate, and boy-hood friend."[20] The shelling also left Private John Mitchell with a shat-tered arm.

Unable to unlimber and return the enemy's enfilading fire, the Ala-bamians found themselves in a desperate situation. Under the circum-stances, there was nothing they could do but move the battery off the road with all possible haste. Fortunately, they succeeded in doing just that and soon were no longer so exposed to enemy fire.

As a result of the artillery barrage, one man had received a mortal wound, and four others had been seriously injured. Though quickly attended to, McCondichie's wound was fatal. Also among the injured, but destined to recuperate and later rejoin the command, were Private John Mitchell and Sergeant James E. Norwood. Mitchell's shattered arm had to be amputated.[21] As for Norwood, his wound was described as severe, but its nature is not known.[22]

Besides the loss of five men, the battery had also seen two of its horses killed and seven others wounded. Additionally, three caissons had been damaged during the bombardment.

Now, even as Reese's company was regrouping from the unexpected shelling, A. P. Hill's men were preparing to resume the offensive. Al-ready, Hill's two available brigades had moved up to the front and were completing their attack formation. It was then about nine o'clock.

Meanwhile, still further to the front, an impatient Jackson had fin-ished reconnoitering, and was hastily riding back to his own lines to speed the next attack. He, however, would never get the chance, for minutes later, disaster struck the Confederate army.

Hill's troops, on edge and all too aware of the possibility of a coun-terattack, had spotted horsemen rapidly approaching their position and opened fire. They did not know that they were firing upon Jackson's own scouting party. During the second volley, they hit Jackson three times, and now seriously wounded, he had to be taken to the rear.

With Jackson out of the fight, command of the Second Corps passed to A. P. Hill. But as the firing on both sides had increased, Hill himself became a victim of the contest. Though not totally incapacitated by his wound (he had been hit in the leg), Hill was nevertheless unable to exercise the kind of effective leadership which the situation demanded. Before long, Crutchfield, himself, would be down with a serious leg wound as well.

Command of the corps then temporarily devolved upon Brigadier General Robert E. Rodes. At the same time, however, a message was sent to Stuart, then several miles away, requesting his presence at the front. Stuart, a more experienced and recognized leader, would eventually take control of the situation.

On the other hand, circumstances had by that time robbed the Confederate forces of the drive needed to resume the advance. The troops were exhausted, and under present conditions, there seemed little advantage to be gained in carrying out the kind of night attack Jackson had urged. Therefore, Stuart decided that the next push would begin at dawn. Thus, it now remained for the Second Corps to hold their positions and do what they could to prepare for the morning offensive.

The Jeff Davis Artillery spent the balance of the night parked with the batteries of Lieutenant Colonel Hilary P. Jones' battalion in the fields surrounding the Dowdall house. The corps' artillery had undergone a temporary reorganization,[23] and for the present, Reese's company was to be attached to Jones' command. As a captain, Jones had first taken command of the battery during the chaotic winter of 1862.

By daybreak, the Jeff Davis Artillery was in line along the Plank Road and was ordered with the battalion to the front. Occupying an area to the left of a schoolhouse, and in proximity to Major Carter M. Braxton's guns, Jones' artillery opened in support of the advancing infantry. The Second Corps, now under Stuart, had resumed its attack.

But this time the Confederates faced a more formidable Union position, much of which had been constructed after the flank attack of the previous evening. Within those lines was a heavily defended elevation known as Fairview, and there the Southern batteries concentrated their fire. In the meantime, more Confederate guns were moving into position on another important part of the battlefield known as Hazel Grove. Earlier, this area had been in Federal hands, but had been abandoned by Hooker who, at the time, was endeavoring to strengthen his army's new defensive line. That was a serious mistake, because the high ground at Hazel Grove actually commanded the area. Already, the newly posted batteries were taking advantage of the situation by adding an ever-increasing fire to that which was coming from the guns nearer the turnpike.

The effectiveness of the artillery was critical to the success of the attack, and during the course of the bombardment, Stuart himself took much personal interest in the deployment of the guns, including those of the Jeff Davis Artillery. John Purifoy recalled:

> Through all this storm, when there was a lull, General Stuart had sat his superb steed and had given personal direction to the artillery. When firing of the enemy's artillery was hushed

by the furious pelting from our guns, there sat General Stuart on his steed with a smile on his face and as superb a figure as I had ever saw. When he ordered the guns forward, he did not say "go forward" but he led the way and gave orders at what point the pieces should locate.[24]

Meanwhile, supported by the massed batteries, the Confederate infantry threw itself time and time again, without much success, into the storm of shot and shell from the guns about Fairview. Not to be thwarted, the gray regiments moved forward once more, and this time captured and held the important position. The loss of Fairview made the remainder of the Federal line untenable, and the Yankees withdrew.

Even as the Confederate brigades rushed forward in pursuit, the artillery was not far behind. Quickly, Jones', Carter's and McIntosh's[25] battalions rushed forward along the road, ascended the slope leading to the now empty defenses and took position on the crest of Fairview. Within a short time, they directed a heavy fire at the retreating Yankees. It wasn't long, however, before the Jeff Davis Artillery had exhausted its ammunition and was sent to the rear for resupply.

Modern view of Federal position at Fairview. Jeff Davis Artillery assisted in the attack, then occupied the enemy works; battle of Chancellorsville, May 3, 1863.

(Author's collection) Wedgewood Studio

It was then about ten o'clock, and already the Alabamians had participated heavily in the struggle for Chancellorsville. As Reese would later attest:

> Our position was in the centre and at one time was a very hot place....The firing was terrific and caused the blood to gush from the nose of one of my gunners, and most of the cannoneers were temporarily deaf when they came out of the fight. I had my horse tied to a small tree which was shot off above his head by a cannon ball. We were firing part of the time at a Yankee battery planted near a large house which the enemy had converted into an hospital, and was filled with wounded, our shells fired the house and burned many of the wounded. In another part of the field the woods were fired and many perished in that way. Oh the horrors of war![26]

Fortunately, during the bombardment of the morning of May 3, the battery itself had sustained little injury, with only two men receiving slight wounds. Still, that is not to say that there had not been a number of close calls for several others belonging to that command. Purifoy, then in charge of one of the guns, was one of those who later recalled a time during the action when his life had suddenly been put on the line: "The gun been charged, and trained preparatory to firing, and the order, 'Ready.' having been given, he [Purifoy] stepped to a favorable position to watch the flight of the ball from the gun and to note its effect. Just as he was about to give the command to fire, he discovered an approaching ball from an enemy's gun."[27] There was hardly time to attempt to escape being hit, so rather than leave his post, Purifoy decided to take his chances with the enemy projectile and issued firing orders to the gun crew. He continued, "...the command was given, and the gun fired, and at the same moment he saw E Carter who was acting No 1 to the gun, fall. This showed that the ball passed a little to his [Purifoy's] right. Carter scrambled off on his hands and knees..."[28]

As events would show, the shot knocked Private Euphroneus Carter down but did not seriously injure him. Both Purifoy and Carter had been extremely lucky as was Reese's young servant, Alfred, who had himself been in the thick of the battle that morning. Several holes had been burned in his clothes by an exploding shell, but no physical injury had been sustained. And, as if that was not enough of an experience for Alfred, "He captured a Yankee and marched him in triumph to the guard in the rear."[29]

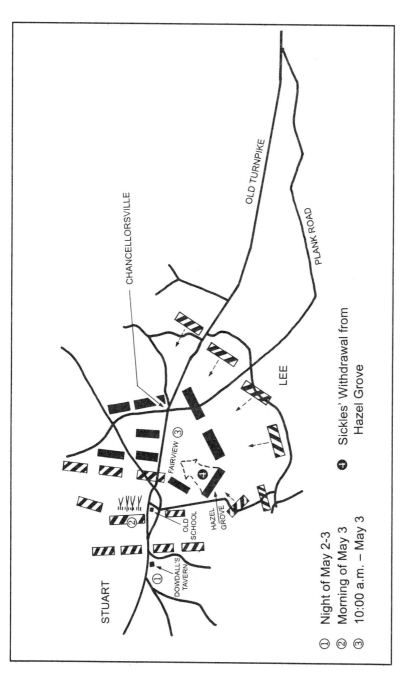

POSITIONS OCCUPIED BY JEFF DAVIS ARTILLERY, MAY 2, 1863 (Also Shows Attack of May 3)

Fredericksburg and Spotsylvania National Military Park (Chancellorsville Troop Movement Map # 8)

① Night of May 2-3
② Morning of May 3
③ 10:00 a.m. – May 3

❹ Sickles' Withdrawal from Hazel Grove

All of the battery's guns, which included two 3-inch Rifles, one twenty-four pound Howitzer and one twelve pound Napoleon, had participated in the fight,[30] firing three hundred and five rounds. The Jeff Davis Artillery had fought hard that morning, and the reprieve that now came about as a result of the need to refill its ammunition chests, was certainly well deserved.

Even as the Alabamians were withdrawing to the rear, the fight for Chancellorsville was reaching a conclusion. In another half hour or so, the Confederates would be in possession of the field. After abandoning their works covering the crucial crossroads, the Union forces took up a new position behind another line of defense closer to the Rappahannock. There, Hooker's army was to make its next stand.

Though flushed with victory, the Confederate forces were, nevertheless, in no condition to immediately follow up their recent success. They were exhausted and somewhat disorganized, and time would be needed to regroup before the advance could be resumed. Therefore, a delay ensued while Lee's men readied themselves for the next assault.

Preparations were completed as quickly as possible, but just about the time that orders for the attack were to be issued, Lee learned from Early of a new threat to the east. Sedgwick had driven Early from the heights above Fredericksburg and was marching in the direction of Chancellorsville. Sedgwick now posed a real threat to the Southern rear, and Lee had to postpone his attack against Hooker.

In an effort to stop Sedgwick, Lee decided to split his available force. McLaws' three brigades, as well as a portion of Anderson's division (Mahone's brigade), were sent back up the Plank Road towards Fredericksburg. Those troops were eventually to hook up with Wilcox's brigade which, at that very moment, was doing its utmost to delay the Federal advance. In the meantime, Stuart's entire force, and the balance of Anderson's division, would be left to hold the bulk of Hooker's army in its works north of Chancellorsville.

That afternoon and evening while Lee attempted (unsuccessfully as it turned out) to destroy Sedgwick, nothing of any consequence had occurred back along the opposing lines to the west. There had been no aggressive movement on the part of the much stronger foe, and for men such as those of the Jeff Davis Artillery, who were back at the front and now occupying works on the Chancellorsville plateau, the time had passed in a most uneventful fashion. Aside from their participating in an occasional artillery duel, the Southern gunners had little to do except remain patiently by their posts. Unknown to the Confederates, however, was the fact that Hooker had no intention of resuming the offensive.

Following the attack against Sedgwick, Lee, on May 5, ordered McLaws and Anderson to rejoin Stuart for a general advance against Hooker. Hooker, however, had already begun to pull back from his defenses before the Southern forces were reunited. Still, Hooker withdrew his forces gradually, actually waiting until the middle of the night before commencing his retreat across the Rappahannock. Thus, the chance of striking a serious blow still existed, and such an opportunity, especially in light of Sedgwick's earlier escape from destruction, was something that General Lee did not intend to miss. By evening, most of the brigades belonging to McLaws and Anderson would be up, and preparations for the grand assault, which had been anticipated by the Confederates for the past two days, could finally begin.

But early in the afternoon, conditions suddenly took a turn for the worse, and in the face of a terrible rain storm, preparations for the Southern advance again had to be suspended. Unlike before, the ensuing delay was to prove a very critical factor, for that night, while the Confederates were waiting out the storm, the enemy began their withdrawal across the river.[31]

By mid-morning of May 6, the Federals had completed their retrograde movement and were already retracing their steps back to Falmouth. That same morning, the Confederate advance was finally resumed, but to Lee's dismay, the enemy works were found to be unoccupied. A pursuit was ordered, but it proved to be a fruitless attempt at retrieving a lost situation, for the Federal army was by then already well out of reach. Though unhappy that Hooker had managed to slip away, the Southern forces at least had the satisfaction of knowing that the Yankee menace no longer had any hold on their side of the Rappahannock.

The Chancellorsville Campaign had come to an end, and by early afternoon, Lee would have most of his force back on the road to Fredericksburg and the camps which had been left behind just one week before.

Certainly, the Army of Northern Virginia had won a great victory, blocking Hooker's plans for the destruction of Lee's forces and the capture of Richmond itself. There had been many bright spots associated with the campaign. Included among those was the army's artillery, which had played a crucial part in the fighting, and by its performance, had proven the effectiveness of its new organization.[32] Even Stuart, in his report of the battle, had noted "...under the happy effects of the battalion system,"[33] how rapidly guns could be concentrated at one place.

Contributing to what had been a fine record had been the Jeff Davis Artillery. Under its new commander, Reese, the Alabama battery had twice been heavily engaged, and had assisted on April 30 in first keeping the enemy pinned down near the Rappahannock, and then on May 3 in driving the Yankees from a strong defensive position. And though once disabled, on the night of May 2 when it was surprised by an enemy barrage down the Plank Road, the company had nevertheless been able to regroup in time to take part in the next morning's fight. Casualties sustained during the campaign had been few, and all things considered, the company had come out of the whole affair in remarkably good shape. Certainly, the Alabamians had begun their second year of active campaigning just where they had left off months before, during the successful operations around Fredericksburg.

And yet, this did not necessarily mean that the Jeff Davis Artillery was operating at peak efficiency as Reese had quickly found out when called upon to engage the Yankees with his entire battery on the morning of May 3. The company still lacked the proper complement of officers, which had placed an enormous burden of responsibility on the new commander. In Reese's own words, "I was the only commissioned officer in the battery during the fight and had to manage everything. Lt Bates had been detailed to act as Qr Master. I made two Sergeants act as Lieuts You may be sure I wished for Robert many times."[34]

With no other commissioned officers on hand, whose specific job would have been to each take complete charge of a section of cannon, Reese was forced to concentrate more on each individual gun crew and less on his battery's overall performance. Most assuredly, Lieutenant Bates would be back on the firing line in time for the next campaign. Even so, it remained to be seen if anything could be done about the vacancy yet to be filled.

Then again, whether the post was quickly filled or not did not seem so critical, especially in light of how well the battery had performed during the fight for Chancellorsville. The men of the Jeff Davis Artillery had quickly proven that they could adapt to such situations, which, in itself, said much about the spirit of the command.

CHAPTER IX

ONCE AGAIN, THE SOUTHERN ARMY
PUSHES NORTH

PART I - REORGANIZATION AND THE START
OF A NEW CAMPAIGN

For several weeks following the battle of Chancellorsville, the Army of Northern Virginia rested and gathered strength in anticipation of the next campaign. The Jeff Davis Artillery occupied a camp in the vicinity of Liberty Mills, Virginia.

That was a critical period, one that witnessed a number of changes among those in the upper ranks, as well as a major realigning of the Army of Northern Virginia. Many of those moves, as it turned out, had a profound effect upon the role of the Jeff Davis Artillery. First, and of great significance, was the decision to reorganize the army from its former two corps arrangement into a three corps system. The purpose of this new design was to reduce the size of each corps, and to hopefully facilitate their movements in the field.

This departure from the old system came on the heels of a great tragedy, the death of Lieutenant General Thomas J. "Stonewall" Jackson. Though originally thought to be on the road to recovery, General Jackson had contracted pneumonia, and on May 10, had succumbed to the effects of the dreaded disease.

Jackson's death had left General Robert E. Lee with a most unenviable task: that of filling the sizeable void then existing at the top of the Second Corps. Certainly, finding someone with Jackson's leadership qualities was not going to be easy. In fact, it looked well nigh impossible.

121

As it turned out, however, the question of Jackson's successor was a problem Lee chose not to deal with directly. Instead, he redistributed his present force so as to create another command, the Third Corps. This new force was composed mostly of brigades taken from Lieutenant General James Longstreet's First Corps, as well as some from Jackson's old command,[1] thereby, at the same time, streamlining the latter two bodies of men. Each of the three corps was left with three divisions. Besides increasing the maneuverability of each corps, the reorganization placed less of a burden on the new corps commanders. In that way, the transition of command could be more easily achieved, and Lee might even come close to making up for the loss of the indomitable "Stonewall."

By the end of May, Lee had selected his new corps commanders. First, there was Lieutenant General A. P. Hill, commander of the hard-hitting "Light Division" of Jackson's Corps. He would lead the newly organized Third Corps. Taking over the reins of the Second Corps, meanwhile, was another man who had served under Jackson, Lieutenant General Richard S. Ewell. Ewell had just returned to the army after recuperating from the loss of a leg, suffered at the battle of Groveton, in August of 1862. Prior to his being wounded, Ewell had shown himself to be a fine leader, and it was hoped that his excellent reputation would carry over and stay with him in his new position.

**LIEUTENANT GENERAL
RICHARD S. EWELL**

Took over command of the Second Corps on June 1, 1863.

(National Archives)

As was to be the case with Longstreet and Hill, Ewell's Corps, besides being comprised of three divisions of infantry, would also have at its disposal five battalions of artillery. Included among the latter would be Lieutenant Colonel Thomas H. Carter's command, which, in addition to Captain William J. Reese's Jeff Davis Artillery, contained the batteries of Captains William P. Carter, C. W. Fry and Richard C. M. Page. As before, Carter's battalion would remain attached to recently promoted Major General Robert E. Rodes' division. As for the other four battalions of artillery, two were to act in a reserve capacity, while the remaining two would be attached respectively to the other divisions of the corps, namely those belonging to Major Generals Jubal Early and Edward Johnson.[2] Lee had moved A. P. Hill's entire division over to the Third Corps.

As already mentioned, the Jeff Davis Artillery was one of those commands whose position relative to the rest of the corps had remained unchanged during the army's reorganization. For the battery, however, this period had been of much significance, not only on account of Ewell's appointment as the new corps commander, but also because the company itself had, during this time, seen some rearranging take place within its own ranks.

First of all, on May 8, Lieutenant Reese had formally taken over the captaincy of the battery. His advancement had come as a result of the receipt of official word from Richmond confirming the promotion of Captain James W. Bondurant to major. That was a move that had been anticipated by the company for some time.

Two weeks later, on May 22, Sergeant Columbus W. McCrary was appointed by Reese to the rank of sergeant major. That was a move that had probably come about as a result of Reese's experiences at Chancellorsville. There, during the heaviest fighting, Reese had been forced to take on the duties usually performed by several different officers. By promoting McCrary, he could not only reduce his own burden of responsibility at the front, but also improve the operation of the battery as a whole. With both Second Lieutenant Dwight E. Bates and Sergeant Major McCrary assisting him, Reese could now devote more of his time to his own responsibilities.

About the same time that McCrary was moving up in the ranks, Sergeant Robert T. Harper had received a promotion, on May 24, to the rank of first lieutenant with the Engineer Corps.[3]

Nine days after Harper received his commission, Private Robert W. Woodward, on June 2, transferred to Company H of the 3rd Alabama Regiment of Infantry. That loss, however, had immediately been made good by R. W. Barlow, who, on that same day, had been received in exchange for the departing private. That, as it turned out, was to be the last turnover for some time.

All during the time that the Army of Northern Virginia was being reorganized, preparations for a major offensive thrust were also being completed. The next campaign was an ambitious undertaking, for Lee planned to strike with his army deep into enemy territory.

By carrying the war north of the Mason-Dixon line, Lee would force Major General Joseph Hooker to vacate his current position north of the Rappahannock River. The Federal army would, in all probability, move in pursuit of the Confederates, and by doing so, would eventually release its grip on the state of Virginia during a critical part of the season, that of harvest time. Additionally, during the course of the invasion, Lee's army would be subsisting, for the most part, on supplies gathered in the North. Consequently, the strain of feeding an entire army would be temporarily lifted from the commissary department, which could then put its efforts towards gathering supplies for the future.

On June 3, all was ready, and on that day, Major General Lafayette McLaws' division of Longstreet's Corps departed Fredericksburg and moved west in the direction of Culpeper Court House. Following them during the next two days were the divisions of Ewell's command. (The Jeff Davis Artillery left camp, with Rodes' division, on the morning of the 4th.) Eventually, only Hill's Third Corps remained to hold a position along the river facing Hooker's army. That was a precautionary measure to protect the Confederate rear. Also, by leaving Hill at Fredericksburg, Lee also hoped to prevent the enemy from learning of his army's real intentions. Later, at the appropriate time, Hill would also leave the Rappahannock line, so to join the rest of the army on its northward trek.

On June 9, the Second Corps could be found in the vicinity of Culpeper Court House. On that day, Ewell was scheduled to start his divisions towards the Potomac River. However, the march was delayed when Major General Jeb Stuart's cavalry, the force which was to guard the army's flank, suddenly became embroiled in a major fight at Brandy Station. It turned out that the Confederate cavalry had been surprised by a sizeable Federal force which, early that same morning, had advanced across the upper fords of the Rappahannock. Only after a severe day-long contest were Stuart's men finally able to force the withdrawal of the Yankees.

Even as the Federals were retreating, Rodes' division was moving on Brandy Station. That force had been sent to help Stuart, but its arrival had come too late to effect the outcome of the battle. Even so, the Jeff Davis Artillery did succeed in firing a few shots at the Federals, who were moving back across the Rappahannock. Still, the battery's efforts came after the fact and had proved to be little more than an annoyance to the withdrawing bluecoats.

Though Reese's company had arrived on the field too late to be of assistance during the battle, the former servant and slave, belonging to ex-Second Lieutenant Edward Knight (one of the officers who had long since resigned from the battery), was captured. He had disappeared during the Maryland Campaign and when taken prisoner at Brandy Station was employed as the servant of a Union officer. Before long, the African-American was sent on his way back to his master in Alabama.[4]

The following day, Ewell's Corps moved towards the Potomac. On June 12, the Confederates arrived at Chester Gap, and after crossing the Blue Ridge Mountains at that point, entered the Shenandoah Valley. Once in the Valley, Ewell split his force. Early's and Johnson's divisions, under the personal direction of Ewell, were sent towards Winchester, Virginia, then occupied by the North. Meanwhile, Rodes' division, accompanied by Brigadier General Alfred G. Jenkins' cavalry, would be marching on Berryville. There, the Confederates were to eliminate another Union detachment. It was important to the success of the campaign that each enemy outpost encountered along the way, such as those at Winchester and Berryville, be taken by the Southerners. Once out of the way, those Federal forces could pose no future threat to the movements of Lee's army.

On June 13, Rodes' division arrived at the outskirts of the town of Berryville, where the Federal, as expected, were in force. Jenkins by then had already pushed back the Yankee cavalry but had himself been halted by the enemy's artillery.[5] By then, coming up on the heels of Colonel Edward A. O'Neal's Brigade was the Jeff Davis Artillery. It and the rest of Carter's battalion then went into position.

The Confederate guns opened fire, but after only a few rounds, the artillerists discovered that their enemy was rapidly withdrawing from the area. The appearance of Rodes' division had obviously taken the Federals by surprise. Though the Confederates attempted to cut off their retreat, they were able to make good their escape, thanks in part to a mismanagement of the forces that opposed them.[6] In their hasty retreat, however, the Yankees did leave behind a large amount of stores which included provisions for the men and provender for the horses. Those supplies were gathered up by the attackers. Purifoy remembered,

> The great quantity of Yankee beans captured in this camp was a novel sight to the men of the Jeff Davis Artillery. This was a new food to them,...Every man supplied himself with a quantity of the beans, as they were among the first to enter the camp and had free access to everything in it.[7]

He also noted that the feed left by the enemy "...came in very nicely for our horses."[8]

After that brief encounter, Rodes' division continued to move northward for a short time before camping for the night. The next morning, the march resumed, and continued with the Confederates reaching the vicinity of Martinsburg, West Virginia, late in the afternoon. There, to the right of the two, Rodes found Union artillery, cavalry and infantry drawn up in line of battle.[9] Jenkins then sent forward an officer to demand their surrender, which was refused.

To that point, the infantry had not yet come up, so Rodes endeavored to use his force at hand, which included both cavalry and artillery, in the most advantageous way possible against the enemy. First, Jenkins was told to move his brigade to the left of the town. Once there, he was to dismount his men, use them as skirmishers, and attempt to gain control of Martinsburg. If successful, the cavalrymen would also be cutting off a route by which the enemy might attempt to retreat.[10]

In addition, Rodes ordered Carter to bring his artillery forward to a position to counter the Federal guns which, by this time, had opened on the Confederates. Carter placed his batteries at three separate points, and it wasn't long before the battalion, including the Jeff Davis Artillery, was "...hotly engaged with a six gun battery of three inch rifles,"[11] commanded by Captain Thomas A. Maulsby. The effect was immediate, as Reese's first shot "...plunged into the farthest section, killing and wounding several horses and demoralizing the infantry support."[12]

By then, however, the Union troops were in full retreat from the town. The Confederates pursued the artillery and cavalry for two miles, and finally forced the Yankees to abandon all but one of their six guns.

Ignored by the Confederates, the infantry was making good its own escape. Actually, that force, it was later revealed, had disappeared down a different road soon after Rodes' attack had begun. The lateness of the Confederate advance and the fast falling darkness had played a part in its escape. As Rodes later reported, "Could the division have reached the town an hour or two earlier, thus giving me time to seize the principal roads leading to Martinsburg, I feel certain that I would have captured the whole force."[13]

Though the Southerners had missed another chance at capturing a substantial force, some consolation for this lost opportunity must have been found in the prizes they had gained. Now in Confederate hands, despite enemy efforts to destroy by fire the stores that had been accumulated in Martinsburg, were 6,000 bushels of grain, approximately 400 rounds of rifled artillery ammunition, various commissary stores, small arms and small arms ammunition, and two ambulances. That came in addition to perhaps the biggest prize of all: five three-inch Rifles, complete with caissons, and most of the horses that went with them.

Obviously, Rodes could make good use of the supplies captured at Martinsburg. As it turned out, however, the Jeff Davis Artillery benefited the most, receiving four of the captured cannon and the horses to pull them.

That move significantly improved the company's effectiveness. No longer would Reese's battery have to find ammunition for three different pieces of ordnance.[14] The command had previously carried two Rome, Georgia rifled cannon, one Napoleon and one twelve pound howitzer.[15] And, never again would one section of guns stand idle because of a lack of proper ammunition or by not having the necessary range.

On June 15, the day following its success at Martinsburg, Rodes' division, this time minus Jenkins' cavalry which had already been sent ahead towards Pennsylvania, again took up its northward march. About dusk, the Confederates reached Williamsport, Maryland. Immediately, Rodes sent three brigades of infantry and three batteries across the Potomac River.[16] He then awaited the arrival of the rest of the Second Corps, which was then concluding successful operations at Winchester.

In fact, the balance of Ewell's command had just won a convincing victory in which they had captured a great number of supplies, as well as most of the force that had opposed them. (Most of this had been accomplished during the night of the 14-15th.) With enemy resistance at Winchester smashed, Ewell then resumed his march towards the Potomac. By late on the 19th, Johnson's division was across the river, and Early's command was within easy reach at Shepherdstown along the south bank. Rodes by then had moved his division to the vicinity of Hagerstown, Maryland. Ewell's Corps was once more reunited.

As for the rest of the army, both corps belonging to Hill and Longstreet, as well as the cavalry under Stuart, were, by that time, also on the move. Those commands had all received marching orders from Lee just days before, when it became clear that the Federals were, at least for the time being, too preoccupied with other things to consider a march on Richmond. Actually, by June 15, Hooker, acting in response to reports of the Confederate movements to the west, had shifted his army north, from its position along the Rappahannock to a point closer to Washington. The Army of the Potomac had then taken up a line west of the Capital, and it was there that the Federal commander now sat with his forces awaiting the next Confederate attack. With the enemy on the defensive, Lee had been able to free up the rest of his army, so it could carry out its own part of the invasion.

While Hill, Longstreet and Stuart all moved north (the latter force screening the movements of the other two), Ewell's corps, which had been held close to the Potomac, waited to resume the march. On June 22, permission from Lee for the continuation of the drive into enemy territory was received.

For the advance into Pennsylvania, Ewell would again divide his force. This time, Early would act independently of the rest of the corps and would take his division first, in the direction of Waynesboro, then later, on an easterly track through the state. Meanwhile, some miles to the west, Rodes and most of Johnson's division (accompanied by the trains of the Second Corps) would be following a route whose course would eventually bring them within reach of the State capital at Harrisburg. Johnson's remaining brigade was to advance farther to the west.

While on the march through Pennsylvania, the Confederates were to collect whatever supplies they could and send them back to Virginia. In addition to conducting an extensive foraging expedition, Ewell was to move against Harrisburg and, if possible, capture the capital city.

By the afternoon of June 22, all of Ewell's Corps were again on the move. Passing through Hagerstown, Rodes' division entered the Cumberland Valley and the state of Pennsylvania. Rodes marched through Chambersburg and Shippensburg and on the 27th arrived at Carlisle. At that time, Johnson's division was also entering the outskirts of the town, though by a different road. The Confederates were now some fifteen miles from the state capital. Early, meanwhile, passed through Gettysburg, and by that time, was just a few miles from York, Pennsylvania. Ahead of him lay the Susquehanna River and, on the other side, important railroad lines of the enemy which he hoped to sever. Finally, already across the Potomac and moving to the support of Ewell's lead divisions, were Hill's Third and Longstreet's First Corps.

Thus far, all was going exceedingly well for Lee's invading army. Great numbers of livestock and other supplies had already been gathered and sent south. Just as important, however, was the fact that the march had, up until now, gone virtually unopposed. Only a few detachments of state militia had been encountered and easily brushed aside.

Unknown to Lee, however, was the fact that Hooker had not remained where he was, but had, during the past few days, moved north of the Potomac.[17] Careful to keep his army between the reported positions of the Confederate forces and Washington, Hooker had begun concentrating his forces in the area of Frederick, Maryland. From there, he intended to move west so to sever Lee's lines of communication with Virginia. If successfully carried out, such a move would also put the enemy in a position threatening the rear of the now divided Confederate army. Lee would then have to react quickly to the Federal presence, or he would run the risk of having his army forced into a battle for which it was ill-prepared.

Meanwhile, the three Confederate corps, still unaware of the menace to the south, continued to make the most of the favorable conditions encountered on their march. The Second Corps, for one, had occupied the town of Carlisle without incident, and Ewell was already preparing for his advance on Harrisburg. In fact, on June 27, the same day the Confederates entered Carlisle, Jenkins' cavalry, which had once again been united with the Second Corps, was sent to reconnoiter the defensive works about the capital city, while Ewell remained at Carlisle.

During the several days the Jeff Davis Artillery joined in the occupation of Carlisle, the artillerists enjoyed certain "luxuries" not already encountered on the rapid trek through the state. First, the company had the opportunity to occupy a portion of the Carlisle Barracks, an historic military post. In addition to sleeping indoors, the artillery men were also afforded the opportunity to rid themselves of the gritty accumulations of the past days. As Purifoy later reported, "Here we found a fine stream of water in which the men plunged, enjoying a bath after their long tramp of weeks."[18]

On Sunday June 28, the Alabamians attended religious services conducted by the corps chaplain, J. William Jones, and were no doubt witness to the raising of the Confederate flag over the Barracks.

The next day, Ewell received a favorable report from Jenkins concerning the defenses around Harrisburg, and quickly started Rodes towards the city during the afternoon. The hours passed, and the time for the advance was growing near, when all of a sudden a Headquarters' courier arrived with new orders for the Second Corps. There had been a change in plans, and Ewell was now to move his command south to Chambersburg, then to Cashtown, so to join the rest of the army. The previous night, Lee had, thanks to a report made by a friendly informant, finally learned of the concentration near Frederick and was now concentrating his own forces. As a result, Ewell was left with no choice but to cancel the advance on Harrisburg.

That same afternoon, Johnson's division was started towards Chambersburg while Early was directed to leave York and move west in order to rejoin the rest of the corps. Rodes' division, on the other hand, was permitted to remain at Carlisle for one more night. He would move out early the following morning.

Near dark on June 29, Ewell received new marching instructions from Lee. He was to send his divisions in the direction of either Cashtown or Gettysburg by way of Heidlersburg. Lee was concerned about a jam at the Cashtown pass, which could seriously delay the re-uniting of his forces and also prove advantageous to the enemy. Though displeased by the discretionary nature of the orders,[19] Ewell issued the necessary instructions to the division commanders and then prepared for his own departure from Carlisle on the morrow.

The following morning, Rodes' division received marching orders, and before sunrise, it, along with Ewell, was on the road to Heidlersburg. The ensuing march was uneventful. Near dusk, Rodes' division arrived at Heidlersburg and then proceeded to make camp. Just a few miles away Early had also halted for the night.

About this time, Ewell received from A. P. Hill, whose corps was presently spread about Cashtown, word of Federal cavalry being seen in the immediate vicinity of Gettysburg. Even so, the situation as it now stood was hardly threatening, and Ewell, who again had been given by Lee the option of marching his corps to either Cashtown or Gettysburg, preferred to wait before committing himself.

Ewell, however, like A. P. Hill, was unaware that the cavalry observed that very day, was actually being used to screen the movements of one wing[20] of the Army of the Potomac, which was not far behind. Just the day before, the Federal army had, in fact, left Frederick moving in pursuit of Lee. Major General George G. Meade had just received from Lincoln command of the Union forces on June 28, following General Hooker's request, on the previous day, to be relieved of his leadership post with the Army of the Potomac.

Soon after he had taken over command of the army, Meade decided rather than strike at Lee's communications, as Hooker had planned, he would move against Lee himself. He issued marching orders for the 29th, and by the end of the following day, most of the army had moved within easy marching distance of the Gettysburg area. Even so, Meade's plans, on the night of June 30, did not call for his army to give battle. Instead, he was inclined to exercise caution maneuvering against the Army of Northern Virginia. Meade wanted to see what Lee's intentions were before committing his own forces.

At the same time, however, Meade made arrangements for a defensive line to the south, along Pipe Creek, and extending from Manchester to Middleburg, Maryland, where, in the event of an attack, he could fall back and concentrate his army for the purpose of checking Lee's further advance. By occupying that line, Meade would not only be forcing the Southerners to meet him on a battlefield of his own choosing, but also would be interposing his entire army directly between them and Washington, thereby effectively blocking the way to the Capital city.

The next morning, that of July 1, found Federal engineers busily at work on the Pipe Creek line. At the same time, however, the bulk of the Yankee army was continuing its advance in the general direction of the region known to be occupied by the Southern forces.[21] And yet, the Federal movements, while conforming to the actions of Lee's army, were not reflecting any specific offensive designs of Meade, who still preferred to exercise caution in his pursuit of the Confederates.

PART II - THE OPPOSING FORCES COLLIDE

Just outside Gettysburg, Federal cavalry under Brigadier General John Buford was battling the lead elements of Major General Henry Heth's Division of A. P. Hill's Corps, which had been sent up the Chambersburg Pike to determine the size of the force occupying the town. Buford's force was greatly outnumbered, but Major General John Reynolds had ordered up his I Corps to support the cavalrymen. Major General Oliver Otis Howard's XI Corps was then also moving in an effort to close up on the I Corps. Howard, however, knew nothing of the fighting at Gettysburg. The remainder of the Army of the Potomac, including its commander, Major General George G. Meade, had also not yet learned of Buford's plight.

At the same time, the bulk of the Army of Northern Virginia was already converging on the Cashtown and Gettysburg areas. Coming up behind Hill's Corps on the Chambersburg Pike could be found the greater part of two of Longstreet's divisions. The third division, Major General George E. Pickett's, had been left at Chambersburg for the time being, to guard the army's rear.

Ewell's Corps, meanwhile, was spread out on the roads north and west of Gettysburg. Johnson's division was marching east from Greenville, while Early was pursuing a southerly route towards Cashtown. Ahead of Early was Rodes' division which had left Heidlersburg and was moving towards Cashtown by way of Middletown. During that march, the Jeff Davis Artillery acted as Rodes' rear guard.[1]

Before reaching Middletown, Ewell received a message from A. P. Hill, telling him of the Third Corps advance on Gettysburg. Not long thereafter, Ewell sent his divisions to Hill's support. Rodes turned his column south at Middletown along what was known as the Middletown Road towards Gettysburg. Early, meanwhile, took the Heidlersburg Road in the same direction. For both divisions, the march, for the most part, proceeded at a normal pace. The only sign of interference was witnessed by the Alabamians while crossing the mountains, when bush-whackers fired on the infantry, causing only a brief halt.[2] No word had as yet reached Ewell about the escalating fight between Heth's division and Reynolds' I Corps, the latter of which had by this time reached the field and beaten back the Confederate advance. The unhurried advance of the Second Corps continued.

All that changed, however, when Rodes, commanding the lead division of Ewell's Corps, reached a point about four miles from

Gettysburg. It was there that the unmistakable sound of artillery fire suddenly became audible. Immediately, there was a new sense of urgency and it wasn't long before there was a dramatic increase in the pace of the division.

As the column pushed ahead, Purifoy recalled that "...the artillery firing seemed to grow in intensity, and couriers met the corps and urged us forward."[3] Pressing on, now almost at the double quick, the Rodes' van soon reached the town's outskirts. Following along the Oak Ridge, the high tree-covered ground located north of Gettysburg, which itself ran north to south and was an extension of nearby Seminary and McPherson Ridges, the Confederates continued to close on the battlefield. In the meantime, Rodes himself moved to a position from which he could scan the entire field before him. It was by then a half past noon.

Just over a half mile to Rodes' front, and beyond, the battle lines of the lead elements of both armies stretched. Heth's division occupied a line facing Seminary Ridge, which it had assumed following its unsuccessful assault earlier that day. Support from the Third Corps had not yet reached the Confederate positions; however, on the opposing side, reinforcements had already come up and taken their place in the Union line. Even so, the Federal flank was undefended, offering Rodes a chance to take the pressure off Heth by dealing a damaging blow to the as yet unsuspecting enemy. In his report, Rodes noted,

> ....I found that by keeping along the wooded ridge, on the left side of which the town of Gettysburg is situated, I could strike the force of the enemy with which General Hill's troops were engaged upon the flank, and that, besides moving under cover, whenever we struck the enemy we could engage him with the advantage in ground.[4]

Quickly, the Confederates prepared to make the most of the opportunity that lay before them. The Jeff Davis Artillery and the three other batteries of Carter's battalion left the road and soon reached a point adjacent to Samuel Cobean's house, located on the each side of the ridge. Rodes began moving his infantry into position for an assault on the Federal right. At the same time, Ewell ordered Carter to occupy Oak Hill, the highest point on Oak Ridge, with his artillery and to begin firing at the enemy's position.

Accordingly, two batteries, William P. Carter's King William Artillery and Charles W. Fry's Orange Artillery, moved to the high ground

Modern view of house of Samuel Cobean, next to which Jeff Davis Artillery stopped before going into battle on July 1. (Gettysburg)

(Author's collection) Wedgewood Studio

and opened fire. In the meantime, R. C. M. Page's Morris Artillery and William J. Reese's Jeff Davis Artillery were held in readiness farther back along the ridge. The Alabama battery now occupied a position near the woods running along the south edge of a pasture on the Cobean farm. It was by then approaching one o'clock in the afternoon.

About that time, the gunners, who had taken up positions on and about Oak Hill, began to enfilade the Federal line. The enemy was startled by the destructive fire.[5] Their infantry was compelled to take shelter in a nearby railroad cut, reported Carter.[6] The Federals now endeavored to adjust their lines in order to meet the new threat on their flank. Accordingly, three brigades of the I Corps began shifting around to the right. By now Howard's XI Corps had also reached Gettysburg, and two of its divisions could be seen moving up to the right of the I Corps.

As the Union line was forming, the Confederate infantry prepared for the advance. Three brigades of the division's five were deployed in a line east and west of the ridge to the Carlisle Road on the other. The remaining brigades held positions a short distance to the rear. Rodes

Modern view of field on Cobean farm occupied by Jeff Davis Artillery on July 1.
(Gettysburg)

(Author's collection) Wedgewood Studio

planned to attack with his right and center with three brigades, one of
which would act as a support for the other two, while holding one brigade, that of Brigadier General George Doles, in a more or less defensive position on the left. He held his last brigade in reserve.[7]

The reason for this strategy was in part due to Early's closeness to
the lead division of the Second Corps. Early was reported to be not far
from Gettysburg and was expected to soon take a position on Rodes'
left nearer the town. With support coming up, Rodes no doubt felt more
comfortable about launching an attack against an enemy whose strength
was growing before his eyes.[8] However, until the anticipated meeting
between the divisions of the Second Corps actually occurred, Rodes,
whose main attention, again, was directed towards the ridge occupied
by the Federal troops opposing Hill's Corps, still had to ensure the protection of his own flank (especially now that Howard's divisions of the
XI Corps were deploying opposite the Confederate left). Therefore,
Rodes decided that Doles' brigade, already in position on the left, would
be held where it was to guard against any turning movement against
the division. That disposition enabled Rodes to strike what he hoped

would be a decisive blow on the right, without being too concerned about what was going on on the left.[9]

Near two o'clock, preparations for the Confederate offensive were complete. However, before Rodes could attack, the Federals began their advance. Immediately, the Confederates moved to the attack. By this time, Rodes had called for the remaining batteries of Carter's battalion. It was time for Reese and Page to move up in support of the infantry.

The Jeff Davis Artillery was placed on a rise just south of the Cobean farm house, while Captain Page's Morris Artillery was positioned at the foot of Oak Ridge. Before long, both batteries had opened fire. At the same time, however, they drew an intense return fire from the guns, now located in the valley north of the town. Page's battery, the more exposed of the two, sustained heavy casualties, having four men killed, twenty-six wounded, as well as losing seventeen horses.

Meanwhile, the infantry, now supported by all the guns of Carter's battalion, continued its advance on the right. But Rodes' assault was delivered in a disjointed fashion, and the attackers found themselves in great difficulty. Colonel Edward A. O'Neal's brigade, one of the two leading the advance, ran into determined opposition and was repulsed with substantial loss. Soon thereafter, the other lead brigade, Brigadier General Alfred Iverson's, was taken in flank. Quickly, the Confederate drive on that portion of the field deteriorated into a desperate fire-fight in which the Southern troops were just barely holding their own.

Farther to the right, Brigadier General Junius Daniel's supporting brigade fared better. Though it too had received a galling fire as it advanced, it kept on and was attempting to drive the Federals from the railroad cut.

Meanwhile, on the Confederate left, Doles' brigade was experiencing increasing pressure from the XI Corps. The Federals had extended their line well to the right and were massing troops both to the front and the flank of the Southern brigade. Fully realizing the danger he now faced, Doles requested artillery support to counter the threat. Accordingly, Carter moved three of his batteries from Oak Ridge to that high ground's eastern base to a supporting position behind Doles' brigade. Captain Fry's Orange Artillery remained at its post on Oak Hill. Reese's battery occupied ground in a wheat field on the east side of the Middletown Road, "...where the grain was nearly as tall as the men."[10]

Once situated, the Jeff Davis Artillery, along with the other two batteries of the battalion, hit the Federals with a concentrated fire. Reese's command focused its attention on Brigadier General Francis C. Barlow's Division and the guns attached to it. Union artillery returned the fire causing "...the stocks of grain to part as the missiles speeded through it."[11] However, the Confederate gunners endured the storm of shot and shell and soon were successful in forcing their opposition to give ground. "Here these batteries rendered excellent service, driving back both infantry and artillery," reported Carter.[12] And yet, in spite of what the Southern artillery had just achieved, the Federal forces were not about to ease the pressure on Rodes' division. The fighting continued to rage on all fronts. It was now nearing half past three.

Already an hour had passed by that time, Lee reached the battle-field near Heth's division's position. In spite of what must have appeared to be a chaotic situation north of the town, Lee, for the present, chose not to interfere. Heth had already asked Lee for permission to resume the attack in hopes of taking some of the pressure off the Second Corps. Heth, however, had to hold his position. Lee did not wish to become any more involved in the fight than he was, that is until Longstreet's Corps, which was on its way from Cashtown, arrived and his army was once more back together. Earlier, Longstreet had been ordered to yield the right of way to Johnson's division of Ewell's Corps. While Johnson was moving on to the Chambersburg Pike, Longstreet's divisions had to wait at Cashtown until the road was clear, thereby delaying their own advance towards Gettysburg.

The events that followed, however, soon caused a complete turn-around in Lee's strategy. Early arrived on the field, joined with Rodes' division and launched his attack. The Confederates, in particular Brigadier General John B. Gordon's Brigade, slammed into the right flank of Howard's XI Corps, forcing the Federals to begin withdrawing toward Gettysburg. All the while, the Jeff Davis Artillery continued "...giving the enemy a hot enfilading fire,...."[13]

About the same time, Rodes resumed the attack, this time with his entire division. The effect of the increased pressure all along the front caused the entire XI Corps' position to weaken. Soon masses of men in blue could be seen fleeing southward.

Lee, having witnessed the sudden change of fortune on the battle-field, gave Heth permission to renew his attack on the I Corps. The enemy stubbornly resisted for a time, but the arrival and advance of Major General William Dorsey Pender's Division forced them to yield their position on Seminary Ridge. A rapid retreat up the Chambersburg Pike commenced.

Soon those brigades, not already exhausted in the previous attacks, pursued the Yankees. The batteries of Carter's battalion also took up the chase with "...a few pieces unlimbering from time to time to break up the formations of the enemy as they endeavored to rally under cover of the small crests near the town."[14]

There was no stopping the Confederates. They pursued the enemy through the streets of Gettysburg. Several thousand prisoners were taken, and before long, the bulk of the Federal forces that remained could be seen making for the heights beyond the town. It certainly appeared that the Army of Northern Virginia was well on its way to achieving a major victory.

Now in control of Gettysburg, Early halted his brigades in order to reorganize. By this time, the Jeff Davis Artillery had reached the northern edge of the town, and had also been brought to a halt. There was now a lull in the fighting.

Near the town's public square,

> Wash Traweek, Gus Acker, and W. J. ("Big Zeke") Melton..., members of Reese's Battery, all noted for their extra qualities for prying into the surroundings when the battery reached a new location, peeped into the cellar of a neighboring residence and discovered Federal soldiers therein. When called out, they found they have five commissioned officers and four private soldiers, who were turned over to the guards.[15]

Just south of the town, at Cemetery and East Cemetery Hills, where a portion of Howard's XI Corps, which had not yet been engaged, had already taken position, the Federals were now starting to rally their own disorganized forces. Still, it would be some time before the greater part of the two Union corps would be able to complete their retreat to the high ground for their next stand. This situation presented the Confederates with an opportunity to strike before the enemy could be fully prepared to defend its new position. If launched without too much delay, such an attack would have a good chance of clearing the Federals from the hills they now occupied, thereby completing the route of the Union forces about Gettysburg.

Though Lee still wanted to avoid a general engagement until his entire force was at hand, he ordered Ewell to resume his advance if the latter felt circumstances warranted such a move. The commander of the Second Corps, however, took no action. Valuable time passes by, and Ewell's lack of resolve in this instance left his officers puzzled as well as frustrated.

General Early suggested that units of the Second Corps be used to seize Culp's Hill, which was located just east of Cemetery Hill and was

Modern view taken from east slope of Oak Ridge (near Oak Hill) looking towards town of Gettysburg. Cannon in foreground is a 3-inch Rifle, the same type gun used by Jeff Davis Artillery.

(Author's collection) Wedgewood Studio

as yet unoccupied. The taking of Culp's Hill was of critical importance because its high ground actually commanded the Federal force's present position. Ewell remained unmoved and delay followed delay.

Union reinforcements were on the way, and the situation at the Pennsylvania town was stabilizing as they continued to improve its position on Cemetery Hill. The commander of the II Corps, Major General Winfield S. Hancock, who had reached the field and taken over command of all the Union forces then at Gettysburg, recommended that Meade bring up the rest of the Army of the Potomac.

Meanwhile, back on the Confederate side, any hopes of a resumption of the attack on July 1 had vanished. It was near dusk, and though Johnson's Division had arrived on the field, that force was in no condition after its hard march to attack. Moreover, a frontal assault by that or any other part of the Second Corps, with so little daylight remaining, could hardly be effectively carried out. The result was that there was no more thought of an attack against Cemetery Hill that day.

For the Alabamians, as well as the other batteries of Carter's battalion, the day's fighting had come to a close. The Jeff Davis Artillery had seen a good deal of action and had performed with its usual alacrity and skill. Though records fail to show specifically how many, if any, men were lost by the battery during the action of July 1, it is very probable that some casualties were indeed sustained.[16] In view of the heavy artillery fire the men of Reese's command had to endure, it is actually highly unlikely that the battery had come out of the action without a scratch.

PART III - TWO MORE DAYS OF BATTLE:
THE ALABAMIANS WAIT...THEN FIGHT

The following morning, July 2, the Alabamians moved from Seminary Ridge to just north of the town, next to the Carlisle Road near John S. Crawford's house. Carter's other batteries joined them there. For the time being, the opposing armies did little more than skirmish. On the Confederate side, Lee had decided to launch an attack with his right, while feinting on his left with a view towards pursuing any opportunity that might develop on that portion of the field. For the attack on the Federal left, three divisions, two from Longstreet's First Corps, and one, Major General Richard H. Anderson's from A. P. Hill's Third Corps, were to be utilized.

Once Longstreet started his attack, the Second Corps' guns on the Confederate left were to open on both Cemetery and Culp's Hills. That demonstration, opposite the enemy's right flank, was designed to prevent the Federals from moving troops from that end of their line to reinforce their left. Ewell planned to use the artillery of Johnson's division, already positioned beyond the Federal flank. Carter's battalion was to remain in their reserve position north of the town.

Meanwhile, just south of Gettysburg, the concentration of the Union army was continuing. Meade himself had reached Cemetery Ridge. Once having surveyed the line his forces had taken up, he had determined that, at least for the time being, he would continue to hold his army in its defensive attitude and await Lee's next move. Meade was still without the services of his largest corps, Major General John Sedgwick's VI, and until it reached Gettysburg (the VI Corps was not expected to arrive at the battlefield until about 4:00 p.m.), the army would not have the reserve strength he desired, especially if an assault against the Southern positions was to take place. Furthermore, Sedgwick's arrival would give Meade the strength he needed to maneuver offensively, while, at the same time, maintaining his line of defense.

And yet, the morning and most of the afternoon of the 2nd was to pass in a relatively quiet fashion. Already it was approaching a half past three, and little more than desultory fire had been in evidence anywhere along the lines. Reese's battery, now acting as part of the Second Corp's reserve artillery, continued to occupy the same ground near the Crawford house, as it had since moving from Seminary Ridge earlier in the day.

Finally, at 4:00 p.m., Lee's assault on the right began. Led by Major General John B. Hood's Division, the attack first took aim at the end of

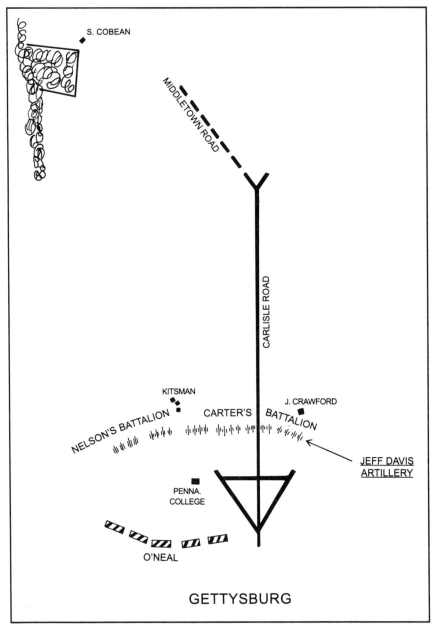

POSITION OF ALABAMA BATTERY-JULY 2ND 1863 – 9:00 A.M.
(remained all day)

Gettysburg National Military Park (After John B. Bachelder – 1883-1886;
Draft Maps of the Battlefield of Gettysburg for July 1, 2 & 3.)

the Federal line, near protrusions called Little and Big Round Top and a boulder filled area known as Devil's Den. After about an hour, the Confederates had gained control of important ground, including Big Round Top, but attempts at taking Little Round Top, the key to the Federal army's position, failed.

Attacks by Major General Lafayette McLaws' and then Richard H. Anderson's division followed with mixed success. The Union III Corps, which had taken up an advanced position away from the rest of the army, was driven from the field by McLaws' troops. The attackers pressed their advantage, but the timely arrival of reinforcements, stemmed the Confederate tide. Brigadier General William Barksdale's brigade, however, charged and made impressive gains, but soon was forced back like its predecessors. Thereafter, firing continued on both sides. By that time, McLaw's brigades had already done their worst.

Anderson's line for a time met with success at several points. Brigadier General Ambrose R. Wright's Brigade even gained a foothold near the Federal center, but was not supported and had to retreat. With that, the Confederate advance came to a halt. Though the Southern forces did have possession of Devil's Den and its surrounding woods, as well as the ground running along the base of the Round Tops, they were not able to inflict any long-lasting damage.

At the same time on the opposite flank, Ewell's divisions were moving against Culp's and East Cemetery Hills.

Following a demonstration provided by the artillery of Johnson's division, which as it turned out, had been severely handled by their Federal counterparts and forced to retire to safety, Ewell had ordered the advance to begin. First to move to the attack were the three brigades of Johnson's division. Their intended target was Culp's Hill.

In the darkness, Johnson's brigades advanced only to meet a stubborn resistance as they moved up the side of the hill. A terrific fight quickly developed on the right where two brigades had all they could do to hold their present positions. On the left, the remaining brigade, Brigadier General George H. Steuart's, established a foothold on the crest of Culp's Hill, but could not drive the well dug in Yankees from their defenses.

Still, the fighting continued, and two of Early's brigades were fully committed to the assault on East Cemetery Hill. In spite of strong opposition, the Confederates had been able to clear their immediate front. Before long, they had captured the summit of the hill and all of the enemy's artillery that had been positioned there. Early had successfully breached the Federal line.

Any thought of achieving a lasting breakthrough quickly faded, though, when Federal reinforcements appeared. The gray attackers were without support, and before long, the Confederates were withdrawing back down the hill.

At the same time that Early was engaged on East Cemetery Hill, Rodes' division (without Reese's battery and the rest of Carter's battalion, which was still sitting idle north of Gettysburg) had been preparing for its attack against Cemetery Hill. Though Rodes was supposed to support Early's advance, his deployment took a great deal of time. Before Rodes could launch his attack, Early's brigades were already falling back. Now unsupported on the left, Rodes halted his attack on Cemetery Hill.

As it turned out, the Alabamians had been unwitting victims of an unfortunate set of circumstances which had caused the Jeff Davis Artillery to remain inactive on July 2. Despite Ewell's decision to launch a major thrust at the Federal right, he had given little attention to the need for proper artillery support for his infantry.[1] His plan had called for only four batteries to participate in the attack. No thought had been given to the possibility of having Reese's battery, or the rest of Carter's battalion, for that matter, lend its support to the offensive.[2] Thus, at a time when that available firepower could possibly have been used to some advantage, the "reserve" batteries were left sitting idle north of Gettysburg. The result was that the infantry had been caused to go into a difficult fight with inadequate artillery support.

Johnson's artillery had been forced to retire from the field having received, as it turned out, assistance from only three batteries from the corps' five remaining battalions. Additional firepower from the reserve artillery on Culp's and East Cemetery Hills would have improved the chances of success for both Johnson and Early respectively. And as both divisions came so close to breaking the Union line, it is probable that use of the corps' full artillery might have made a difference.

Yet, even if the Jeff Davis Artillery had been forced to spend an inglorious day behind the lines, that still did not mean that the Alabamians' work was done.

At 4:30 on the morning of the 3rd, the action resumed on the Federal right in the area of Culp's Hill. There, Steuart's brigade suddenly came under a heavy bombardment. The Yankee artillerymen were trying to drive it from the side of the hill. As it turned out, however, the cannonade had little effect, but it wasn't long before the firing became general all along the lines, as the brigades advanced in an effort to dislodge the Union troops from their commanding position. That same morning, Johnson had received reinforcements from both Rodes and Early and was attacking with six full brigades, but they were repulsed with heavy losses.

For nearly five hours, the Confederates launched attack after attack, but by 10:00 a.m., Johnson's men had given their best and were exhausted. Before another hour had passed, the Southerners had begun to withdraw from their positions on the hill, relinquishing any gains made the previous evening.

Johnson's attack had failed, and the Yankees were once again in full possession of Culp's Hill. Ewell, considering the strength of the position, and the high cost of the latest assault, gave no further thought to renewing efforts to take it.[3]

During Johnson's attack, there had been a noticeable absence of artillery support. That time, however, the reason was not due to an oversight, but rather to the topography of the area. Nowhere could the gray cannoneers find suitable ground upon which to position their guns so to provide effective fire during the fight. The result was that a number of batteries had unavoidably been left standing idle.

Even so, that did not mean that all the corps artillery had themselves been left idle while Johnson was engaged. Specifically, Reese had been moved, with the six other rifled guns of Carter's battalion, as per the instructions of the Second Corps' Chief of Artillery, Colonel John Thompson Brown, to the high ridge on the right and left of the railroad cut.[4]

That move was part of Lee's plan to assault the Federal center. Lee felt that during the previous day's attack, Meade had weakened his Federal center and right in order to reinforce the left. This meant that at the Union center, where Confederate units had already met with success on July 2, there existed what Lee thought to be the best opportunity to cut Meade's line.[5] Once he achieved a breakthrough, he would have the tactical advantage.

Longstreet would be in charge of the offensive, for which he had nearly 11,000 men in nine brigades (the three of Pickett's division and six taken from Heth's and Pender's divisions) for his assault. In addition, Brigadier General Cadmus Wilcox's and Colonel David Lang's men, along with the three remaining reserve brigades belonging to Anderson's division, were to support the attack, should the need arise.

Before reaching the Federal line, the Southern forces would have to advance over about 1400 yards of open ground. Hence, to cover that attack, artillery was being massed all along the Southern line. That initial bombardment would involve batteries or parts of batteries taken from each of the three corps (more than 140 guns in all) and was de-signed to soften the enemy's positions along Cemetery Ridge, thereby reducing the threat from Meade's artillery. The main target areas in-cluded Cemetery Hill and Little Round Top, positions from which the enemy, if allowed, could rain a deadly flank fire upon the infantry. A lot, therefore, depended on the artillery doing an effective job of neu-tralizing the Northern guns.

Obviously, the task that lay ahead for the gunners serving the four 3-inch Rifles of Captain Reese's command was an important one. Hav-ing already completed about a half hour's move from their former po-sition along the Carlisle Road to the ridge traversed by the railroad cut, the Alabamians awaited the orders that would permit them to play their part in the grand offensive.

Just a few minutes past 1:00, Longstreet's order to open fire, which had been received by Colonel James B. Walton, Chief of Artillery of the First Corps, was transmitted to Captain M. B. Miller's battery. Two cannons were fired, the signal to start the bombardment, and the Jeff Davis Artillery joined in opening upon the Federal positions. Soon, an artillery duel of proportions never seen before on the continent had commenced.

For the next hour and a half, an incessant rain of iron was sent to-wards the Union lines. And yet, even with all that firepower, the Con-federate batteries achieved only limited success. Though the Yankee front line suffered some damage at the outset, it was actually its close supporting and reserve artillery in the rear that sustained the most hits. Because of the dense smoke that soon covered the target area, the Con-federate gunners lost the ability to sight their pieces and had, for the most part, overshot their main objective. Still, this did not necessarily mean that the bombardment was ineffective in certain locations, such as Cemetery Hill. Colonel Thomas W. Osborn, Chief of Artillery of the XI Corps, whose guns came under the fire of Reese's Jeff Davis Artil-lery, recalled that, "...many, very many, shells and solid shot fell among the batteries and many shells exploded just in front of them, the frag-ments scattering among the men and horses."[6] At that stage of the fight, the work of the Alabama battery was particularly impressive as borne out by the following excerpt:

> A hush of death brooded o'er the bloody field. The vet-erans of Pickett had marshalled to charge and die, and leave behind (fit emblem of glorious defeat) the laurel and the cy-press around the Southern brow entwined.

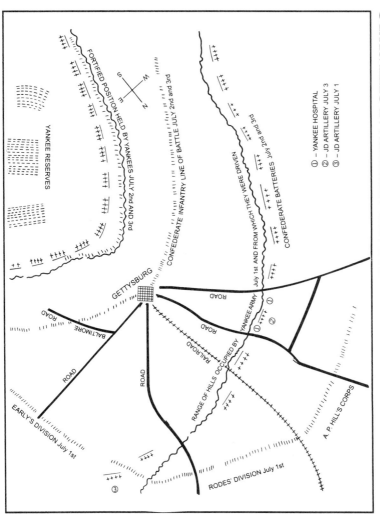

JEFF DAVIS ARTILLERY AT GETTYSBURG
Recreated from a drawing by William J. Reese
(Courtesy of R. Brooks Traweek, Richmond, Virginia/Gettysburg National Military Park)

The highest of the ridge on the southern side was swept by nineteen guns which Lee wished silenced. The Jeff Davis Artillery, manned by Dallas County boys and commanded by Lieut. Bates and Captain W. J. Reese, were picked out for the position and work. Everything was arranged for death or victory.

The duel began. As men fell, others quietly stepped into their places until the nineteen guns ceased firing, and their men scattered out of sight.

Think of it, men and women of Dallas! Four guns silenced nineteen! Your fathers, sons, and brothers were there, and the heritage of their deathless achievement is yours! Lee rode rapidly up to the begrimmed heroes of that awful half hour, saluted and thanked them for their "unsurpassed chivalry."[7]

It was now past 2:30, and the infantry had to attack without further delay. The batteries had by then used so much of their ammunition, that if the current rate of fire continued much longer, there soon would not be enough ammunition available for the artillery to properly support the infantry. The artillery train had been sent to the rear and could not be drawn from in time to resupply the batteries. Moreover, it was also beginning to look as if the bombardment had finally had the desired effect. By that time, Federal return fire had slowed significantly and had even ceased entirely at Cemetery Hill and on Cemetery Ridge at the Union center.

Subsequently, the Confederate infantry moved to the attack. By then, the cannon on both sides had ceased firing altogether. The Federals, as it turned out, had done so in an effort, not only to cool their guns in preparation for the expected assault, but also to deceive the Confederates into thinking they had silenced the guns on Cemetery Ridge.[8] The Southern artillery, meanwhile, had halted its fire to conserve ammunition.

Advancing at a steady pace, the gray brigades passed through the long lines of the silent Southern artillery. Soon the attacking forces were within range of the enemy's guns, many of which now opened. Quickly, Pickett's men became the victims of a damaging barrage. The Confederate artillery itself rejoined the contest in hopes of taking the pressure off of the infantry. For the most part, however, its fire was ineffective in stopping the Yankee barrage.

The Southerners were obviously going to have a difficult time of it during the advance, and yet, it might have been even worse at the outset, especially had all of the available Yankee guns been used against them. Unknown to them was the fact that a number of batteries at the center were deliberately holding their fire, waiting for the Southern lines to move closer. Those batteries, in fact, had used up their long range ammunition and could only fire effectively at close range.

Moving still nearer to the enemy's position on the ridge, the gray-clad forces now found themselves being hit in front and on both flanks by an even more effective fire. In spite of what Lee had hoped, the Federal artillery had not been significantly weakened. Huge gaps appeared in the gray lines, and the much exposed brigades on the left, which contained some of the least experienced of all the attackers began to waiver. Some began to leave the ranks.

Ironically, it was by that time that the Southern artillery had again reduced its own fire. Ammunition was low and had to be conserved or else there would not be enough when it became time to follow-up the advance of the infantry.

Before long, the most advanced of the brigades crossed the Emmitsburg Road and were pushing up the slope of Cemetery Ridge, on whose crest, behind a stone wall, lay the Federal infantry supported by numerous cannons. Volleys were exchanged and canister now filled the air as the waiting guns opened with fearful effect on the still advancing Confederates. Now charging forward, the Southerners reached the enemy's works at the center and for a time, took advantage of the cover afforded by the stone wall. Then advancing once again, several hundred of the attackers attempted to carry the Federal position. However, after a fierce hand to hand struggle, those few, who still remained, were forced to retreat. By then, Union troops had swung around both flanks of the attackers and were pouring a murderous fire into them from three sides. Meanwhile, on the right and left, others who had also fought their way up Cemetery Ridge now began to fall back. Officers attempted, often unsuccessfully, to rally the survivors streaming back towards Seminary Ridge. The men were too badly shaken from their ordeal.

Even as his men were trying to regroup, Longstreet was preparing to repulse the expected counterattack. Longstreet, however, was unaware that Meade was satisfied with what had already been achieved. Moreover, his men were exhausted, and he had no intention of sending them against what was still a very formidable foe. Meade's decision not to take the offensive gave the Southern forces the opportunity to regroup after the bloody contest.[9]

The cost of the attack had been enormous. From beginning to end, the Confederates had suffered more than 7,000 casualties (killed, wounded and captured) out of a total of about 12,500 participants. This includes Wilcox's and Lang's brigades which had advanced even as the attack was being repulsed.

Pickett's division had been cut to pieces. Of its three brigade commanders, Brigadier Generals Lewis Armistead and Richard B. Garnett had both been killed, while Major General James L. Kemper had been seriously wounded and would later be captured. Only one field officer had escaped injury, and overall, the division had suffered nearly 70% casualties. In addition, a number of Third Corps' brigades had also been similarly decimated during the attack on Cemetery Ridge.

The artillery, on the other hand, was still intact. It had suffered its share of casualties during the opening bombardment, but thereafter, had gone relatively unscathed. In view of the day's event, that was indeed fortunate. And yet, the artillery's activities on the 3rd of July had served to raise serious questions about the role of the various battalions in the hours and days ahead. It was already a well-known fact that the Southern batteries had seriously depleted their supply of ammunition during the day's action.

There was on hand only enough ammunition for one more day of fighting. Most of the available shot and shell was still some distance to the rear in the supply train. Distribution of that ammunition would take time, and if the enemy, as expected, had resumed the contest, the Confederate batteries, with their limbers now nearly empty, would no doubt soon have found themselves at a serious disadvantage. And yet, even if the prospects did seem particularly grim following Pickett's Charge, the Southern artillerymen displayed no loss of resolve and stood defiantly in place, prepared to defend their positions at any cost.[10] Still, Lee was left with no recourse but to withdraw back towards the Potomac.

Lee wanted the vehicles, carrying the wounded, and the supply train with any prisoners taken during the battle, to lead the way back to Virginia. Following them would be the Corps of Hill, Longstreet and Ewell, in that order. For the first part of the march, a detail from the Second Corps would serve as the rear guard.

Meanwhile, the next morning, July 4, Lee's army waited to see if an attack would come. The forenoon, however, passed in a quiet fashion. Midday came and went, and still there was no unusual or threatening movement by Meade. Near one o'clock, one brigade did push forward. But, it formed in line of battle and advanced no further. By then, a heavy rain was soaking the battlefield.

There was no renewal of enemy activity during the afternoon. That same afternoon, Lee's trains, complete with cavalry escort, were started on their way. The Southern army's grand exodus had begun.

PART IV - THE RETREAT

Just after dark, on July 4, the Third Corps withdrew from its position along Seminary Ridge and left Gettysburg by way of the Fairfield
Road. Next to evacuate the ridge were Longstreet's divisions. Rain continued to fall, delaying the withdrawal.

That night, the Jeff Davis Artillery joined Carter's battalion on the
road, but had hardly moved before coming to a halt. As Purifoy remembered, "In diminished quantities, though sufficient to soak the
soldiers clothing, the rain continued a steady downpour."[1] After remaining in the same position on the road for some time, a tired Purifoy,
availed himself of a nearby fence to get some rest. "I soon placed myself in a recumbent position on the slanting rails and, with my knap-
sack under my head, though the rain continued to patter down, I was
soon lost to the surroundings."[2]

The following morning brought no change in the battalion's position, as the artillerymen waited for the troops up ahead to take the road.
Purifoy, meanwhile, sat on the fence and remembered watching the
movements of the Federal troops on Cemetery Ridge, as well as the
activity on the road his battery would soon be travelling.[3]

Finally, near midday, after a wait of nearly sixteen hours, the Jeff
Davis Artillery took up the march with the rest of Ewell's Corps. Late,
on the afternoon of July 5, the Second Corps reached Fairfield. There,
the entire column stopped for the night.

The men of Reese's battery, however, were not as yet afforded the
opportunity to rest. Federal cavalry had been discovered moving on
Fairfield, and it was now necessary to take up a defensive posture. Consequently, the Jeff David Artillery went into position with the infantry
just beyond the town.

A few shots were exchanged, but the firing quickly subsided. For
the moment, the threat had passed. The Alabamians now bivouacked
for the night.

The encounter at Fairfield had, again, only been against Federal
cavalry. As for Meade's infantry, it had not taken up the pursuit of Lee's
army until the afternoon of the 5th and was experiencing serious delays because of the poor road conditions. For the present, only the
enemy's cavalry was interfering with the movements of the Southern
forces.

Just before midnight on July 4, Brigadier General Judson Kilpatrick's
cavalry had cut off and either captured or destroyed a good portion of
Ewell's trains near Monterey, on the South Mountain range, west of
Fairfield. All of the wagons belonging to Carter's battalion were lost.

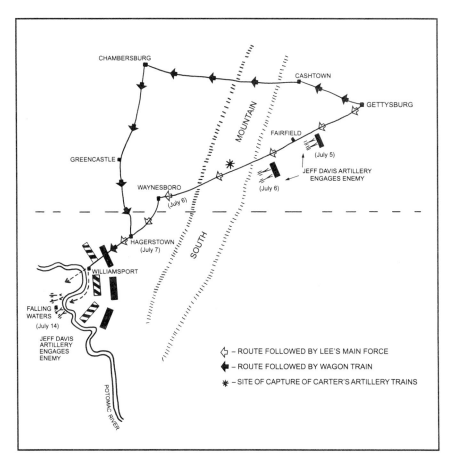

CONFEDERATE RETREAT FROM GETTYSBURG – JULY 4 - JULY 14, 1863

Recreated from Plate XLIII-7 of _The Official Military Atlas of the Civil War._

During that attack, the drivers of the battery forges and wagons of the Jeff Davis Artillery were taken prisoner. Those captured were privates John R. Busby, George Champion, James M. Powell and William T. Wade along with four of the battery's five artificers, James C. Gates, John J. Howell, John J. Humphries and Charles Kuhne. The company's only remaining artificer now was John Cochran, who normally accompanied the gun crews themselves while on the march.[4]

Following their capture, the prisoners from the Jeff Davis Artillery had been sent to Fort Delaware, a prison where conditions were terrible. In fact, "No other Northern prison was so dreaded in the South as this."[5] On July 26, 1863, a Northern surgeon reported the following about conditions at the prison: "A thousand ill; twelve thousand on an island which should hold four;...; twenty deaths a day of dysentery and the living having more life on them than in them."[6]

While at Fort Delaware, Wade and Private M. M. Dingler, who had also been taken prisoner on July 4, contracted smallpox and died.[7] Kuhne and Howell, meanwhile, both survived and were discharged in the Fall of 1864. After his release, Kuhne was placed on detached service back in Selma, Alabama. Howell received a forty day furlough after his release, but after that, it is not known whether or not he reentered the military. Champion remained in Union custody for only several weeks before receiving his parole on July 30, 1863. It is not known whether or not he returned to Confederate service. At the same time, both Busby and Gates eventually took the oath of allegiance to the United States, with Busby later joining the U. S. Army.

Powell endured over one and a half years of prison, first at Point Lookout, Maryland, then at Elmira, New York before falling victim to disease. Humphries, on the other hand, barely survived nearly fourteen months of prison life. He was exchanged on September 18, 1864, already in poor health and died one month later in a Richmond hospital.

Certainly, the march from Gettysburg had already been a costly one for the Jeff Davis Artillery. In a matter of minutes, the battery had lost more men than it had during the entire first month of the campaign.

As a result of the attack on the train, Carter's entire battalion was left without cooking utensils, and no one to borrow from within the command.[8] Nevertheless, Purifoy recalled:

This destitute condition of the men caused their ingenuity to launch many makeshifts, some of which had been previously developed by similar trials. Every old Confederate soldier remembers the split Yankee canteen, each half of which could be readily turned into a helpful convenience. A frying pan, a stewpan, and a corn and roasting ear grater are a few of the useful implements into which they were usually transformed....The same old soldier has seen the bark slipped from certain trees in the early spring, and the sections divided equally, each of which made an excellent substitute for a bread tray....The makeshifts noted comprise but a few of the many expedients which the necessities of the Confederate soldier compelled him to devise.[9]

That evening, after having assisted in driving off the Federal cavalry, and with pickets in place, the artillerymen felt secure.[10] As Purifoy recalled, the men "...quietly partook of their meager rations, spread down their blankets, and had a quiet night's sleep; he horses were unhooked from the gun and caisson carriages, and, harness remaining on them, they were given their provender."[11]

The following morning, July 6, while breakfast was being eaten by the artillerymen, they discovered a skirmish line advancing towards them from Wright's Division of Major General John Sedgwick's VI Corps. Dole's and Daniel's brigades stopped them without too much difficulty. They, as well as the remaining troops of Rodes' division, plus a section of guns from the Jeff Davis Artillery, served as the army's rear guard on that day.

The Second Corps again took up the march. Upon reaching South Mountain, that particular section of Reese's command, which was located at the rear, went into position, while the rest of the marching column, including the other section of guns belonging to the battery, moved on. A sharp fight took place at the foot of the mountain, but after a time, the Yankees were driven off. During that engagement, the cannon of the Jeff Davis Artillery had been silent. The enemy, as it turned out, had never concentrated their numbers enough to present the gunners with a suitable target.[12] The Alabamians then limbered up and crossed South Mountain, without further hindrance. Upon reaching the crest of the mountain gap, the rear guard section of Reese's battery came to a halt. While stopped on the road, Purifoy took note of his surroundings.

...From that point one of the picturesque rural scenes greeted my vision that I remember to have seen before or since. For miles, yes, as far as the vision would permit, toward the east a plain of unbroken forest – save the numerous interspersed farms which dotted the vast expanse, each with comfortable farmhouse and the other essential buildings – was spread out before me....Until the rhythmic tread of the Confederate soldier echoed through the valleys and gorges of this grand panorama, the blighting touch of war was perhaps never known in it. What a contrast with similar sections of the "Old Dominion!"[13]

The march resumed and while proceeding down the western slope, the men saw the burned remains of the wagon train that the Federal cavalry had fallen upon, on the night of July 4. Once past the mountains, the artillerymen moved at a steady pace until they reached Waynesboro. There, they went into camp and were once again reunited with their comrades.

The next day, July 7, the march towards the Potomac continued. Ewell's Corps reached Hagerstown, Maryland about noon, and there the entire command halted pending further orders. At the same time, the van of the main army was already arriving at Williamsport, where the northward crossing of the Potomac River by the Jeff Davis Artillery had taken place some weeks before.

Up until now, the withdrawal through Pennsylvania and Maryland by Lee's three corps had gone off exceedingly well. However, upon reaching Williamsport, Lee, who had been accompanying the lead corps, found his wagon train of wounded stalled on the north side of the river. Because of recent rains, the Potomac had become swollen and was now well past fording, even at the normally wadable Williamsport crossing site. Moreover, the pontoon bridge, which had been located a few miles down stream at Falling Waters, had been recently destroyed by the Union forces. With the bridge now gone, there was no way for the army and its trains to cross to the safety of the Virginia shore.

Lee was left with no alternative but to have his army dig in along the river and protect the crossings until a new bridge could be constructed. That same day, July 7, the army began taking up a position along a six mile front between Hagerstown and Williamsport. Dispositions were completed during the next few days, with Rodes' division and Carter's battalion occupying the extreme left of the line, on the heights west of Hagerstown. The Jeff Davis Artillery took its place along the line on July 10.[14]

Still short of ammunition, Reese's battery received orders to fire only on any advancing lines of Federal infantry. Artillery duels were definitely out of the question. Such restrictions on the use of firepower could certainly put the battery at a disadvantage.

Fortunately, the restraints put on the artillery were short-lived, thanks to the timely arrival of supplies from south of the river. On July 8, Lee received word that ammunition was on the way from Winchester. At that time, it was expected that the wagon train would reach the Potomac on the following day. Assuming that the wagons had arrived on schedule, it is likely that by July 10, the resupplying of the different battalions had already begun. Although, it is conceivable that the distribution had not yet occurred on the extreme left where the Jeff Davis Artillery was currently posted. Otherwise, that battery would not have been restricted in the use of its guns, as it was when it first went into position on the line on the tenth.

Indeed, the ammunition arrived at a most opportune time, because it had also been on July 9 that information had been received reporting the main Federal army's approach from Frederick, Maryland. Such news convinced Lee that another major battle could not be too far off.[15]

The Federal advance had been a steady one out from Frederick, and by July 10, Meade's entire army was within close striking distance of the Confederate works. He then spent two days preparing for the assault. Finally, on the afternoon of Sunday, July 12, all was ready. However, sudden bad weather, just as orders for the attack were about to be transmitted, caused Meade to postpone the advance. Another day passed, during which demonstrations aimed at feeling out the Southern positions took place. It would not be until the morning of July 14 that Meade would again be ready to attack. However, by then it would be too late, for most of the Confederate army would already be well out of reach.

On the evening of the 13th, the Confederate engineers had completed their work on the pontoon bridge at Falling Waters. By that time, the Potomac River had also fallen sufficiently, so that the Confederates could ford it. As a result, Lee's withdrawal began during the afternoon, with the artillery and wagons being the first to move towards the bridge. They were followed after dark by the First and Third Corps in that order. Meanwhile, the infantry belonging to Ewell's Corps would be moving across the Potomac at Williamsport.

The Jeff Davis Artillery began what was to prove a memorable journey downriver to the crossing at Falling Waters. As Private John Purifoy wrote of the march made that night of July 13:

I think the night we made this march was one of the darkest I ever under-took to move in. The rain was falling in torrents, and the mud was terrible. Our movements were ex-

158

ceedingly slow. The battery was moving from near the extreme left of the army to the extreme right. When we started out in the beginning of our enlistment, when accoutrements and ammunition were furnished, among the supplies given us, were a lot of port-fires, socalled. These were long paper tubes, enclosing a combustible composition that, when lighted burned slowly producing, a beautiful flame. During our two years of previous service we had never found any use for these. During this dark march an enterprising comrade suggested that the port-fires might be used to light our way. The suggestion was carried out and in extremely dark places during that miserable night's march these torches served a useful purpose. We were on the move the entire night, though we had to move but a short distance.[16]

Finally, at about seven o'clock on the morning of July 14, the Jeff Davis Artillery reached the pontoon bridge. The battery crossed over and went into position on a high bluff overlooking the crossing site. There, they were joined by the other batteries of Carter's battalion.

Once they had been situated on the other side of the Potomac, the by now exhausted men of Reese's command collapsed on the ground next to their guns. The artillerymen were soon asleep and oblivious to all that was going on around them.

Some time later, the gunners were roused and told to be ready to engage the enemy. Purifoy recalled that, "On awakening a roar of musketry on the opposite side of the river greeted his ears,..."[17] The Federals had by then begun their much delayed advance, and Heth's division, which was acting as rear guard, was now attempting to hold them off while the second of A. P. Hill's three divisions made its way across the bridge at Falling Waters. By then only Heth's and part of the center division from the Third Corps remained north of the river.

Heth's delaying tactics were successful, and soon only his division remained on the opposite shore. Now moving towards the bridge, it suddenly was itself in danger of attack. A Federal battery had rapidly come up to the rear of the gray column and was now assuming a position from which it could challenge his intended crossing.

The appearance of the artillery had been seen from across the river, and the Jeff Davis Artillery opened upon it. At once, all the battery's guns were in action. "From the right and left also came echos of our reports from two or three onther batteries of the battalion,..."[18] The aim of the Confederate gunners was without fault, and the Federals, now suddenly finding themselves the object of a murderous fire, were forced to make a hasty retreat without firing a single round.

A short time later, Northern skirmishers were seen advancing. As before, artillery again provided cover for Heth's men to prevent the bridge from being captured. That time, however, the Jeff Davis Artillery alone was selected for the important work.

"The battery...was instructed to shoot with shot or shell at as many as two or three of the enemy when such a group showed itself."[19] Reese's gunners went to work, and with uncanny accuracy hit their mark time after time. The result was that the enemy became cautious and slowed their pursuit, thus allowing the last Confederates to get safely across the river allowing there was ample time for the destruction of the pontoon bridge. "The gunners of the Jeff Davis Artillery were complemented by General Lee, who witnessed the work done. He was at that particular point supervising matters in person."[20] Thanks in part to the Alabama battery, the Army of Northern Virginia was now safely back on Southern soil.

Many years after the war, Purifoy received a letter from A. F. Southworth of Huntington, West Virginia (Formerly of Page's battery), who remembered and attested to the expertise shown by the Jeff Davis Artillery in the incident just described. Mr. Southworth remarked:

> Do you remember when you crossed the Potomac? We had reached the Virginia side and all had gone into position, (the battalion) and your battery was firing at the Federal sharpshooters who were firing on the Confederates, who were attempting to take up or destroy the pontoon bridge. Your battery stopped them from firing on our men. You made some of the finest shots I ever saw fired."[21]

This was quite a compliment made by a fellow artillerymen of Carter's battalion.

The defense of the Falling Waters bridge had been, as far as the men of Captain Reese's command were concerned, strictly a one-sided affair. The company had sustained no casualties, nor come under fire at any time during the action. Even so, Privates John Burwell and John Duhig, were now found to be missing from the ranks. As it turned out, Burwell had deserted at Williamsport and had fallen into enemy hands. Duhig, meanwhile, had been separated from the company some time during the march to Falling Waters and had never made it across the bridge. He, too, was a prisoner of war. Whether or not Duhig would ever have the opportunity to rejoin the battery is something not made clear by the company records. What is known, however, is that he would spend the following months in Washington's Old Capitol Prison.

Following its encounter at Falling Waters, the Jeff Davis Artillery moved south with the rest of the army. By the 16th, it had reached the Darkesville/Bunker Hill area. There, the army halted, resupplied itself and rested.

On July 21, Ewell moved his entire corps against a force protecting the Baltimore and Ohio Railroad, situated between Hagerstown and Hedgesville. The Federals, however, withdrew before the Confederate advance and escaped.

Following its unsuccessful mission, the Second Corps turned around and headed back down the Shenandoah Valley. By that time, the main Union army had itself crossed the Potomac and was moving south along the eastern side of the Blue Ridge Mountains in pursuit of Lee. At Berryville, an encounter took place during the dark of night. Throughout the course of the engagement, the flashes from the guns of the Jeff Davis Artillery drew return volleys from the enemy, whose target was otherwise shielded from sight by the cover of darkness.[22]

After the engagement at Berryville, Reese's command took part in a running fight with a cavalry regiment in the vicinity of Front Royal. In that instance, the Confederates were actually the pursuers, chasing the Federals in a northerly direction through a gap in the mountains.

Next arriving at nearby Manassas Gap (on the 23rd), Ewell found Wright's brigade, Anderson's division, Third Corps, deployed in line of battle against a much larger force.[23] (Wright had been left behind to hold the gap until Ewell's arrival. In the meantime, Longstreet's First and the rest of Hill's Third Corps had been completing their withdrawal through the mountain towards Culpeper Court House.) Rodes' division and Carter's battalion were immediately brought up in support of Wright.[24] O'Neal's brigade took up a position with the men of the Third Corps, while the rest of the division, including Carter's battalion, was placed in a second line not far to the rear.

> The enemy attacked in force, driving the front line of skirmishers back slowly. Wright's men fought obstinately, as did the sharpshooters. After obtaining possession of the ridge occupied by the first line of skirmishers, the enemy attempted to make a farther advance in line of battle,..., but failed signally,...
>
> ...A few shots from Carter's artillery and the skirmishers' fire halted them, broke them, and put a stop to the engagement...[25]

Thereafter, only Page's and Fry's batteries kept up a leisurely fire which served to stop the Yankees until dark when the Confederate force was withdrawn.

Another skirmish took place soon thereafter, farther south at Chester Gap, but with the coming of nightfall, the Federals withdrew. Ewell then moved rapidly up the Shenandoah Valley. Reaching a point near Luray, located on the south fork of the Shenandoah River, the Confederates halted and encamped for a few days. After that brief halt, Ewell crossed the Blue Ridge Mountains and marched to Madison Court House. From there, he moved to Orange Court House where, by August 4, he had taken up a defensive position on the south side of the Rapidan River with the rest of the army. That marked the close of the campaign.

After a most auspicious start, the Gettysburg Campaign had certainly ended on a sour note for the Confederate army. Even though Lee had successfully returned his forces to a position of relative safety along the Rapidan, the fact remained that his army suffered much while in the end achieving very little of major importance. Casualties at Gettysburg alone had robbed Lee of more than one third of his effective strength.[26]

But the men of the Jeff Davis Artillery could certainly look back with pride at their performance over the past month or so. At Gettysburg, the Alabamians had played a significant role in assisting their fellow infantrymen during two major offensive thrusts. During the lst and 3rd days of the mammoth battle, the battery had fired a total of 229 rounds against both infantry and artillery. So impressive was their fire, that it had brought favorable comment from Lee himself.

Next when called upon to protect the army during the withdrawal from Pennsylvania, Reese's command had again done its part, in a distinctive fashion, as during the action at Falling Waters bridge. There once again, the gunners had won praise for their action.

Fortunately, losses suffered during the campaign had been comparatively light, and had not seriously affected the battery's performance. No detailed report of the Jeff Davis Artillery's casualties at the battle of Gettysburg exists. For the campaign, Carter's battalion's totals were: 6 killed, 35 wounded and 24 captured or missing. Of his four batteries, Carter's and Page's had been far and away the most severely injured, and that just during the afternoon of July 1 when they dueled with the Federal artillery. Between the two batteries, 6 men had been killed and another 33 wounded.[27] At the same time, just over half of those who had been counted among the battalion's captured or missing were from the ranks of the Jeff Davis Artillery. All those losses had, again, occurred during the Army's withdrawal from Pennsylvania and Maryland.

CHAPTER X

ATTEMPTING TO BEAT THE ODDS

August found the Army of Northern Virginia and the Army of the Potomac occupying approximately the same lines as they had before the Gettysburg Campaign. The armies held positions on opposite sides of the Rapidan River, within easy striking distance of one another, and yet, neither Lee nor Meade wanted to take the offensive. Both were content to rest and gather strength in preparation for the next encounter.

Carter's battalion needed time to recoup its losses. Brigadier General William N. Pendleton, Lee's Chief of Artillery, had recently reported that the battalion was without sufficient transportation and had been forced to borrow forges from another command because of the loss of its own during the retreat from Gettysburg.[1] Moreover, its casualties had not been replaced.

Fortunately, recruiting efforts had increased in Alabama, largely due to a revision of the conscription laws of April 6, 1862 which now allowed men from the ages of 18 to 45 to be drafted. By August 31, seven men had signed up with the battery. They included Privates G. H. Ball, Obediah Belcher, A. M. Blackmon, James Bulger, W. M. Walker, Joseph Defreese and William Farrar. They would help make up for almost half of the losses of the past few months. During September, eight more men enlisted for the Alabama battery. And in the months that followed, the list of new recruits continued to grow.

Unfortunately, however, it would take months before most of the recruits would reach the battery. In fact, only four of all those who signed up in August and September would arrive in camp before the end of October: Privates J. W. Barlow, John M. Peebles, F. M. Callahan and W.

J. Harris. The reasons for the long wait before the arrival of the rest of the men are not known.

But, their arrival came at a critical time. Lieutenant General James Longstreet with Major Generals John B. Hood's and Lafayette McLaws' divisions of the First Corps were to be sent to reinforce General Braxton Bragg's Army of Tennessee defending Chattanooga and the vital passes near that town.[2] Opposing Bragg was the Army of the Cumberland, led by Major General William S. Rosecrans.

In the meantime, however, the temporary loss of the two First Corps divisions would leave the Confederate forces, then facing the Army of the Potomac, at a two to one manpower disadvantage. Even so, Longstreet believed that Lee would not be in much danger from Meade's army, still little inclined to attack.[3] The Confederates had shortened their lines, and if it became necessary, could pull back to the formidable defenses about Richmond. Nevertheless, they would be in considerable difficulty if the Federals should move aggressively without warning across the Rapidan. On September 13, with Longstreet's divisions well on their way, Federal mounted troops advanced across the Rappahannock and forced the Confederate cavalry, located between the Rappahannock and the Rapidan, back across the Rapidan River.

The next day, the 14th, another small confrontation occurred along the Rapidan at Summerville Ford involving both the Jeff Davis Artillery and the King William Artillery took part. During that fight, Private John Hartigan, of the Jeff Davis Artillery, who had been accepted earlier in the year as a substitute for John Billingslea, was killed. No other casualties were sustained by the Alabama battery. Carter, on the other hand, lost seven killed and wounded when a shell exploded near one of his guns.[4]

Reports of a new Yankee offensive persisted for the next couple of weeks, but during that time, no unusual movement was detected. Then on September 27, Lee learned of a plan to transfer two Federal corps under Major General Joseph Hooker to the West. Seven days earlier, Bragg's army, with Longstreet in command of the Left Wing, had won an important victory at Chickamauga, near the Georgia-Tennessee border. Now, reinforcements were being sent to Rosecrans who, by that time, had retreated to the defenses around Chattanooga.

Meanwhile, with the Union army now reducing the number of troops along the front, and at the same time not showing any aggressive tendencies, Lee decided to take the offensive with his present force.

Though the expected return of Longstreet had now been delayed indefinitely by the failure of Bragg to achieve a complete victory, Lee felt that the absence of the First Corps would not weaken his chances of success.[5] He planned for the Second and Third Corps to turn the enemy's position, which on one end extended to the Rapidan, and then attack the Federals while they were in retreat.

BRIGADIER GENERAL ARMISTEAD LINDSAY LONG

Promoted to Chief of Artillery of the Second Corps on September 23, 1863.

(The Museum of the Confederacy, Richmond, Virginia) Library of Congress

On October 8, the flanking maneuver began with the advancing of the artillery battalions of the Second Corps from their positions along the Rapidan to the vicinity of Pisgah Church. The next day, the Jeff Davis Artillery, which had spent the better part of the past three weeks in the vicinity of Morton's Ford, joined Ewell's Corps as it moved towards the Rapidan. The corps' artillery was now commanded by Brigadier General Armistead Lindsay Long, who had been promoted on September 23 to take the place of the still ailing Colonel Stapleton Crutchfield.

All of the battalions, excepting that of Lieutenant Colonel Hilary P. Jones, which followed Early's division and crossed at Peyton's Ford, waded the river at Barrett's Ford. Once the crossing was completed, Carter's battalion fell in behind Rodes' division on the road, with one division of cavalry leading the way and another guarding its flank. The Second, as well as the Third Corps, which had by that time also started its march, moved in the direction of Madison Court House.

Pushing on in a northwesterly direction, the army marched until it reached the vicinity of Jack's Shop. There, it made camp for the night. The following morning, October 11, the gray columns reached Madison Court House. Passing through the town, the Confederates turned eastward towards Culpeper Court House. The Yankees, as it turned out, had recently vacated that place and were now withdrawing in a northerly direction along the Orange and Alexandria Railroad.

The Southern forces arrived in the vicinity of Culpeper Court House before midday, then moved past the town and bivouacked at Stone-House Mountain. There they rested and ate. Thus far, no contact had been made with the enemy by either the Second or Third Corps. The lead cavalry division, on the other hand, had already fought with the Yankee rear guard near Brandy Station, and had successfully pushed it back across the Rappahannock River.

The next morning, Lee placed his two corps on separate roads in hopes of intercepting the retreating enemy. Hill was to take the more circuitous of the routes. His corps would be marching towards the Orange and Alexandria Railroad by way of Little Washington while Ewell followed a shorter track closer to Meade's line of retreat. Eventually, the Second and Third Corps would form a junction at Warrenton, from which they both would continue the chase along roads parallel to the Orange and Alexandria railway.

During the forenoon of the 12th, while the cavalry was continuing its close pursuit, Ewell was moving at a fairly rapid pace in the direction of Warrenton Springs, the point at which his command was to cross the Rappahannock. In the evening of October 12, the Second Corps finally arrived at the west bank of the river. There, they found both cavalry and artillery, positioned to block any Confederate attempt to cross. Subsequently, Reese's battery, and the rest of Carter's battalion, were brought up. After taking their places on high ground opposite the Federal position, the artillerymen opened fire. The bombardment that followed lasted about twenty minutes and drove off the Yankees. Rodes' division then moved across with Carter's battalion close behind. The bulk of Ewell's force, save Lieutenant Colonel R. Snowden Andrews' and Hilary P. Jones' battalions, as well as the reserve artillery, soon had successfully crossed the Rappahannock, and halted for the night.[6]

The next morning, the Second Corps travelled as far as Warrenton, where it halted in order to await the arrival of the Third Corps, which was still on the road. By then, the cavalry had sent word to Lee, then accompanying the Second Corps, that it had been sighted Yankees a few miles east of Warrenton Junction. There, they were burning stores to prevent their falling into Confederate hands. Already, the Southern forces had significantly closed the gap between themselves and Meade's army.

The next day, October 14, Lee split his forces, directing Hill to take the road to Greenwich by way of New Baltimore, and Ewell to march to the former by way of Auburn. Once at Greenwich, Ewell was to follow Hill's advance towards Bristoe Station.

Thus far, the Yankees had offered little resistance. Hill's Corps set out for Greenwich, and once there, found the still burning campfires of the enemy. The Confederates pushed on towards Bristoe Station, finding "Guns, knapsacks, blankets, etc. strewn along the road...."[7] The enemy was not far ahead. Hill's men pressed on rapidly in pursuit both to prevent the blue clad soldiers from building strong defenses and from destroying their stores.

Ewell, meanwhile, was some distance behind the Third Corps. His advance had been slowed on the way to Greenwich, soon after daybreak on the 14th, by the outposts of Major General Gouverneur K. Warren's II Corps located near Auburn. Artillery, infantry, and cavalry occupied a ridge that stretched on either side of the road upon which Ewell was moving. Moreover, the Federals had placed their three six-gun batteries in such a way that they commanded all approaches to the town.

Following an examination of the enemy's position, Long deployed his batteries in the following manner:

> ..,Carter's battalion was directed to a position on the right and ordered to occupy it, being supported by Rodes' division. Jones' battalion, in conjunction with Early's division, made a flank movement to the left to gain the enemy's rear. Andrews' battalion was ordered to occupy the center, and to operate with Johnson's division. Hardaway's and Nelson's battalions, under the command of Colonel Brown, were held in reserve to be applied at the most favorable points as soon as the forces should become engaged.[8]

After a time, Rodes' sharpshooters advanced on the right. It was not long thereafter, however, that the blue clad infantry was seen withdrawing from the ridge. The cavalry and the three batteries stayed behind to cover the retreat.

Without delay, Andrews' battalion came up and opened fire upon Captain John G. Hazard's Federal artillery. Part of Carter's battalion, including the Jeff Davis Artillery, also joined in. The cannonade soon forced the Federals to retire. Before long, Warren's entire force disappeared from Auburn.

With the road now cleared, the Second Corps resumed its advance. The march to Greenwich was made without incident, and by mid-afternoon, Ewell had begun following the road to Bristoe Station. At first, the movement from Greenwich proved to be uneventful. Then, towards evening, the sound of heavy gunfire suddenly became audible. Immediately, the pace of the gray column quickened.

Ahead, at Bristoe Station, Hill's Third Corps was involved in a sharp fight with the Federal V Corps. About midday, Hill had come upon what appeared to be the last part of the Army of the Potomac moving across Broad Run, a stream, which the Orange and Alexandria Railroad crossed just north of Bristoe Station. That force was actually Major General George Sykes' V Corps.

The Federals were unaware of the approach of the Third Corps, and Hill had immediately prepared to attack. Quickly, Colonel William T. Poague's artillery had moved into position and had begun shelling the unsuspecting soldiers who fled in disorganized fashion across Broad Run.

Soon thereafter, Major General Henry Heth's three brigades began to push towards the stream. Before long, however, reports of a heavy Federal force threatening Heth's right began to reach Hill. But, rather than halt Heth and investigate these reports, he kept the advance moving forward. Major General Richard Anderson's division would soon be up, and it could take care of the enemy still on the near side of the Run. Unknown to Hill, however, was the fact that the force which had been spotted opposite the Southern flank was actually part of Warren's II Corps, the army's rear guard deployed in line of battle behind the railroad embankment. The Third Corps was walking into a trap.

When Heth's men had neared Broad Run, they had, at once, found themselves exposed to a terrible flank fire. After being momentarily stunned, the brigade on the right of the advancing line instinctively swung around to meet the attack head on. The next or center brigade then moved in support of the first, and both had quickly become involved in a terrific struggle for possession of the ground along the railway. Anderson's division, most of which had not yet come up, could do little to help Heth. As it turned out, the Confederates could not drive the Union from its position behind the embankment, and had been forced to fall back after sustaining very heavy casualties. Warren then took advantage of Heth's withdrawal to advance and capture some of Hill's artillery.

It was not long thereafter that the van of Ewell's column reached Bristoe Station. The Third Corps was still then actively engaged with

Warren's II Corps. After examining the front, Long brought up a battery from Jones' battalion to bolster Hill's line. The battery took its position and soon became fully engaged. At the same time, however, Long did not call upon any other portion of Ewell's artillery to join the battle. By then it was nearly dark, and little could be gained by sending more guns into action at that late hour.

In the meantime, though, the various brigades of Ewell's Corps had been moving into position on the right of Hill. During the deployment, which had already taken what remained of the afternoon, there was a good deal of skirmishing along Ewell's front, but at no time was there any aggressive movement on the part of either side. Though it had been several hours since the repulse of the Third Corps, neither side was prepared to bring on another major confrontation at Bristoe.

Even though most of the Second Corps was at hand, Lee, who was still unsure of the enemy's exact strength or position, had elected to wait until Ewell's entire force arrived before resuming the offensive.

Warren, on the other hand, was already at a serious numerical disadvantage. Still, he had decided that even in the face of increasing odds, it was best not to attempt a withdrawal, but to stay where he was. His force was well screened, and in Warren's words, "To move was to disclose my comparative weakness and invite immediate attack,..."[9] At the same time, he was hoping that darkness would prevent Lee from attacking his position.

Just before nightfall, Confederate artillery, located in Ewell's sector, did open an enfilading fire on Warren's position.[10] Quickly, Federal artillery behind the railroad answered back, and a cannonade started which lasted until well past dark. The fire fight, however, proved of little consequence. By nine o'clock, all firing had ceased, marking the end of the fighting at Bristoe Station.

That night, the Confederate army bivouacked at Bristoe Station. Warren, meanwhile, withdrew his forces across Broad Run, north along the railroad towards Manassas Junction.

The latest engagement with Meade's rear guard resulted in nearly 1,900 Third Corps casualties, including those taken prisoner, while inflicting only about 300 total on the Union side.

Thus far, the Jeff Davis Artillery's part in the campaign had been one of assisting in driving off the Federal army's rear guard whenever encountered. At both Warrenton Springs and Auburn, that had been achieved without difficulty, which more than the efficiency of the gunners, was probably an indication of the enemy's intention not to stay and fight, but only to delay their pursuers. The next day, Lee's cavalry again took up the pursuit.

Following the railroad, the Confederates pushed on towards Manassas Junction. Near there, where two Southern victories had previously been won, Lee hoped that Meade would turn to confront him. In that, however, Lee was to be disappointed because Meade only had Warren stop and dig in at Manassas, while his main force pushed on in a northerly direction to the Centreville-Chantilly Ridge. There the Union army dug in and awaited the Southern forces' next move.

Lee now had to determine whether or not there was still an advantage to continuing his present campaign. At present, his army was low on food and could not expect subsistence from the war-ravaged territory it now occupied. Additionally, the Confederates could expect little relief from their inadequate supply trains. Nor could the railroad be depended upon because Meade's forces had destroyed the major railroad bridges as they moved north. Soon, Lee would have to find another source of supply or his army would starve.

But, even if Lee found provisions for his army and continued his campaign, there was actually little, if any, chance of the Confederates making any significant gains. If outflanked by the Southern army, Meade would then retreat towards the heavily fortified Washington defenses, against which the Confederates would not have the strength to launch a successful attack. There certainly seemed little advantage in continuing an offensive campaign against Meade. Ultimately, Lee withdrew his forces back down the Orange and Alexandria railway towards the Rappahannock.

On October 16, the bulk of the Southern artillery started for the river. Then, the following morning, the main army itself left Bristoe Station. As they moved south, the Confederates destroyed the segments of the Orange and Alexandria Railroad not already wrecked by the Union forces. By doing that, they prevented Meade from rapidly following the Southern withdrawal. At the same time, Lee, in a letter to President Jefferson Davis, even went so far as to suggest that, "The destruction [of the railroads]..., may prevent another advance of the enemy in this direction [towards the Rappahannock] this season."[11]

During the withdrawal, the Jeff Davis Artillery, and the rest of Carter's battalion, accompanied Early's division. The cavalry, meanwhile, served as the army's rear guard.

On October 18, the Confederate army, except for the cavalry, re-crossed the Rappahannock and took up positions along the south bank of the river. Carter's and Andrews' battalions subsequently went into camp near the railroad bridge which crossed the Rappahannock. At the same time, though, three batteries were taken for picket duty at the bridge itself.[12]

The securing of the Rappahannock line by the Confederates marked the end of the Bristoe Campaign. All in all, the just completed campaign had to be considered a success. First, the Confederate army had outflanked and forced the sixty mile withdrawal of forces much larger than their own. Furthermore, Meade's retreat had relieved the pressure which his presence on the Rapidan had placed on the Confederate capital itself. After all was done, total casualties on both sides, in spite of the one-sided affair at Bristoe Station, were almost equal, thanks in a large part to the work of the cavalry during the campaign. Stuart's men had, in fact, inflicted three times the injuries that they themselves had sustained. At a cost of 408 casualties, Stuart's cavalry had inflicted more than 1,200 on the enemy.

Over the past week and a half, the Confederates had accomplished much. At the same time, however, reaction among the ranks to what had just occurred, was not altogether favorable. Purifoy, in a statement made years later about the march to Bristoe, probably expressed the feelings of many when he said, "This flank movement had not been made with the old time celerity that was practiced by Stonewall Jackson. The army had gone in four days only about as far as Jackson would have gone in a day or two at most."[13] Comparisons between the popular Stonewall Jackson and later commanders were probably inevitable.

Fortunately, though, the company was already used to conditions experienced while on that march. In fact, according to Purifoy, "...the hardships from hunger and fatigue were not as severe as in some former campaigns,..."[14] At the same time, though, Purifoy could not forget that "The wading of the rivers on this campaign was severe, the cool nights of October making the water exceedingly chilly."[15]

Finally, during its advance and subsequent withdrawal, the Jeff Davis Artillery itself, even with its involvement in the fights at Warrenton Springs and Auburn, had suffered only one casualty. On October 17, Private Joseph Blankinship was given a furlough of forty days in order that he might have ample time to recuperate from the explosion of a cartridge.

In the days that immediately followed the main army's return to the Rappahannock line, all was quiet along the front. Accordingly, the men took advantage of that lull to catch up on their rest. That respite, however, only lasted a little more than a week.

By October 20, the Federal infantry had begun to move south. Preceding the infantry, meanwhile, was the cavalry with which Stuart's horsemen were keeping contact during much of the time.

By October 25, Brigadier General John Buford's cavalry had reached a point near Bealeton Station, about five miles north of the Rappahannock River Bridge. At the same time, just a short distance away was a supporting brigade of infantry from the III Corps under Colonel Benjamin F. Smith.

The following morning, the cavalry, plus Johnson's division of Ewell's Corps, to which the Jeff Davis Artillery was temporarily attached, moved against the blue coats. They made contact just south of Bealeton, and before long, had pushed the Federals back toward the town. The men in gray pressed forward and soon drove the Yankee cavalrymen past Bealeton, at which point they rallied and turned.

The Federals now pushed the Southerners back as far as Bealeton, but once at that place, the Yankees halted in the face of stiff resistance. The Yankees could not make any headway, and it wasn't long before the tide of battle again turned with the Southern forces driving the Federal cavalry back to their infantry support farther up the line between Bealeton and Germantown.

In a short time, the Jeff Davis Artillery had also opened upon the Yankee brigade. Federal cannon answered, and the following firefight raged for some time. It was then that an enemy shell exploded over the heads of the Alabamians, its iron fragments hitting both Private Abraham Adams and Captain Reese. Adams was only slightly injured, but Reese received a serious shoulder wound. Disabled, he had to turn over command of the Jeff Davis Artillery to his second in command, First Lieutenant Dwight E. Bates.

Near the middle of the afternoon, the firing on both sides began to slacken. Not long thereafter, the guns grew quiet, marking the end of the fight.

Early the next morning, Johnson's infantry and the Alabama battery retired across the river to their former positions. The Southern cavalry, however, remained on the north side of the Rappahannock, presumably to keep watch on the Yankees.

During the action at Bealeton, the Confederates had successfully pushed back the Federals, but as the records indicate, there was more behind the Southern presence north of the river than simply counter-ing the enemy's advance. At midnight of October 27, General Buford wired Lieutenant Colonel C. Ross Smith, of the 1st cavalry division, as to what he supposed had been the main purpose of the Confederate sortie across the Rappahannock. "I believe they came after railroad iron, as portions of it below Bealeton have been removed."[16] In his own re-port, Smith confirmed that when he stated that the Southern advance had been "...to carry off the railroad iron of the torn-up track between Bealeton and Rappahannock Station."[17]

Meanwhile, the wounded Captain Reese soon returned home to Alabama to recuperate, while Bates, the battery's only commissioned officer, was left in command. At the same time, however, any rights that Second Lieutenant John Mitchell, also of the battery, might have had were simply ignored. Mitchell had been elected lieutenant by the company the previous December, but had never received his commis-sion, nor had he been permitted to perform the duties of his new rank. Later, Mitchell had received a serious wound at the battle of Chancellorsville, losing an arm. Then, following a lengthy hospitaliza-tion, he returned to duty on September 22 and renewed efforts to re-ceive his commission. The military authorities, however, refused to recognize his officer status, which consequently left Bates alone in con-trol of the battery.

The day following the return of the Jeff Davis Artillery to its posi-tion near the Rappahannock Bridge, Lieutenant Colonel Carter assigned Cadet Richard H. Christian, formerly of the 12th Virginia Infantry, to the battery. Christian would hold the rank of Junior Second Lieutenant with the company. Presumably, he was to assist Bates. But, as events would show, Christian had higher ambitions.

On November 4, the Jeff Davis Artillery, and the rest of Carter's battalion, were withdrawn from their position near the Rappahannock Bridge to the vicinity of Cedar Mountain. The following day, Federal patrols were spotted on the north side of the Rappahannock. Then on November 7, it was reported that Meade's entire army was moving towards the river in two columns, one towards the Rappahannock Bridge and the other in the direction of Kelly's Ford, five miles downriver.

Just after midday on the 7th, a Federal force pushed rapidly across the river at Kelly's Ford and succeeded in capturing the majority of two regiments which had been posted at the crossing. The Yankees then threw a pontoon bridge across the river, and soon thereafter, large numbers of reinforcements poured over the south bank of the Rappahannock.

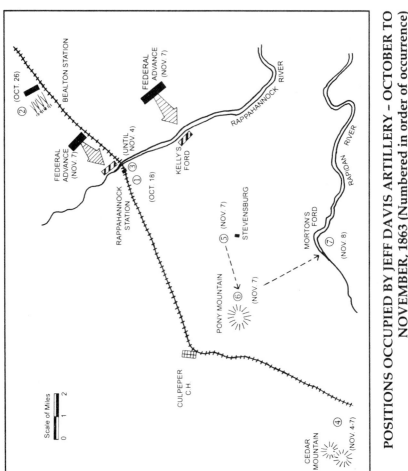

POSITIONS OCCUPIED BY JEFF DAVIS ARTILLERY – OCTOBER TO
NOVEMBER, 1863 (Numbered in order of occurrence)
Recreated from Plate LXXXVII-2 of The Official Military Atlas of the Civil War.

The loss of the lower crossing was of great significance, but, at the same time, it did not necessarily mean serious trouble for the Confederate army. In fact, Lee, who would not learn of the Federal crossing at Kelly's Ford for hours, had been prepared for such an eventuality. The Confederate position on the south bank of the river at Kelly's Ford was vulnerable because of the commanding nature of the ground on the opposite side of the Rappahannock. The troops defending the crossing were only to delay any advancing Federals until reinforcements could arrive. At the same time, a strong demonstration at the bridgehead upriver was to occupy the main Union force and prevent reinforcements from being sent to Kelly's Ford.

In spite of the surprise attack at Kelly's Ford, Rodes' division was well positioned to block any further Union advance. Moreover, Johnson's division had moved up in support of Rodes. If conditions along the rest of the line did not deteriorate, Lee's plans for the recapture of the crossing might still be carried out.

Meanwhile, a considerable force was closing on the bridgehead on the north bank of the Rappahannock. That defensive position, commanded by Major General Jubal Early, was held by two brigades of infantry plus artillery.

At dusk, the Federals launched their attack. Though repulsed at first, the weight of the enemy's advance began to tell, with the Confederate defenders soon being overwhelmed. They lost 1,600 men, but fortunately, the pontoon bridge to the rear of the Southern works was destroyed, preventing the Yankees from advancing any further.

The loss of the bridgehead forced Lee to change his plans for any attack at Kelly's Ford. With the enemy not only on the south side of the river, but also in force opposite the much weakened lines at the railroad bridge, holding his present position was no longer practical, so Lee withdrew to the Rapidan.

All the while that events had been unfolding along the Rappahannock, Carter's battalion had been shifting positions to the rear. Earlier in the day, the entire command had been ordered to leave its encampment near Cedar Mountain and to move to Stevensburg, which was several miles to the east of Culpeper Court House. Then, on the night of the 7th, the time of Lee's withdrawal from the Rappahannock line, the battalion was reunited with Rodes' division and fell back with the infantry to the base of Pony Mountain.

The following day, the Confederate forces were formed in line of battle because the Union forces had begun their pursuit and were not far behind, but nothing developed. After dark on November 8, Lee's army recrossed the Rapidan, and Carter's battalion returned to its old camp near Morton's Ford. Not long thereafter, the Yankees reclaimed their former position on the opposite side of the Rapidan.

For two and a half weeks following Lee's occupation of the Rapidan line, it was relatively quiet, with only skirmishes at different points along the river. At Morton's Ford, where during the entire time Carter's battalion had been performing picket duty, two such engagements took place. On November 15, Carter's battery had a confrontation with a small cavalry and artillery force. Then on the 26th, Fry's command engaged a similar force. Neither of the fights developed into anything serious.

There is no mention in the records of the Jeff Davis Artillery engaging the enemy at any time. From all indications, there had been comparatively little for the company to do besides picket duty since its return to the Rapidan. And now, with the month of November into its final week, it was beginning to look like there would be no more active campaigning for the Alabamians in 1863.

Then, on November 26, the same day that Carter's battalion had last been engaged, Meade's army started to move towards the lower fords of the Rapidan and Lee set his army in motion towards it. On the 26th, Hill's Corps moved from its position on the left to join Early, temporarily in command of the Second Corps, having taken the place of Ewell, who was sick. Early was then occupying the Confederate right. The following morning, the Second Corps led the advance. During the march, the Jeff Davis Artillery, and the rest of Carter's battalion, moved with Rodes' division.

Advancing in an easterly direction, Rodes' command and its supporting artillery crossed Mine Run and then proceeded on towards Locust Grove. In the meantime, the other two divisions of the Second Corps marched on separate roads in a similar direction.

The Federal army was by then moving west, on the same side of the Rapidan as the Confederates, in anticipation of soon encountering the flank of Lee's force. That, except for one critical factor, was in accordance with Meade's plans, which had called for the entire Federal army to first cross at the lower fords of the Rapidan, and then rapidly march west for a sudden strike against the Confederate flank before Lee could bring up the necessary counterforce. The only problem, however, was that the Union army had not been moving with the necessary speed.

As a result of French's tardy advance, one full day behind schedule, Meade had lost any tactical advantage that he might have had. Not only had the Confederates had time to concentrate their forces, but they could move to block Meade. Unknown to Meade, the III Corps was on a collision course, not with the vulnerable flank of the Southern army as anticipated, but with Early's three divisions.

It was at Locust Grove that Rodes' and Major General Harry T. Hays' pickets first made contact. Johnson's division, however, had not yet come up, so Lee decided that an engagement would not be brought on until all three of Early's divisions were in position.[18] Rodes and Hays then formed a line of battle and awaited Johnson's arrival. Carter's battalion, meanwhile, took up a position in the rear of Rodes' right flank.

Before midday, the head of Johnson's column began forming on Rodes' left. Then, shortly past noon, Johnson learned that the rear of his column had come under fire. Quickly, Brigadier General George H. Steuart's Brigade, acting as rear guard, engaged the Yankees. After examining the situation in person, Johnson ordered the rest of his division into the fight. A confused struggle ensued, in which the tide of battle swung back and forth numerous times. The fighting continued throughout the afternoon and finally ended with darkness. In the end, Johnson's division carried the field. During the engagement, Rodes and Hays had been involved in skirmishing with the Federals, but no serious fighting had developed on their front. The role of Carter's battalion during the engagement, if any, was not specified.

On the night of the 27th, Early withdrew his forces back across Mine Run, where the Confederates established a strong line of defense. The next day, the Army of the Potomac appeared on the opposite side of the Run and began to entrench. Meade was planning an assault aimed at Early the morning of November 30. His artillery on the right and center was to open prior to the infantry's advance, which was to be aimed first against the right, then the left of the Southern line. A successful attack would force Lee's withdrawal and leave his army open for destruction.

The following morning, the Federal guns opened as planned, but the infantry did not go forward. A further examination of the Southern works on the left found those defenses, which had been strengthened overnight, too formidable. Therefore, Meade called off the offensive.

That same morning, Carter's command came under fire from the enemy's artillery, but did not respond. Later in the day, however, two batteries did open "..upon a body of skirmishers advancing, with considerable effect."[19]

There were no further attempts by Meade's forces to breach the Confederate line. On the night of December 1, the Federals, who were running low on supplies, began their withdrawal back towards the Rapidan.

In the meantime, Lee had been working out plans for an offensive thrust of his own. When the anticipated attacks of both November 30 and December 1 did not materialize, as he had anticipated,[20] Lee began shifting troops for an assault against the Federal left which his cavalry had reported to be resting on air. Two of Hill's divisions were to be used in the attack which was scheduled for dawn on December 2.

Preparations were complete, and at the appointed hour, Hill advanced. The Confederates, however, found no enemy in their immediate front. Quickly, Lee sent his cavalry and infantry in pursuit of the Federal army.

During the chase, the Jeff Davis Artillery took the lead of the battalion, with Carter riding at the head of the battery. And it was then, while on the move towards the Rapidan crossing site, that the following incident took place:

> While riding along a straight stretch of the road, some distance ahead were seen two men of the enemy, serving as rear guard. A young man, acting courier for Col Carter, obtained permission to attempt their capture. Along both sides of the road the woods was very thick. Knowing that the men would make for the river as soon as they moved, our scout deflected to the left, through the woods. The advance along the road was continued. Soon our gallant young scout came into the road not far from the object of his persuit and then began a race, the two blue coats urging their steeds forward. They were soon lost sight of, to the marching column, as they had turned into the road to the ford. Soon we reached the point where the Kelly's ford road deflected and turned into it. After going a short distance we met our scout coming back, having captured one of the enemy. It developed that our scout had succeeded in making the capture of the man, who was well armed while the confederate had no arms at all, not even a sabre. Our blue coated friend was terribly distressed at the fact that he had permitted himself to be captured by a man without arms, and that he had suffered himself to give up his arms under such circumstances, and was escorted to the rear with these. I regret that I have not the name of the young southerner. Such heroic deeds should be preserved.[21]

As it turned out, the rest of the army had none of the scout's good fortune. The Federals had too much of a head start on the pursuing Confederates and were able to recross the Rapidan unscathed.

On December 3, the Southern forces returned to their positions along the Rapidan. For the Jeff Davis Artillery, that meant going back to their camp at Morton's Ford. The campaigns of 1863 were over.

Looking back, the second full year of active military service for the Alabama battery had been a memorable one, evidenced by important leadership changes, as well as the continuation of an excellent record on the field of battle.

For the fifth time in two and a half years, the Jeff Davis Artillery had undergone a change in command. Fortunately, though, the company's captain, William J. Reese, who had taken over active at the start of the spring campaigns, had already seen prior service with the battery. He knew many of its members which had contributed much towards making a smooth change of command take place. And from the battery's performance in the months following Reese's appointment, there can be little doubt that the Alabamians were once more in very capable hands.

Additionally, also since the spring of 1863, the battery had been acting as part of an artillery battalion, not as an independent command attached to an infantry brigade, the arrangement used earlier in the war. Reese's command had certainly profited by that new system, which by its very nature had meant better artillery support for the infantry, as well as improved maneuverability and quicker deployment of the batteries attached to Lee's army.

During the crucial Chancellorsville and Gettysburg campaigns, the Jeff Davis Artillery had proved its mettle on numerous occasions. There had not been any instance when the company, even when involved in a hot fight, had failed to provide an effective, if not destructive, supporting fire for the infantry. At the same time, however, it can be deemed fortunate that there had been only one instance over the past months, when the company itself had been victim to an extremely damaging fire. That had been during the unexpected artillery barrage on the night of Jackson's flank attack at Chancellorsville. All in all, the Alabamians had suffered relatively little material damage on the battlefield in 1863.

Casualties sustained over the past months had also been fairly light. Only two men had been killed in action. At the same time, a good number of the company had received wounds, but most of the injured had subsequently recovered and returned to the battery. The greatest single loss in manpower had occurred during the withdrawal from Gettysburg, when the pursuing Federal cavalry had intercepted the trains belonging to the Second Corps.

Earlier in the year, the Jeff Davis Artillery had also seen its numbers reduced by disease, but such losses were for the most part temporary, with the majority of those who had been struck down, recovering and resuming active service. And yet, more than twenty men, whether it be due to promotion, detached service, ill health, desertion, etc., had been lost during the course of the year and for the duration of the war. Such losses had, as indicated earlier, had been made good in part by recent recruiting efforts, but the company had still never actually recouped the reduction in manpower it had undergone during its first year and a half of service, when sickness had been all too prevalent with the command.

Nevertheless, the ranks of the Jeff Davis Artillery, as we shall see, were destined to grow again, thanks to continued recruiting efforts in Alabama. In fact, as it entered its third winter, the company would actually be as close to full strength as it would ever be again.

CHAPTER XI
MORE CHANGES WITHIN THE ORGANIZATION

For several weeks following the end of the Mine Run Campaign, the Jeff Davis Artillery remained at the encampment at Morton's Ford. At that time, a number of important events took place which had both short and long term effects on the company.

First, during the early winter of 1863, that the battery's chronic manpower shortage, at least for the time being, suddenly became a thing of the past.[1] Specifically, those final weeks of the year saw the arrival at the camp near the Rapidan of more than forty men from Alabama. All were conscripts, and included among them were many of those men who had enlisted as early as the previous August, but had never been sent east to join Reese's command. Most had enlisted at Talladega, and were between thirty and forty-five years of age. But, they had, however, not yet received instruction on the workings of a light artillery battery. In order to prepare them, the non-commissioned officers, whose task it was to drill the new recruits, would have to work extra hard. But according to Purifoy, "...many of these [conscripts] were averse to army life, and not inclined to make progress in the drill,..."[2] At the same time, though, one of the conscripts had taken steps to ensure that his service in the military would not be so disagreeable. Soon after his arrival, that particular individual was joined in camp by his wife. As Purifoy remembered, "She accepted the camp life of her husband and followed the company around until we reached the point at which we went into winter quarters,..."[3]

Even as the conscripts were becoming acquainted with the rigors of life in the military, a disquieting affair involving their unit's new

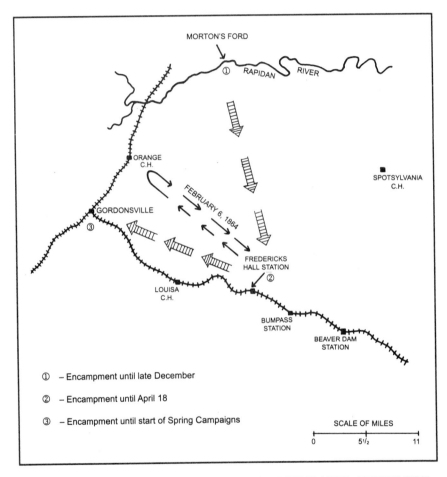

**MOVEMENTS OF JEFF DAVIS ARTILLERY –
DECEMBER 1863-APRIL 1864**

Recreated from Plate XVI of The Official Military Atlas of the Civil War.

leadership took place. During December, Second Lieutenant Richard H. Christian replaced Dwight E. Bates as commander of the battery. As it turned out, Bates was actually placed under arrest in order to ensure that Christian's ascent to the top would be unobstructed.[4]

Once the change in command was effected, Bates was released. He immediately tendered his resignation, but it was not accepted. Thereafter, there is nothing to indicate that Christian's new position was ever challenged. For the present, he would hold command of the battery.

Near the end of December, the Jeff Davis Artillery moved from its camp on the Rapidan River to Fredericks Hall, about twenty-one miles to the south and immediately adjacent to the Virginia Central Railroad to establish its winter quarters.

Purifoy remembered that, "...[the new recruits] kept with us very well, until we reached Frederick Hall, and went to work and built winter quarters, as the veterans did."[5] But on December 28, two of the draftees, Privates David M. Messer and Jefferson Tiner, deserted, never to be seen again.

Other conscripts were not able to tolerate the hardships of camp life during the colder months of the year, and they fell sick. Already by the latter part of December, three of the battery's newest members, Privates Obediah Belcher, Albert Gulbrith and Thomas Knight, had become ill. Knight contracted Typhoid Pneumonia and spent all of the next year in the hospital or on sick leave at home. Gulbrith developed a bad case of asthma, and Belcher was described as suffering from some physical disability. Both were discharged early in 1864.[6]

In the meantime, food and clothing shortages continued to be a problem. In order to supplement the poor fare provided them by the commissary department, the men conducted numerous raids on the pig pens and chicken coops of the nearby city. Eventually, the depredations became so great that those in command were forced every night, regardless of the severity of the weather, to order roll call without warning at some very late hour. That was done in hopes of catching those responsible. In those situations, however, those who were out foraging at the time actually had little to worry about, because when their names were called, they were answered for by a friend. Many times the officer in charge could not detect the deception in the darkness, and even if he did, would just as soon look the other way, for he knew that the foragers were merely attempting to get enough to eat and nothing more. Purifoy later wrote, "Our big hearted lieutenant, Dwight Bates, I have always thought, performed his duties in this matter, in a perfunctory manner."[7] The end result was that the late night roll calls did little to forestall the raids on local livestock.

It was also during the long winter months that the men of the Alabama battery sought to amuse themselves by taking part in a variety of activities. "Snow balling was a favorite sport."[8] In addition, the men like Corporal Frank Wootan, who were especially adept at telling amusing anecdotes, were called upon quite regularly. Those story-telling sessions would even attract listeners from neighboring camps. Then, finally, there were the foraging expeditions themselves, to which there must have been attached some sense of adventure and from which an interesting story or two must have originated. Even with all the internal and external problems now plaguing their organization, the Alabamians were obviously doing their utmost to make the best of their situations.

On January 13, Captain William J. Reese returned to command of the Jeff Davis Artillery. The journey by rail from Alabama to Fredericks Hall had taken nine days to complete, and to the captain's gratification, he received a warm welcome from his company upon his arrival at the camp. At the same time, though, his return had been anticipated for some time, as he wrote the day after he reached his destination. "I found the company in 'winter quarters' and they had built me a nice house with two rooms and a fire place to each, so that you see there is a chance for me to be comfortable."[9] With Reese back, Christian was reassigned to duty elsewhere.

Not long after his return, Reese reversed a demotion made the previous month of two of his veteran non-commissioned officers. Specifically, on December 27, both Corporal George Y. Higgins and Sergeant Robert E. Cobb had been reduced to the ranks. The company records, however, failed to indicate why those steps had been taken. Even so, the action against the men in question must have been unjustified, because both were restored to their former ranks by Reese before the month was out.

The latter part of January, as it turned out, would also see more changes in the battery's personnel. First, on January 18, Private A. Nance was discharged from the service. It had been discovered that Nance, one of the newest members of the battery, was in fact a minor. About the same time, though, G. F. Davidson and Cicero Woodruff were added to the company rolls. The addition of those two would help to offset the manpower loss that the battery had experienced in recent weeks.

By the end of January, conditions were back to normal, and judging by what had already been experienced in previous years, there was little reason for the men of the Jeff Davis Artillery to expect that the balance of the season was to be evidenced by anything but winter's normal monotonous routine.

Less than one week later, however, the battery was suddenly called upon for field service. On February 6, the Jeff Davis Artillery, and the rest of Carter's battalion, were instructed to leave Fredericks Hall to move to Orange Court House. That same day, the Federals had advanced in strength to Morton's Ford and other points along the Rapidan. Ewell had mobilized the Second Corps to counter that threat.

As it turned out, though, the Federal army's movements were only a diversion for an operation aimed at the same time against Richmond. Major General Benjamin F. Butler, commander of the Department of Virginia and North Carolina, had advanced against Richmond with the hope of capturing the city. The success of that operation, however, depended on the ability of the other Federal forces to prevent Lee from reinforcing the defenses of Richmond.

In order to accomplish this, Butler asked Major General John Sedgwick, temporarily in command of the Army of the Potomac (Meade was ill and was away from the army), to keep the Confederates busy by conducting demonstrations along the Rapidan line. Sedgwick complied with the request, and on the morning of the 6th, while Butler's men were pushing towards Richmond, part of the Army of the Potomac closed on the crossings of the Rapidan.

Major General Gouverneur Warren's II Corps conducted the advance on Morton's Ford and, according to a circular received the previous day from Headquarters, was to, "...make demonstrations to cross the river at that point [Morton's Ford] or in that vicinity, through Saturday, Sunday, and Monday, returning to its present camp Monday evening, unless otherwise ordered."[10] Already by eleven o'clock that same morning, however, the II Corps had crossed the Rapidan and overwhelmed one lieutenant and twenty-five men, posted on the south bank. Earlier, Warren had also been told by Sedgwick: "The movement was intended as a demonstration only, but if, in your judgement, you can attack the enemy successfully, without great loss, do so."[11]

Warren did not stop once he was in possession of the works on the south bank, but continued to move inland. Soon he reached a point about three quarters of a mile from the ford. Not far ahead, and by then quite visible to the Federals, were the camps of the Confederate infantry. By that time, however, the enemy's progress had already been slowed, thanks to an effective resistance being offered by First Lieutenant Robert M. Anderson's First Company of Richmond Howitzers of Colonel Henry C. Cabell's artillery battalion. That battalion had been occupying several strategic points along the river including one position about one mile from Morton's Ford, and it had been the battery situated at these which had first opposed the Union advance. In the meantime, Cabell had also called up a reserve battery. Soon the infantry arrived and took positions near the blazing cannon of Cabell's command.[12] By then, Ewell had also arrived to take overall charge of the defense near Morton's Ford.

The Union troops now found themselves up against a force of considerable strength, and elected to hold their present position, hopefully to avoid bringing on a major engagement. Near dusk, however, Ewell launched an attack against both the enemy's flanks. Although the Confederate thrusts were repulsed, they forced the Federals on that very night, and two days sooner than originally anticipated, to retire back across the river. The following morning, that of the 7th, Warren's Corps returned to its winter camps. That same day, the remaining forces on the south side of the Rapidan were also withdrawn. Ewell's Corps had successfully defended its position along the river.

On February 7, Butler's army reached Bottom's Bridge, twelve miles from the city, only to find a formidable line of defenders. It then retreated, thus ending that threat to the capital of the Confederacy.

Following the encounter at Morton's Ford, the Jeff Davis Artillery returned to Fredericks Hall. Reese's command, as it turned out, had not been called to play an active part in the defense of the Rapidan line. But during the march from Fredericks Hall to Orange Court House on February 6, seven of the conscripts had deserted.[13] None of them would ever be seen again, and that, in Purifoy's words was, "A clear proof of the adage that you may 'carry a horse to water but you cannot make him drink.'"[14]

Fortunately, just a few days after the mass desertion, three more men enlisted and were assigned to the Jeff Davis Artillery: John F. Methvin, J. D. Watson and T. P. Webster. Even so, the new recruits were not coming in fast enough to compensate for the battery's manpower losses. Since the latter part of December, the company had lost twelve, or more than one fourth, of its newest members. At the same time, only five more men, including those just mentioned, had enlisted and been assigned to serve with the Alabama battery. That gradual depletion of the ranks was to continue during the remaining months spent in winter quarters, and beyond. Though the company would eventually see several new faces join its ranks, the effective strength of the organization would never again be anything like what it had been during the first weeks of December 1863.

But the battery was still lacking officers. Just a few days before the advance to Orange Court House, Reese renewed his efforts of the previous spring, aimed at getting Second Lieutenant Robert S. Walker, then serving with Company I of the 43rd Regiment Alabama Volunteers, Brigadier General Archibald Gracie's Brigade of Longstreet's Corps, to rejoin the Jeff Davis Artillery. On February 2, Reese asked General Samuel Cooper, the Adjutant and Inspector General of the Confederate Army, directly, to transfer Walker. That letter contained sixty-eight signatures of members of the Alabama battery, including that of Reese. That represented a majority of those with the company at the time. By its very nature, then, that petition confirmed the election of Walker to the grade of second lieutenant with the battery.[15]

Brigadier General William N. Pendleton, the Army's Chief of Artillery, approved the transfer. But nothing ever came of that request.[16]

About that time, John Mitchell again took up his fight for a commission as junior second lieutenant with the battery; a post which he had previously been denied by the military authorities in Richmond. Mitchell's appeal eventually reached the highest ranking officials of the Confederacy. His case would even go before Jefferson Davis himself, but there is no record that Davis made a final decision. Some five months later, Mitchell's name would be dropped from the rolls of the company.[17]

There were no further efforts made to fill the vacancies in the upper ranks of the battery. Reese and Bates remained as the company's only commissioned officers.

For three weeks following the action at Morton's Ford, little of real importance took place concerning the Jeff Davis Artillery. But then during the last days of February, the Federals started another raid which quickly caused waves of excitement to spread through the artillery camps at Fredericks Hall. On February 28, Brigadier General Judson Kilpatrick's cavalry crossed the Rapidan and began a movement whose object included the destruction of the Virginia Central Railroad at or near Fredericks Hall, as well as the release of Federal prisoners then being held at Belle Island, Richmond.[18] Kilpatrick planned for his cavalry to cross the Rapidan at night, and then go to Spotsylvania Court House, where they would divide into two columns. Kilpatrick would then push southward, first towards Beaver Dam Station, then on to Richmond, with the larger force, while the other detachment, led by Colonel Ulric Dahlgren, would move in a southwesterly direction towards Fredericks Hall. Once Dahlgren had completed his mission of destruction along the railroad, he was to head south and, if possible, work with Kilpatrick during the final critical phase of the mission, the freeing of the Federal prisoners at Belle Isle. It was an ambitious plan, and certainly one that could mean serious trouble for the artillery units encamped near Fredericks Hall. And yet, because of the efforts of Brigadier General Armistead Lindsay Long, the Chief of Artillery of the Second Corps, the numerous companies then occupying winter quarters near the Virginia Central Railroad were not totally unprepared for an attack.

Anticipating just such a move, Long had asked for infantry support for his artillery, but they arrived too late. Taking matters into his own hands, Long then procured a large number of muskets which he had distributed among the batteries of his command. The result was that each battalion now had its own company of sharpshooters attached to it. In that way, Long achieved his infantry support, but whether those riflemen would prove capable of defending his guns remained to be seen.

By eight o'clock, on the morning of the 29th, Dahlgren left Spotsylvania Court House for Fredericks Hall. In three hours, his men had already moved to a point which was less than three quarters of a mile from Fredericks Hall Station.

During their approach, the Federals had also "...captured 16 artillery soldiers belonging to the Maryland battalion."[19] Those men informed their captors that "...at the station there were three different camps, eight batteries in each, in all about ninety-six guns; that there was a regiment of infantry near at hand and a battalion of sharpshooters in each camp."[20]

In addition to the artillerymen, the enemy also took prisoner, twelve officers of a court-martial which was then in session. Long later explained: "A vacant house some distance from camp had been selected for the meeting of the court, and the movement of the enemy was so sudden there was not time to notify the court of their approach."[21]

Long was himself apprised of the Yankee cavalry's approach near midday, and immediately moved his forces to defensive positions. The battalions of Colonel John Thompson Brown and Lieutenant Colonel Carter M. Braxton were placed in the first line of defense, while the Jeff Davis Artillery, the rest of Carter's command, and all of Major Wilfred E. Cutshaw's battalion were placed a short distance to the rear. Once the artillery was deployed, 120 men armed with rifles were brought forward in support. Now, all that remained was for the cannoneers of the Second Corps to await the enemy's attack.

Shortly, the Federal cavalry closed to within a half mile of the most advanced of the Confederate defenders. An attack seemed imminent, but the enemy quite unexpectedly changed direction and moved off to the left of Long's position towards Bumpass Station.

As it turned out, Dahlgren had been surprised by the presence of sharpshooters in his path. He had only expected to be opposed by un-supported artillery, which he might have been able to attack success-fully. But with both infantry and artillery in his front, Dahlgren thought it too risky to assault the Confederate position. Consequently, he moved in a southerly direction away from the forces at Fredericks Hall.

In the end, Long's foresight had prevented a catastrophe from be-falling the artillery of the Second Corps. The value of having even a small amount of infantry support for the guns had certainly been proven. Even so, Long was not totally satisfied with what had come out of the near confrontation with the enemy. In his report, he would not only express his disappointment about having been left to fend for himself, but also concerning the kind of strategy he had to employ. In Long's words, "I greatly felt the want of a few hundred infantry. With these I am sure I could have inflicted a severe chastisement upon them... My sharpshooters were too few, and I had too much at stake to hazard any movement against them."[22] Even if circumstances had not allowed Long to take the attack to the enemy, he still thwarted the Federal cavalry.

After having avoided a confrontation with Long, Dahlgren's men pushed on in a southerly direction until they reached a point along the Virginia Central Railroad between Fredericks Hall and Bumpass Sta-tion. There, they tore up rails and cut the telegraph before moving on towards the Confederate capital.

By the following morning, March 1, Dahlgren and Kilpatrick had moved to within easy striking distance of Richmond itself. Continuing their advance, the two Federal columns at first met with little or no opposition. That, however, began to change once they came within five miles or so of the city. By then, its defenders were mobilized and ad-vancing to meet them.

At the outset, Kilpatrick, who was pushing down the Brook Turn-pike, had little difficulty in pushing aside the resistance he was meet-ing, but when within one mile of the Capital, he encountered a formidable force, which left him with no choice but to withdraw.

Not far to the west, Dahlgren had, in the meantime, been pursuing a destructive course, burning a number of mills, warehouses, canal boats, etc., as he moved east along the north bank of the James River. Initially, nothing had stood in the way of Dahlgren's raiders, but once they had penetrated to within five miles of the city, the road became more difficult. The first pockets of resistance were handled with comparative ease, but it wasn't long before the Federals ran into determined opposition and were forced to withdraw. During the retreat, Dahlgren was killed and nearly eighty of his men fell into Confederate hands. Except for the damage done to the Virginia Central Railroad and the destruction of mills along the James River, the raid had resulted in nothing more than anxious moments for Richmond.

Back at the winter camps of the Second Corps artillery near Fredericks Hall, conditions returned to normal. In March, Special Order #77 from Headquarters reorganized the artillery of the Army of Northern Virginia. It reassigned selected batteries and confirmed, as Pendleton had previously recommended, the promotion of numerous officers within the different corps.

In Carter's battalion, of the Second Corps, there were three important changes made among those in the higher ranks. Of those moves, two promotions in particular would impact directly upon the Jeff Davis Artillery.

First of all, the battalion's celebrated leader, Lieutenant Colonel Thomas H. Carter, was promoted to colonel. That advancement was not only a reward for past service, but as events would show, also a step that was to lead to an important organizational change within the Second Corps and new responsibilities for him.

At the same time, Captain Richard C. M. Page, of the Morris Artillery, was also promoted to major. An accomplished officer, Page was to still serve under Carter, but at the same time, was to be in direct charge of the battalion. Captain S. H. Pendleton replaced Page in command of the Morris Artillery.

A few weeks later, on April 7, Special Order #13 was issued, announcing that the five battalions of the Second Corps, namely Braxton's, Brown's, Carter's, Cutshaw's and Lieutenant Colonel William Nelson's "...will hereafter be organized into two divisions,..."[23] Colonel John Thompson Brown would command the First Division, which contained Nelson's, Braxton's and Lieutenant Colonel Robert A. Hardaway's battalions.[24] Carter, meanwhile, was selected to lead the Second Division, made up of Cutshaw's and Carter's (now Page's) battalions.

That creation of two separate divisions simplified the chain of command. Under the new system, the two division leaders, and not the five battalion commanders, were to report directly to the corps' chief of artillery. With the spring campaigns now just weeks away, that change could not have come at a more opportune time.

Just about ten days after the reorganization, the artillery was relocated to various grazing camps to the west. There, the horses would be ensured more forage.

On April 18, the Jeff Davis Artillery left Fredericks Hall. Two days later, it arrived in camp near Gordonsville. The battery spent the better part of the next two weeks there.

By that time the Jeff Davis Artillery settled into camp near Gordonsville, two events had already taken place which were to have a significant effect on the future operations of both the Army of Northern Virginia and the Federal Army of the Potomac. And, of course, the battles in which the Alabamians were to participate.

First of all, General Longstreet and his corps had been recalled from Tennessee, where he had ultimately failed in his second attempt at semi-independent command.

On April 11, following more than three months spent in winter quarters in northeastern Tennessee, Lee brought Longstreet back to Virginia. On April 20, Longstreet was encamped not far from Gordonsville, at Mechanicsville, Virginia, in a position to reinforce the Rapidan line.

The fact that Longstreet's First Corps, about 10,000 men, could now once again be available to Lee was of considerable importance for several reasons. First, it was believed that with the onset of spring, the Union army would soon be advancing from its camps beyond the Rapidan. Essentially, Longstreet's presence both allowed Lee to cover a much wider defensive front than before. At present, the Second and Third Corps were in a position to guard the lower crossings of the Rapidan, while Longstreet was now situated at the upper fords.

By that time, the effective strength of the Federal army had grown to a total of just over one hundred thousand men, and would soon be increasing even more when Burnside arrived from Centreville. The Confederates, on the other hand, could muster only about 64,000 men.

Almost a full month before Longstreet received orders to return to Virginia, an important change had taken place within the Federal high command. Specifically, it had been on March 9 that Ulysses S. Grant was appointed lieutenant general and put in charge of all the United

States' land forces. Grant had commanded armies in the Western theatre, and while there, had won a number of great victories. In the process, he also had gained the reputation of being a fighter.

Following his appointment, Grant established his headquarters with
the Army of the Potomac. From there, he would plan the overall strategy of the army which had been battling the Army of Northern Virginia for nearly two years. At the same time, he left Meade in command
of the Army of the Potomac. That combination of the steady Meade
and the aggressive general from the west would, in all probability, provide Lee with a more troublesome foe than he had faced in any of the
previous campaigns. Still, nothing was assured, and not until the two
sides again encountered one another on the battlefield would the ad-
vantages, if any, of the Federal army's new system of command become evident. As it turned out, however, the test by fire was not too far
off, for by now April had passed into May and already signs of unusual
activity were in evidence on the north side of the Rapidan. The Federal
army was preparing to move.

CHAPTER XII

TWO MAJOR BATTLES; TWO DIFFERENT ROLES

PART I - MUCH WAITING IN THE WILDERNESS

South of the Rapidan, the Confederate signal station on Clark's Mountain watched for signs that the Army of the Potomac was again on the move. It was by then the morning of May 3, and from what had already been observed, there could be little doubt that some significant maneuver was about to occur. That morning, and all during the day, they saw heavy smoke, probably caused by the burning of supplies not needed on the march, as well as dust clouds caused by the marching of troops.

Then, near midnight, on Clark's Mountain, the signalmen spotted lines of troops marching past the distant campfires. Major General George Meade's army was on the move.

It was too dark to ascertain which way the Federal columns were moving, though Lee had already guessed that once put in motion, they would push towards the lower crossings at Ely's and Germanna Fords.[1] As an added precaution to prevent his being outflanked, Lee also had Lieutenant General Richard S. Ewell, whose troops were located on the Southern right, prepare to march at dawn. Lee told Lieutenant General James Longstreet to extend part of his command farther to the northwest to be in a better position to block any movement against the Confederate left.

The next day, Lee's predictions were borne out when it was observed that long columns of troops, as well as the Federal army's trains, were indeed moving to the right. Before long, Lee's three corps were

193

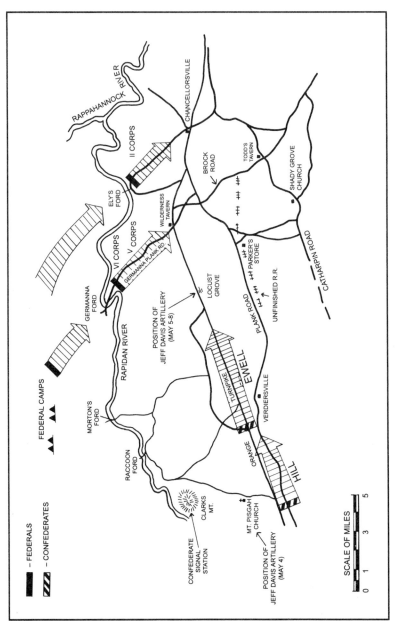

BATTLE OF THE WILDERNESS – MOVEMENTS OF MAY 4, 1864

Recreated from Plate LXXXI-1 of The Official Military Atlas of the Civil War.

moving along three separate routes towards an area known as the Wilderness, an area covered with tangled overgrowth, in which the movement of troops would be hampered and where the numerical advantage of the enemy could have little bearing on any battle fought there.

Ewell's Corps, the first to march, was to proceed in an easterly direction up the Orange Turnpike, while Lieutenant General A. P. Hill's Corps was to move along the Orange Plank Road, a route which ran parallel to and just south of the Turnpike. At the same time, Longstreet, who had the longest distance to march, had cross Brook's Bridge on the North Anna River, then to follow both the Orange Plank and Catharpin Roads into the Wilderness. If all went as planned, Ewell would occupy the left, Hill the center and Longstreet the right during the advance and subsequent attack.

At nine o'clock on the morning of the 4th, Ewell's divisions commenced their movement along the Orange Turnpike. At the same time, the Jeff Davis Artillery, and the rest of Major Richard C. M. Page's Battalion, which had recently left Gordonsville and relocated to camps near Pisgah Church in the vicinity of Raccoon Ford, also took up the march. Meanwhile, the rest of the Second Corps artillery, most of which was still situated near Gordonsville, broke camp. That included two battalions of Colonel John Thompson Brown's Division and Major Wilfred E. Cutshaw's battalion of Colonel Thomas H. Carter's Division. Major William Nelson's battalion, of Brown's division, was already at the front.

Hill's Third Corps, on the other hand, had received its marching instructions much later than Ewell, and would not be starting out for another two hours. Consequently, Lee told Ewell to slow his rate of advance, so as not to get too far ahead of the Third Corps' divisions.

As it turned out, the marches of Lee's three corps, made on May 4, were all conducted without incident. Ewell eventually halted his divisions for the night at Locust Grove. That same evening, the Second Corps artillery closed up behind the infantry. Hill's Corps, meanwhile, after detaching Major General Richard H. Anderson's division at Orange to guard the upper fords of the Rapidan, had proceeded as far as Verdiersville before stopping for the night. Then there were Longstreet's two divisions, which had crossed the North Anna and were now camped near its north bank. It was expected that the First Corps would be joining the rest of the army by night fall of the 5th. Early the following morning, Lee would launch his attack.

But Lieutenant General Ulysses S. Grant's plans, which assumed that the Confederates would fall back before his advance to a new position, in fact called for a rapid advance through the Wilderness. Then, providing all went as expected, he would meet Lee's forces in the open, where the North's numerical superiority could be used to advantage.[2]

By the afternoon of May 4, the first, and one of the most critical phases of the Federal offensive had been completed. Specifically, the crossing of the Rapidan, at both Ely's and Germanna Fords by the three corps of the Federal army.[3] The cavalry had crossed the Rapidan the night before to establish a bridgehead and scout ahead. After that, it only remained for the army's wagon train and Major General Ambrose E. Burnside's IX Corps, which was on its way to join the main army, to complete their movements to the south of the river.

Once on the opposite bank, each of the Federal corps had moved in a southeasterly direction, but had gone only a short distance before making camp. Major General Gouverneur Warren's Corps, for one, had gone only as far as Wilderness Tavern, which was about six miles from the river. At the same time, Major General Winfield S. Hancock had stopped his command a shorter distance from the Rapidan at Chancellorsville, the site of the great battle, of the same name, fought exactly one year ago. Major General John Sedgwick, meanwhile, had followed Warren and had encamped along the road leading to Wilderness Tavern.

The army's supply train had not yet completed its crossing of the Rapidan. It was not expected to be south of the river until later on the 5th.

Accordingly, marching orders for the following days were again governed by the slow progress of the wagon train. Warren was to proceed as far as Parker's Store, Hancock to Shady Grove Church, and Sedgwick, after leaving a division to guard Germanna Ford, to Wilderness Tavern. All were within the confusing terrain of the Wilderness.

The following morning, that of May 5, Hancock's, Warren's and Sedgwick's corps stepped off in a southerly direction towards the roads that would eventually take them out of the Wilderness. They did not know that they, at that very moment, were themselves being pursued by every available division of Lee's army.

Early that same morning, the three corps of the Confederate army had resumed their eastward march towards the flank of the moving Federal columns. Ewell's command was now moving up the Orange Turnpike, with Brigadier General John M. Jones' Brigade of Edward Johnson's division leading the way. Nelson's artillery battalion accompanied the lead division. At the same time, Hill's Corps, which was still without Anderson's division, was continuing its own advance up the Plank Road to the south. As on the previous day, Lee had Ewell regulate his march with that of Hill's command, which was still some distance to the rear. The rest of the Second Corps artillery, meanwhile, was being concentrated at Locust Grove. There, the Jeff Davis Artillery took up a position along the Turnpike with the rest of Page's battalion.

Ewell's Corps continued its advance until ten o'clock, when suddenly it was brought to a halt about two miles from the point where the Germanna Ford Road crossed the Turnpike. Up ahead, Federal troops were moving south through the intersection of the two roads. Quickly, Ewell deployed his entire corps on either side of the Turnpike and prepared to meet the enemy. Lee reminded Ewell that he was not to bring on a major engagement until Longstreet arrived. Accordingly, Ewell told his division commanders, then later the officers of the most advanced brigades, to retire slowly if pressed by the enemy. Besides Jones, that included Brigadier Generals Cullen A. Battle and George Doles, who had moved up in support of the lead brigade.

By that time, however, Grant was advancing in force to meet the threat on his right. Just hours before, Union Headquarters had learned of Ewell's advance up the Orange Turnpike, and Meade had immediately ordered Warren, all of whose divisions, except one, had already moved past the intersection of the Turnpike and Germanna Ford Road, to reverse his corps and attack the Southern force.

It was near eleven o'clock when the V Corps' lead division first made contact with Jones' brigade. At first, the firing was comparatively light, but then the bluecoats launched a furious attack. That caught Jones' men somewhat by surprise and soon they broke to the rear. Before long, Battle's brigade, which had been posted behind Jones, was also caught up in the confusion, and was left in a temporary state of panic. The Second Corps was now in a desperate situation.

Fortunately, though, Ewell quickly brought up Brigadier General John B. Gordon's brigade which soon checked the Union's advance. Pressure increased as other gray brigades, including Battle's command, entered the fight, and it wasn't long before the Federals were outflanked and forced to withdraw. Reinforcements (two full divisions) were moving up by then, but they could do nothing to stall the Confederate counterattack.

Before long, Ewell's men had regained the ground lost at the outset of the struggle. But, he halted his brigades where they were and had them dig in on both sides of the road. Eventually, the Confederate works would extend for about a mile to points north and south of the Turnpike. For the balance of the day, Warren would attempt, without success, to drive the Second Corps from its defenses.

The fight along the Orange Turnpike had offered little opportunity for the use of artillery. At the start of the fight, it in fact had been necessary to withdraw Captain John Milledge's Battery from its position near Jones' brigade, not only because of the threat of it being overrun, but because the tangled growth which covered the area prevented an effective use of its guns.[4] Following the initial struggle along the Turnpike, Nelson's battalion occupied various positions to the rear and on the right of the Confederate line. From there, its guns were "...used with effect in repulsing partial attacks of the enemy."[5] As for the Jeff Davis Artillery, and the rest of the batteries belonging to Page's battalion, they had not been required to leave their reserve positions at Locust Grove.

About four o'clock, and the same time that the action along the Orange Turnpike was winding down, another battle was rapidly developing a few miles to the south in the vicinity of where the Brock Road crossed the Orange Plank Road. There, Major General Henry Heth's Division of Hill's Corps was now being rocked by the divisions from both Sedgwick's VI and Hancock's II Corps. That attack, like the one launched against Ewell, came without much warning.

By early afternoon, Heth's division had only met some cavalry which it easily pushed aside while going up the Plank Road. Then, at about one o'clock, the Confederates made contact with the skirmishers of Brigadier General George W. Getty's Division of the VI Corps. Heth had halted and deployed in line of battle. About that time, Lee had discovered that a dangerous gap now existed between the Second and Third Corps which might prove Hill's or even Ewell's undoing, especially if the enemy found that unprotected area and struck the exposed flanks of the divisions near what now constituted the Confederate center. To prevent that, Lee had Major General Cadmus Wilcox's Division, then located behind Heth on the Plank Road, march to the left and form a line beyond Heth's unprotected flank.

Skirmishing continued along the front, and for the next couple of hours, there was no fighting on the Southern right. By then, Lee was considering the possibility of making an attempt to drive along the Brock Road, splitting the Federal army in two. Heth felt he would have to use his entire division to do it and had been awaiting further instructions when he was suddenly attacked.

For the next several hours, a fight, hotter than most of the participants had ever seen or would ever see again, took place.[6] At first, the Federal assault fell entirely upon Heth's unsupported division. Though outnumbered more than three to one, the Confederates successfully withstood the enemy's advance, while inflicting heavy casualties. Hancock threw more men into the fight, thereby increasing the pressure on the already hard-pressed defenders. He advanced again and again, and soon the weight of the attack began to tell. A portion of Heth's line was now in danger of giving way.

At the critical moment, Wilcox, who Hill had ordered to assist Heth, arrived and saved the Southern line. In the meantime, Lieutenant Colonel William T. Poague's artillery battalion also came up to support the infantry. Together, the two gray divisions then continued to thwart the efforts to drive them back down the Plank Road. When darkness finally settled upon the area, the fighting ceased, with the opposing forces occupying basically the same positions they had held when the bitter struggle had begun.

Several times, Heth asked Hill's permission to form a new line behind the present one; however, his requests were denied. The men were exhausted and should be allowed to rest. Moreover, Longstreet and Anderson were expected to arrive before morning and would then form a new line, thereby relieving both divisions. Unknown to Hill, however, was that Longstreet's progress on the march had been slower than anticipated. His corps would not be arriving until some time after first light. Just hours before dawn, with still no sign of the promised relief, Heth and Wilcox brought up the pioneers in hopes of at least providing some protection for their exposed troops.

At five o'clock, Hancock launched a massive attack whose design was to hit Hill in front then on the left flank, ultimately resulting in the destruction of the Third Corps. To prevent reinforcements from being sent by Ewell to assist Hill, simultaneous attacks were also made against the Second Corps.

The defenders on the Southern right offered some resistance at first, but the weight of the Federal offensive quickly began to tell. Men started to fall back, though they continued to challenge the advancing foe as best they could. Even so, the retrograde movement continued. Soon a number of the withdrawing Confederates reached Poague's battalion, located in a clearing just north of the Plank Road. The Federals were not far behind, and before long, the gunners of all twelve pieces had opened a withering fire upon the pursuing enemy.[7] They succeeded in slowing the Yankee advance, but it looked to be just a matter of time before the battalion's position was itself overrun.

At the critical moment, however, Longstreet's First Corps reached the field and began a furious counterattack which forced the Federals back. By ten o'clock, Longstreet's men had regained the ground lost earlier in the day. Anderson, by then, had also come up, and was moved up on the right in support of the First Corps, while Hill's men filled the gap between Longstreet and Ewell.

Meanwhile, to the north, the strength of Ewell's line had enabled his troops to withstand a number of heavy assaults. The artillery, as it turned out, had also played an important part in the defense of the Confederate left. During an advance against Gordon's brigade, batteries concentrated at that point "...were used with considerable effect in assisting to repel this attack."[8]

That same morning, a major portion of the Second Corps artillery, from the reserve at Locust Grove moved to the front. Directing part of the advance was Carter, who had been given charge of the guns on the left side of the Turnpike (Brown had been in command of the batteries on the right) and had, as per instructions, moved a number of guns to the extreme left to guard Ewell's flank. About the same time, Braxton's, Cutshaw's and Lieutenant Colonel Robert A. Hardaway's battalions were also brought forward to occupy ground on both the right and left of the Turnpike. Meanwhile, Nelson's battalion, which had been positioned along the line, was relieved. At the same time, there was no change in disposition for the Jeff Davis Artillery. It, and the rest of Page's battalion, still occupied their reserve position at Locust Grove.

At about eleven o'clock, the fighting on the Southern right intensified once again. Longstreet, making use of an abandoned railroad cut, struck Hancock's left flank and drove it north towards the Plank Road. The Confederates also struck in front, and the combined pressure forced the Federals back to the works along the Brock Road.

Having achieved his objective, Longstreet then planned another flanking movement to force the Yankees from the crucial intersection of the Brock and Plank Roads. Instructions were issued to the various brigade commanders, then Longstreet moved up the Plank Road to be nearer the action. Suddenly, some of his men opened fire on some stragglers from another gray brigade which had been mistaken for the enemy. Longstreet rode ahead to stop the firing, but he himself was seriously wounded and was taken to the rear. Confusion followed which ended any plans for an immediate attack.

When the Confederates finally went forward, some four hours later, the results were disastrous. They ran into a strengthened Federal line, and after a difficult struggle, were repulsed. The fighting now wound down on the Southern right.

Meanwhile, on the opposite end of the line, Gordon's scouts had long since observed that the North's flank was unsupported and vulnerable to attack. Once having confirmed that report, Gordon had apprised Ewell of his findings, but Major General Jubal Early, who was in attendance, thought such a move too risky. Ewell then had decided to take no action until he could examine the situation in person.

The entire afternoon passed, and not until about half past five when Lee arrived at the Second Corps Headquarters, was the attack ordered. Near six o'clock, the Confederates surged forward, and as expected, were able to roll up the Federal flank. By the time darkness fell and brought the fighting to a close, the Southern forces had pushed Grant back about a mile. In the end, more than one thousand Yankees were counted among the killed, wounded and captured.

That action on the Confederate left was the last major confrontation to take place between the two armies in the Wilderness. The following morning, that of May 7, there was little more than light skirmishing between the opposing lines. More important, though, was the fact that, since first light, there had been signs indicating that Grant was preparing to move from Lee's front.

Early that morning, it had been discovered that the North had withdrawn its forces from the line opposite the extreme left of the Confederate position. Later, in an effort to learn more about Meade's intentions, Brigadier General Armistead L. Long, with infantry and two battalions of artillery, scouted in the direction of Germanna Ford, a crossing which the enemy had left heavily guarded on previous days. Upon reaching a point on the Germanna Plank Road, which was about a mile from the ford, Long encountered Federal cavalry. It, however, had soon been "...driven away by a few well-directed shots,..."[9] from the artillery. Those horsemen, as it turned out, had been the only hostile force discovered in the area. From all indications, the enemy had all but abandoned their position near the ford.

A few hours later, officers of A. P. Hill's staff had also discovered that an artillery park, adjacent to what was believed to be Grant's Headquarters, had been broken up and its batteries put on the road leading to the Union left. That, combined with other reports of enemy activity beyond the Confederate right flank, convinced Lee that the Yankees were about to attempt another turning maneuver in the direction of Spotsylvania Court House, located to the southeast of his army's present position. Once having learned the enemy's intentions, Lee had to abandon his own position for one farther to the south, in the immediate vicinity of Spotsylvania Court House. If the Federals should win the race to the Court House, they would be between the Southern army and Richmond, and in position to threaten the capital.

Late on the afternoon of the 7th, Lee evacuated his Wilderness line. On the left, Long was told to prepare his artillery for the movement. In his own words, "Nelson, Hardaway, and Cutshaw were directed to encamp at Verdierville. Braxton and Page were ordered to remain with the infantry and move with it."[10] To that point, the Jeff Davis Artillery had still not moved from Locust Grove, a point they had been occupying since May 5.

By early evening, Lee had issued marching orders to Major General Richard H. ("Dick") Anderson, who had succeeded the wounded Longstreet as commander of the First Corps. His two divisions occupied the right of the line, a circumstance which caused them to be closest of any Southern force, except the cavalry then operating beyond the flank, to Spotsylvania Court House. It, therefore, would be up to the First Corps to occupy it before Grant arrived.

PART II - AN URGENT APPEAL, THEN CATASTROPHE AND NEARLY THE END OF AN ORGANIZATION

At approximately nine o'clock on the night of May 7, Major General Richard H. Anderson began pulling his men back from the main line in order to afford them some rest before setting out for Spotsylvania. The twelve mile march that lay ahead was to start, as per General Lee's instructions, before 3:00 a.m.[1] Anderson, however, had already decided that he would start for Spotsylvania Court House at 11:00 p.m. Following the First Corps, when circumstances permitted, would be Ewell and Hill, in that order. The Jeff Davis Artillery was to accompany the Second Corps on the march.

The route to Spotsylvania, at least at the outset, was not to be an easy one. Initially, the First Corps would have to follow a newly cut trace through the woods, giving it a more direct route to its destination, which was full of stumps and other portions of trees not yet removed. Moreover, the march over that rough ground was to be made in the dark.

Anderson, meanwhile, was frustrated in his efforts to find a suitable bivouac for his troops. The surrounding woods which had caught fire during the battle, were still burning.

Circumstances demanded a change in plans. Rather than rest his troops, Anderson started them to Spotsylvania Court House. Though it would be a difficult journey, the early start improved the Confederates' chances of getting there first.

As it turned out, the march through the Wilderness consumed the entire night. Not until 5:00 a.m., did Anderson's men finally emerge from the tangled terrain and fall out along the road to rest and cook breakfast. They were then three miles west of the Court House. About that same time, Reese's Alabamians were just beginning their own movement from the left of the Wilderness line.

Even as Anderson's men ate, they could hear the gunfire coming from the north. Major General Fitzhugh Lee's cavalry was, as it had been for the past several hours, contesting Merritt's cavalry coming up the Brock Road.

Two miles from the Court House, Yankee cavalry attacked a hastily constructed line of works which the Confederates had thrown across the road. The enemy's advance was unsuccessful, but reinforcements were on the way. Coming up behind the Federal horsemen was Warren's entire V Corps. Against so formidable a force, the Confederate cavalry could hardly be expected to hold their position for very long.

Major General Jeb Stuart sent a courier requesting assistance. By chance, the courier came upon Major John C. Haskell, whose artillery battalion was leading the First Corps advance. Haskell immediately sent his batteries to the aid of the cavalrymen. A bit later, Anderson himself received an urgent request for help from Fitzhugh Lee and responded by sending two brigades of Major General Joseph B. Kershaw's Division to assist him. The reinforcements arrived just in time and played a major role in stopping the Federal advance. Another assault followed, but was repulsed after a sharp fight.

Eventually, the entire First Corps was strung along a line stretching about a mile to the west and half a mile to the east of the Brock Road. Once again, the enemy advanced against the Southern line, only to be forced back as before.

Soon, however, three divisions of Sedgwick's VI Corps reached the field, giving the Yankees a numerical superiority. Moreover, they began extending their left to threaten Anderson's right flank. By then, the First Corps was stretched to its limit along the present line and could not effectively counter that maneuver.

At five o'clock, the Yankees attacked. Despite being hit by heavy artillery fire, their advance on the right could not be stopped. Anderson was in danger of being taken in his flank. At the critical moment, however, the Second Corps reached the field.

Major General Robert E. Rodes' division, leading Ewell's advance from the Wilderness, moved forward and took up a position on the endangered right. Soon a galling fire was being delivered by the gray infantrymen into the Federal ranks. Realizing that they now faced a reinforced foe, the Yankees quickly broke off the attack and retired to their own lines. Part of Rodes' division pursued the Federals, but were unable to force them out of their works. That marked the end of the day's fighting, Lee's forces had successfully thwarted Grant's turning maneuver, and despite some anxious moments earlier in the day, Spotsylvania Court House remained in Southern hands.

That night, in an effort to further strengthen his position, Ewell placed Major General Edward Johnson's division on Rodes' right. At the same time, Early's command was placed in a supporting position to the rear. Early, however, was not with his men. He had taken charge of the Third Corps for Hill, who was too ill to exercise command. Brigadier General John B. Gordon was now in charge of Early's division. In the meantime, the Third Corps had the responsibility of guarding the rear of Lee's army. Not until the following day would it move into position on the Spotsylvania line.

The Jeff Davis Artillery did not reach Spotsylvania until 11:00 p.m. on the night of the 8th. The battery's late arrival indicates that it had occupied a post near the rear of Ewell's column during the march from the Wilderness. Reese's Alabamians had been on the road for close to eighteen hours. Fortunately, though, the route they took had been less difficult than what Anderson's divisions had encountered. They, and the Second Corps, had followed the Orange Plank and Shady Grove Church Roads to Spotsylvania.

On May 9, the Confederate lines were firmly established, and Major Richard C. M. Page's and Lieutenant Colonel Carter M. Braxton's battalions positioned along the works occupied by Johnson's division. The Jeff Davis Artillery was now located on a section of the line known as the "Mule Shoe." That particular part of the Southern defenses was so labelled because of its curved shape. The Mule Shoe contained "...two salients - one at Rodes' right brigade (General Doles'), the other at Johnson's center,..."[2] Those two salients were known respectively as the West and East Angles.

The position occupied by Ewell's troops was well fortified against attack, but at the same time, it was not a place where artillery could be used to its best advantage. Brigadier General Armistead L. Long described the terrain as follows: "This position, like the one at the Wilderness, was not well adapted to the effective use of artillery, the view being obstructed by forest and old field pine. The artillery was, however, carefully posted, with the view of rendering the most effective support to the infantry."[3]

That day, there was some heavy skirmishing along the lines, but the artillery saw little action. The next morning, that of May 10, both Page's and Braxton's battalions were relieved after their picket duty and sent to the rear. The batteries belonging to Lieutenant Colonels William Nelson and Robert A. Hardaway now took their turn occupying the front line.

Towards evening, Colonel Emory Upton's Brigade of the VI Corps launched an attack against the left side of the Mule Shoe salient, occupied by Brigadier George Doles' Brigade of Rodes' division. Owing to the density of the terrain to its front, Doles' command was caught by surprise, and soon was driven from its position on the right. A battery, belonging to Hardaway's battalion, fell into Northern hands, and for a time, conditions were desperate for the Confederates.

Fortunately, reinforcements were rushed towards the breach. "Battle's brigade and Gordon's division were rapidly brought up, and the former thrown across the head of the enemy's column, while the leading brigade (R. D. Johnston's) of the latter, with the remnants of Doles' and the right of Daniel's brigades, struck them on one flank, and the Stonewall (Walker's), of Johnson's division, on the other."[4] Hardaway's battery was recovered, and Upton was soon driven from the Southern works.

The following morning, May 11, Page's and Major Wilfred E. Cutshaw's battalions were positioned along the front. A heavy rain fell throughout the day, and there was no serious fighting anywhere along the lines.

Then, late in the afternoon, reports of what looked to be an enemy withdrawal began coming in. In fact, troops could be heard leaving Anderson's front and moving to the right. It appeared that Grant was again attempting to outmaneuver Lee though his exact designs could not be determined.

So that he would be in a better position to pursue, regardless of Grant's line of march, Lee issued orders for his chiefs of artillery "...to have all the artillery which was difficult of access removed from the lines before dark,..." and informed them "...that it was desirable that everything should be in readiness to move during the night;..."[5] Brigadier General Edward Porter Alexander, Chief of Artillery of the First Corps, whose route away from the front was not that difficult, had his limbers moved to within easy reach of his guns, so that a quick withdrawal could be effected. Long, on the other hand, removed all but two batteries of Cutshaw's battalion from his section of the line. The road to the rear of his present position was much more treacherous, and with the night promising to be very dark, it seemed prudent to withdraw the bulk of the Second Corps artillery without delay.

Therefore, it was before dusk that the remaining two batteries of Cutshaw's command, as well as all of Page's battalion, began making their way to the rear. Passing through the woods near the McCoull house, the artillery column continued to push slowly ahead until it reached a point about one and a half miles to the rear of the salient. There, the battalion, except for one section of Captain Charles W. Fry's company, which was sent off to escort a wagon train, was parked for the night. Horses were unhitched, and what few tents that could be found were set up to afford protection from the rain. The men settled in and in Page's own words, "...the whole camp reposed in a state of most profound security."[6]

While there was no reason for concern among the artillerymen, their move had not sat well with the troops still occupying the Mule Shoe. Long's decision to remove the guns of the Second Corps had left the infantry there without proper artillery support hence more vulnerable to attack. At first, the men had been a bit puzzled, if not surprised by the departure of the batteries.[7] Even Johnson had been caught unaware by the decision to remove the guns.[8]

Near midnight, however, feelings of apprehension replaced those of surprise, when the rumbling sound of troops on the move were overheard coming from the position across the way. Brigadier General George H. Steuart, a brigade commander in Johnson's division, whose troops occupied the right side of the salient, soon was convinced that the noise meant that an attack was forthcoming.[9]

That was certainly not the sound of withdrawal. What Steuart heard was the noise made by the men of Hancock's II Corps, 15,000 in all, who were massing for an early morning attack against the salient. Grant had learned a valuable lesson from the temporary success that Upton's brigade had achieved two days before and was preparing to launch an attack of similar design, but of much greater proportions than the earlier assault. The II Corps advance was to be supported by Burnside, who would be sending his divisions against the Southern right. Not long thereafter, Major General Horatio G. Wright would assault the left side of the salient while Warren struck Anderson on the Confederate left.[10] That strategy, Grant believed, would result in a permanent breakthrough and ultimate victory for the Union forces.[11]

Meanwhile, sensing that an attack was forthcoming, Steuart went to Johnson and requested that the artillery be returned to the front. Ewell was then apprised of the situation, and he sent orders by messenger to Long, telling him to have his batteries reassume their position along the salient about 2:00 a.m.

Back at the front, the hours passed, and two o'clock came and went without any sign of the promised artillery. More concerned than ever about the situation along the front, Johnson sent another messenger to seek out Long.

Finally at 3:30 a.m., Long "...received a note from Johnson, indorsed by directing me to replace immediately the artillery that had been withdrawn the evening before; that the enemy was preparing to attack."[12] Ten minutes later, Major Page was awakened and received orders from Long to move his battalion with all possible speed to the aid of Johnson. The men were aroused and there occurred the following exchange in the camp of the Jeff Davis Artillery, as remembered by Corporal John Purifoy:[13]

"Hello, Jack! Get up! Orders for the battery to move to the front immediately." "Ha, ha, what is it?" The writer inquired

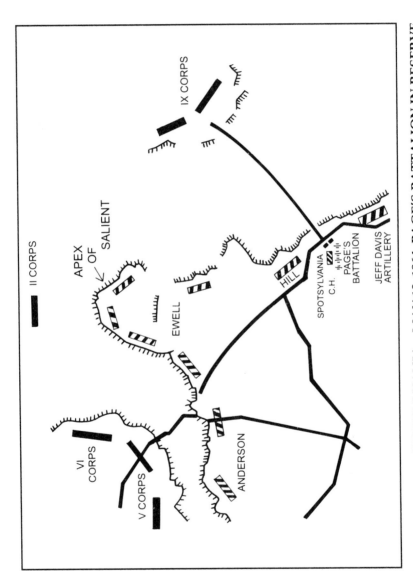

SPOTSYLVANIA – MAY 10, 1864, PAGE'S BATTALION IN RESERVE

Fredericksburg and Spotsylvania National Military Park (Spotsylvania Troop Movement Map – Sheet #3)

as he was aroused from a sound sleep, anywhere from 12 o'clock midnight to 3 a.m. on the morning of the 12th of May, 1864, by Sergt. C. W. McCreary, of the Jeff Davis Artillery, acting orderly sergeant. "Get up! The battery has orders to move to the front at a double quick." "We had no supper, how about breakfast?" was the surly inquiry. "Breakfast, nothing! This is no time to discuss breakfast! You'll have as good breakfast as you had supper last night."[14]

In no time at all, the camp was full of activity. Horses were harnessed and hitched to their respective vehicles. At the same time, Page consulted with Colonel Thomas H. Carter concerning the repositioning of the artillery at the salient, and "...it was fully understood that Carter's battery, two rifles and two light twelves, should take the lead and occupy the salient itself - to be followed in order by Montgomery, four light twelves, who was to take position just to the left of Carter; Fry, two rifles under command of Lieutenant Deas, to take position about one hundred yards to the right of Carter; and Reese, four rifles, about fifty yards to the right of Fry."[15] Preparations were soon completed, and the artillery started towards the front.

The battalion quickly ascended the hill leading to the road, which it had used when withdrawing the evening before. Still, even with their rapid start, it was doubtful whether the batteries would reach the front in time to prevent a disaster from befalling the Southern army. Already by 3:45 a.m., Hancock had written the following message to Major General Andrew A. Humphreys, the Chief of Staff of the Union army: "My troops are nearly formed. As it is misty I think I shall wait until it is a little more clear, by which time my troops will be formed."[16] It was now just a matter of time before the Federals launched their attack.

Meanwhile, to the rear of Johnson's position, the darkness and dense fog, not to mention the rough road which in Purifoy's words, "...tortuously wound its way through dense undergrowth, thickly interspersed with shortleaf pines, briar thickets, trickling streams, and oozy marshes,"[17] served to hinder somewhat the progress of the artillery column. And yet, with so many obstacles in its path, the battalion moved at a surprising pace. "On the drivers sped with a daredevil recklessness, thrusting in Providence to guide them over the dangerous quagmires, around the many pines among which the indistinct roads wound,..."[18] The corporals and cannoneers, meanwhile, followed their respective guns on foot.

The drivers, sergeants, quartermaster, and commis-
sionary sergeants, and all commissioned officers of the artillery, were mounted on horseback. But the corporals and
cannoneers, who were expected to handle the guns and ammunition and do all other necessary work, must not be en-
cumbered with such useless trumpery, nor be permitted to
ride and increase the loads on the half-starved horses.[19]

The perilous journey to the front continued. The drivers did their
best to keep their vehicles on the road, but an occasional mishap could
not be avoided. Early on, an accident occurred involving one of Captain Charles R. Montgomery's guns, and it had to be left behind.[20] Then,
with more than half of the journey completed, a caisson belonging to
the Jeff Davis Artillery, specifically the one "...following gun number
two, section number one,..." bogged down in a marsh and also had to
be temporarily abandoned.[21]

Near dawn, Page's battalion finally reached the salient. "There was
a heavy fog and some scattering musketry, but no enemy visible,..."
remembered Page.[22] Carter and Montgomery received instructions from
Page concerning the placing of their guns, and immediately moved towards their respective positions along the line. Page then rode off in
the opposite direction, towards the right side of the salient, to personally direct the emplacing of the two guns of Fry's battery. Having completed that particular task, Page then rode to see Reese to issue
instructions regarding the positioning of the four rifled guns belonging
to the Jeff Davis Artillery. Shortly thereafter, the battalion commander
departed in order to check the progress of Montgomery's battery.

The Alabama battery, meanwhile, took up its position on the right.
Its four pieces were aligned in the following manner: guns numbered
one and two, of the first section of the battery, were placed on the right
side of the angle, while guns three and four, of the second section, were
put on the left side of the angle. The position occupied by the second
section of guns would, as it turned out, be the most difficult of the two
sides of the angle to defend. The slope of the ground to the front of that
section of the line was such that an advancing enemy could not be spotted until they were about one-hundred and fifty yards away, or actually at the edge of the plateau upon which the Southern lines were
located. That fact, combined with the poor visibility caused by the dense
fog and light drizzle, which was continuing to fall, would give any
attacker on the left a certain element of surprise, especially if there was
a lack of vigilance on the part of the defenders. As for the right side of

the angle, there was a more open field of fire and less opportunity for a force to approach unscathed to within easy reach of the Confederate works.

Also occupying the angle currently being held by Reese's command were the regiments of Steuart's brigade. Pickets had long since been sent out to guard against an enemy advance. To that point, no alarm had been sounded by the pickets, and the officers and men of the infantry could be found relaxing behind the works. On the other hand, the men of Captain Reese's command were alert. The great haste in which they had been returned to the front could only mean that serious business lay ahead. Purifoy recalled that, "...the surroundings for a short time bore an ominous silence."[23]

By that time, Page had returned to the opposite side of the salient, where, to his horror, he had found that the Federals had already overrun that part of the line. While he was busy arranging the guns on the right side of the salient, the first line of the advancing enemy had made contact with Johnson's division a little past 4:30 a.m. Despite the gallant efforts by the late Brigadier General John M. Jones' and Brigadier General James A. Walker's brigades, the surging mass of bluecoats could not be stopped, and soon had pushed over the Southern works. In short order, the enemy had captured many prisoners, including Johnson himself, and all the guns of the batteries belonging to Montgomery, Carter and Fry.

Only two of Carter's guns had been in position to resist the attack, and the gunners had gotten off only two rounds before falling into enemy hands. Montgomery's guns, meanwhile, had never even gotten into position, and as for Deas' section, it had succeeded in firing only once before being captured.

Seeing that the situation was hopeless on the left, Page whirled his horse around and rapidly rode in the direction of the Jeff Davis Artillery to see if that battery could be saved. By then, however, the Alabamians were already involved in a crisis of their own.

Reese's command had scarcely gotten into position when suddenly a wave of Federal infantry appeared within canister range of a section of guns. Emotions ran high as the gunners yelled for permission to fire their pieces, and "...the two gun corporals actually ordered canister and began firing."[24]

The canister had a destructive effect, causing the Yankees to slow their advance and even halt temporarily. "Each discharge had cut a lane through the ranks of the assaulting column. As the column was

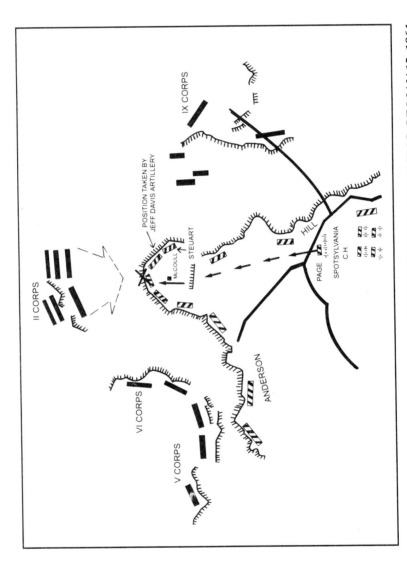

SPOTSYLVANIA – PAGE IS ORDERED FORWARD – MORNING OF MAY 12, 1864
Fredericksburg and Spotsylvania National Military Park (Spotsylvania Troop Movement Map – Sheet #5)

several lines deep, the destruction wrought was heavy."[25] Corporal George G. Jackson, in charge of gun No. 3 remembered:

> Shot six rounds and killed forty three Yankees, or at least, that was the number "Big Zeke" Melton reported. He jumped over the breast works and robbed the dead Yankees and brought back fifteen watches, and forty or fifty dollars in green backs. He was No 1 at my piece. About this time General Stuart ordered us to cease firing, that his pickets had not come in. Captain Reese also very excitedly gave the same order.[26]

In spite of the orders to cease fire, the gunners, who could only see blue to their front, kept to their work. Steuart soon realized that he had seen the last of his pickets. There had been no warning of the attack, and that could only mean that the men assigned to watch the front had been surprised and swallowed up during the early stages of the Federal advance.

The situation was growing more desperate by the moment, not only for the artillerymen, but for Steuart's own men who had also entered the fight. The latter offered a stubborn resistance at first, but there were just too many coming. Jackson continued; "By this time our front was covered with Yankees, nine lines deep. I fired into them and the trail of my gun rebounded and knocked General Stuart down and I threw him into the ditch.

PRIVATE MATTHEW TUCKER

Jeff Davis Artillery; post-war view.

(Courtesy of Maurice B. Andrews, Chickasaw, Alabama)

Before I could fire again the United States flag was planted at the trail of my gun and I was ordered to surrender."[27]

The action then shifted to the next piece or gun No. 3, where gunner Private Matt Tucker was stationed and later recalled:

> As a cannoneer I had charge of the lanyard and primer,...The Corporal was standing at the trail of the gun. I could have touched Captain Reese with my left hand...You could not

distinguish a man ten paces from you. The first thing I knew the enemy's line of battle was coming over the temporary works at my gun, and one slapping his hand on the gun opposite me said, "Surrender." The gun being loaded, the primer placed, the lanyard attached and in my hand, my first impulse was to turn loose with that load and save myself if possible. I passed by Yankees and Confederates as I came out. Everything was in confusion and I took advantage of this circumstance and came out.[28]

Two of the Alabama battery's guns were by that time as good as lost. Ironically, though, the Federals had not as yet appeared in front of the first section of the battery, located to the right of the apex. It wasn't long, however, before those previously idle gun crews were fully involved in the fight, within the very works they were defending.

The enemy, as it turned out, had crossed the works on the left side of the angle and were approaching the two remaining pieces of the Jeff Davis Artillery from the rear. Both guns were immediately reversed to face the enemy, and in Purifoy's own words:

At the same instant I heard Corporals Blankinship and Wootan and Sergeants Cobb and Norwood,.., call for canister. Having anticipated the call, I held a charge of canister in my hand when number five approached and he immediately double quicked on return, when it was inserted into the muzzle of the gun and rammed home. I heard Corporal Wootan give the command to fire, and almost simultaneously I heard Blankinship, at the other gun, give the same command, and the explosions of the guns were in quick succession. The charge of each whizzed by me with a striking resemblance to the noise made by a covey of quail when suddenly flushed. As I was situated in front of the two guns,.., I realized that there was danger in the shots of friends as well as those of foes. During the firing of these guns I saw the infantry, which was not over thirty steps from me, fire a volley into the same mass of Federals....It was about this time that the halted and confused enemy opened with musketry, the first that I had seen proceed from their line. The bullets were flying thickly around me.[29]

Corporal Francis M. Wootan, in charge of gun No. 2, also remembered:

> I reversed my gun in the works and loaded with a double
> charge of canister and told the boys when I fired I was going
> over the breast works. I waited until the gun above me sur-
> rendered, this was "Hickory" (G G) Jackson's, and then I
> enfiladed the whole concern, went over the works in a hoop,
> followed by no one except John Oliver. I got my clothes full
> of holes and my shoes soles shot off.[30]

Wootan was able to make good his escape, but the fighting was far from over for that particular gunner.

Page now arrived and immediately attempted to save what he could of the Jeff Davis Artillery.

Riding to gun No. 1, he issued orders for its immediate withdrawal. The men reacted quickly. The limber was brought forward, the cannon hooked to it and it was rapidly driven off away from the firing.

At the same time, Page continued to the limber chest of Corporal Wootan's adjacent gun, and ordered that its accompanying piece also be removed from the front. Once having issued his instructions, the battalion commander went no further but instead, "...immediately re- turned in the direction from which he came, not attempting to reach the other two guns, which I am sure had fallen into the hands of the enemy."[31]

The cannoneers of gun No. 1, as it turned out, had made good their escape, but with the guns of the Jeff Davis Artillery now idle, the en- emy recovered his nerve and resumed the advance. Purifoy, who was in charge of the limber chest of the second piece with his gun crew, would have to act quickly if they were to get away from the Federals.

Immediately, Purifoy ordered the drivers to mount and move to- wards the artillery piece. Two of the drivers reacted promptly to the command, but the third, a conscript, refused to move. The critical na- ture of the combat had caused a fright that had effectively immobilized him. That particular driver's actions, however, especially since he was in the heat of battle for the first time, could not have been considered a total surprise.

Purifoy repeated his order, but the man would not budge. The Yan- kees were now approaching fast. Still, Purifoy was not about to give up on his efforts to save the piece.

> I then attempted to draw the gun to the limber, thinking to
> have his horses mounted by another. I was making progress

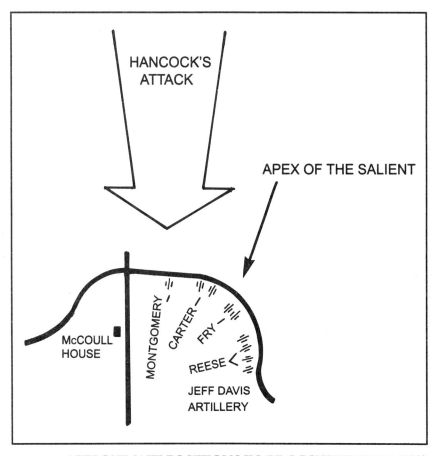

**APPROXIMATE POSITIONS TO BE OCCUPIED BY PAGE'S
BATTALION ON MORNING OF MAY 12, 1864**

*Fredericksburg and Spotsylvania National Military Park
Recreated after Jedediah Hotchkiss (Position of Confederate Batteries at Capture of Salient at
Spotsylvania C. H. May 12th, 1864.)*

when, looking toward the limber, I saw it at least forty yards away, the wheel horses lying on their backs dead and the other horses sprawling on the ground also, two of the drivers having been killed and the third, the one who failed to mount his horses when ordered, was severely wounded and fell into the hands of the enemy. The derelict driver had mounted when I turned my back, and they had attempted to escape but veered too far to the right and ran into a column of the enemy, who had used their muskets as mentioned. Sergeant Cobb at my gun was severely wounded...[32]

Purifoy had lost any chance of saving the gun, and the Federals were almost upon him. At that juncture, the Yankees were screaming, "Surrender, you damn rebel sons of bitches,..,"[33] and Purifoy had no choice but to make his escape by jumping over the earthworks. Seconds later, gun No. 2 was overrun by the enemy.

The battery had been broken up, and what still remained of it was now pressing rearward, both individually and in small groups, towards the far end of the salient.

During its short-lived defense of the angle, the Jeff Davis Artillery had come as close to being destroyed as it had ever been in any previous campaign of the war. Besides the loss of three of its four guns, the company had twenty-two of its horses killed. Casualties among the men and officers were also unusually high, with forty of the company being lost. Both Reese and Bates, as it turned out, had come out of the fight without a scratch, but they, like many others, had the misfortune of falling into enemy hands. Those who had made it to safety could consider themselves extremely lucky.

In spite of such devastating results, Reese's command could be proud of what it had achieved. By its heroic defense, the Jeff Davis Artillery had bought the Southern army some valuable time. The numerous rounds of canister that the battery had been able to fire had checked the enemy long enough to allow the start of efforts aimed at retrieving the situation within the salient. Even now, reinforcements were rushing to plug the gap in the line.

Once apprised of the breakthrough, Gordon, whose division was being held in reserve, had advanced Brigadier General Robert D. Johnston's Brigade which had had little success in slowing the Federals. Without hesitation, Gordon had then begun deploying his old brigade along a line of incomplete works, located about a half mile to the rear of the apex of the Mule Shoe. Those infantrymen succeeded in checking the Federal drive for a time.

By that time, many from the Alabama battery, who had been able to escape, had also reentered the fight. Corporal Joseph Blankinship, in charge of the only gun of the battery to come out of the struggle at the angle, had already unlimbered his piece and begun firing away at the enemy. Purifoy recalled, "The men who escaped with the gun that was saved stopped at the first point which offered a prospect of rallying the demoralized troops."[34] About the same time, another gun which had been abandoned earlier in the day was brought up and also manned by the Alabamians.

During the crisis within the salient, Gordon was the master of the situation. At great personal risk, with bullets flying all around, he endeavored to put together what remained of his command, as well as those troops which were available from Johnson's shattered division. Before long, his deployment was completed, and the Confederates counterattacked.

The Yankees soon started to give ground. Though they had superior numbers, the Federal thrust had lost momentum, as it overrun the Southern works and a confusion about what should be done next spread through the ranks. Moreover, the attacking force, thanks in part to an effective fire from the gray troops opposite its flanks, had been contained in a relatively compact area, within which maneuver soon had become difficult. The situation worsened for the enemy as reinforcements continued to pour in from the rear, causing the loss of organization throughout. Under such circumstances, a proper defense was, again, impossible. That left the enemy with no alternative but to fall back before the Southern advance. Soon, the Federals were rapidly withdrawing up the salient.

The Confederate counterattack was succeeding and gained more strength as Major General Stephen Dodson Ramseur's brigade of Rodes' division, which occupied the west side of the salient, swung around to the north and joined the fray.

Meanwhile, not too far away, the Alabama battery's own Corporal Wootan, who had just recently made good his escape, was himself rejoining the contest. In Wootan's own words:

> I made swift time to the next hill, when I found General R E
> Lee on his horse, at an unimployed brass napoleon piece, the
> gunner was killed. The General seeing my stripes, asked me
> if I was a gunner, and answering him in the affirmative, told

me to take charge of it, which I did. At the same time Gordon's
division at a double quick, was passing and rushed into the
fight and soon had possession of the breast/works. The shot
of canister I threw into them, before leaving the angle, demoralized them so much that they did not move in some
time, giving Gordon's division time to meet them in the right
place. I was ordered to a point where there was a gap in the
breastworks, where I fought sharpshooters all day, loosing
twenty men out of twenty five.[35]

With the support of guns manned by men from Reese's command,
as well as other batteries brought up and posted along the base of the
salient, the Confederate infantrymen continued to force the Federals
back as far as the northeastern tip of the salient. But there, their resistance suddenly proved to be quite strong. All efforts to dislodge the
Yankees failed, and a terrific struggle along the works ensued.

Meanwhile, on the Confederate right, enemy pressure had eased
somewhat. Burnside's Corps, which had moved against that side of the
salient at the same time that Hancock struck the apex, had been repulsed with severe losses. In that instance, the Southern artillery had
played a major part in stopping the assault. There was a continuing
fire-fight in that particular sector, but no new movement on the part of
the Federals.

The situation had stabilized on the right, but for the Confederates,
conditions on the opposite side of the salient were beginning to deteriorate. It was by then past 6:00 a.m., and Wright was throwing the full
weight of the VI Corps against the defenders. Rodes' men were hard
pressed to hold off the enemy, and before long, it began to look as if it
was just a matter of time before the enemy broke the gray line. To prevent a second disaster, it was essential that Rodes receive reinforcements.

Fortunately, three brigades of Brigadier General William Mahone's
Division of the First Corps were already on the way. Though at first
intended to be used in support of Gordon, the men of the First Corps
were redirected to assist Rodes. The result was that the Union forces
were defeated in their attempt to take that portion of the line immediately to the left of the apex.

The repulse of the Federals, however, did not lead to any slackening of fire along the salient. On the contrary, the fighting there became
even more fierce, as the opposing forces battled each other at close range

over the very works which Hancock's troops had swept over less than two hours before.

> Troops were killed by thrusts and stabs through chinks in the log barricade, while others were harpooned by bayoneted rifles flung javelin-style across it...Down in the trenches, dead and wounded men were trampled out of sight in the blood-splotched mud by those who staggered up to take their posts along the works,...[36]

While the fighting raged, Warren's V Corps moved out to attack the Southern left, which was still being held by Anderson's Corps, about 9:00 a.m. The Federals, however, came under a destructive fire before the assault could gather any momentum and were beaten back. No further advance was attempted on the left.

For the balance of the morning and throughout the afternoon, the struggle along the salient, later to be dubbed "The Bloody Angle", continued, with neither side gaining any significant ground. Lee threw all his available men into the fight, and by doing so, was able to prevent not only further damage to his lines, but to also relieve those men already left totally exhausted by the contest.

Though the Confederates were holding their own, nevertheless, the Yankees had breached their defenses and were now in possession of a portion of the works near the apex. Under those circumstances, holding the Mule Shoe salient for any longer than was necessary to resist the enemy made little sense. Consequently, a new defensive line was drawn across the base of the salient, and the balance of the day was spent strengthening that position. Once work on the defenses was completed, it was intended that the forces, still occupying the salient, would be withdrawn to the new line.

In the meantime, the fighting along the front continued. Dusk turned into night, but there was no order to pull back. As it turned out, the defenses to the rear were not yet ready to be occupied.

Several hours passed, with the bitter struggle showing little sign of winding down. Then, near midnight, word that the works were completed was finally received. Gradually, the Confederates withdrew back to the new line throughout the night, and finally completed their daybreak retreat. With the coming of first light, there was no effort on the Federals to pursue. The battle for the angle was over.

Only by the extraordinary efforts of its officers and men had the Army of Northern Virginia been able to escape what at first must have looked like certain disaster. Gordon's effective deployment of the reserve forces had checked Hancock, then led to a Confederate counterattack, which had resulted in the regaining of much of the lost ground, as well as the reestablishing of the Southern line near the tip of the salient. Then, only because the old line was no loner tenable, did the Confederates finally relinquish their position.

Lee's forces had, in the end, inflicted close to 7,000 casualties, though at a terrible cost. They themselves had lost more than 6,000 killed, wounded and captured. Johnson's division alone suffered more than 2,500 casualties, the vast majority of those losses having been incurred when Hancock's Corps overwhelmed the Southern position at the tip of the Mule Shoe. In addition, Generals Johnson and Steuart had both been taken prisoner early in the fight.

Page's battalion, meanwhile, had dissolved before its commander's eyes during the initial stages of the battle for possession of the salient. In the end, twenty guns and a great many cannoneers had fallen into enemy hands.[37]

As mentioned, the Jeff Davis Artillery had itself suffered heavily during the few minutes in which it had opposed Hancock's infantry. Aside from the loss of three guns, the company had lost a total of twenty-two horses, as well as two caissons, and all the equipment that went with them.

The fight had also left the Alabama battery without any commissioned officers. Besides Captain Reese and First Lieutenant Bates, six noncommissioned officers were now also prisoners of war. Included among them were Sergeants Joseph J. Barlow, Robert E. Cobb (he had also been wounded), John Fox Maull and Augustus B. Patton, as well as Corporals George Y. Higgins and George G. Jackson.

In addition, Privates Andrew J. Blanks, Thomas M. Bradley, William Batton and W. R. Harris had been killed, while several men, including Privates E. Miner and J. V. F. Walker, had received wounds. At the same time, twenty seven from the ranks had been taken prisoner during the early morning attack. Altogether, the Jeff Davis Artillery had lost forty men, or better than *fifty percent* of its effective force.

Though its ranks had been decimated and left scattered, the battery still had never lost its identity. As mentioned, the survivors had regrouped near the base of the salient where they had then manned two guns and rejoined the fight.

That day, the solid reputation of the Alabama battery had certainly been upheld. Despite having suffered the humiliation of losing three guns and having been driven from the front, Reese's command had, prior to that unhappy occurrence, been most active in its defense of the salient. Records indicate that the company had gotten off "...twenty five rounds of case + canister,"[38] before finally relinquishing its position to the enemy. The men of the Jeff Davis Artillery had been conspicuous for their gallantry during the early morning attack, but that does not mean that the battery's performance over the rest of the day had been any less courageous. There, in fact, was one particular instance where individual gallantry had been cited. Specifically, it was ·Wootan, who had won the plaudits of his fellow soldiers for his actions with the brass Napoleon on May 12. In the corporal's own words,

> The officers next day thought I had played thunder and wanted to promote me. I told them that I had all the office I wanted, but they could give me a sixty day furlough if they wanted to, and it came in due time while we were enroute to join Early in the Valley. The furlough was a meritorious one from General Lee which I have always been proud of.[39]

By the following day, May 13, Reese, Bates and the others from the Alabama battery, captured in the battle for the Angle, had been sent to Belle Plain, a vast holding area located on the Potomac River from which they were to be transported by train to some Northern prison. Ultimately, both Reese and Bates were sent to Fort Delaware. The remaining men were transported to other prisons, some to Point Lookout, Maryland, others to Elmira Prison in New York. Later, most of the men sent to Point Lookout were transferred to Elmira. In the end, a number of the men would die as a result of the conditions to which they were exposed during their confinement.

May 13 also marked a day of reorganization for the artillery of the Second Corps. Page was left in command of what still remained of his battalion - four guns, two belonging to Fry, and one each to Montgomery's and Reese's batteries. In addition, Page was also given charge of the remnants of Major Wilfred E. Cutshaw's battalion (two batteries). Cutshaw, meanwhile, had been assigned to Lieutenant Colonel Hardaway's battalion. Hardaway had been wounded during the fight of the 12th.

Though the Jeff Davis Artillery had been reduced to less than one half its effective strength, there were still more men than were needed to serve its one surviving gun. There was no alternative but to make some drastic changes within the old organization. Therefore, a sufficient number of men were selected to man the lone field piece, and

FORT DELAWARE PRISON

Where Captain William J. Reese was imprisoned following capture at Spotsylvania Court House; modern view.

(Author's collection) Wedgewood Studio

they were attached to Fry's Orange County Artillery. Fry's command now consisted of just one section of guns, which had been on detached service while the attack on the salient was taking place. From that day forward, that one section, as well as the one three-inch Rifle belonging to the Alabama battery, were to be used in concert against the enemy.

That still left twenty men of the Jeff Davis Artillery without assignments. Whether they all would be attached to one particular command or split up among several others was a question presently left unanswered. What was known, however, was the fact that Reese's battery had, as of May 12, 1864, ceased to exist as an individual fighting unit with the Army of Northern Virginia.

CHAPTER XIII

ANOTHER TRANSFER AS THE BATTLE LINES MOVE SOUTH

On May 13, Page's newly reorganized command took its place with the rest of Carter's division along the recently completed line of works at the base of the salient. Included among the gun crews on hand was the Jeff Davis Artillery detachment of the Orange County battery which, in Fry's own words, had been "...thrown, though not consolidated with mine."[1]

That day there was some skirmishing and artillery fire along the lines, but it was, for the most part, a day of rest for both armies. In fact, Grant had made plans designed to turn Lee out of his works in front of Spotsylvania. To achieve his goal, Grant had decided to shift Warren's V Corps from his right over to the left during the night, then to attack the unsuspecting Confederate right at dawn. Wright's VI Corps would follow-up and support Warren.

That night, the Federal withdrawal from the works opposite Anderson's Corps began. Before long, Warren's entire corps was pushing eastward towards the assigned jump off point. Terrible road conditions, however, slowed the movement and caused much straggling.

The next morning, troops were late moving into position after the previous night's march. More delays followed, and the assault against Lee's right was called off.

Meanwhile, on the Confederate left, troops had advanced to occupy the abandoned Federal works. Then, on the night of the 14th, Anderson's divisions were themselves shifted to the right of Early's position, thereby extending the Southern lines as far south as Snell's Bridge on the Po River. By doing that, Lee was merely conforming to the enemy movements of the night before.

All the while, things remained comparatively quiet along Ewell's front. On May 15, Private John V. F. Walker, who had been captured during the fighting of the 12th, rejoined the Jeff Davis Artillery. Walker, the brother of Robert Walker, whose services Reese had been seeking for the past year and a half, had escaped from a Union field hospital to the safety of the Southern lines.

Considering the Alabama battery's present state of affairs, that bit of good news about Walker could not have come at a better time. The Alabamians must have been still smarting from the treatment they had received on May 12, and had to be anxious for another shot at Meade's forces.

Appropriately, Grant was planning yet another assault against Lee's well-entrenched army. Major General Horatio Wright, believed that the Confederate left, then occupied by Ewell's Corps along the base of the old salient, must have been weakened in order to counter the shifting of Federal troops over to the right, making it vulnerable to attack. Consequently, Grant decided to return those troops, just withdrawn from the Union center, to points opposite the Southern left for an assault there. Wright's VI and Hancock's II Corps were to make the attack, with Burnside's command being used to divert attention away from the movement.

On the morning of May 18, Federal troops moved up in the pre-dawn darkness to take their positions within the northern tip of the salient. This time, however, Long's artillery was ready for the attackers. Twenty-nine guns from both Page's and Hardaway's battalions, including the lone piece being served by the Jeff Davis Artillerymen, had been positioned along the base of the salient. At the same time, the Confederates had already correctly learned the enemy's intentions.

Since first light, Long's gunners had waited for the first signs of enemy activity opposite their position. Then at 8:00 a.m., a good deal of movement was suddenly apparent in and about the works which the Confederates had abandoned several days earlier. Such activity was unmistakable. The anticipated attack had begun.

Immediately, the Southern artillery opened, sending shot and shell into the first visible ranks of the enemy, as well as into the surrounding woods through which the attacking force was advancing. Soon, long blue lines, which stretched from one end of the salient to the other, emerged from the tree-covered terrain. As the Federals advanced, the Confederates rained a steady, damaging fire upon them.

The enemy moved still closer to the Southern works and were momentarily staggered by an increased fire from the massed batteries. Recovering their composure, the Federal infantry pressed forward at a much more rapid pace. Then, as Long reported, the enemy "...was allowed to come within good canister range of our breast-works. Carter's division of artillery then opened a most murderous fire of canister and spherical case shot, which at once arrested his advance, threw his columns into confusion, and forced him to a disorderly retreat. His loss was very heavy; ours was nothing."[2]

As soon as the Yankees disappeared back into the woods, the Southern artillery ceased firing to conserve ammunition. In the end, the well-served guns of the Second Corps had easily repulsed an attacking force estimated to have contained between ten and twelve thousand infantry. Following that one-sided affair, Grant abandoned the idea of trying to break Lee's grip on the Spotsylvania line by frontal assault.

The morning of May 19, there was no activity anywhere along the lines. Lee, however, suspected that his adversary was again shifting his forces to the left, and ordered Ewell to demonstrate along his front in order to see if the enemy was still there. Fearing that such a move might prove costly, Ewell requested that he be allowed to maneuver around the enemy's flank instead. His suggestion was accepted by Lee.

Just past midday, all of the Second Corps infantry, and six guns from Lieutenant Colonel Carter M. Braxton's battalion, were withdrawn from their positions on the left and started on a circuitous march towards the Union right. Two brigades of Major General Wade Hampton's cavalry were sent along to cover the flank movement. Meanwhile, the remainder of Long's artillery continued to occupy the same position which it had held on the previous day.

The roads used by Ewell had been kept soft by recent rains, and travel became more difficult as the march progressed. In fact, conditions along the route were so bad that: "After proceeding 2 or 3 miles the roads were found to be impracticable for artillery, and Braxton was ordered to return to his former position."[3] Ewell's infantry and his cavalry escort, however, pushed on and soon had crossed the Ni River. To that point, no enemy had been encountered.

Then, when less than a mile beyond the river, the Confederates ran into a full division of Warren's V Corps. Rather than be caught off balance by an enemy advance, Ewell elected to take the initiative and attack the division. At first, he was successful in driving the Yankees back, but Warren received reinforcements from Hancock's Corps, and they, combined with the unchallenged fire of the Federal artillery, soon halted the attackers. Quickly the tide of battle turned, with the outnumbered and out-gunned Ewell eventually retiring back across the Ni River. As it turned out, only the efforts of the artillery belonging to Hampton, which had been able to check the advancing enemy long enough to allow Ewell's withdrawal, had saved the Second Corps from disaster. In the end, Ewell's flanking maneuver had confirmed that the Federals were present in strength opposite his front. That, however, had been a costly mission, with nine hundred men being counted as casualties on the Southern side.

That action involving Ewell and the Federal V and II Corps was the last fighting to take place at Spotsylvania. The night of May 20, Hancock vacated his position opposite the Confederate center and moved off in a southeasterly direction towards Guiney Station. Not long thereafter, each of the three remaining Federal corps were also pulled from the line, and were started on a track similar to that of the II Corps. Just as on May 8, Grant was attempting to steal a march on his adversary.

As it turned out, Lee had already anticipated Grant's next move. The Federal army's departure necessitated a countermove. Lee decided to shift his army southward to a strong defensive position along the North Anna River. Just south of the North Anna was Hanover Junction, where railways from the south and west met, and where reinforcements totalling 8,000 men from both the Shenandoah Valley and near Richmond would be arriving. Troops had been made available, thanks to a pair of tactical victories scored by Major General John C. Breckinridge and General Pierre G. T. Beauregard at New Market and Drewry's Bluff, Virginia respectively.

Near dawn of the 21st, the evacuation of the Spotsylvania line began, with Ewell's Corps being withdrawn from the left and started in a southerly direction towards the Po River. Fry's battery, including the remainder of Reese's command, and the rest of Page's battalion accompanied the infantry, though the exact position taken by the artillery during the march is not known.[4] After reaching the Po, Ewell crossed to the south side of the river on Snell's Bridge. Once across, the Second Corps was brought to a temporary halt.

About midday, the march was resumed, with Ewell moving south along the Telegraph Road. Several hours later, Anderson's divisions also started for the North Anna, using the same route taken by Ewell. In the meantime, the Third Corps, with the somewhat recovered A. P. Hill again at its head, was held in position at Spotsylvania, with orders not to move until well past nightfall or when the enemy had completely abandoned their works, whichever came first. When Hill left the Court House, he was to follow a more westerly route, enabling him to guard the army's trains.

On the morning of May 22, Ewell's Corps reached the North Anna River and started across by way of the Chesterfield Bridge. Once on the south bank, it took up a line running from the bridge to just beyond the point where the Richmond and Fredericksburg Railroad crossed the North Anna, about a half mile downriver. Long's artillery, meanwhile, took up a position which covered two fords located on the right. In that particular instance, the exact disposition of Fry's battery is unclear.

As an extra precaution, two bridgeheads were also established on the north side of the river. Besides covering the bridges, Ewell's present position served to protect Hanover Junction itself, which again was a short distance to the rear.

Just past noon, Anderson's Corps arrived and went into position on Ewell's left. The Confederate line now extended upriver as far as Ox Ford. Breckinridge, who had already arrived at Hanover Junction, was posted between Anderson's right and Ewell's left. Major General George Pickett's Division, just sent north by Beauregard, was also on hand and was to join Hill's Corps upon its arrival south of the river.

On the morning of the 23rd, the Third Corps concluded its march and stopped to rest about one and a quarter miles southwest of Ox Ford, at Anderson Station on the Virginia Central Railroad. That period of relaxation, however, was short-lived. Meade's army had come up, and Hancock's II Corps was already threatening the defenses north of the North Anna. At the same time, Warren's V Corps was preparing to force a crossing upriver at Jericho Mills.

Back at Ox Ford, the Confederate batteries opened upon the advancing foe. Soon, the Federal artillery answered back, and fire-fight ensued.

In the meantime, Warren had pushed across the river and had begun advancing along the south bank towards Lee's left. Hill immediately sent Wilcox's division to confront the Federals. Not long thereafter, the Confederates hit and pushed back Warren's most advanced division. The Southern forces, however, soon became disorganized and quickly lost any advantage they had held. Wilcox's men fell back and were pursued until a heavy rain forced an end to the action. Warren then fortified his position.

Even as the action upriver was ending, the fighting on Anderson's and Ewell's front began to escalate. In an attempt to capture the Chesterfield Bridge, Hancock sent two brigades against it. The Southern positions were overrun, and the Federals soon had possession of not only the approaches to the crossing, but the bridge itself.

Even so, the recent Federal gains did not present a serious problem for Lee. By then, he had devised a plan by which his army would take up a new position. The Southern forces were to occupy a line resembling an inverted "V," whose apex was in the vicinity of Ox Ford, which by reason of its topography was virtually impregnable to attack. Extending from the apex, both up and downriver, but at ever-increasing distances from the North Anna, would be two well-protected lines of defense.

Lee hoped that Grant would advance against both sides of the "V." Because he held the interior lines, Lee could easily shift troops back and forth as needed to repel the enemy attacks. More important, though, was the fact that this defensive arrangement would cause the two wings of the Federal army to be isolated from one another, thereby giving Lee an excellent opportunity to strike a decisive blow against either force. In addition, any Federal troops being shifted up or downriver would be forced to cross the North Anna twice before they could reach the front.

On the morning of May 24, while Ewell and Anderson fortified the center and right of the line, Lee instructed Hill concerning the position he was to occupy on the left. Before long, the men of the Third Corps were hard at work constructing defenses of their own.

While the Confederates continued to strengthen their lines, Meade's army began its advance. Upriver, Warren started his troops in the direction of the works occupied by the Third Corps. Moving up behind him was Wright's VI Corps, which had crossed at Jericho Mills that very morning. Meanwhile, downriver, Hancock had crossed the Chesterfield Bridge and was moving towards the Confederate right. At the same time, Burnside was preparing to attack the defenses at Ox Ford.

Both up and downriver, the Federal forces conducted a cautious advance. So far, they had only run into the slightest opposition, and had become apprehensive about what lay ahead.[5] Up until then, everything was proceeding just as Lee had anticipated.

But, Lee had become incapacitated by an intestinal disorder and was unable to direct the movements of his army. Moreover, there was no one that he could turn the operation of the army over to while he was bedridden. Both Hill and Ewell were unwell, while Anderson, though physically fit, did not have the necessary experience. Consequently, as the enemy drew near, the Confederates did little more than continue working to improve their defenses.

During the afternoon, the Federals arrived opposite the Southern works and had their men dig in. Grant cancelled his attack, and for the rest of the afternoon and through the night, he worked on his own positions in anticipation of an attack by Lee.

Also on the 24th, those men from the Jeff Davis Artillery, who had been left without a unit as a result of the May 12 fight at Spotsylvania, were finally reassigned to another battery. That latest reorganization left twenty-one Alabamians attached to Captain Charles B. Griffin's Salem Flying Artillery of Lieutenant Colonel Robert A. Hardaway's Battalion.

LIEUTENANT COLONEL ROBERT A. HARDAWAY

Commanded portion of Jeff Davis Artillery from May 1864 to March 1865.

(Photograph courtesy of W. S. Hoole Special Collections Library, The University of Alabama)

Those just transferred to Griffin's command were: Sergeant Columbus W. McCrary, Corporal J. M. Jones, and Privates W. S. Blackburn, A. Blackstock, William H. Dunn, H. Edmondson, B. Franklin Ellis, J. P. Ellis, M. Gorman, John Hill, Benjamin Jackson, Littleton G. Jackson, C. S. V. Jones, Albert W. Metcalf, John F. Methvin, Solomon M. Peak, D. J. Pendergast, Wiley J. Polk, W. M. Walker, W. F. Ward, and T. P. Webster.

It became increasingly evident that those veterans were not at all pleased with the new arrangement. As Purifoy later explained, "Thus it will be seen that we who were not in Yankee prisons, became quasi Virginians....we had, in a measure, lost our identity, and we felt that whatever might be accomplished by us, we would, perhaps not get credit for it, as Alabamians."[6]

While the men attached to Griffin's battery became acquainted with their new surroundings, little of importance took place in the vicinity of the North Anna River. Some long range skirmishing did take place, but there was no significant movement on the part of either side.

Grant had already decided that it would be best to pull his army back across the North Anna as soon as circumstances allowed. On May 26, there were demonstrations all along the Federal lines. Then, once night had fallen, he withdrew his forces back across the river. By the morning of the 27th, the Union army had left Lee's immediate front and had begun moving downriver. As on previous occasions, Grant was trying to get the advantage of position over the Confederates by conducting a turning movement around the Southern right.

Lee reacted to Grant's latest sidling maneuver by immediately putting his own army in motion. That same morning, Carter's division, including the two batteries between which the members of the Jeff Davis Artillery had been divided, went into column and commenced a rapid march, with the rest of the Southern army in the direction of Atlee Station.

By sundown of the 28th, the Confederates had reached Atlee Station and had begun taking up a position near the Totopotomoy River, from which they could cover the approaches to Richmond. The Second Corps, with Early in temporary command for the ailing Ewell, was on the right, about four miles from Atlee Station, in the vicinity of Pole Green Church. As it had been at the North Anna, Hill took the left and Anderson the center of the line. Now all that remained was for Grant to make his appearance.

Then early on the morning of May 29, Lee received word from his scouts that a portion of the Union army had crossed the Pamunkey River at Hanovertown, eight miles east of Atlee Station. Unsure of whether the crossing had been made by cavalry, infantry or both, Lee sent his own cavalry on a mission to learn more about the Federal force and its destination.

Meanwhile, back on the Southern right, a position bolstered by Long's well placed batteries,[7] the Alabamians set up camp with their respective battalions in the vicinity of the Mechanicsville and Old Church Roads. For veterans like Purifoy and McCrary, who now occupied separate camps, the return to the Mechanicsville area must have brought back memories of the battle of Seven Pines, where their battery had received its first real baptism of fire. There, the Jeff Davis Artillery had established a record of dependability and efficiency in the field, a trait that had continued over two years of campaigning. With the battery broken up, things now were different. The dramatic changes of the past two weeks had ensured that the Alabamians, under present circumstances, could hardly have the kind of impact on any future battle as they had had on May 31, 1862.

On the road from Hanovertown, at Haw's Shop, the Southern cavalry had made contact with the Yankee horsemen. By the end of a seven hour battle, in which both sides incurred heavy casualties, the Confederates had determined that Federal infantry was, indeed, present in strength west of the Pamunkey River. At the same time, the enemy's intentions could not be ascertained, causing Lee to hold the bulk of his army where it was.

By midday of May 30, the Federals had arrived opposite the Southern army's position and begun to mass troops all along the front. On the left, Grant established his flank beyond that of the Second Corps. Lee ordered Early to attack. He was to be supported by Anderson's First Corps. That same day, Early attacked, but it was poorly handled and ended in a repulse. That night, Hardaway moved up to the front line, with Page's battalion being kept in reserve.

By that time, Lee had learned of a large force made up of portions of the XVIII and X Corps commanded by Major General William F. Smith, being sent by Major General Benjamin F. Butler, to reinforce Meade. Believing its destination to be the Federal left, Lee immediately requested troops from Beauregard, who complied. By mid-morning of the 31st, Major General Robert F. Hoke's Division of 7,000 men was on its way to the front.

In the meantime, Lee had instructed his cavalry, pending Hoke's arrival, to hold the vital Cold Harbor crossroads, the point he expected Butler's men were to occupy. Later that same day, Federal cavalry attacked Fitzhugh Lee's force, and the detachment from Hoke's command which had been sent to assist him, and forced them to relinquish the crossroads. As yet, no Yankee infantry had made its appearance.

The following day, Lee, determined to drive back the Federal horsemen, and any reinforcements that may have arrived, from the crossroads, ordered Anderson to launch an attack, supported by Hoke's division. The morning of June 1, Anderson moved forward, only to be repulsed by the enemy. Once driven back, the Southern troops entrenched and awaited developments.

Late in the afternoon, Wright's VI Corps and Smith's detachments from two corps, which had reached the field, launched a furious attack against Anderson's position. Though hard pressed, the defenders held their ground, thereby preserving Lee's right.

That same day, fighting had also taken place along that part of Early's line defended by Griffin's battery of Hardaway's battalion. The

former occupied a position at Pole Green Church and took part in the action described below:

The enemy charged about 6 p.m., and owing to the proximity of the lines got quite close to our line of battle before they were observed. A few rounds of canister broke them. They were easily repulsed without the aid of infantry.[8]

Casualties, though, were high, and Hardaway was relieved by Colonel William T. Poague's battalion. From all indications, this was the first time since their transfer on May 24 that the men of the Jeff Davis Artillery had the opportunity to serve the guns of Captain Griffin's battery.

To that point, Fry had not yet been called up from his reserve position.

LIEUTENANT COLONEL WILFRED E. CUTSHAW

Commanded battalion to which the Jeff Davis Artillery was attached from May-June 1864 to April 1865.

(The Museum of the Confederacy, Richmond, Virginia. The Long Arm of Lee.) J. P. Bell Co.

Meanwhile, Major Wilfred E. Cutshaw, who had assumed temporary command of Hardaway's battalion, while the latter recuperated from his Spotsylvania wounds, had replaced Page. Cutshaw's new command consisted of his own, plus Page's two batteries. Page was later assigned to Major Edgar F. Moseley's battalion, then serving with Beauregard.[9]

The following morning, that of June 2, there was skirmishing all along the front, but no advance by the enemy. During the day, Lee sought to lengthen his lines and also improve his position in case of attack. Near three o'clock in the afternoon, successful attacks were launched from both the far left and right of the Southern line. The one on the right had enabled the Confederates to seize high ground for the artillery's use, while the other action felt out the Federal positions. By day's end, Lee's line had been extended from the Totopotomy River on one end, to within a half mile of the Chickahominy River on the other.

Grant, meanwhile, had decided, in view of Lee's proximity to Richmond, to attempt to carry the Southern works by direct assault. The main thrust, originally scheduled for June 2 but postponed because of the two flank attacks, was to be aimed at the right and center of Lee's line.

At dawn of June 3, the attack commenced. Three corps, or more than sixty thousand men, were sent forward, only to be hit by a terrible storm of lead and iron once within range of the Southern works. Acting independently of one another, each corps soon also came under an increased flank fire. Casualties on the Union side increased rapidly, and except for a temporary lodgement made on Lee's right, the attackers were easily repulsed. Combat followed until 1:30 p.m. when Meade's orders cancelling the offensive were received.

Meanwhile, on the left, Early had also come under attack. Both Fry's and Griffin's batteries took part in the action, a fight in which "...Hardaway secured a most effective oblique fire on the enemy..." while Cutshaw "...opened a terrific enfilade fire upon the column which assaulted Rodes' works."[10] The Yankees were beaten back, thanks in large part to Long's artillery.

That same day, Private John Peebles, a member of the Jeff Davis Artillery serving with Fry's battery, was killed by a sharpshooter's bullet. Peebles had been with the company since the Fall of 1863.

For the next few days, Griffin's battery was itself under fire or participated in the shelling of the enemy. On June 7, Lee sent Early on a turning movement near Matadequin Creek. Griffin went along and provided a flank fire against the enemy. The flank attack, however, failed to achieve much, mainly because of the difficult terrain.

During the next several days, things remained relatively quiet along the lines, with only light skirmishing taking place. At the same time, however, the activities of other Union forces operating around Petersburg and to the west were a cause of great concern at Southern Headquarters.

A Federal army, led by Major General David Hunter, had marched up the Shenandoah Valley, and on June 5, soundly defeated the only force of sufficient strength to impede his progress in that area. Hunter then destroyed a large number of stores at Staunton and headed south, threatening Lynchburg, an important rail hub and supply depot.

In the meantime, Major General Philip Sheridan's cavalry had been sent west to assist Hunter on his mission of destruction. In addition, June 9, a Federal force consisting of cavalry and infantry attacked Beauregard at Petersburg. The enemy, however, gained little ground, and the fighting ended with darkness.

Two days later, the Southern cavalry, commanded by Major General Wade Hampton, intercepted Sheridan in the vicinity of Trevilian Station. There on June 11 and 12, both sides engaged in a fierce series of battles. In the end, the Confederates were left in possession of the field, Sheridan having abandoned his mission.

By that time, Lee had already sent Breckinridge and his two divisions against Hunter. Breckinridge, though, as it turned out, was badly outnumbered and could do little to stop the Yankee force of destruction. As a result, Lee decided to detach the Second Corps from the army to deal with Hunter, then possibly move to threaten Washington itself.

A still ailing Ewell, who was soon to take command of the Richmond defenses, had been replaced by Early, who was to take three full infantry divisions plus Nelson's and Braxton's battalions commanded by Brigadier General Long for the confrontation in the valley. Hardaway and Cutshaw were to remain with the main army.

By the morning of June 13, Early had departed. That same day, Lee's forces discovered that Meade's army had pulled back from its works about Cold Harbor. That withdrawal had actually begun about dusk of the previous day. During the retrograde movement, Hancock and Wright had occupied a newly constructed line to the rear in order to guard against a Confederate night attack while the rest of the army was on the move. Smith's Corps, meanwhile, had pushed in the direction of White House Landing on the James River, where transports awaited its arrival. Grant intended to cross the river to the south side and move against Petersburg.

Lee had not yet determined what Grant's exact intentions were, so he sent his cavalry forward. It, however, ran into a screen of Federal horsemen which could not be penetrated. As a precaution, though, Hoke's division was relocated to a position from which it could easily move to Beauregard's assistance, if the need arose. At the same time, the rest of the army was shifted to the south so that its right rested on Malvern Hill, just north of the James River. In that way, the Confederates could still cover the approaches to Richmond while keeping a close watch on the enemy's activities to the south.

On June 15, Union cavalry, plus Smith's entire XVIII Corps, which had crossed over the James that very morning, moved against Petersburg. Brushing aside token resistance a few miles from the city, the Federals advanced to within easy striking distance of the main defenses. At 7:00 p.m., they attacked, and within an hour's time had taken possession of more than a mile of the Southern lines. Petersburg was close to falling.

The attack, however, was not followed up. Smith decided to wait for Hancock, who was by then moving to this support. Later, Smith decided to postpone the assault until morning.

That night, Hoke's division took its place along the Petersburg defenses. Still fearing that his present force was hardly sufficient to stop the enemy, Beauregard stripped the Howlett line, which guarded the railroad between Petersburg and Richmond, of its defenders. That left Butler's army, which was then occupying a position opposite that line, virtually unopposed. Lee reacted to Beauregard's latest move by sending two of Anderson's divisions across the James to preserve the Howlett Line, which the enemy would have certainly overrun before help arrived.

On June 16 and 17, the reinforced, though still badly outnumbered Beauregard, barely held his own against a number of disjointed and partially successful attacks. In fact, the Confederate center had, in fact, been pierced late on the 17th, but a counterattack plugged the gap in the line. After dark, Beauregard pulled his troops back to a new defensive line nearer the city.

By early morning of June 18, Lee was finally convinced that Meade's entire army had been shifted to the south. He responded by ordering the last of Anderson's divisions and Hill's entire corps to Petersburg. At the same time, Cutshaw's and Hardaway's battalions, each with their detachments from the Jeff Davis Artillery, were held north of the James for the purpose of patrolling the river. Carter was to direct their movements.

That same day, the enemy launched a general assault against Petersburg's outer works, only to find them already abandoned. Later, a thrust, directed against the newly constructed line closer to the city, was repulsed with heavy loss. For the present, the crisis on the South side had passed. Petersburg was safe.

Meanwhile, by the 17th of June, Early, and much of his force, had reached Lynchburg. The men of the Second Corps and those belonging to Breckinridge had then occupied strong positions beyond the two and prepared to meet Hunter's army which had already made its appearance. That day, the only significant action was between the opposing artillery. Early wanted to assume the offensive, but the rest of his force had not yet come up by rail, forcing him to hold his ground.

On June 18, a few minor assaults were beaten back by Early, who still was awaiting the arrival of the remainder of his corps. Finally, by days end, all the Second Corps' infantry was on hand. An attack was scheduled by Early for the 19th. That night, however, Hunter began a rapid withdrawal from the area.

At first light, the Confederates moved in pursuit of the enemy, but only succeeded in catching and skirmishing with Hunter's rear guard. The Federals got away virtually unscathed, but the threat to Lynchburg and its connecting railroads, had been effectively neutralized. Grant's attempts to get at and destroy the rail lines upon which not only Lee, but the Southern Capital itself depended for supplies, had been thwarted.

Meanwhile, back along the north bank of the James River, the Alabamians and their respective batteries had commenced a tour of duty not unlike what they had experienced prior to the battle of Fredericksburg. It was then that they had used their guns to drive off Yankee vessels. Now, as then, the artillerists had been given the job of trying to interrupt, if not stop altogether, enemy boat traffic on the James. At the same time, they were to keep watch for any Federal troop movements along the river.

For the men formerly attached to Reese's Alabama battery, that kind of field service, regardless of its contribution to Lee's overall defensive strategy, could hardly compare to those other assignments normally given the light artillery. Though the Alabamians would no doubt make the best of their present situation, they were to regret more and more the position into which the fates had placed them.

 HAPTER XIV

FROM ONE THEATER OF OPERATIONS TO ANOTHER

PART I - MUCH ACTION ON THE NORTHSIDE

The job of patrolling the James River promised to be an undertaking filled with a host of new adventures for the men from Reese's battery. Even so, that type of duty did not, as it turned out, ease the feelings of dissatisfaction felt by the artillerists. There seemed little hope of the Jeff Davis Artillery regaining its former status within the Second Corps, that is not to say, however, that efforts were not being made to bring the company back together. On June 22, Private Abraham Adams, then attached to Fry's battery, wrote Governor Thomas H. Watts of Alabama proposing just such a reorganization. As Adams wrote:

> I have the honor in behalf of the "Jeff Davis" Artillery to solicit your aid and influence in obtaining a transfer for said company to the local defense of either Selma, Mobile or any place your excellency's judgment may suggest.
>
> In the recent sanguinary battles in defense of our capitol, said company has had the misfortune to loose its commissioned officers and guns.
>
> While the exigencies of the service demanded its men to fill the depleted ranks of other companies and battalions, they cheerfully submitted to dismemberment and being scattered throughout the corps; confidently expecting to be reassembled in the organic form of a company of artillery. But owing to the superabundance of artillery in the corps, it is

currently rumored in official circles that reorganization is hardly probable....

During the three long, bloody years in which said company has been anxiously toiling and battling, it has offered up from its ranks some of Alabama's noblest and bravest sons as sacrifices upon scores of our country's reeling alters: and, is still willing to struggle and suffer on through an indefinite period of years to come, in defiance of the high and holy principles of political right and religious freedom in the corporate capacity of a company. But for its members to be segregated and scattered, to become absorbed in other companies, to the permanent destruction of its personal identity in the far famed army of northern Virginia; and its name to be obliterated from its brilliant records which it has never stained by a single act of cowardice, or acted in any way to tarnish the burnished and shining glories of its noble state, is doing it a moral and practical wrong which will naturally tend to engender a demoralizing influence whereby a majority may be rendered indifferent, and many worthless as soldiers. Our great and wise representatives in order to avoid these baleful consequences, and in their anxious solicitude to promote the general good and comfort of the toil-worn soldier have provided the legal means by which they may be relieved from the embarrassing and unpleasant association of strangers and foreign companies. After three years battling amid the dangers, sufferings and privation of a foreign cl___, to be transferred to serve amid the scenes of childhood, and around the homes of their nativity, would be a grateful respite from the toils of war; infusing a moral courage and inflexible determination in battle, complete with their acquired skill in the use of sponge-staff, and small proficiency in the science of gunnery, would exert an influence upon the raw material now garrisoning either of the above mentioned places, that would be highly beneficial. Thus the shattered fragments of this company might be able in these dual functions to serve those liberal and generous patriots of Alabama who furnished their horses, harness, equipments and other outfits at the breaking out of the war.

If the above mentioned reasons should meet with the concurrence of your excellency's good judgement, it would

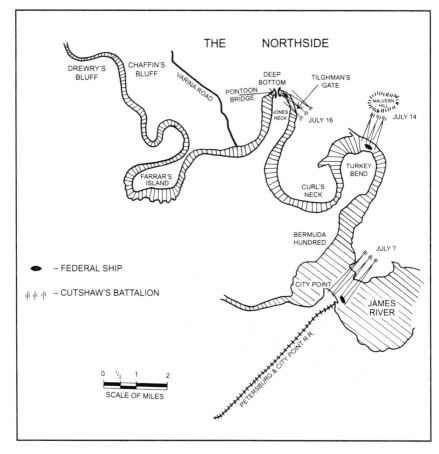

PATROLLING THE JAMES RIVER

Recreated from Plate LXXVII-3 of The Official Military Atlas of the Civil War.

be highly gratifying to the remaining eighty odd members of this veteran company.[1]

Watts, however, felt it would not be appropriate for him to ask for the transfer on behalf of the members of the Jeff Davis Artillery. In Watts' own words, "It would be interfering with matters over which I have no control."[2] He referred the matter to the proper military authorities, but unfortunately, there is no record of anything ever coming of the request made by Private Adams.

In the days that followed, enemy activity along the James River kept Carter's gunners busy, but the Confederate artillery proved ineffective in stopping Federal shipping.

During the first days of July, the enemy had occupied the area known as Deep Bottom, opposite Jones' Neck, on the north side of the James River. There, the Yankees had also constructed a pontoon bridge much to the chagrin of Lee. On July 6, he sent a message to Ewell, who had since been given command of the Richmond defenses, expressing his dissatisfaction with the situation along the river. In his correspondence, Lee stated, "I do not like the continuance of the enemy on the north side of James River and the maintenance of the pontoon bridge at Deep Bottom.... I had hoped that Colonel Carter would have been able to have annoyed, if not injured, his transports on the river,....Please see if anything can be done to drive the enemy from the north bank and interrupt his communications, & c."[3] In his message to Ewell, Lee also suggested that a special battery be organized for use against the enemy's transports.

Before three days had passed, Carter had placed a detachment of his artillery near Deep Bottom. According to Ewell, Carter's gunners subsequently "...drove off a gun-boat of the enemy, bringing a monitor to take its place, but owing to distance and limited field of fire, could not stop the navigation."[4]

Then, on July 13, Carter moved Cutshaw's battalion to Walker's Farm on the James River. By late afternoon of that same day, Cutshaw's command was in position. The battalion was armed with five Napoleons, three 3-inch Rifles (one of which was the one surviving gun of the Jeff Davis Artillery), four 20 pounder Parrotts and one Whitworth gun from Hardaway's battalion.

At 5:30 p.m., the Confederate gunners began firing on two enemy vessels moving along the river. One ship was hit repeatedly, while the other was forced to turn around and head back upriver.

The following day, "...the Whitworth gun was posted on Malvern Hill and drove off the picket gun-boat opposite Turkey Island House."[5]

On July 16, the four 20 pounder Parrotts of the Rockbridge Artillery were placed at Tilghman's Gate in order to bombard the enemy's camp and pontoon bridge, as well as a Federal gunboat, then located at Deep Bottom. The attack proved successful, and according to Carter, "The gun-boat was struck three times before it retired under the bank of the river....The camp was put in great commotion by the shelling....The pontoon bridge was fired at several times,..."[6]

The attack on Deep Bottom was followed some time later by another aimed at the Federal base at City Point.[7] Once in position, Cutshaw's gunners began the action by firing upon a Yankee transport. The ship was hit several times and was forced to return to its landing. Next, the gunners turned their attention towards a Federal camp located on the opposite side of the river. The three 3-inch Rifles of Fry's Orange County battery shot at the encampment, but they failed to reach their target. The camp was too far away. It was then that the Whitworth gun joined the action. Immediately, the superior range and accuracy of that piece began to tell. As Purifoy remembered, "...the Whitworth threw its shots into their [the inhabitants of the camp] midst. These produced a perfect stampede. We would see the dust stirred up, showing that a considerable commotion was going on."[8] Soon thereafter, several Federal gunboats made their appearance, forcing the artillerists to pull back out of range.

Towards the end of July, Grant decided to attempt another raid on the Virginia Central Railroad. As before, Sheridan's cavalry was selected for the mission. This time, however, the foray against the railroad would be covered by a simultaneous movement aimed at Richmond's outer defenses, and in particular, Chaffin's Bluff, where the Federals hoped to establish a foothold and block Lee's attempts to send reinforcements to the Northside. That diversionary attack, designed to catch Lee by surprise, was to be carried out by a large force consisting of both infantry and artillery, which was to be assembled at Jones' Neck.

Unknown to Grant, however, was the fact that the increased activity near the crossing site had not gone unnoticed. Even before the movement got underway, Lee knew about the enemy buildup. He responded on July 23 by ordering Kershaw's division of Anderson's Corps back across the James River.

Three days later, twenty-thousand infantry belonging to Hancock's II Corps, four batteries and all of Sheridan's cavalry, conducted a night crossing, using the pontoon bridge situated at Deep Bottom. Hay and other materials had been spread over the bridge to muffle any noise.

At dawn on the 27th, the Federals began their advance against Richmond's outer defenses. Opposing the enemy, and occupying a line of works which "...ran along the edge of a wooded crest covering the New Market and Malvern Hill road,"[9] were Carter's two battalions, supported by Kershaw's division under the direction of Anderson himself.

The enemy attacked, and before long had succeeded in flanking Kershaw. The Confederate infantry withdrew rapidly, exposing the four guns of the Rockbridge artillery. Its gunners continued to resist, but soon their position was overrun. The four guns were captured, and the Yankees pressed forward in pursuit of the withdrawing Confederates.

Despite his early success, Hancock quickly realized that both his and Sheridan's missions were not to be so easily accomplished. A large number of Confederate troops were obviously already on the Northside, and "...as all chances of surprising the enemy had passed it was a question whether General Sheridan's cavalry should attempt to break through the enemy's lines for the purpose of making a raid as had been contemplated, or whether the cavalry should wait until the infantry advanced farther."[10]

While the alternatives were being weighed, Hancock's infantry continued to push ahead. They soon, however, came to a halt in the vicinity of Bailey's Creek. Just beyond the stream, they had discovered a second line of well-fortified works. Any plans of attack were cancelled, and the balance of the day was marked by heavy skirmishing along the opposing lines.

The following morning, the Confederate forces took the offensive, with Kershaw attacking the position being occupied by Sheridan's cavalry. At the outset, the Southern infantry was successful in driving the enemy, but the Yankee horsemen regrouped and pushed back the attackers. For the rest of the day there was more skirmishing, but no serious movement on the part of either side.

That night, Major General William H. F. Lee's cavalry, Poague's artillery battalion, Captain Nathan Penick's Pittsylvania Battery and Heth's division of the Third Corps came up. Lee had sent them to the support of the troops already on the Northside. The next day, Major General Charles W. Field's Division, of the First Corps, was to come up as well.

On July 29, there was more demonstrating along the lines, but no attack took place. Then late in the afternoon, orders from Union

Headquarters directed that Hancock withdraw back across the river after dark. The II Corps was to support an attack to be launched by Burnside's IX Corps against the Petersburg defenses the following day.

Just after nightfall, the Federals began their withdrawal as instructed. For the present, the danger to the Virginia Central Railroad, and the Capital itself, had passed.

Even as Hancock's Corps was slipping back across the James, final preparations were being made for a pre-dawn attack against a section of the Southern works known as Elliott's Salient. The Federal assault was to follow immediately on the heels of a below ground explosion, originating from the end of a tunnel dug beneath the Confederate works, which was expected to blow a huge gap in Lee's lines.

At about a quarter to five on the morning of July 30, after a delay caused by a faulty fuse, an enormous blast shook the ground. Men, guns, carriages and timber were blown skyward. A portion of Captain Richard G. Pegram's Petersburg Battery, occupying the salient at the time, had ceased to exist. The Federal artillery opened, and the assault of the IX Corps began.

The lead brigades advanced, but what was to have been an attack across a wide front quickly became an advance through a narrow space, because of a failure to clear the field of defensive obstacles which included "...a log-and-dirt trench eight feet deep, with a heavy barrier of abatis out in front."[11] The Federals, as a result, moved straight ahead right into the crater where they became mixed up and the attack lost momentum. Not until another division moved around the disorganized mass of infantrymen did the attack then show a promise of success. By then, however, Southern troops were advancing to plug the gap in their line. Those troops crowded in the crater became easy targets, and it was just a matter of time before they were driven back with heavy losses. Following that disastrous assault, Grant was content to conduct siege operations against Petersburg. As it turned out, though, that period of active campaigning had also seen a change of personnel within the old artillery organization.

In the weeks following the Wilderness Campaign, five more men signed up for duty with the Jeff Davis Artillery. They included: John W. Blackmon, J. L. Cauley, S. J. Lee, Henry Smoke and Rufus P. Stuart. By the second week of June, those new recruits had joined Fry's command on the Northside,[12] and most no doubt had participated in some of the fights along the James River. For Privates Smoke and Blackmon, however, their new career in the military had hardly begun in an auspicious manner. Early on, those two men had become sick and had already spent weeks in the hospital. It was actually five months before Blackmon would again be fit for active service. By July 1, Smoke had resumed his duties, but, he was destined to return to the hospital for an extended period of time before the summer was over.[13]

Then on July 25, Private Thomas Glaze was discharged because he was too old. On November 7, 1863, Glaze had enlisted at the age of forty-seven, two years older than the limit set by the conscription laws. About eight months had passed since his illegal enrollment into the service, and why his age had suddenly become an issue is unclear. Whatever the reason for the disclosure, the fact remained that the Jeff Davis Artillery had lost the services of another man for the rest of the War.

For the Alabamians serving with Fry's command, the business of patrolling the James River soon came to an end. In fact, before August was a week old, Lee had decided to send Major Cutshaw's battalion to Early, whose Army of the Valley had been not only operating with great effectiveness in the western part of the State, but in enemy territory as well.

On July 11, after pushing aside a Union force at the Monocacy River, Early had brought his army to the outskirts of Washington. An attack had been planned by him for the following morning, but the city's de-fenders had received heavy reinforcements from Meade's army, mak-ing, as it turned out, such an assault impracticable. The night of July 13 Early had withdrawn his forces back towards Virginia.

Once the Army of the Valley was back in the Dominion State, the Federal forces in that region, had begun to move against him. During the last two weeks of July, a number of minor engagements took place in the Valley.

On July 30, the Confederate cavalry had rode into Chambersburg, Pennsylvania. After a demand for $100,000 in gold had been refused by the city officials, the gray troopers had set its business district on fire.

Within four days of the burning of Chambersburg, Lee had received reports that Federal troops were being loaded on to transports at City Point. Those forces, he believed, were being sent against Early, who as a result, would soon be badly outnumbered. Two days later, Lee had ordered Kershaw's division, Fitzhugh Lee's cavalry and Cutshaw's bat-talion, under the command of Lieutenant General Anderson, west to cooperate with Early.

For the men of Reese's command, that new assignment would mean a return to an area with which most were quite familiar. During the two invasions of the North, it had been there that the Jeff Davis Artillery had been involved in numerous engagements. Then, the battles had been fought to either clear the way for a Southern advance, as at Martinsburg in June of 1863, or to block a Federal force bent on the destruction of Lee's army, as when Meade had pursued the Confederates into Virginia after Gettysburg. This time, however, the Alabamians would be endeavoring to help defend the Shenandoah Valley, an area upon which the main army depended heavily for supplies.

On the same day that Lee ordered Anderson to the Valley, Sheridan arrived at Monocacy Junction to assume command of the forces being concentrated there, for use against Early. Sheridan's army, then more than 30,000 strong, was also to render the Valley useless to the Confederates. Additional reinforcements were also moving to join him, and by all estimates, Sheridan's force would soon total some 48,000 men. Early, on the other hand, even with the addition of Anderson, would still have just under half that number of effectives available to him. Against such odds, he would certainly be hard pressed to keep Sheridan from carrying out his destructive mission in the Valley.

PART II - A MONTH SPENT PROTECTING 'THE VALLEY'

By August 11, the Alabamians accompanying Anderson's command, which again included Kershaw's division, Fitzhugh Lee's cavalry and Cutshaw's artillery battalion, were well on their way to the Shenandoah Valley. Leaving Mitchell's Station on the 12th, they continued to move west, and two days later reached Front Royal. From that location, adjacent to the south fork of the Shenandoah River and just west of the Blue Ridge Mountains, Anderson was in a position from which he could not only guard the Luray Valley, but also be of assistance to Early's army, located to the west near Berryville.

For the next several weeks, Anderson cooperated with the Army of the Valley by conducting maneuvers designed to confuse the enemy and give them a false impression of Confederate strength. During that time, there were a number of engagements with the Federals.

On August 16, Anderson sent a detachment, including Cutshaw's artillery, to the vicinity of Cedarville, in order to seize Guard Hill, a location from which they could cover a nearby crossing site along the Shenandoah River. There, the Confederates encountered the enemy's cavalry, which after a sharp fight, they succeeded in driving back. The next day found Anderson over the river and in pursuit of the Federals on the Winchester Pike. At the same time, it was noted that, "The enemy retired, burning the grain, barns, and grass as he marched."[1]

Before another week had passed, Anderson was pushing for Charlestown, along the old Charlestown Road. When about six miles from Summit Point, he encountered Federal cavalry. It was forced back, but, at the same time, succeeded in slowing Anderson's advance enough so that he could not join with Early in an attack, initiated by the latter, against Sheridan. That night, August 21, the Confederates encamped at Summit Point.

Sheridan subsequently retired to Halltown. The Southern forces pursued him, and a few days thereafter, Anderson was left to confront the Federals while Early attempted a flanking maneuver aimed at Sheridan's rear. During that operation, Early succeeded in driving some Yankee cavalry, but that was all that was accomplished. As the month of August came to a close, Early was back at Winchester.

To date, Sheridan had not made use of his superior force against Early and Anderson, and at times had even seemed overcautious. That was because Grant believed that the entire First Corps had reinforced Early, giving him a force nearly as strong as Sheridan's. Later, when he learned that only one division had gone west, Grant told Sheridan to still exercise caution until Meade's army could exert enough pressure on the Richmond-Petersburg line to cause a return of the troops Lee had sent to assist Early.

By that time, Meade's army had conducted offensive operations against both the Northside and the Weldon Railroad, south of Petersburg. Initially, on August 14, Hancock's Corps had again assaulted the Richmond defenses, only to be stopped with heavy loss. Hancock was then held north of the James, where Lee had already concentrated his forces, while Warren moved a against the lightly defended Weldon Railroad. On August 18, he succeeded in getting possession of the railway at Globe Tavern and then pushed northward destroying the tracks, until attacks by first Beauregard, then A. P. Hill, halted his progress. The Yankees had cut an important supply line. Lee, who was soon forced to extend his lines to counter a similar movement made by the enemy, decided to recall Kershaw and Cutshaw in order to strengthen his position. On September 15, that force, led by Anderson, began its trek eastward.

Prior to being recalled, the Alabamians attached to Fry's battery had seen a good deal of action against the enemy. Even so, the morale of those artillerists, and their comrades on the Northside, was not as it had been earlier in the War, because the dissolution of the old command was still a source of continuing dissatisfaction. As stated by Sergeant Columbus W. McCrary, "The rolls at this date will show the number of men still attached to this command to be sufficient to form a full Battery and will exhibit the injustice of dividing and apportioning men who have conducted themselves so gallantly into + for the benefit of organizations from another state."[2]

The latter part of the summer had also seen the departure of Second Lieutenant John Mitchell. He had been with the Jeff Davis Artillery since July of 1861 and for the past year and a half, had been trying without success to have the War Department recognize his rank. In August, Mitchell's military career abruptly came to an end when he received notification from the War Department that he had been dropped from the rolls.[3] As a result of that action, the Jeff Davis Artillery had lost the closest thing to a commissioned officer it had had since the disaster at Spotsylvania.

As unfortunate a development as the discharge of John Mitchell might have been, that was not, as it turned out, the worst of the news concerning the battery's personnel. During the last days of August, two of its members died of illness. Those latest victims of disease had been

Privates Z. C. Canterberry and G. F. Smart. Both men had enlisted in the Fall of 1863, and though no record has been found indicating when they first became ill, it is known that they spent their last days in a Richmond hospital.

By that time, illness had also robbed Early of the services of Long, his chief of artillery. Long had been first stricken in mid-August and had temporarily relinquished his post to Lieutenant Colonel William Nelson. Then later, when it became increasingly evident that Long would not soon be in any condition to resume his duties, a more permanent replacement for him had been sought by Early. Colonel Thomas H. Carter had been summoned from the Northside, and on September 9, had succeeded Long as Early's chief of artillery.

With Carter a week in his new position, the Alabamians found themselves pressing on in an easterly direction with the rest of Cutshaw's battalion. Even as Anderson's force was increasing the distance between itself and Early, plans were being finalized at Harpers Ferry, where Grant had just arrived for a consultation with Sheridan, for a movement up the Shenandoah Valley.

On September 19, Sheridan advanced towards Winchester. Just east of that town, and some distance from the rest of Early's army, which was presently spread out to the north in such a way as to confuse the enemy as to its strength, was posted Major General S. Dodson Ramseur's lone division. Sheridan planned to attack Ramseur, then turn on and destroy the rest of Early's army.

As Sheridan advanced, Early discerned his designs and immediately prepared his own forces for the attack. Ramseur was placed in line of battle, while Gordon and Rodes moved up to occupy ground on his left.

The Union attack was two pronged, with an assault on Ramseur's position, as well as a flank maneuver aimed at the Southern left. Ramseur's line held, while Gordon and Rodes advanced against the Federals on the left. After a sharp fight, they succeeded in driving the Yankees back. During that action, however, Rodes had been mortally wounded.

After a lull in the action, Sheridan again advanced, that time forcing the cavalry, located on the left, to retire. That attack was stopped by Breckinridge, who had since come up. Soon thereafter, Early pulled back to a new position nearer the town. The fighting continued, with Early later ordering a general withdrawal when he received word that his right was being turned. The report was in error, but it was too late to stop his army's retrograde movement which continued, except for a temporary halt beyond the town, until the Confederates reached Fisher's Hill, some twenty miles from Winchester.

The fight of September 19, called Third Winchester, had cost Early more than 4,500 men or about forty percent of his effective force. Lost forever were the services of Major General Robert E. Rodes, to whose division the Jeff Davis Artillery had been attached during the campaigns of 1863. Carter had also been wounded, and while he recuperated, his place was taken by Nelson.

Once at Fisher's Hill, Breckinridge's command was detached from the Army of the Valley for duty to the southwest. At the same time though, Early was assured by Lee that Kershaw's division, Cutshaw's artillery, with its detachment of Alabamians, and more cavalry would soon be on their way to join him. Those additional troops could not arrive too soon, for already on September 20, Sheridan had begun massing his forces opposite the Confederate works on Fisher's Hill.

PART III - YET ANOTHER TRANSFER FOLLOWING MORE ACTION IN THE EAST AND TO THE WEST

Even as Early was preparing for the next confrontation with Sheridan, there was unwelcome news, concerning one of the Jeff Davis Artillery's own, from north of the James River. Private C. S. V. Jones, a member of the battery since March of 1862, was dead. On September 19 he had been killed in action at Fort Harrison, located along Richmond's outer defenses.

Less than ten days later, that same work, near where the nineteen remaining Alabamians of Griffin's battery were posted, was again targeted for an attack. Grant had decided to use Butler's forces for a strike against the defenses on the Northside. Butler ultimately decided to use the two corps of Major Generals Edward O. C. Ord and David B. Birney, the XVIII and II respectively,[1] plus Brigadier General August V. Kautz's cavalry, to attack Harrison and nearby Fort Gilmer. Both forts were of strategic importance because they covered the defenses located at Chaffin's Bluff. The assault was to take place early on the morning of September 29.

After crossing the James on the night of the 28th, Ord launched his attack against Fort Harrison as planned. The Federals encountered little opposition and succeeded in overrunning that position. Next was Fort Varina, where the members of the Jeff Davis Artillery were manning the guns. Private John F. Methvin recalled, "The negro troops charged our Fort Varina and in the charge came within 10 to 15 yards of our fort. With the aid we got from an enfilade, or cross fire, from the artillery guns at Fort Gilmer and Fort Fields on either side, we repulsed the negroes and they fled in confusion, leaving at least half their number dead on the ground."[2]

An hour or so later, the Yankees massed in the woods for an attack against Fort Gilmer, located to the left of the position occupied by the Alabamians. Methvin continued:

> ...we opened fire on them with solid shot and tore the line of cord wood down and killed many of the negroes with wood; they then charged Fort Gilmer and more than 1,000 of them reached the fort and fell into the ditch around the fort. From their conduct we thought they were partly drunk.

From the ditch many of them got on the shoulders of others and attempted to crawl into the fort, but our boys were standing with loaded guns and when one put his head above the ground he lost that head...

Our boys took shells and set them up on the breastworks, put a 15 second fuse in them, lit them off with a m..tch and rolled them off into the ditch among the negroes;...[3]

Ultimately, the Federals were forced to retire, with "...Griffin aiding materially in their repulse by firing canister into them at close range."[4] With the failure of the attack against Gilmer, the enemy concentrated their efforts on making preparations at Fort Harrison to meet the Southern counterattack, which was expected to occur at any time.[5]

On September 30, the Confederates launched fierce assaults in an effort to retake Fort Harrison. Lieutenant General Richard Anderson, who had returned from the Valley, commanded some 10,000 plus artillery, but failed in his efforts to dislodge the enemy.

The following day, there was no resumption of the offensive. Only the artillery was active. Having failed to retake Harrison, the Confederates proceeded to construct a new line of works to the rear of the fort.

As it turned out, the recent fighting on the Northside had not been the only important action to take place along the Richmond-Petersburg front. On September 29, while the attacks against the Capital defenses were in progress, Federal cavalry and two divisions each from the corps belonging to Warren and Major General John G. Parke, who had replaced Burnside following the failed attacked of July 30, had moved from Globe Tavern against the Boydton Plank Road and the Southside Railroad, the only two remaining supply routes leading into Petersburg. Should those vital lines be cut, the city would fall.

Some two miles from their starting point, and about halfway to the Boydton Plank Road, the Federals had met strong resistance, first from Hampton's cavalry, then from A. P. Hill's Corps. After suffering heavy casualties, they had abandoned its westward push. Still, even in defeat, the Union forces, by that movement, had successfully extended their lines a bit further to the west, and by doing so, had forced Lee to widen his own front.

With the conclusion of that latest Federal operation on the Southside, came a period of relative quiet along the Petersburg front. Action, however, continued on the Northside, with fighting taking place on both October 7 and 13. The earlier of the two engagements was the most noteworthy, with Lee's forces making an attempt to wrest part of the lost outer works from the enemy. The attack, as it turned out, was unsuccessful.

In the days that followed,[6] an important development having to do with the Alabamians attached to Griffin's battery, took place. As per the orders of Brigadier General E. Porter Alexander, Chief of Artillery of the First Corps, they were transferred to Captain James N. Lamkin's Battery of Colonel John C. Haskell's Mortar Battalion. Lamkin's command, also known as the Nelson Light Artillery, was armed with four Coehorn mortars. It had already seen action on the Southside, particularly on the day the mine was exploded outside Petersburg.

After the Yankees captured Fort Harrison, Lamkin had been moved by Alexander to the Northside, where he had taken up a position along the outer defenses. The mortar battery had then taken part in the counterattack against Harrison, in which it had been "...assigned the task of shelling the hostile works..."[7] Following that engagement, Lamkin had occupied an advanced position along the line, bearing on Fort Harrison.[8] That is where the nineteen former members of the Jeff Davis Alabama Artillery joined their new battery.

To the west meanwhile, Early had been exercising more caution than in previous months. That change in strategy, however, had not been due to a lack of boldness on Early's part, but was, in fact, more a result of the action at Fisher's Hill.

On September 22, just three days after the Army of the Valley had retreated from Winchester, Sheridan had attacked Early. In that battle, the Federals had succeeded in routing the defenders on the far left, then had forced the rapid withdrawal of the rest of Early's army from Fisher's Hill by increasing pressure all along the line. During the retreat twelve unsupported guns had to be abandoned.

Once having been driven from Fisher's Hill, the Confederates had retreated up the Valley until September 28, when they reached Waynesboro, a town located opposite Rockfish Gap, at the foot of the Blue Ridge Mountains. Sheridan had pursued Early as far as Mount Crawford, then had stopped to rest his army.

The Army of the Valley had suffered two disastrous defeats in less than a week, but Early was still as determined as ever to drive Sheridan from the Valley. Even then, he still wanted to return to the offensive.[9]

That kind of strategy was possible because of the arrival of assistance from the east. By that time, Early had already received most of his promised reinforcements. In fact, it had been on September 26 that both

Kershaw's division and Cutshaw's battalion had passed through Brown's Gap and joined Early's forces. That same day, Colonel Carter had also resumed active field duty, replacing Lieutenant Colonel Nelson.

Nine days later, Brigadier General Thomas L. Rosser's cavalry brigade had arrived in the Valley. With those reinforcements, the Army of the Valley was of sufficient strength to make things difficult for Sheridan.

Meanwhile, in the vicinity of Harrisonburg, Sheridan had made preparations aimed at resuming his own operations in western Virginia. He, at the time, was of the opinion that Early no longer posed a serious threat and had decided that Wright's VI Corps could be spared for use on the Petersburg front. Prior to the detaching of the VI Corps, however, Sheridan wanted to move back up the Valley in order to burn the crops and destroy anything else that might prove useful to the Southern forces.

On October 6, the Federal forces left the Harrisonburg area. As Sheridan moved north "...the cavalry was deployed across the Valley, burning, destroying, or taking away everything of value, or likely to become of value, to the enemy..."[10]

Early had pursued the enemy, with his cavalry leading the way. Several skirmishes had taken place between the mounted troops of each side. Then on October 9, Rosser had been routed, along with the cavalry commanded by Major General Lunsford L. Lomax, by their Federal counterparts. On that occasion, Brigadier General Alfred T. A. Torbert, who was the enemy's cavalry chief, had been ordered by Sheridan to "...whip the rebel cavalry or get whipped..."[11] Following that one-sided affair, the northward movements of both armies had continued.

On October 10, Sheridan's army had crossed Cedar Creek and gone into position along the stream's north bank. Two days later, Wright had begun his march towards Petersburg. Early, meanwhile, had reached the vicinity of Fisher's Hill. There, he had awaited the enemy's next move.

Shortly after the Southern army's arrival at Fisher's Hill, the Jeff Davis Artillery detachment, and the rest of Fry's battery, had been placed on picket duty on Hupp's Hill, just above the town of Strasburg. Sergeant James Norwood commanded the gun being served by the Alabamians.

The enemy, as it turned out, had been in close proximity, and the Jeff Davis Artillerists, who had been relaxing awaiting orders to prepare for action, suddenly became the targets of Federal sharpshooters.

For a time, the bullets had whizzed harmlessly past the men, but then "...that familiar 'chuck,' indicating that someone had been hit with a minnie ball, was heard,..."[12] Norwood, who had been sitting astride the trail of his gun had been struck. He had received a serious thigh wound and was subsequently carried from the field.

Norwood had also been wounded at the battle of Chancellorsville on May 2, 1863. Though he would recuperate from his latest wound during a several month stay in a hospital, he did not return to active service. According to Purifoy, "...he was ever afterward compelled to move about with crutches."[13]

On that day, October 13, Gordon's division and Brigadier General James Conner's Brigade of Kershaw's command had felt the brunt of a Union assault. Fry's battery had blasted away at the advancing enemy and was conspicuous in helping to repulse the Yankees, who suffered heavy loss.

Over the next several days, there had been no movement on the part of either side. By then, however, Sheridan, who had since been made aware of Early's reinforcements, had recalled Wright. On October 16, Sheridan was summoned to Washington for a strategy conference with Grant leaving Wright in command of his army, still at Cedar Creek.

Meanwhile, Early was running out of provisions, and since the nearby countryside was totally devoid of supplies, they could not remain where they were for very much longer. He had either to retreat to where stores could be readily procured, or to attack. Though outnumbered two to one, he decided to take the offensive.

CHAPTER XV

NEWS, BOTH BAD AND GOOD

PART I - A BOLD DESIGN, FINE EXECUTION, BUT THEN...CATASTROPHE

For the men who belonged to the Jeff Davis Artillery detachment of Fry's battery, October 18, the fifth day of picket duty on Hupp's Hill, proved uneventful. That night at roll call, however, they learned that Early had decided to attack the Federals on the north bank of Cedar Creek. At the same time, orders outlining the plan of battle, which had been scheduled for the following morning, were read to the men. That in itself was something of a surprise for the Alabamians.[1] Never before had they received advance information concerning an upcoming battle.

The plan of attack was fairly complex and would involve Early's entire army. That same night, Gordon, who was given command of three divisions of the Second Corps (his own, Pegram's and Ramseur's), was to move around to the right and march east, following the Shenandoah River's north fork, until he reached Bowman's Ford. There, Gordon was to halt until the signal was given to cross the river. Once on the other side, he was to move to a point next to the house of J. Cooley, which was near the Federal left, and prepare for the attack. Gordon's immediate objective was a farm known as Belle Grove, which Sheridan was thought to be using as his headquarters. One cavalry brigade, whose task was to capture Sheridan, would accompany the Second Corps.

While Gordon moved against the Federal left, Kershaw's division was to pass through Strasburg and proceed in a northerly direction to Bowman's Mill on Cedar Creek. Once there, Kershaw was to push across the stream and drive straight ahead into the Union left which Gordon was also attacking.

At the same time, Brigadier General Gabriel C. Wharton's Division was to advance up the Valley Pike and leave a sufficient force to guard the bridge crossing Cedar Creek, then move to the attack. Rosser, meanwhile, was to move against the cavalry located on the far left. The rest of the Southern cavalry, under Lomax, was to move around by the right and reach a point in the vicinity of Winchester, where it was to make contact with the retreating Yankees. Carter's artillery, in the meantime, would occupy Hupp's Hill, a position from which it could easily advance to support the offensive. The attack was to begin at 5:00 a.m., with Rosser beginning the action, followed by Gordon and Kershaw, in that order.

Just before first light on October 19, Gordon's divisions arrived at Bowman's Ford as planned. Even as they massed opposite the crossing, Kershaw's men were already pushing across Cedar Creek. Thus far, the Northern guns had been silent.

It was 5:00 a.m., and all at once, the sound of Rosser's cannon opening up on the left, as well as the crack of rifles to the right, could be heard. Before long, both Gordon and Kershaw were driving for the Union left, a position protected by a line of entrenchments and occupied by Major General George Crook's VIII Corps. Caught by surprise, the Yankees attempted to make a stand before the advancing gray lines, but it was of no use. In short order, the Confederates had overrun their position and forced a rapid withdrawal across the Valley Turnpike. Hundreds fell into Southern hands.

Having routed the VIII Corps, the Confederates pressed ahead toward the elevated ground to the right of the Turnpike which Major General William H. Emory's XIX Corps was holding. Though more prepared to meet the gray onslaught, it had no more success than Crook in checking it. By that time, Carter's massed batteries on Hupp's Hill, had also begun sending shot and shell into the Federal ranks. That barrage, combined with the volleys being delivered by both Gordon's and Kershaw's divisions, was too much for the XIX Corps. Emory's men broke for the rear, as brigade after brigade were routed by the Confederates.

In the meantime, Major General Horatio Wright's VI Corps had arrived on the field and taken up a position north of Belle Grove and west of the Turnpike. Before long, however, Wright, realizing that the collapse of the rest of the army had made the new line untenable, ordered his corps to withdraw to a more defensible position. That was done, but the persistent attacks of the Confederates soon succeeded in forcing two of Wright's three divisions from the field. The remaining force, that of Brigadier General George W. Getty, had also pulled back,

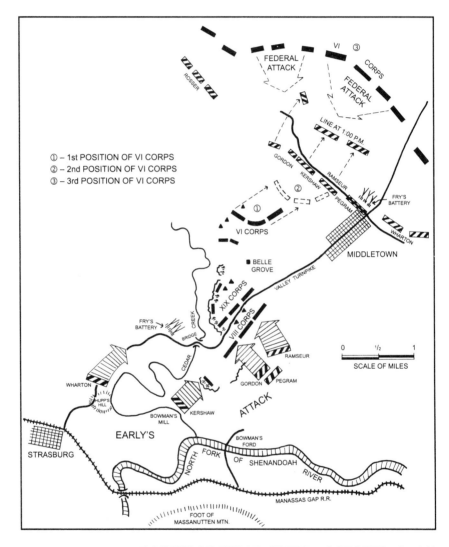

BATTLE OF CEDAR CREEK – OCTOBER 19, 1864

Recreated from Plate LXXXII-9 of <u>The Official Military Atlas of the Civil War</u>.

but to a strong position at the Middletown cemetery. There, it held on despite heavy assaults, and being bombarded by twenty-one guns of Carter's artillery, until it was flanked and forced to withdraw.[2] Beyond the town, Getty's division joined the rest of the already rallying Union army.

By then, Fry's battery had itself moved from its initial position south of Cedar Creek. Crossing the stream, the Orange County men and their detachment of Alabamians had followed the victorious infantry, advancing swiftly up the Turnpike as they did. Passing through the captured camps of the enemy, the battery had reached, then moved through Middletown, and had taken up a post immediately adjacent to the Valley Pike. Skirmishers had also been sent forward to guard against an attack.

It was just past 10:00 a.m., and already the Southern troops had succeeded in achieving what their commander considered to be a great victory.[3] Early's outnumbered Army of the Valley had driven three full Federal corps from the field with comparative ease. Though the Yankees were reforming north of Middletown, the advantage still lay with Early's forces, and it now remained for them to complete the destruction of Sheridan's army.

Gordon urged his commander to resume the offensive, but Early was, in fact, satisfied with the results already achieved and felt it was only a matter of time before the enemy retreated from his front.[4] Gordon also added that the Federal VI Corps would have to be driven from its present position, but Early stood by his decision. Scattered fighting continued, but there was no further movement on the part of either side.

By that time, however, some disconcerting news had reached Early concerning the situation to the rear of the Southern army's position. Indications were that a substantial number of his troops were involved in plundering the captured camps. According to Corporal John Purifoy, "The starved and hungry Confederates were not accustomed to see such rich booty as these captured camps presented, and the temptation to tarry and plunder them was so great..."[5] Early immediately dispatched members of his staff to the rear, to put an end to the looting and get the men back into line.

In the meantime, Yankee cavalry had massed opposite the Southern right, where, as it turned out, only a single brigade of mounted troops protected the flank. That was also of great concern to Early. And yet, nothing more than heavy skirmishing was to take place in that sector. The Federals were content to stay where they were, occupying the Union left, and holding the Valley Pike.

For the balance of the morning, the Southern forces exchanged shots with the enemy. During that time, however, there was no significant movement on the part of Sheridan's force. The eventual withdrawal, as predicted by Early, had still not taken place. Colonel Carter went to Early and told him that the men, puzzled by the delay in resuming the advance, were anxious to attack.[6] Early remained unmoved.

By midday, the enemy, in fact, was more determined than ever to hold on to its present position. Having taken advantage of Early's lack of aggressiveness, most of the men who had been routed from their posts along the Valley Pike, and sent reeling beyond Middletown, had rallied and joined the line of battle north of the town. That had come about largely because of the efforts of Sheridan, who had ridden back to join his army.

At about one o'clock, Early finally permitted Gordon to go forward in an attempt to drive the enemy from the ground it occupied beyond the town. The Confederates advanced, but they were unsuccessful in their efforts to dislodge the Federals. A lull in the action followed.

As the afternoon wore on, Early's subordinates, including Gordon, became more and more concerned about the possibility of a counterattack, something for which they were ill-prepared. As a result of the present arrangement of Early's forces, the southern left was somewhat exposed, and should an attack fall there, the results could prove disastrous. Early suggested that Gordon extend his flank and bring up more artillery in order to strengthen that part of the line. Accordingly, "...six of Cutshaw's pieces and two of Jones' were posted to guard the interval between Gordon and Rosser."[7] Even with those measures, however, the troops occupying the left were still spread very thin.

About 4:00 p.m., the entire Federal line advanced and before long had launched an oblique attack against the Southern left and center. The two left brigades of Gordon's division became separated, and despite gallant efforts to hold on, the men quickly realized that their situation was hopeless and began to withdraw. Seeing the collapse of the line on their left, both Kershaw's and Ramseur's divisions began to abandon their positions along the center. Carter's gunners, however, did not budge, and did their utmost to cover the withdrawal. To the right, meanwhile, both Pegram and Wharton also continued to hold their ground.

Already by that time, the Federal cavalry had advanced against the gray line on both sides of the Pike, including the ground being covered

by the guns of Fry's battery. The Confederates, however, had little difficulty in repulsing the Yankees. Purifoy remembered that, "It was fun
to drive them back, and kill their horses and men. Great lanes were
plowed through their ranks and soon the charging column was in the
utmost confusion and retreating to the cover from whence they had
come."[8] The artillerymen had had an easy time of it, but the fun was
soon to end.

With great difficulty, the Southern officers back on the left and center of the line, soon succeeded in halting the retrograde movement of
portions of the infantry. By that time, however, the men were already
badly shaken, and it took only the loss of a few of those officers, including Dodson Ramseur, who fell mortally wounded to cause a resumption of the retreat. Before long, Pegram and Wharton, both of whom
still held their respective positions on the right, were also ordered by
Early to withdraw.

Carter's artillery held its position along the disintegrating line as
long as practicable. Then, when the danger of capture by the advancing foe became too great, Early ordered it to limber up and start for the
rear. Fry's men began to move back down the Valley Turnpike in a de-
liberate fashion. John Purifoy remembered, "...we could see the entire
line of infantry to our left retiring in disorder."[9]

As they moved towards the rear, the artillerymen begged the retreating infantry to stop and make a stand against the pursuing enemy,
but all efforts aimed at checking the withdrawal failed.

On occasion, the battery unlimbered and fired several rounds at
the Union troops, but even those momentary halts were not enough of
an inducement for the infantrymen to stop and support the guns. "These
men who had faced the enemy on a half hundred battle fields, and had
snatched victory from a large majority, were completely demoralized,
and no amount of begging and persuasion could induce them to face
about and show their old time courage."[10]

Not long after the Jeff Davis Artillery detachment started back down
the Valley Pike, a projectile felled one of the Alabamians' wheel horses,
forcing the limber to a halt. With the Federals in pursuit, there was no
time to procure another horse. Unless something was done to get under way, all would be lost.

Quickly, Private Joseph Blankinship stepped in and took matters
into his own hands. He unhitched the dead horse, took over the vacated wheel position and told the drivers of the limber to continue on.
Blankinship assisted in moving the gun for some distance, and by his
action, saved the piece from capture.

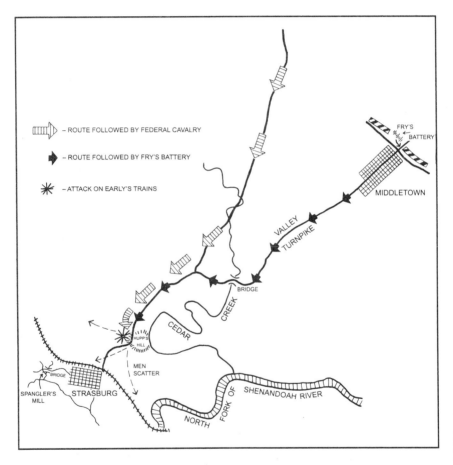

WITHDRAWAL OF FRY'S BATTERY – OCTOBER 19, 1864

Recreated from Plate LXXXII-9 of The Official Military Atlas of the Civil War.

The Army of the Valley continued its rapid withdrawal, crossing Cedar Creek and moving south in the direction of Strasburg. All the while, Carter's gunners did their best to keep the pursuing enemy in check. Finally reaching the Creek crossing themselves, the artillerymen moved over to the far side of the stream without incident. It was now dusk, and though Early's army was retiring in disorder, it appeared that the Confederates had successfully escaped Sheridan's forces. That was hardly the case, because even as Carter's guns were rolling south towards Hupp's Hill, yet another catastrophe was about to befall the Army of the Valley.

Rosser's cavalry, which had held the far left of the line, had finally been compelled to relinquish its position. As they withdrew, Rosser's men had only limited success in slowing their mounted pursuers. The retrograde movement continued, with the result that the enemy was soon able to gain the Valley Turnpike just west of the Cedar Creek crossing. Just ahead, in the vicinity of Hupp's Hill, was the slow moving column containing many wagons and the bulk of the Southern artillery.

Spurring ahead in the darkness, the Federal horsemen soon reached the unsuspecting column. As reported by Brigadier General Pendleton, "...the enemy's cavalry charged the train on the right flank, and by their bugle blasts, cheers, horses' feet clattering, and pistol shots in the darkness, occasioned an incurable panic in the infantry, already seriously disorganized."[11] At the same time, part of the enemy force rode west to Spangler's Mill and destroyed the bridge located there, thereby cutting off the retreat of that portion of the train located between the Mill and Hupp's Hill.

Along the road, everything was confusion as the Yankees "...dashed along, killing horses and turning over ambulances, caissons, and c., stampeding the drivers,..."[12] Not having any muskets to defend themselves and their guns, the artillerymen pleaded desperately with the infantry for their rifles. The gunners' pleas, however, fell on deaf ears. The situation was hopeless, and they had to flee for their own safety. "The men were completely demoralized and fled to the mountains. Some waded the Shenandoah River to the left of the turnpike, others in darkness crossed the road the enemy had advanced on and ecaped to the west of the turnpike and along the old railroad track to Fishershill."[13]

The Federal cavalry captured forty-three pieces of artillery, including all the guns taken by the Confederates earlier in the day. At the same time, a number of ordnance wagons and medical vehicles also fell into its hands. In Early's own words, "...the rout was as thorough and disgraceful as ever happened to our army."[14]

At Hupp's Hill, Carter had witnessed the wrecking of a greater part of his artillery. He later commented, "One hundred men in an organized state, with muskets,... could have saved the train."[15]

For the Alabamians, the disaster on Hupp's Hill was like Spotsylvania all over again, with nearly one-third of the old command being captured by the enemy. The list of those taken prisoner included: Privates C. A. Cobb, James W. Cox, Henry Gayle, James A Parish, Asbury Payne, John B. Stuart, William R. Stewart, Ira Y. Traweek, John V. F. Walker and J. D. Watson. All would eventually be sent to Point Lookout Prison. Only J. D. Watson would fail to survive his confinement there.

That was the second time that Walker had fallen into enemy hands. This time, however, he would not have the good fortune of being able to escape from his captors, as he had at Spotsylvania, the previous May.

Not included among those captured on the evening of the 19th was Private J. J. Jones. According to company records, he had received a serious wound during the fighting in the vicinity of Cedar Creek. It is not known, however, if he was wounded on Hupp's Hill, or elsewhere.

The bad news for the Alabama detachment did not end there. During the assault on the artillery column, it had also lost its most prized possession, the 3-inch Rifled gun that had been with them since June of 1863. To further complicate matters, Fry's Virginians had also lost their two Napoleons during the retreat. The Orange County battery was now weaponless.

For the men from the Jeff Davis Artillery, it had certainly been an unforgettable day. An unexpected twist of fate had turned the glorious achievements of the morning, in which Fry's battery and its Alabamians had played an important role, into a humiliating defeat by evening for Early's Army of the Valley. Besides the enormous loss of artillery, the Confederates had sustained nearly 3,000 casualties although Union losses totalled just over 5,600.

It had indeed been a sad day for the Southern army, but there was nothing but praise from Early for the artillery of the Second Corps. In his own words,

> The artillery throughout, from first to last, in this as well as in all the actions I have had, behaved nobly, both officers and men, and not a piece of artillery had been lost by any fault of theirs. I attribute this good conduct on their part to the vast superiority of the officers. Colonel Carter and all his battalion commanders richly deserve promotion. They not only

fought their guns gallantly and efficiently, but they made the most strenuous efforts to rally the infantry.[16]

All through the night of October 19-20, the retrograde movement continued. At Fisher's Hill, Early attempted to reassemble his army to make a stand the next day, but it was no use. The retreating army continued to push on in a southerly direction.

That same night, a few men from the Alabama battery did meet with one another on Fisher's Hill but, after a brief interval, were ordered to keep moving. Some time after first light, on the morning of October 20, the artillerymen reached Woodstock. It was there that a sad sight met the eyes of Corporal Purifoy. "Looking forward along the turnpike the writer saw a moving mass of disorganized humanity."[17]

The retreat up the Valley continued. Sheridan's cavalry moved in pursuit of the Confederates, but Early's forces kept the horsemen at bay. That night, the defeated army finally reached New Market. There, the men made camp, and a semblance of organization returned as companies and regiments were reformed. Fry's command was itself pieced together, though it was more than a week before the remaining members of the company, who had fled to the mountains, reached the camp. While in New Market, horses and guns were resupplied to the artillery. It was there that the three guns lost by Fry's battery were replaced by two twelve pound Howitzers. For the next month or so, the Army of the Valley remained in the vicinity of New Market, moving through the Upper Shenandoah from time to time in search of forage.

PART II - THE GRAND EXODUS FROM ELMIRA

While the Army of the Valley was still at New Market, an event took place which provided a much needed lift to the members of the Alabama battery. The cause of the excitement in camp was the arrival of Sergeant John Fox Maull, Corporate George G. "Hickory" Jackson and Private William H. Templin of the Jeff Davis Artillery, who, just a few weeks before, had escaped from New York's Elmira Prison. Actually, it had been on the night of October 7 that ten prisoners of war had gained their freedom by way of a tunnel dug beneath the prison stockade. Two others from the Alabama battery, Privates John P. Putegnat and Washington B. Traweek, had also taken part in the escape.

The formulation of a plan of escape had, in fact, begun a short time after the transfer from Point Lookout Prison to Elmira, on August 15, of thirty-five members of Reese's command who had been captured at Spotsylvania. It was then that John Fox Maull and Frank Saurine, of the 3rd Alabama Infantry Regiment, had decided that the best way to gain

ELMIRA PRISON, ELMIRA, NEW YORK

Where many men from the Jeff Davis Artillery were imprisoned and from which seven tunnelled out on October 7, 1864.

(The Chemung County Historical Society, Elmira, New York)

their freedom was by digging a tunnel. Work on the tunnel had begun on August 24 from within a tent which was located some sixty feet from the stockade wall. A spade, "borrowed" from within the prison yard, had been used in order to start the hole, but it made so much noise that it was discarded in favor of a knife. From that point on, that was all that had been used to dig the tunnel.

The dirt taken from the initial shaft, and then the tunnel itself, had been carried out of the tent in small bags made from a shirt, and then had been dumped into the waters of a nearby sink. "These bags held about a pint. The man who carried the dirt wore a jacket and cape. The lining on the inside was slit, so two or three sacks of dirt could be stowed on each side and carried away without attracting notice."[1] Much care had to be taken to avoid being spotted by the guards or the spies that moved about the prison grounds.

The tunnel was just large enough for a man to crawl through. Initially, the only ventilation available to the men had been at the mouth of the tunnel, which though proving a handicap because it provided a limited amount of air, had at the same time ensured that the men below could work without being detected. Later, a hole poked through the ground using a ramrod, had provided more air to the tunnelers.

Still, their had been other problems which the diggers had been forced to overcome. Early on, the work had begun to sap the strength of the men. Fortunately, arrangements had soon been made with the "Sick Sergeant" J. P. Scruggs to obtain extra rations.[2] That did much to improve the condition of the workers, and had helped them see their way through to the conclusion of the project. At the same time, more men had been taken on to assist with the work.

The inability of the diggers to keep the tunnel going in the proper direction had also proved to be a problem. At one point, when they wanted to check on their progress, they had made an unhappy discovery. The tunnel, instead of moving directly towards the prison wall, was actually curving away from the stockade. As it turned out, the men had used their right hand to dig and had done so in a way that caused the tunnel to curve around to the right. The problem, however, was soon rectified.

On October 7, or approximately six weeks after the first spadeful of dirt had been removed from the tent, the tunnel had finally been completed. Just before four o'clock in the morning, Washington Traweek had broken through the surface outside of the stockade and disappeared into the darkness. The remaining nine men had followed immediately behind.

The first stage of the escape, as it turned out, had not been without its complications, for just across a road, located near where the break out had occurred, were a half-dozen soldiers gathered around a camp fire. Fortunately, all the escapees got past the Federals without being challenged.

Once having made their escape, all the men, save one, had moved off in groups of two or three. The three Alabamians who had eventually found their way to Early's army had been together since first light of the 7th. Their story, based upon a postwar account written by Sergeant Maull, follows:[3]

SERGEANT JOHN FOX MAULL

(Of Jeff Davis Artillery) and family, postwar view; he escaped from Elmira Prison on October 7, 1864. *(The Chemung County Historical Society, Elmira, New York)*

After having spent the first day following their escape on the side of the mountain which over-looked the prison, the three artillerists had begun their southward journey. Not long after starting out, the Alabamians, who had had little to eat over the past two days, came upon an apple orchard. Soon they had not only eaten their fill of the fruit, but had also stuffed their pockets full of the valuable foodstuff.

Some time later, the three men had come upon a house located not far from the five mile post south of Elmira. There, they had stopped and asked for something to eat. They had been told to come in, and even though these Confederates were deep in enemy territory, they had quickly found that the occupants of the house were, in fact, sympathetic to their cause. The following exchange, as remembered by

Maull, took place between the lady of the house and the escaped prisoners: "I bet you fellows are rebel prisoners that escaped last night." We told her she was mistaken. "I am sure of it," she said; "if I didn't think so, I wouldn't give you a mouthful of supper; I do wish every rebel prisoner would get away: I'm so sorry for them."[4]

Following that friendly encounter, the escapees had continued to move south. At one house, the men "captured" a pail, which was later used to cook whatever food was procured along the journey. From a nearby barn, the Alabamians took a buffalo robe. "We took it and cut parts of it off, and made gloves for each of us, and then I cut a hole in the middle and put my head through it. I have never repented taking it; it provided us lots of comfort."[5]

The men had eventually passed through Williamsport, Pennsylvania. Then after following the railroad for some distance, Maull and his companions had made camp. Near dawn of the following day, however, they had been forced to make a quick exit when a group of men had come looking for them.

The next night, they found a boat and traveled down the Susquehanna River towards Harrisburg. After a while, though, they abandoned the boat in favor of a nearby turnpike. In Maull's own words, "...we got so cold we could not stand it to sit still, so we pulled for the bank."[6]

Reaching Harrisburg, the Alabamians had not lingered, but instead had turned immediately towards Carlisle. On the way, an interesting incident took place, as Maull recalled; "It was about ten o'clock at night. We met a group of boys and girls. As they passed us one of the girls gave a jump, exclaiming 'See the Rebels!' One of the others said, 'Don't be silly, supposed they were Rebels sure enough!' – Little dreaming they had seen the real article, they passed on."[7]

By the following morning, the three reached Carlisle. There they had spent the entire day in the vicinity of the U.S. barracks. The next night, they had moved in the direction of Chambersburg. When nearing that town, they had come upon a large number of Federals and had to take great care so not to have their true identities discovered by the soldiers.

Then, after a few close calls with hunters below Chambersburg, the Alabamians, who were following in reverse the same route that the Southern army had used during the Gettysburg Campaign, reached Hagerstown, Maryland. After a short respite at that place, the three men had travelled to Williamsport where they had waded across the Potomac.

The next stop had been near Falling Waters, the exact spot where Lee's retreating army had crossed the Potomac after Gettysburg, a crossing where an endless stream of enemy traffic was in evidence. After moving from the bridge site, the by now exhausted escapees had determined that they would attempt to pass through, rather than go around, Martinsburg, a town crawling with Yankees.

After encountering guards on several streets, the Alabamians had made good their escape. They found their way to the Winchester Pike, but had soon run into trouble.

> ...Near the big spring we ran into a picket. We had noticed fires along the pike in several places, which we took to be picket fires, and had gone around them, but this time we made too small a circuit, and on coming back to the pike we run right on to him. He cried "Halt!" but we did not stop. He then raised his rifle and fired. The cap exploded but did not fire the charge, and we ran. Soon we heard a great commotion. Orders were shouted, and the cavalry horses' hoofs began to ring on the pike. The pike was getting too warm for us, so we made for the mountain.[8]

That night, the Alabamians had gotten lost, but had been able to get back on the right road the following morning, thanks to a young couple who they had come upon in a nearby farm house. Sympathetic to the Southern cause, they recommended that the three escapees head for the house owned by a man named Webster, who could provide them with accommodations and further assist them on their journey.

At Webster's, the Alabamians received directions to the house of a man named Kelso, who could provide them with assistance in getting back to the Southern lines. Four days had been needed to reach Kelso's house, which was some hundred miles away, but once there, Maull and his companions were glad they had taken Webster's advice. Kelso had connections with numerous Confederate sympathizers, and within a couple of days had made arrangements for the safe passage of the three through the neighboring countryside.

Not long thereafter, the travellers had reached Brigadier General John D. Imboden's headquarters. He, as it turned out, had learned of their movements and had been expecting them. Two days later, Maull, Jackson and Templin were directed to Gordon's headquarters and reunited with what still remained of their old command. As Hickory Jackson recalled, "All the boys were as glad to see us as we were to meet them again."[9]

The day after the three men rejoined the army, they reported to Early, who gave them all thirty day furloughs "...in consideration of our escape and prompt return to our command."[10] Both Jackson and Templin later returned to the service and saw action with their old batterymates. Maull was assigned to duty with Hardaway's battalion.

By the time the three Alabamians had reached camp, the other two members of the Jeff Davis Artillery who had escaped from Elmira had also experienced their share of adventure while pursuing the road to freedom. Washington Traweek, for one, had departed the stockade in the company of J. W. Crawford, of the 6th Virginia Cavalry.

After eluding the soldiers outside the stockade, Traweek and Crawford had crossed the Chemung River, then had climbed to the top of a hill south of the prison. It was then time for roll call and Traweek remembered, "With a little spyglass we looked down on

PRIVATE WASHINGTON B. TRAWEEK

(Of Jeff Davis Artillery) postwar view; he escaped from Elmira Prison on October 7, 1864.

(The Chemung County Historical Society, Elmira, New York)

the confusion which was created when they missed us. We could also see the cavalry rushing around through the valley in search of us."[11]

Both men then followed the Williamsport and Elmira Railroad until they reached the west branch of the Susquehanna River near Williamsport, Pennsylvania. Stealing a boat, they floated down the river for an entire day before heading for shore. After that, the escapees had left the river and moved up into the nearby mountains. In a village that was soon encountered, Traweek and Crawford entered a house and took two suits of clothing and a pepperbox pistol. Both men had then discarded their Confederate uniforms, donned their newly found clothes, and proceeded to borrow a horse and buggy which they drove "...until the horse gave out."[12]

After that, the two men had shared a couple of different horses, as well as another buggy, all of which they had procured during their southward journey. As they moved through enemy territory, Traweek and Crawford had had several close calls, not only with the citizenry, but with some soldiers as well. On one particular occasion, Traweek remembered, "We 'touched' another quiet Yankee farmer for two horses and a buggy, which took us twenty-five miles nearer our goal. The next day seven Yankee cavalrymen swooped down on us in a tight place · and we had to run for our lives."[13]

The pair eventually made their way to Edwards' Ferry on the Potomac, where, after eluding a picket line, they crossed the river. Later, both men had come upon Colonel John S. Mosby's partisan rangers which they then had accompanied as far as Winchester, Virginia. From there, both had departed for their homes, Crawford in Virginia, and Traweek to Alabama. The fighting was over for Traweek, who remained at home for the duration of the War.

Then there was Private John P. Putegnat, also of the Jeff Davis Artillery, who had made his escape in the company of Cecrops Malone of the 9th Alabama Infantry Regiment. Once beyond the stockade, those men, unlike their comrades, had struck out in a northeasterly direction towards the Erie Railroad. They had then followed Newton Creek for a while before heading for the mountains.

The escapees had then moved east, then north along different roads until they had come to within a half dozen miles of Ithaca, New York. After getting directions and breakfast at a nearby farmer's home, Putegnat and Malone had proceeded to Ithaca. They passed through that town about dusk and moved on to Varna, where they had taken a room at a hotel. It was there that both had had an extremely close call. As Malone recalled,

PRIVATE JOHN P. PUTEGNAT

(Of Jeff Davis Artillery); he escaped from Elmira Prison on October 7, 1864.

(The Chemung County Historical Society, Elmira, New York)

...As we sat by the stove in the evening, warming ourselves, two soldiers came in and we thought we were caught. The landlord said, "Boys, have you heard the news from Elmira?" They said, "No, what is it?" He replied, "Ten Rebel prisoners have just escaped from the prison by a tunnel." We could have sunk through the floor we were so scared. A few comments were made, and then the two soldiers, without noticing us, went out and we were safe. I had two suits of citizen's clothes when I was captured. I put on one of them before we left the prison, and gave the other to Putegnat. This is all that saved us from detection by the soldiers.[14]

Soon after that encounter, Putegnat and Malone had resumed their northerly trek. The next day, the two men had asked about getting work at a house which they had come upon while on the road. The owner had given them some work, and after that, they had helped another man gather his crops.

Once the work at the farm had been completed, the escapees had travelled to Auburn, where they worked at a machine shop in hopes of getting enough money to pay for the trip home. After earning enough money, Putegnat and Malone left Auburn. Eventually, they reached their respective homes in Texas and Arkansas. For Putegnat, like Traweek, the days spent as a member of the Alabama battery were over.

The escape of the ten men from Elmira Prison was no doubt the topic of conversation in both Northern and Southern camps for some time to come. The courage and daring displayed by the escaped prisoners, not only during the tunneling operation, but also on their respective journeys back to the safety of the Southern lines, certainly had to be admired. All things considered, the achievements of the ten, especially in light of the dangers encountered along the different escape routes, had been nothing less than extraordinary.

The days following the receipt of the glad tidings concerning the former prisoners of war saw little change in the dispositions of the opposing forces in the Valley. To the East, however, Grant was preparing to undertake yet another flanking maneuver against Lee's forces, with the greatest number of troops used to date against the Petersburg line.

Postwar view of those who tunnelled out of Elmira Prison; seated at left: George G. "Hickory" Jackson; next to him: Washington B. Traweek; standing at left: William H. Templin; next to him: Berry Benson; in center circle: Cecrops Malone; in left circle: John Purifoy.

(The Chemung County Historical Society, Elmira, New York)

HAPTER XVI

THE FINAL CAMPAIGNS OF 1864 AND NEW
ATTEMPTS AT REORGANIZATION

PART I - CONTINUING TO COMBAT THE ENEMY
ON TWO FRONTS

It was October 26, and preparations were being made by the Federals for an attack, which was to be launched the following day against both ends of the Richmond-Petersburg line. Grant's plans called for Butler to cross to the Northside and make a feint in the direction of the Confederate Capital. While Butler demonstrated north of the James, the three corps belonging to Parke, Warren and Hancock were to move against the Southern right, specifically in the area of Burgess's Mill, where the Boydton Plank Road crossed a stream known as Hatcher's Run. While Parke hit the end of the gray line, Hancock and Warren were to swing around the Run and gain possession of the Southside Railroad.

The Union offensive commenced the next morning as planned, with Butler advancing in the vicinity of Fair Oaks. Meanwhile, to the south, the three Federal corps moved against the Southern right flank.

Almost from the beginning, however, things began to go wrong for the attackers below Petersburg. Parke's Corps ran into heavy resistance and was prevented from reaching its objective. Hancock did reach the Plank Road, but while awaiting the arrival of Warren, who had a more difficult marching route to follow, he was attacked by A. P. Hill and Wade Hampton and was eventually forced to withdraw. In the meantime, Parke and Warren were repulsed at Hatcher's Run.

To the north, meanwhile, Butler had been held in check by Lieutenant General James Longstreet, who had since returned to active duty. Though Haskell's battalion had played an important role in the fighting, the role of Lamkin's battery and its detachment of Alabamians, if any, is unclear. In any case, the Federals subsequently withdrew back across the James River. By the first days of November, siege operations had again resumed along the Richmond-Petersburg front.

Meanwhile, in the vicinity of New Market, Early's Army of the Valley continued to move about in search of forage. At the same time, Sheridan's forces were posing no real threat. Such inactivity convinced Lee that it was an opportune time to recall some of the troops on loan to Early from the main army. Two weeks later, on November 15, Kershaw's division marched east to rejoin the First Corps, located north of the James.

About December 1, Early's remaining forces began to move back down the Valley. Their destination was Fishersville, just about five miles east of Staunton, and along the Virginia Central Railroad. There the army was to go into winter quarters.

As soon as Early reached Fishersville, the construction of crude shelters began. Work for some, however, soon came to a halt because of new threats being posed by Brigadier General George A. Custer's cavalry now active in the lower Valley. A force was assembled to drive off the Federals, including the men from the Alabama detachment of Fry's battery.

The Confederates started in pursuit of the enemy before dusk, and as Corporal Purifoy recalled, "The evening we started out the clouds got thick and portended approaching snow. Such little things, however, were never permitted to deter a soldier from going when it was necessary."[1]

After travelling some distance, the Southerners encamped on a newly cleared section of land. Fires were built to keep the men from freezing. Overnight, the weather took a turn for the worse, and by morning, the men awoke to find themselves covered with several inches of snow.

The snow was still falling when the column moved on later the same morning. As the Confederates pushed on, conditions became even more disagreeable when the snow turned to sleet and ice, making the roads treacherous. The men suffered greatly from the cold. Their thin clothing was hardly adequate protection against the elements. Purifoy remembered that "...he had on a pair of pants, which, having been worn out at the knees, some time previously, had split down the legs from opposite the crotch, to the hem at the bottom."[2] Still, in spite of such difficult conditions, Purifoy had what might have been considered an advantage over many of his comrades. He had been chosen as battalion flag bearer on that campaign, and was allowed the privilege of being on horseback.

Progress was exceedingly slow on the icy roads. Both men and horses were constantly losing their footing and falling on the ice, resulting in a number of broken legs. Any horse that had the misfortune of breaking a limb, had to be destroyed, a loss that the artillery could ill afford.

Only about ten miles could be made each day. When it came time to make camp for the night, "...the snow and ice were raked away to make place for the men to sleep. Straw stacks near the camps suffered, as we robbed them to get beds to sleep on."[3]

Finally, after three or four days of marching, the chase was abandoned and the column was about-faced.[4] The men retraced their steps back to Fishersville. Once back in camp, the Alabamians set about completing the work they had started on their winter quarters. For them, another year of active campaigning had come to a close.

It had certainly been a trying, if not frustrating, period for that group of veterans from Alabama. Following the near destruction of the battery at Spotsylvania, the Alabamians had witnessed the dissolution of what remained of the old company, which had resulted in their being thrown together with the remnants of Fry's battery. Though they were not at all pleased with that new arrangement, they had nevertheless continued to fight with the same alacrity and skill.

All during the summer, whether it had been while fighting the Federal Navy along the James River or while maneuvering against Sheridan in the Shenandoah Valley, the Alabamians had done their part in all the actions in which they had been engaged. Although, from June through September there had been only one recorded casualty. Moreover, only a handful of men had been forced to take temporary leave because of some physical ailment. In addition, there had been only two others from the unit, Lieutenant John Mitchell and Private Thomas Glaze, who had been discharged from the service for different if not curious reasons. All in all, that particular detachment from the Jeff Davis Artillery had come through the summer in good condition.

The month of October, however, had, after promising results achieved in the field on the 13th and morning of the 19th, turned noth-

ing short of nightmarish for the Alabamians. Left weaponless following the catastrophe at Cedar Creek, they had, for all intents and purposes, lost whatever individuality they had maintained. Nevertheless,
during the year's remaining campaigns, they had continued to carry
out their duties with their old time determination.

In the meantime, the nineteen other Alabamians who had been attached to Hardaway's, then Haskell's battalions, continued to maintain a defensive posture in the vicinity of Fort Gilmer, along Richmond's
outer line of works.

Like their comrades who had been attached to Fry's battery, those
so-called "Quasi-Virginians" were not at all pleased with their current
status. They would hardly be expected to fight with the same pride as
members of some other state's artillery unit as they had when repre-
senting Alabama. Still, despite their obvious displeasure with their new
assignment, they too had put feelings aside and performed their duties
as if nothing had changed. During the engagements near and at Cold
Harbor, Griffin's battery had fought with distinction, no doubt due in
part to the skill of the Alabamians.

Later, after having spent some time patrolling the James River with
Hardaway's battalion, the "nineteen" had taken part in the hard fought
defense of Richmond. Then as part of Lamkin's mortar battery, they
had been relegated to doing what, in effect, was nothing more than
picket duty.

Though virtually stripped of all identity, these Alabamians at least
had had the good fortune of not seeing their numbers diminish only by
one during their six months of service around Richmond. Whether or
not their luck would hold, now that winter had arrived, was something
that would have to be left up to the fates to decide.

Even as the two detachments from the Jeff Davis Artillery attended
to their respective tasks at Fishersville and on the Northside, more significant changes were taking place with regard to the troop strength of
the two Southern armies operating in Virginia. In fact, Lee's forces about
Richmond were again increased at the expense of Early's Army of the
Valley. Wright's Corps, of Sheridan's army, had gone east to bolster
Meade's forces along the Richmond-Petersburg front, and Lee sought
to counter that increase by returning Gordon's and Pegram's divisions
to the main army. By December 10, both had departed from the Lower
Valley.

A short time later, when snowy weather had rendered the roads in
the Upper Valley impassable, and put a halt to all activities, Lee also
recalled Major General Bryan Grimes' (formerly Rodes') Division. That

left Early with only Wharton's division of infantry, Rosser's cavalry and several battalions of artillery with which to confront Sheridan.

Though bad weather had already halted operations in the Valley, enemy activities to the east had not yet subsided. In fact, even before Gordon and Pegram had left the Shenandoah, a force mainly of troops from Warren's Corps had been sent against the Petersburg and Weldon Railroad. The object of that movement had been the destruction of a substantial portion of the railway below Stony Creek, thereby further disrupting that line of supply and increasing the distance that future supplies from North Carolina would have to be hauled by wagon.

In the end, about sixteen miles of track had been torn up before local resistance, poor weather and diminishing rations had forced a withdrawal by the enemy. Though A. P. Hill's divisions and Hampton's mounted troops had been sent to drive off, if not destroy the enemy force, they had arrived too late to do little more than harass the retreating blue column.

Two weeks later, the Federals sent a force against Gordonsville, on the Virginia Central Railroad. This time, however, the Confederates arrived in time to thwart the designs of the enemy. After that, the Federals remained quiet. The campaigns of 1864 were finally over.

PART II - A MOST DIFFICULT AND FRUSTRATING WINTER

Though winter weather had brought a halt to active campaigning in both eastern and western Virginia, that did not mean that the days ahead were not to be without their share of strife in and about the camps of the Southern armies. For the Confederates, the struggle to get both sufficient rations to the troops and provender to the horses continued. Now that the farms of the Valley had been stripped bare and the lines of supply reduced to a critical few, feeding the army had become nothing less than a monumental task.

As December drew to a close, the very future of the Second Corps artillery itself was jeopardized by a supply problem of a sort that had actually been plaguing the cavalry for quite some time. Specifically, the number of horses available to the different battalions for future service in the field had been reduced to a dangerous level. There were just not enough horses to replace those that had been lost in battle, had been left totally useless by months of hard campaigning, had died or had to be killed as a result of disease of injury. Without a sufficient number of horses to pull the guns, limbers and caissons, the battalions, not to mention the individual batteries, would be rendered totally ineffective for active field service.

Within a couple of weeks, however, what could be considered at best, a partial solution to the aforementioned problem had been worked out back at Army Headquarters. General Lee had himself recommended that two of Early's four artillery battalions be unhorsed and sent east. And it was on January 17 that Brigadier General Pendleton wrote to Colonel Carter and outlined what had been decided concerning the future disposition of the artillery under his command. In his correspondence, Pendleton stated,

> ....The general [Lee] leaves it very much to General Early, yourself, and myself to determine which two battalions shall remain there and which come down. [to join the main army] They are all such good commands that no particular preference need be expressed. You can converse with General Early and the battalion commanders, and either determine on some grounds thus developed or have it decided by lot.
>
> The service indicated by General Lee for those that come is working some of the powerful guns defending James River from Drewry's Bluff to Howlett's – a noble charge, that will

try the best officers and men if the enemy pushes up his monitors, as the general seems to anticipate. Some may also be needed here at Fort Clifton, on the Appomattox....[1]

Pendleton then put forth his own opinion as to which commands should be transferred from Early's current force. In his own words,

...On some accounts, I should venture to suggest Colonel Nelson's and Major Cutshaw's battalions to come; and if Major C. prefers more active duty, and would like service with the cavalry, I may get for him one of the battalions of horse artillery which it is proposed to arrange. The idea is to form five such battalions of two batteries each, each battalion to have its own major commanding, with a quartermaster and ordnance officer, the whole to be supervised by Chew, made lieutenant colonel. I merely suggest this, however, for Major Cutshaw's consideration. The composite nature of his companies since Spotsylvania Court-House, and the fact that there are already on duty with this army a number of detailed men belonging to his companies, which men had best be with their own commands, [sic] his, in my judgment as one of the battalions to come.[2]

For the first time since the start of the War, the Alabamians had to face the possibility of having to relinquish their present status as members of a light artillery command for garrison duty. The prospects certainly looked grim, especially in light of Pendleton's recommendations. Even so, there were four battalions, all of which were "such good commands," and there was still a chance that Cutshaw might just be selected to remain in the Valley.

By the end of January, all had been decided. Both Braxton's and Cutshaw's battalions were to leave for Richmond. Carter, as it turned out, would also be making the eastward journey. The reason for his departure was the return of Long to active duty. With Long back on the scene, Carter was freed of his responsibilities with the Army of the Valley.

On February 2, the men from the Jeff Davis Artillery boarded the train that was to take them, and the rest of Cutshaw's battalion, to Richmond. Upon their arrival at the Capital, the Alabamians received their new instructions. They were to man the heavy guns of Fort Clifton, located on the west bank of the Appomattox River, about one and a half miles downriver from the city of Petersburg.

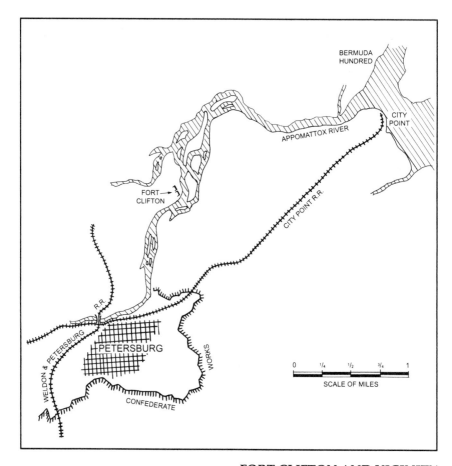

FORT CLIFTON AND VICINITY

Recreated from Plate LVI-1 of The Official Military Atlas of the Civil War.

The fort itself was constructed entirely of earth, and was situated on a bend in the river, near where obstructions had been sunk in order to hinder the Federal Navy. The walls of the fort faced both in an easterly and northeasterly direction, thereby affording its gunners a broad field of fire. Also of importance was the fact that Fort Clifton was only about one mile from the northern tip of the line of works which guarded Petersburg. The bastion's guns, therefore, also covered the interval between the fort and the city's defenses.

Though the Alabamians had been charged with an important duty, the change from active field service to a life spent behind great walls of earth would certainly take some getting used to. Still, they made the best of a difficult situation. John Purifoy observed, "Our little band, of Jeff Davis Artillerymen, were all cheerful and ready to cross sabres with our foes."[3]

For numerous others, however, the extreme hardships were more than even they, the veterans of many a tough campaign, could endure. Desertions were not uncommon, with a number risking their lives while attempting to reach the enemy lines. Many others just headed for home, some with hopes of joining up with some local militia.

With all that was going on around them, the Alabamians still managed to keep an eye focused towards the future. In fact, on January 21, Sergeant Columbus W. McCrary, then attached to Lamkin's battery, had written to the Honorable William P. Chilton of the House of Representatives in hopes of releasing his comrades from their duties both at Fort Clifton and north of the James. In the letter, McCrary suggested,

> If we find the company can not be reorganized, then try and disorganize it as an Artillery Co + try + get the Company ordered to Alabama to procure horses for Cavalry Company. many if not all the men can get horses in Alabama whilst there is not one who could furnish himself with a horse in our present condition. We have been in service since July/61 + I have been at home 12 days since that time + this is the case with the Majority of the Co. If we are allowed to go to Alabama we will furnish ourselves with good horses + will report where we are ordered + will give a good account of ourselves.[4]

The sergeant's suggestions followed a discussion, about the Jeff Davis Artillery rearming, held at a recent meeting he had held with Chilton. In his correspondence, McCrary had added weight to his argument by praising the merits of the company. "...the battery has never faltered upon any occasion the truth of which the officers who commanded will testify Col. Thos H. Carter Comdg Arty. 2nd Corps. Maj R. C. M. Page. Maj Genl D. H. Hill. + many other gallant + distinguished officers who have fallen would testify to the conduct of this command."[5]

In addition, McCrary had mentioned that there were at least one hundred men from the Jeff Davis Artillery listed on the Army's muster rolls.[6] If the different segments of the old command were reunited, it would have had the necessary strength to act as an independent unit, whether it be of cavalry or artillery.

Just three days after McCrary wrote his letter, Chilton expressed his opinion to Secretary of War James A. Seddon that, rather than disbanding the command, strong consideration should be given to reforming it into a cavalry or even as infantry company. In his letter, Chilton had also stated that, "It will, my humble judgement, be a pity + a considerable loss [word missing] our Army to have the Jeff Davis Artillery Co. disbanded."[7] With a member of the House working on the Alabamians' behalf, perhaps the future of the Jeff Davis Artillery did indeed hold some promise.

For Privates J. L. Cauley, J. W. Johnson, James M. Powell and Joseph D. Stuart, however, there would be no more active field command. Cauley, who had been captured the previous October at Hupp's Hill, and had been held at Point Lookout Prison since that time, died on January 26, the victim of chronic diarrhea. Powell, captured in 1863 during the Gettysburg Campaign, had spent a year at Point Lookout, before being transferred to Elmira. There he breathed his last on February 22. As for Johnson and Stuart, both had been taken at Spotsylvania and confined at Point Lookout before also being moved to Elmira. While there, Johnson fell victim to what was described as general debility on February 13. Stuart, meanwhile, had contracted Variola and had died six days earlier.

Even as other Alabamians continued their struggle for survival in Yankee prisons, the others attempted to make the best of a difficult situation along the Richmond-Petersburg front. By March 1, conditions within the gray lines had grown worse. Though the commissary department was sending food to the troops, the rations were barely enough to keep them going. "The daily ration seldom consisted of anything beyond a pint of corn meal and an ounce or two of bacon."[8]

Also desertions had reduced the Army's numerical strength. The Southern forces could only boast an effective strength of just over forty thousand men, about one-third of the total number of troops arrayed against them.

Moreover, the Confederates had, just weeks before, been forced to extend their thin lines to the right to counter new Federal gains. On February 5, Warren and Humphreys, with two divisions each, plus Major General David M. Gregg's cavalry, had moved against the Boydton Plank Road, the route Grant mistakenly believed was used by Lee's supply wagons. Only a few wagons were taken, and after a sharp fight at Hatcher's Run, the Yankees had withdrawn. Afterwards, a new line had been drawn which extended Meade's left another three miles. The Confederates had no choice but to conform to that maneuver. For the next few weeks, there had been no other significant movement by either side.

On March 2, Sheridan routed what was left of Early's Army of the Valley at Waynesboro. Immediately following the defeat, Early, Long and a few others headed east in order to join Lee's forces. The Army of the Valley was no more.

Meanwhile, on the Richmond-Petersburg front, the men of the Jeff Davis Artillery assigned to duty at Fort Clifton continued to lead a boring existence. As Purifoy remembered, "While on our immediate part of the line little occurred to break the monotony, we witnessed, nightly, brilliant displays of fireworks in the nature of shellings from mortars."[9]

To date, no action had been taken on McCrary's suggestions concerning the future of the Alabama battery. Before the month of March was a week old, however, recently promoted Lieutenant Colonel Wilfred E. Cutshaw, displeased about the recent unhorsing of his battalion, wrote to General Samuel Cooper, the Adjutant and Inspector General of the Confederate armies, on his artillerymen's behalf. In his correspondence, dated March 6, Cutshaw proposed:

> If it meets the approbation of the general-in-chief and the department, I respectfully ask that my command be charged to cavalry and organized into a regiment. The command now constitutes a light artillery battalion,...
>
> There are officers enough to give two to each company, besides four vacancies which can be filled without interfering with the rank of the other officers now in prison. Both officers and men are extremely anxious for this change, and will do their best to render themselves useful and reliable in this branch of the service. We have the advantage of a discipline that very few commands can compare with, and the men have learned to give that attention to their horses without which no cavalry can remain efficient.[10]

Cutshaw also suggested that squads of his men be sent to capture horses in the Valley if the government was unable to furnish them, arguing, "Our object in seeking this change is to get into mounted service with a more active life. Our past service as light artillery gives us some claim, and I am sure the opinions of the superiors officers as to the conduct of officers and men on the field must have some weight as a recommendation."[11]

Cutshaw also outlined the strength of his batteries. Reese's was shown to have forty men present for duty. Meanwhile, another forty-seven men had been reunited, which, upon their arrival, would raise the battery's effective strength to eighty-seven. That did not include another fifty-nine men who were either absent, sick or listed as prisoners of war.

In his letter, Cutshaw had presented a strong case. It remained to be seen if Cooper would take any action.

By coincidence, only a few days later, McCrary's own request for a reorganization of the Jeff Davis Artillery finally reached Lee. But, he recommended, for the present, that no action be taken. The date was March 11, 1865.

Certainly, Lee's decision must have come as a major disappointment for McCrary. Fortunately, though, that was not the only action affecting the Alabama battery.

It was also about that time, that the nineteen men who had been serving with Lamkin's battery on the Northside, were reunited with the rest of their old company at Fort Clifton.[12] After ten long months, the Jeff Davis Artillery was once more intact.

It is not known whether or not Lieutenant Colonel Cutshaw's letter to General Cooper made the difference, but on March 16, Special Order #11 was issued from Artillery Headquarters with new instructions for the battalion:

> Col. Thomas H. Carter will proceed to rearrange the refit the artillery battalion of the Second Corps on the following plan, viz:..., McLaughlin's (King's) to be called in and assigned to duty at Fort Clifton instead of Cutshaw's, and the latter to be rendered efficient for the field;...[13]

Accordingly, it would only be a matter of time before the Jeff Davis Artillery left the fort and returned to field service as part of a light artillery battalion.

The following day another more detailed statement, concerning the future of the Second Corps' battalions, was issued by Artillery Headquarters. Its first part read:

> First. That the battalion commanded by Lieutenant Colonel King and Major McLaughlin, now in Giles County foraging, be assigned to Fort Clifton, instead of Lieutenant Colonel Cutshaw, the horses, guns, and c., being turned over to the latter that it may be fitted for the field....King's men are not comparable to Cutshaw's for thoroughly efficient service in the field, and besides Cutshaw's command is abundantly large to bring up Nelson's and Braxton's battalion to a proper standard of strength.
>
> Second. Nelson's battalion to be re-established by using, in suitable ways, some of Cutshaw's surplus men and obtaining guns and horses that may be available.[14]

The details of the artillery's reorganization had been worked out. The question was just how long it would take to prepare the battalions for active field duty.

Nothing new took place within the corps over the next couple of days. Then on March 20, Special Order #13 was issued by Army Headquarters. That part which concerned itself with the Second Corps artillery read as follows, "Nelson's, Braxton's, and Cutshaw's battalions, Second Corps, will be re-equipped for the field under command of Col. Thomas H. Carter as soon as possible."[15]

The need for quick action, as far as the refitting and mobilization of the artillery was concerned, could easily be understood, especially when considering the circumstances under which Special Order #13 was issued. The end of March meant a gradual improvement in weather conditions and the resumption of active campaigning. If Lee was to have any hopes of effectively countering the movements of the numerically superior Grant, he would have to have every available battery of his army in as ready for action as possible.

At the same time, there was a very real possibility that the Confederate army would soon be forced to abandon its defensive position and undertake an active campaign against the Federals. In order to relieve the pressure being exerted along the Richmond-Petersburg front, the two Southern armies operating in the Eastern theatre, the Army of Northern Virginia and General Joseph E. Johnston's Army of Tennessee, then in North Carolina, might just have to coordinate their campaigns and take to the offensive. If the junction of the two armies could be successfully carried out, both could move against Major General William T. Sherman, whose campaign had also brought him to North Carolina. Once Sherman was out of the way, the Southern forces would strike out for Meade's army to the north. Such strategy would mean the temporary loss of both Richmond and Petersburg, but the sacrifice of the two cities was necessary if Lee was to be free to maneuver.

Up until that time, the military authorities also entertained the belief that Johnston might defeat Sherman and march to the relief of Lee's army. By March 21, however, any hopes of victory in North Carolina quickly faded when reports of the battle being waged between Johnston and Sherman at Bentonville came in. Despite early gains, the tide had turned and Johnston's army was doing all it could to maintain its present position against a hostile force which was actually more than twice its size.

Then on March 23, a plan to both ease the pressure along the front and disrupt the enemy's offensive designs was developed at Southern Headquarters. Major General John B. Gordon, who had recently been given command of the Second Corps in place of Early, had worked out a plan which called for the launching of a surprise night attack against Fort Stedman on the Petersburg line. Once its defenders were overwhelmed, the Confederates were to advance further, with the intentions of not only capturing the works adjacent to Stedman, but also several forts to its rear. From the latter works, the attackers were expected to deliver a destructive fire into the Federal rear. If all went according to plan, the enemy would have to send reinforcements from the left (and by doing so shorten his own front) in an effort to plug the gap in his line.

The attack was scheduled to be launched in the pre-dawn darkness of March 25. Reinforcements from both Hill and Anderson brought the attacking force, exclusive of a cavalry division which was to exploit the breakthrough, to a total of nearly 12,000 men, or half of the force defending the Southside. Later, Gordon requested that Pickett's division of Longstreet's Corps also be made available for the attack. It was, but did not arrive in time to be of assistance.

On the morning of March 25, while final preparations were being made for the assault on Fort Stedman, the garrison of Fort Clifton, including the men of the Jeff Davis Artillery, was put on alert. Fort Clifton was located on the opposite side of the river from Stedman, and its defenders would have to be ready to take appropriate action should the enemy attempt a crossing of the Appomattox. Since Lee had weakened his lines in order to enable Gordon to have sufficient attacking force, a Yankee advance, the purpose of which was to take advantage of the changed situation along the front, could not be ruled out. As a result, Corporal John Purifoy was sent out, some distance from the fort, in order to watch for any sign of enemy movement along the river.

At 4:00 a.m., the Southern assault commenced. The enemy's picket line was quickly overrun, and in short order, axe-men had begun chopping their way through the obstructions in front of Fort Stedman. A passageway was completed, and the Confederates surged into the fort. The defenders were taken completely by surprise, and the position was soon in Southern hands.

Three hundred of the attackers, including some artillerymen, moved to gain control of the forts to the rear. Meanwhile, more troops moved up and endeavored to widen the breach caused by the initial attack. Two other Union positions, Batteries 10 and 11, were taken with little difficulty. All seemed to be going exceedingly well for Gordon and his men.

It wasn't long, however, before conditions on the battlefield began to take a decidedly negative turn for the Confederates. First, word came to Gordon that the forts to the rear could not be found. Therefore, the expected supporting fire from them, which was crucial to the success of the attack, would not be forthcoming. About the same time, Yankee artillerymen located further down the line began firing at those men holding Fort Stedman and the other nearby works. Federal infantry was also massed for a counterattack.

Quickly, the Confederates found that the ground they occupied offered virtually no protection from enemy fire, and could not possibly be held without great loss. They were hemmed in, and nothing could be accomplished by staying where they were. To prevent a major disaster from befalling Gordon's command, Lee ordered a withdrawal.

Breaking off the engagement, however, was no easy task. In order to reach the safety of their own works, the Southern troops had to re-cross an area between the lines that was being swept by Federal artillery fire. Rather than risk being killed as they moved back across the field, many chose to remain where they were and surrender. Hundreds fell into enemy hands. For the others who decided to retreat, it was truly a race with death. In the end, nearly 3,500 men, or better than twenty-five percent of the attacking force, were lost.

Some time after midday, the Federals, who had concluded that the rest of the Southern line had been weakened in order to provide proper support for the movement against Fort Stedman, attacked A. P. Hill's position in the vicinity of Hatcher's Run. More than nine hundred defenders were taken prisoner during the assault. Such losses were irreplaceable.

Meanwhile, back at Fort Clifton, there was nothing of interest to report. During the fighting in and around Stedman, no enemy force had appeared along the river.

It had already been a week since the latest directive had been issued concerning the reorganization of Cutshaw's battalion, but the Alabamians had seen no hint that they were about to be rescued from their present predicament.

Four days later, on March 29, a message sent by Longstreet to Colonel Walter H. Taylor, of Lee's staff, gave a good indication of what the future held in store for Reese's old command. The message read as follows, "Can I get either Braxton's, Cutshaw's, or Nelson's battalions to man guns on intermediate line from Brook pike to James River, above Richmond? Artillery horses cannot probably be furnished soon to equip them again."[16]

That just about settled it. Horses were in much shorter supply than first thought, and there were just not enough of them to permit the refitting of Cutshaw's command, let along the other two battalions of the Second Corps.

Though it represented the breakdown of an important facet of the Confederate supply system, the inability of the army to remount its light artillery battalions was nowhere near the worst of the difficulties facing the Southern High Command. By that time, the tactical situation, as concerning both Confederate armies in the East, had, in fact, grown even more critical than it had been in previous weeks. Already, Lee had received word from Johnston telling him that the forces in North Carolina were so badly outnumbered that they could do little more than annoy the enemy. Sherman's army, therefore, was free to march north and form a junction with Meade's forces around Petersburg. With Lee's lines already stretched to the breaking point, the joining of the two Federal armies could only lead to one possible outcome.

That unwelcome news, combined with the costly reverse suffered at Fort Stedman, had left Lee with no recourse but to begin planning for the evacuation of the Richmond-Petersburg line and the eventual hookup with Johnston in North Carolina. Regardless of when the withdrawal finally commenced, the Southern forces were to move in such a way that would allow them to make full use of the rail connections between Petersburg and Johnston's army. Once the Confederates had abandoned their positions in front of Petersburg, they would move west, following the Southside, then Richmond and Danville Railroads, until they reached Danville. Later, the army would pick up the Piedmont Railroad, which they would take south to Greensboro, North Carolina.

The success of the movement depended largely upon Lee's ability to keep the enemy from gaining control of the Southside railway. That line also constituted the main supply route for the army.

Just when the necessity of keeping the railway out of enemy hands was greater than ever, some discomforting news had been received at Southern Headquarters. Union cavalry was reported moving towards the Federal left. That meant a new threat to the Southside Railroad.

CHAPTER XVII

THE FINAL CAMPAIGN

It was March 29, and what the Confederates perceived as just a cavalry raid aimed at the Southside Railroad was actually only part of a much larger movement being undertaken by the Federals. Grant, in fact, had mobilized most of his army and was shifting it towards the left so that his infantry would be in a better position to exploit any gains made by the mounted troops.

Grant hoped that the cavalry, commanded by Sheridan, who had since returned from the Valley, would gain possession of Five Forks, a critical intersection located three miles from the railroad, and from there move against the Confederate flank and rear. He also hoped that Lee would weaken his center in order to bolster the threatened right, leaving the Federal troops with an excellent opportunity to attack and overrun the stripped defenses.[1] With its line broken, the Confederate army would have no choice but to retreat or attempt to make a stand and fight.

Lee, in the meantime, had already begun to take steps aimed at strengthening his endangered flank. Pickett's division, which was still on the Southside, was ordered to move to the right and take up a position just beyond Hatcher's Run. With Pickett, and under his command, would be two brigades taken from Anderson's Corps. At the same time, three cavalry divisions, led by Fitzhugh Lee, William H. F. Lee and Thomas Rosser, were to be assembled in the area of Five Forks. It was there that Pickett, in command of all the Southern forces, would rendezvous with the mounted troops and move against the enemy.

The following morning, the Yankees were reported to be at Dinwiddie Court House. That afternoon, Pickett advanced in the direction of Five Forks. Federal cavalry harassed the marching column all the way to the important intersection, which was finally reached at about 4:30.

The next day, March 31, Pickett, whose cavalry support had come up, advanced towards Dinwiddie Court House. During the march, Union cavalry was again encountered but was easily dealt with. By nightfall, the Confederates were within a half mile of the Court House.

That night reports came in from outposts on the far left of the capture of two men from Warren's V Corps. That meant Sheridan had infantry support. Finding himself up against a more formidable force than first thought, Pickett pulled back, during the early morning hours, to Five Forks.

The next day, the Federals closed on the intersection. By mid-afternoon, the V Corps had come up and begun forming for the attack. The enemy had vastly superior numbers on their side, outnumbering the Confederates 3 to 1. Moreover, both Fitzhugh Lee and Pickett were absent from the field and had not told those left in charge where they had gone.

At 4:00 p.m., the enemy attacked. On the right, the defenders facing Sheridan's cavalrymen, provided a stubborn opposition. On the left, however, where Warren's V Corps attacked, the Federals proved unstoppable. Before long, the Confederates were in full retreat. The troops on the right held firm for a time but soon had to withdraw. Both cavalry and infantry joined in the pursuit of the shattered gray-clads.

About that time, Pickett reached the field, but he could do nothing to retrieve the situation. The contest had already been decided, and more than half of his men had been killed, wounded or captured.

The chase of the fleeing Southerners continued until near dusk, when Sheridan halted his men a few miles short of the Southside Railroad. There, he prepared to meet an expected counterattack, which, in fact, never came.

The defeat of Pickett's forces left Lee with no choice but to shift troops from his already weakened right to support whatever force still remained in front of the Southside Railroad. The call went to three brigades of Anderson's Corps, and the result was that three miles of the defenses were left virtually unoccupied. At the same time, however, Field's division of Longstreet's Corps had been ordered to the Southside to bolster the line. Back at Fort Clifton, meanwhile, the Alabamians saw no change in their disposition in spite of the disaster on the right.

While Lee did what he could to prevent another disaster from be-falling his army, Grant issued orders for what he hoped would be the final blow against his adversary. At first light on the morning of April 2, a general assault was to commence against that part of the Confeder-ate line which ran from the Appomattox River to Burgess's Mill.

At about 9:00 p.m. on the night of April the 1st, Union artillery began bombarding the Southern positions targeted for the assault. The noise of the guns grew louder as dawn approached. Then at just a little past 4:30 a.m., the Federal advance began.

A. P. Hill's thin lines were struck and their defenders could do little to stall the attacking VI Corps. They gave way, retreating to the west towards Anderson, and east towards the works before Petersburg. Not long thereafter, Hill was killed as he rode to rally his troops.

Meanwhile, farther to the left, Gordon's men were having a better time of it. Though they had been pushed from their works to a second line, they offered a stiff resistance and frustrated the enemy.

Off to the far right, Anderson, who had failed in his efforts to find Pickett, was ordered by Lee to march to Bevill's Bridge, which crossed the Appomattox, and await the arrival of the rest of the army, which was to evacuate Petersburg that night.

By that time, the enemy had gained possession of the Southside Railroad, and the situation on the right had grown even more critical. Field's division had not yet arrived, leaving only about six hundred men of Brigadier General Nathaniel H. Harris's Brigade and Wilcox's division to man the works, known as Forts Gregg and Whitworth. Fac-ing them were thousands of infantrymen from Major General John Gibbon's XXIV Corps.

At one o'clock, Gibbon sent one division against Fort Gregg. The Yankees, however, came under a very destructive fire and were repulsed. Numerous times they attempted to advance, only to be driven back again and again.

Finally, Gibbon sent a larger force forward, and after a tremendous struggle, during which "..,wounded gray-backs loaded rifles taken from the dead and dying, and passed them up to rapid-firing marksmen perched atop the walls,"[2] they finally succeeded in overwhelming the fort's defenders. The Southerners suffered 86% casualties during the fight, but had gained three precious hours for their army. Once Gregg had fallen, Fort Whitworth became untenable and its defenders were forced to withdraw.

Field's division had arrived by that time and had occupied the works beyond the two forts. Gibbon, finding a formidable force drawn up be-fore him, elected not to attack. For the present, Lee's right was secure.

With the situation along the front more or less stabilized, Lee issued orders to his commanders, both north and south of the James, telling them that the evacuation of the Richmond-Petersburg line was to commence at 8:00 p.m. that night. The various elements of the army were to move west towards Amelia Court House, located on the Richmond and Danville Railroad, and some forty miles away, where they were to concentrate before moving on. The army would then follow the railroad by way of Burkeville for an eventual hookup with Johnston's army beyond Danville, some hundred miles from Amelia Court House.

Near eight o'clock, the withdrawal began with Brigadier General Pendleton who withdrew his guns from the Southside. The artillery was in turn followed by Field's division and the rest of the forces occupying the Petersburg defenses.

Back at Fort Clifton, Cutshaw's command had not learned about the evacuation until ten o'clock when a messenger suddenly arrived and announced that the battalion had been instructed to leave the fort. "In a few minutes orders were received to destroy what could be destroyed without noise or fire."[3] After that, the men of the Jeff Davis Artillery formed a line outside of Fort Clifton with the rest of Cutshaw's battalion, and were issued muskets. There were, however, an insufficient number of guns to go around, so some of the Alabamians were left without weapons. Active field duty had finally come to the men from Reese's old command, but certainly that was not the kind of service they had anticipated. Instead of being refitted as a light artillery command or even a cavalry unit, the battery had been transformed into a detachment of foot soldiers.

Soon it came time for the garrison of Fort Clifton to move out; that is, except for a small detachment of men which was to stay behind long enough to spike the guns and blow up the magazine. The Jeff Davis Artillery marched away from the fort with their battalion for a rendezvous with the rest of the army. Not long thereafter, the blackened skies were lit by the flash caused by the exploding magazine of the fort.

Some time before three o'clock in the morning, while Cutshaw's battalion was pushing towards the Richmond Road, the Second Corps, which was acting as the main army's rear guard, completed its crossing of the Appomattox River. Immediately thereafter, the bridge it used was set on fire.

Gordon's Corps then moved west following the River Road. Cutshaw's command, meanwhile, pressed ahead in the same general direction. As the two columns got farther and farther away from

Petersburg, the reverberations and flashes caused by the exploding magazines, forts and gunboats continued to fill the night air.[4]

The Alabamians pushed ahead in the darkness. Soon the skies began to brighten, indicating the start of a new day. The column, however, like the rest of the scattered army, did not stop but continued to press on in a westerly direction.

It was April 3, and the day that was to see the reuniting of much of the Southern army in the vicinity of the upper crossing of the Appomattox River. In the afternoon, what remained of that portion of Heth's and Wilcox's divisions, which had been cut off during the Federal attack of the 2nd, formed a junction with Longstreet's marching column. Longstreet, by that time, had already assumed command of the remaining men from Hill's Corps.

Near dusk, Anderson reached Bevill's Bridge and that night was joined, west of the Appomattox, by the greater portion of Longstreet's command. That same evening, Pickett's force, now numbering only a few hundred men, also came up.

Meanwhile, behind Longstreet were Gordon's Second Corps and Mahone's division, the latter of which had been withdrawn from the Howlett Line, north of Petersburg, and had the greatest distance to cover of the two commands before reaching Goode's Bridge. At the same time, Lieutenant General Richard S. Ewell, who commanded all of the forces from the Northside, was on the march from Richmond, but had not yet made contact with the rest of the retreating army.

The exact position of Cutshaw's "Infantry" battalion, on the night of April 3, is not known though it is believed that it had moved within a few miles of Goode's Bridge.

Though much of the Southern army had succeeded in forming a junction near the Appomattox River, it had not been achieved without some sacrifice. "The miles came hard to many stiff, blistered, often unshod feet, torturing the muscles of legs for which nine months of normally sedentary siege life had made fast marching a dim memory. Where they could they stopped to rest, to cook what pitiful rations they had brought with them, or to forage the already stripped land for what food could be found."[5]

Even though the few provisions remaining to the army had been quickly exhausted, there was to be relief for the half-starved troops. Supplies would be awaiting the army at Amelia Court House. It was, for most of Lee's present force, less than a day's march away, and the knowledge that food was not that far off had helped to instill new feelings of hope within the ranks.[6]

Thus far, there had been little interference from the enemy. Grant, as it turned out, had not sent his forces in pursuit of the fleeing Confederates until the morning following the evacuation.

Leading the advance was Sheridan's cavalry, which had been instructed by Grant to move west towards Jetersville, on the Richmond and Danville Railroad and ten miles southwest of Amelia Court House, in order to block what was believed to be Lee's shortest route to North Carolina. Coming up behind Sheridan was Griffin's V[7], Humphreys' II and Wright's VI Corps. To the south, but following a route that was parallel to the road being utilized by the aforementioned troops, were Parke's IX Corps and three divisions of Ord's Army of the James. That force was to cut the Danville line at Burkeville, should the Confederates elude Sheridan and attempt to move in that direction. With his path blocked at Burkeville, Lee would be forced to march much farther west before turning south for the eventual hookup with Johnston.

The morning of April 4, the Jeff Davis Artillery and the rest of the garrison from Fort Clifton, resumed the march. At the same time, the greater portion of the Southern army, with Longstreet in the lead, took up the march to Amelia Court House. As the army pushed west, there was some skirmishing with Federal cavalry which had made its appearance on the flank.

At about 8:30, the lead elements of the Confederate army arrived at Amelia Court House. It, however, was quickly discovered that there was, in fact, no food awaiting the hungry soldiers. All that was found was a large shipment of ordnance supplies. There had been a mix-up at the War Department. The rations, which, just days before, had been requested by Lee, and were to have come from storehouses in Richmond, had never been shipped out.

The discover that there were actually no provisions at Amelia had a devastating effect on the army. In John Purifoy's own words, "This unlooked for calamity created a dismay in the troops that would have to be seen to be appreciated; no fact wore a heavier shadow than that of General Lee."[8] A number of men, who were no longer able to cope with the hardships of the campaign, left the ranks and disappeared.

The army was in serious trouble. Without food, the Southern troops could hardly be expected to maneuver effectively before the pursuing enemy. Immediately, Lee sent a request to Danville for 200,000 rations for his army. At the same time, he held his forces at the Court House while wagons were sent scouring the countryside in search of supplies.

During the course of the day, the rest of the army closed up on Amelia. Just past midday, Wilcox's division arrived. Not long thereafter, Heth's troops came and shared in the great disappointment being felt by the provisionless army. In the meantime, Gordon halted his command some five miles away, in order to wait for Mahone's division which had already reached Goode's Bridge and was holding it for Ewell, whose whereabouts were still a mystery.

Then finally during the late afternoon, word was received from Ewell, stating that he would be across the Appomattox well before midnight. Instead of crossing at Goode's, Ewell had elected to use a railroad bridge, nearer to his line of march, in order to get to the west shore.

After travelling all day, Cutshaw's battalion itself finally reached Moore's Church, about five miles from Amelia Court House. There, the column was brought to a halt.

Then, after an all too brief rest, the battalion was roused while it was still dark in order to resume the march. On the morning of April 5, Cutshaw reached Amelia Court House and a short time thereafter was attached to Brigadier General James A. Walker's Division of Gordon's Corps.

That same morning, the commissary wagons, which had been sent out to gather provisions, returned. With the arrival of the foraging parties, however, came even more bad news. That portion of Virginia, already overtaxed by four years of war, could offer up but little in the way of food. The army would have to hold out until it met the supply train from Danville. Unknown to the Confederates, however, was the fact that no more trains were operating on the Danville line.

Having already wasted a day awaiting supplies, Lee resumed the march. To facilitate better movement along the roads, the number of vehicles and artillery accompanying the army were reduced by nearly one-third. At the same time, the reserve caissons and ammunition, which had been accumulated at Amelia, were destroyed.

On the way to Burkeville, the troops and wagons moved along separate but parallel routes. Soon, the sound of gunfire was heard to the south. Just this side of Jetersville, about five miles from Amelia, the Confederates had come upon Federal cavalry occupying works blocking the road to Burkeville. Not that far away, and rapidly moving up, were Griffin's V and Humphreys' II Corps.

The delay at Amelia Court House had cost Lee whatever lead he had gained since leaving Petersburg. If he was to reach Burkeville, and the provisions supposedly coming up by rail, he would have to cut his way through Yankees located across his path.

After examining the Federal position, Lee decided that it was too strong to assail. Instead, he decided to have his army deflect to the west and move in the direction of Farmville, located on the upper Appomattox. To that place, reserve supplies being held at Lynchburg could be shipped by rail for his starving men.

Near dusk, on April 5, the march resumed. Leading the advance was Longstreet, including both Field's and Mahone's divisions, followed by Heth and Wilcox, Anderson, Ewell and Gordon in that order. That march was the most torturous journey of all for the men of Lee's army.

For the first five miles or so, the infantry had a clear path. After that, both trains and foot soldier shared the same road. "Through a night that grew blacker as the hours passed, the men groped their way alongside an endless tangle of wagons. Then as always, the strong and experienced officers of resolute character kept their men under control, but among the more discouraged and weaker units, command collapsed."[9]

> ...Hundreds lost their grasp on reality, mumbled incoherently, wandered off into the woods to fall down in a stupor, or panicked at the slightest provocation.
>
> Several times firing broke out as the men shot at shadows, or, worse, each other...."[10]

Still, the vast majority pushed on. The morning of April 6, the van of the Confederate army moved towards Rice's Station, which was, at most, a couple of hours march from Farmville. At the latter place, according to information received from Commissary General Isaac St. John, who had caught up with the army at Amelia, 80,000 rations were awaiting the starving troops. To get there, however, the Southern forces would have to outdistance their pursuers who were pressing their flanks and rear.

The army continued to push ahead, but soon a gap developed between Mahone's division and the head of Anderson's column. (At that time the army's order of march was as follows: Longstreet-Field, Heth, Wilcox and Mahone, First Corps Trains, Anderson, Ewell, Second and Third Corps Trains and Gordon, which included Cutshaw and the Jeff Davis Artillery.)

As it turned out, Ewell had halted his and Anderson's men without notifying the troops up ahead. The cause of the halt was increased pressure from Federal cavalry, which had been snapping at the wagon trains located between Ewell and Gordon.

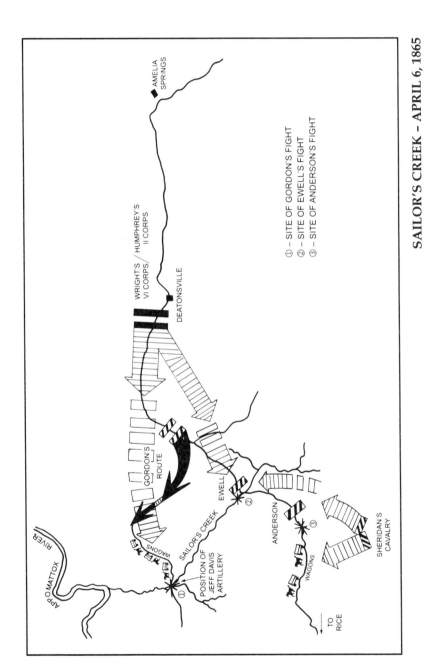

SAILOR'S CREEK – APRIL 6, 1865

Recreated from Plate LXXVII-4 of The Official Military Atlas of the Civil War.

The Federals had been repulsed. But to better protect the wagons, and also decrease the distance he might have to move to support Gordon in the event of attack, Ewell had stopped so the long line of vehicles could move ahead.

Before long, a large part of the undefended wagon train had moved on to an open stretch of road between Anderson and Mahone. Seizing at the opportunity that lay before him, Sheridan attacked. During the assault, the Federals captured and burned hundreds of wagons. Sixteen artillery pieces were also taken.

Anderson moved to the attack, but could not drive the enemy from the road. Ewell then endeavored to save the rest of the train. The wagons were near a fork in the road, the upper part of which ran parallel, for a few miles, to the lower branch which was the route followed by the army. Without delay, the vehicles were moved off to the right, along the upper fork, in order to bypass the Yankee horsemen. Gordon, who was close behind, followed, not having been told of the change in routes. He pressed on ahead, leaving Ewell and Anderson quite isolated from the rest of the army.

To make matters worse, two divisions from Wright's VI Corps was approaching the unprotected rear of Ewell's command. With a formidable foe on both front and rear, the question was whether to try to escape or attack. Ewell, though the senior officer, deferred any decision making to Anderson, who favored launching an attack in front, while Ewell took care of holding off the Federals to the rear.

Anderson moved forward, and at first succeeded in driving a portion of Sheridan's force. Sheridan, however, brought up supports and contained the attackers. Not long thereafter, another cavalry division advanced, carried the Southern position and drove most of the gray infantry back in confusion. Brigadier General Henry A. Wise's Brigade eluded the grips of the enemy, but the rest of Anderson's fleeing command was at the mercy of the blue-clad horsemen. In the end, some fifteen hundred Confederates, or half of Anderson's force, were killed or captured. Anderson, though, escaped.

Back up the road, Ewell was also under attack, but his men provided a stubborn defense against superior numbers from a ridge west of a stream known as Little Sailor's Creek. Suddenly, Sheridan's cavalry, fresh from its victory over Anderson, joined the fight, striking the Southern flank and rear. The Confederates resisted the attack for a time, but the situation was hopeless. Except for a few hundred infantrymen who escaped, Ewell had no choice but to surrender. His command was no more.

Meanwhile to the northwest, Gordon was himself facing possible annihilation. He was then battling Humphreys' II Corps in the vicinity of two different crossing sites along Sailor's Creek. At the Jamestown Road crossing, the wagons which Gordon's command had been protecting, had quite literally bogged down in the marshy surroundings of the stream. As a result, his men had been forced to halt in order to assist the teamsters in freeing the vehicles. During that delay, the Federals had struck Gordon's rear.

The Confederates had immediately formed a line of battle across Lockett's Hill, some 500 feet from Sailor's Creek, and prepared to beat back their attackers. Cutshaw's battalion had taken up a position on both sides of the Jamestown Road. The men of the Jeff Davis Artillery took their place in the line with Fry's battery, to the left of the road.

The enemy had advanced, only to be forced back by a deadly volley from Gordon's men. Again and again, the Federals moved forward, but each time they were brought to a halt by their adversary. They advanced once more, in greater numbers than before. The pressure was too great, and the defenders began falling back towards Sailor's Creek.

Attacked in front and on both flanks, the Confederates resisted as best they could. It, however, was a hopeless situation, and some began to lay down their arms. Those that could get away, rapidly retreated across the stream and up the opposite slope. Fortunately, artillery and cavalry had been posted beyond the Creek, which provided cover for the withdrawing troops. Once having reached safety, the remaining men of the Second Corps did their best to reform their ranks.

The fighting broke off some time after nightfall. The losses had been heavy, with about 1,700 men falling into enemy hands. In addition, much of the wagon train had been captured.

For Cutshaw's battalion, one casualty in particular had stood out. Lieutenant Colonel Cutshaw had gone down with a serious leg wound that would necessitate the amputation of the limb. He had been taken from the field in an ambulance and left in a nearby house, where he was later captured. With the loss of Cutshaw, command of the battalion passed to Captain Charles W. Fry.

That night, the men of Reese's battery fell in line with the rest of Cutshaw's battalion and marched in the direction of the Appomattox River. Gordon's force, which included the survivors of Anderson's command, was to cross at High Bridge, where there were actually two spans; a railway (High Bridge) and an adjacent wagon bridge. The crossing site, covered by Mahone's division, was finally reached. After crossing the wagon bridge, Gordon's command halted and bivouacked for the remainder of the night. The next day, both bridges would be burned in order to slow the pursuing enemy.

For the Alabamians, the march from Amelia Court House to the Appomattox River had proved to be quite an experience. Though their command had finally once again crossed swords with the enemy, it had not done so without significant loss. During the course of the day, a dozen Alabamians had been captured by the Federals. All had been taken prisoner in the area of Jetersville and Burkeville. They included Privates Thomas A. Burroughs, Richard G. Clarke, O. Denson, H. Edmondson, Samuel Edwards, B. Franklin Ellis, John W. Eubanks, Michael Gorman, Benjamin Jackson, John B. Jackson, Littleton G. Jackson and Edward D. Wright. It is not known whether or not those men had been captured during one of the many skirmishes that took place that day, or had just not been able to keep up with the rest of the army and were swallowed up by the advancing Yankees.

In addition, it is interesting to note that of the dozen men, most, as indicated by the company service records, were also supposedly captured at Farmville on April 6. That is an impossibility, for the Alabama unit would not arrive at that place until the following morning. More than likely, the Alabamians were seized sometime before the affair at Sailor's Creek. Since Farmville was the next closest populated area, its name appears in the records.[11] More importantly, though, was the fact that the enemy now held twelve artillerymen from Reese's battery.

Early on the morning of April 7, the Jeff Davis Artillery marched off in the direction of Farmville with the rest of Gordon's command. The journey proved uneventful, and before several hours had elapsed, the Alabamians had reached the rail depot, where they were issued two day's rations from the waiting train. While the food was being prepared, Longstreet's men began arriving. They had crossed the Appomattox River using the Farmville bridge, which, along with an adjacent railroad bridge, were to be set on fire in order to prevent a crossing by the Federal infantry.

Then, all at once, events took a totally unexpected turn. About mid-morning, Lee received word that the Yankee foot soldiers were in fact on his side of the river. There had been a delay in burning the spans at High Bridge. Though the engineers had begun their destructive work, it had been interrupted by the appearance of Humphreys' II Corps. The enemy had put out the fires on the wagon bridge, and by nine o'clock, one Federal division had made its way across the river. Mahone had attempted to drive the Yankees back, but succeeded in only temporarily slowing their advance.

Marching orders were immediately issued to the Southern forces at Farmville. The trains and the provisions they contained were sent on their way towards Lynchburg. Men, who had not completed cooking their rations, had to throw the food away.

The Confederate army was to move north towards Cumberland Church, some three and a half miles away, then turn west and follow the road to Lynchburg. That route would eventually bring the Southern forces to a place near the Southside Railroad where the provisions could again be distributed. In the meantime, Lee directed Mahone's division to occupy a position at the intersection of the roads leading to Cumberland Church, in order to block the approaching enemy.

Before Gordon's command left the Farmville area, however, it was involved in a rear guard action just north of the town with Major General Francis C. Barlow's Division of Humphreys' II Corps. The enemy was pushed back, and a number of prisoners were taken. Following the engagement, Gordon proceeded on his way towards Cumberland Church and assisted the cavalry in covering the movements of the army's trains.

When about two or three miles north of Farmville, a portion of those troops guarding the wagons was driven back in confusion by the enemy. Walker's division was immediately instructed to drive off the menacing force. A line of battle was formed, with Cutshaw's battalion on the right, and soon the whole concern was pressing forward in the direction of the enemy.

It was here that the Jeff Davis Artillery made its first charge as infantrymen. The advance was very well executed, and the Federals soon commenced a rapid retreat before the attackers, whose enthusiasm caused them to continue to press forward despite the urgings of a courier who had been sent out after them to stop the movement. Finally, a high ranking officer rode up and ordered a halt. Only then did the division stop. By then, the enemy had been driven back far enough to prevent them from being a further threat to the trains.

Cutshaw's battalion's attack had proved quite successful and, as it turned out, had not gone unnoticed. General Lee was nearby and had witnessed the entire affair. As John Purifoy remembered, "Our first charge was made under the eye of our great Commander, and the battalion was complemented for its bearing."[12]

During the assault, several prisoners had been taken by the Confederates. And as reported by Corporal Purifoy, "It was the duty of the writer [Purifoy] to take charge of these prisoners and deliver them to the provost guard."[13]

Meanwhile, in the vicinity of Cumberland Church, Mahone had just enough time to take his position and throw up a line of earthworks before two divisions of Humphreys' II Corps appeared on his front. The Yankees advanced, and a sharp skirmish ensued. Both Gordon and Longstreet later came up in support, and the enemy was checked in convincing style. Near dusk, the fighting came to an end.

Then, at about 9:00 p.m., a message from Grant, asking for the surrender of the Army of Northern Virginia, was delivered by way of flag of truce. When shown the note, Lee, who hoped that a peaceful solution to the present hostilities could still be reached without him having to surrender his army, sent a reply asking Grant's terms. When Lee's answer reached Federal Headquarters, Grant decided to withhold his response until the following day.

That same night, the Southern forces resumed their march, this time in the direction of New Store, which was about ten miles from Cumberland Church. After reaching New Store, the army was then to proceed in the direction of Appomattox Station, on the Southside Railroad. There, more supplies were awaiting the Confederates. On the way, Longstreet's command would act as rear guard. Gordon, who had been almost continuously engaged during the retreat, was to take the lead.

By first light of April 8, the Southern forces had passed through New Store and begun closing on Appomattox Station. The morning wore on, and during that time, the enemy was conspicuously absent. Into the afternoon, the march continued, and still there was no real threat from the Union forces.

The rigors of the journey, however, was too much for some. They could be seen "...lying prone on the ground along the roadside, too much exhausted to march farther, and only waiting for the enemy to come and pick them up as prisoners..."[14]

Along the road from New Store, bits of wreckage from the slow moving army were not an infrequent occurrence. "...at short intervals there were wagons broken down, their teams of horses and mules lying in the mud, from which they had struggled to extricate themselves until complete exhaustion forced them to wait for death to glaze their wildly staring eyes."[15]

The uncontested, but terrible march towards Appomattox Station continued until late in the afternoon. By then, the head of Gordon's column had arrived at a point about two miles north of Appomattox Court House, and five miles from the railroad depot, where the desperately needed supplies awaited the army. There, above the Court House,

Lee's forces were to rest until 1:00 a.m., on the morning of April 9, when they would resume the march.

While Gordon's troops established a temporary camp, Brigadier General Pendleton road south towards Appomattox Station. He was going to check on the rest of the army's artillery, commanded by Brigadier General R. Lindsay Walker, which had preceded the main column during the retreat from Amelia Court House, and was purportedly located a mile or so from the railroad. Pendleton located the artillery train. Then at 6:00 p.m., he witnessed a surprise attack, made by Custer's cavalry division, against Walker's camp. It was a desperate situation. "To avert immediate disaster from this attack demanded the exercise of all our energies,"[16] reported Pendleton.

The attack was repulsed, due in large part to the efforts of two companies of artillerists serving as an infantry guard. Their musket fire had slowed the Yankee advance and allowed Walker to bring up several pieces of artillery, whose fire permitted the withdrawal of the rest of the train.

With the repulse of the enemy, Pendleton headed back to Headquarters. For a time the return ride was uneventful, but when just a short distance from the Court House, the enemy's cavalry suddenly appeared on the road. Pendleton "...only escaped being shot or captured by leaping my horse over the fence and skirting for some distance along the left of that road toward our column then advancing, and until I reached a point beyond where the enemy's charge was checked."[17]

In the meantime, the Federals launched several more assaults against Walker's position, but each time the artillerymen beat off their attackers. Then at 9:00 p.m., Custer ordered a general advance. This time, the Confederate gunners were forced to give ground. In the end, their position was overrun, with the loss of "...twenty-four pieces of artillery, all his trains, several battle-flags, and a large number of prisoners."[18] as reported by Custer. The Federal horsemen were finally halted at Appomattox Court House by some infantry, which had been moved up to meet the attacking force.

The loss of Walker's artillery and its accompanying train was serious, but not the worst of the news from Appomattox Station. Upon Custer's arrival at the depot, just prior to the attack on Walker, he had captured three trains loaded with supplies intended for the Confederates. Once in enemy hands, the locomotives and cars had been moved back to Farmville.

The Southern forces were again without provisions, and to further complicate matters, the route south was blocked by the enemy's cavalry. Furthermore, as the night progressed, much of the Federal infantry which had pursued Lee had also come up. The glow of the Yankee campfires could be seen in every direction, except to the north. The Confederates were almost surrounded.

That same night, a conference was held between Lee, Longstreet, Gordon and Fitzhugh Lee, in order to decide what should be done next. By that time, Lee had heard from Grant and had sent a second message in which he had expressed his desire to set up a meeting in order to discuss ways of bringing about a peaceful settlement to the present hostilities. At the same time, Lee had indicated that he saw no need, at present, to consider the surrender of his own army. Grant had not as yet responded to the latest correspondence. Therefore, it was decided by those present that some concerted action should be taken in hopes of rescuing their army from its predicament. As yet, Pendleton had not reached Headquarters, and nothing of what he had witnessed near Appomattox Station was known by Lee or his generals.

Ultimately, the commanders decided that an attempt would be made to break free of the Federals. At 1:00 a.m., on the morning of April 9, the Confederates would endeavor to wrest the road to Lynchburg away from the enemy. Once that was accomplished, Lee's army could continue the march towards Johnston's forces to the south.

The plan was for Fitzhugh Lee's cavalry to open the attack, supported by Gordon's entire command. Once the assault had commenced, the Southern forces were to undertake a turning movement to the left, in order to cover the passage of the army's trains over the just recovered roadway. At the same time, Longstreet would move up behind the vehicles, and by doing so, protect the army's rear.

Before the conference at Headquarters broke up, Fitzhugh Lee requested that he be allowed to leave the field with his command, with intentions of riding to North Carolina in the event they could not achieve their objective, and surrender of the army seemed imminent. Lee gave his permission for the attempted break-out.

Sometime between midnight and 1:00 a.m., Pendleton finally arrived at Headquarters. He immediately told Lee what had transpired earlier that night. From all indications, the enemy was present in greater strength than had first been anticipated. Accordingly, Lee told Fitzhugh Lee to reconnoiter the Federal position and see what the Confederates were actually up against. He was also given permission to delay his attack, if circumstances demanded, until first light. As it turned out, the advance was indeed postponed until later in the morning.

The night of April 8-9 had also witnessed the return of Corporal Francis M. Wootan, of the Jeff Davis Artillery, to the main army. Three days earlier, following the disaster at Sailor's Creek, a despondent Wootan had met up with an old friend, Dr. Conrad Wall, Chief Surgeon of Brigadier General Archibald Gracie's Brigade.[19] Together, both men had left the field on Wall's horse and had ridden until they had reached Farmville. At that particular town, Wootan had been treated to a hearty meal by the doctor.

The following day, Wall had procured a mule for Wootan, and both men had ridden south beyond their army's line of march, in search of more provisions. Once just south of the Appomattox River, they had encountered some Federal infantrymen, who, as it turned out, had just stolen some horses from a nearby farmhouse. In Wootan's own words, "At the instance of the Doctor, I took his pistol and soon caught them, and by flourishing my weapon and other threats, induced them to give them up. I led them back to the great delight of the old gentleman and family, who treated us magnificently."[20]

While dining at the farmhouse, a Negro from a neighboring farm had arrived out of breath and had announced "...that the Yankees were killing and robbing everything on their place."[21] Upon hearing that, Doctor Wall, Corporal Wootan and the farmer's son decided that they would go and drive off the bluecoats.

After arriving at the neighboring property, Wall and the farmer's son had exchanged a number of shots with the Federals. After a time, the thieving Yankees had been driven off.

There, however, had been little time to celebrate the victory. A company of Federal cavalrymen, alerted by the firing, was rapidly approaching. As Wootan and Wall were south of the Appomattox, the enemy was endeavoring to cut them off from the river. "But by a desparate race for life, we made it through the farms, by knocking down and jumping fences, and crossed the river as the enemy descended on the opposite side. We turned up the swamp and eluded them."[22]

Soon after the near brush with the Yankees, Wall had suggested that they return to a mill located near the ford they had just crossed, to get some flour. It was a dangerous mission, with an enemy picket nearby, but Wall had insisted on going through with it. In the end, the doctor had gotten his sack of flour, but not before a number of shots from the picket had just missed Wootan's head. The noise had also attracted the attention of some cavalry, who had then given chase. As before, both riders had escaped their pursuers.

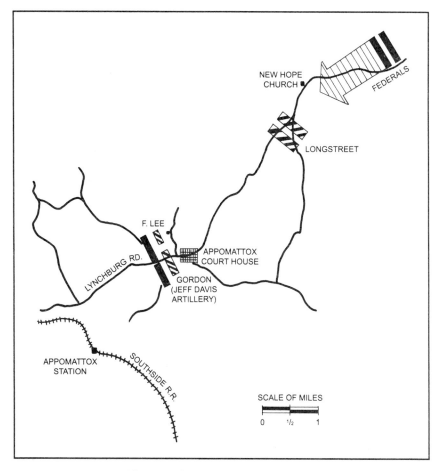

MORNING OF APRIL 9, 1865 – PRIOR TO ATTACK

Recreated from Plate LXXVIII-2 of The Official Military Atlas of the Civil War.

Wootan and Wall had finally reached the vicinity of Appomattox Court House after dusk on April 8. They spent the night sleeping between the then active skirmish lines of the opposing armies.

At first light on the morning of April 9, both Fitzhugh Lee and Gordon studied the Federal position, which stretched across the Lynchburg Road to their front. There was some disagreement about whether the enemy forces being scrutinized were in fact infantry or dismounted cavalry. After much discussion, the infantry was finally sent forward, supported on the right by Lee's mounted troops. John Purifoy recalled,

> When General Gordon, with that gallant five thousand, moved forward with the old time fire and showed that he and his men had lost none of the courage that had carried them through four years of brilliant achievement, and a determination to do or to die, no more grand sight was ever presented to living man. The fragment of the Jeff Davis Artillery formed in this line and moved with it. Their old time impetuosity still inspired them. Away went the line with flags flying and the old time yell.[23]

There was heavy firing on both sides, and before long a member of the Alabama battery fell to the ground. That was Private John Thompson. He had been struck, though not killed, by a Yankee bullet. The advance continued, and it took but a short time for the gray-clad attackers to overrun the Federal position.

With the enemy driven from the front, the Confederates executed the turning movement to clear the Lynchburg Road and allow the army's trains to proceed on ahead. Gordon's men were now facing south.

All at once, however, the situation south of the Court House began to deteriorate. Gordon received word that Federal infantry were present in strength beyond the Southern right (Fitzhugh Lee's position) and rear.

In less than an hour, the Yankees struck the Confederate cavalry's position and forced the mounted troops back on Gordon's flank. Not long thereafter, more infantry were spotted moving as if to cut off Gordon and Fitzhugh Lee from the rest of the army. About the same time, the enemy's cavalry began putting pressure on the Southern left.

Gordon was battling the enemy on three sides in a veritable fight for survival. The men of the Jeff Davis Artillery, like the rest of their comrades, fought with an unyielding determination, giving their all to the struggle. Though up against enormous odds, they were determined to fight on.

Meanwhile, supporting them were the well-served batteries of the army. Joining the bombardment, and in command of one section of Parrott Rifles belonging to Captain Valentine C. Clutter's Richmond Battery of Colonel Marmaduke Johnson's Battalion, was none other than Corporal Francis Wootan. That morning, he had come upon the battery in position on the road near the Court House and had been given charge of the guns. His section occupied a piece of tree-covered ground on the Southern left, and was involved in a sharp fight with some Federal cavalry. In Wootan's own words, "We were confronted by cavalry skirmishers, who kept a continual fire on us, to which I heartily responded..."[24]

In spite of the gallant efforts of Wootan and others from Reese's battery, the situation was hopeless. Gordon could not possibly continue his own fight unless heavily reinforced. And such assistance could only come from Longstreet, who was preparing to meet a heavy force which was advancing against the army's rear.

Back at Southern Headquarters, Lee realized that there was little point in continuing the struggle. Accordingly, a message was sent by him to Grant asking for terms. Quite unbelievably, the end of the four year struggle for Southern Independence was at hand. Lee was about to surrender his army. Before long, a cease-fire was put into effect along both lines.

For a short time, though, Corporal Wootan either refused to acknowledge what was occurring or was not aware of the cease-fire. His two artillery pieces continued to send their missiles at the Federals. Not until Brigadier General Long rode up and ordered his commander to stop firing did his guns fall silent.[25] Wootan later wrote, "I am satisfied that I fired the last cannon fired by Lee's Army."[26]

The silencing of the guns, which seemed to confirm the notion that surrender was imminent, caused shock waves to roll through the ranks of the Army of Northern Virginia. The brave veterans could scarcely believe what was happening, and began to wonder what was to be their fate. In the words of John Purifoy,

> Four years of unparalleled fighting, four years of intense suffering, four years of extreme suspense, four years of ardent hope, all went for nothing, worse than nothing. He [Purifoy] had lost all. He was a human being without a country. Federal prisons with all their horrible suffering stared him in the face. The horrible ghosts of our comrades, who had been starved in these war "hells", came trooping before him by regiments and brigades.[27]

Not wishing to wait to hear the terms of capitulation, a number of men from the Jeff Davis Artillery decided to take advantage of the cease-fire, to leave the field. They would attempt to make their way to Johnston's army in North Carolina. Included among them were Corporals John Purifoy and Thomas G. Traylor, as well as Privates Jake Jones, John Dunn, John Methvin and Halsey Smith.

In that instance, Purifoy was accompanied by Meredith Hogan, a member of Fry's battery. Hogan was familiar with the countryside, and felt confident in his being able to get both himself and Purifoy out of their predicament.

Soon after starting out, however, they encountered an unexpected obstacle. According to Purifoy,

> We immediately began to move and had not gone far until we were overtaken by General Fitzhugh Lee, with his flowing brown whiskers, on his iron gray charger. He asked, "Where are you men going?" To this question no reply was made. He immediately said, "Go back to your command," and rode steadily on. To give us the appearance of obedience, we halted for a moment and watched the General as he rode out of sight, up the mountain. We were not long in concluding that he had given us an order that he was himself unwilling to obey, and as soon as he passed out of sight we continued our movement.[28]

In fact, Fitzhugh Lee had found a way out of the Federal encirclement, and he and his cavalry did escape from the Court House while flags of truce were being passed.

The first part of the journey from the Court House proved most difficult, with Purifoy and Hogan having to elude enemy pickets as they moved through the woods. By nightfall, however, they had succeeded in getting beyond the left flank of the Federal army. That same night, they arrived at the home of a man named Arrington, and asked for some supper as well as a place to sleep. The home-owner was, at first, suspicious as to the exact identity of the two strangers, but after asking many questions, was satisfied that they were indeed Confederates. Arrington then asked about General Lee and was told of the surrender. And "...while he did not express a doubt, I [Purifoy] thought he was disposed not to credit our story. He acknowledged, however, that he had heard heavy firing early in the morning and that it had ceased about the hour we said General Lee had surrendered."[29]

The Army of Northern Virginia had indeed been surrendered. Among the men who laid down their weapons were Corporal Wootan and more than twenty other officers and men from the Jeff Davis Artillery. Their names were as follows:

Sergeant-Major Columbus W. McCrary
Corporal Joseph Blankinship
Corporal Christopher DuBose
Corporal James M. Jones   Bugler James A. Melton

Private John Blackmon   Private William Breithaupt
Private W. M. Callihan   Private S. M. Carter
Private J. P. Ellis   Private G. A. Jant
Private J. D. Garrard   Private Adam Hasselvander
Private A. W. Jones   Private G. W. Lee
Private S. J. Lee   Private John A. Logan
Private John A. Oliver   Private Wiley J. Polk
Private A. W. Skinner   Private Davidson Stoker
Private W. M. Thomas   Private Matthew Tucker
Private W. F. Ward   Private A. A. Young[30]

As was the case with all those from Lee's army included in the terms of the surrender agreement, the men of Reese's battery were to be paroled and sent home. The actual paroling procedure was to begin the next day, on April the 10th. Two days later, the formal surrender would take place.[31]

John Purifoy and his travelling companion meanwhile moved in the direction of Maryville (Hogan's home town). Along the way, they had an interesting encounter with a Confederate dressed in a surgeon's uniform. After being questioned about whether they were from the Army of Northern Virginia, they told the surgeon "...that Lee had surrendered. He seemed to have become indignant that we should have made such an answer. His air showed that he believed Lee was invincible. He replied 'I don't believe a word of it.' 'You are skulkers,' and turned and immediately walked away."[32]

The two "fugitives" resumed their journey, and some time after dark reached Hogan's home. There, Purifoy remained for the next few days.

Back at Appomattox Court House, the formal surrender, the laying down of arms, and turning over of flags of the Southern army took place as planned on the 12th of April. Following what, for all the Confederates, was a most humiliating experience, it was time for the men of Lee's former command to go home. "The men received paroles that obligated them not to enter the ranks and engage in fighting again until duly exchanged. These paroles permitted them to go to their homes wherever located."[33]

"Appomattox Court House, Va. April 10th, 1865. "The bearer, private J. A. Logan, of Reese's battery, of Cutshaw's Battalion, a paroled prisoner of the Army of Northern Virginia, has permission to go to his home, and there remain undisturbed.

> W A Deas, lst L't, Act,g,
> Commanding Battery."

On the back of this was <u>stamped</u> the following:

> "A Gilchrist
> April 13th, 1865,
> Cap't and Pro. Marshall."

> "Q M Capt. City Point, Va.
> April 17, 1865
> Free transportation,
> Sam'l Gibson, Capt, and A Q M."

> "Office P. M. G.
> April 17, 1865
> To Ft Monroe."

No. 696   "Office Provost Marshal, Mobile, Ala. May 4, 1865.

The bearer, John Logan, Reese's Battery, paroled prisoner of the Army of Northern Virginia, had permission to proceed by steamer, to his home in Lowndes County, Ala. and there remain without molestation, so long as he observes the condition of his parole and regulation and laws in force at the place of his residence.

By order of S O Lewis, Major and Provost Marshal."

Endorsed on the back;

> "Office Provost Marshal, Mobile Ala, May 4, 1865.
> Quarter Department will furnish the necessary transportation.
> By order of S O Lewis
> Major and Provost Marshall.

> S H Beard
> Capt, and Ass't Pro Marshal."[34]

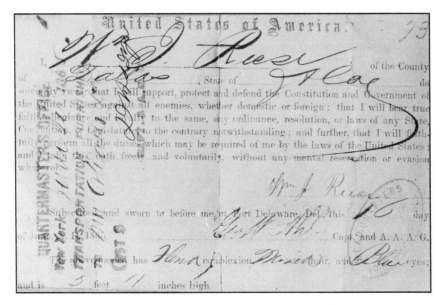

Captain William J. Reese's Oath of Allegiance.

(Sturdivant Hall Museum Association, Selma, Alabama)

As shown above, transportation was made available to those officers and men who wished an easier way of reaching their respective destinations. Many men from Reese's command elected to take advantage of that offer.

Two days following the event at Appomattox Court House, Purifoy left Maryville and resumed his own southward journey. By then, some of the recently paroled soldiers from Lee's army had already reached the town.

A short time later, after crossing the border into North Carolina, he turned himself into a Federal cavalry unit and received his parole. Purifoy then continued travelling, mostly on foot, until he reached his home in Alabama.

As for Dunn and Methvin, two others who had attempted to escape to North Carolina, both had surrendered with Lee at Appomattox. Apparently, neither one had been able to get through enemy lines. As for Halsey Smith, there is nothing to indicate where and when he received his parole, or if he ever eluded the Federals.

One member of the Alabama battery, however, did eventually reach his objective. That was Private John Thompson, who had been wounded during the last charge on the morning of April 9. Once the fighting had ceased, Thompson had been removed from the battlefield and taken to the U.S. Hospital in Farmville.

Not wishing to remain in Federal hands, he had escaped from the hospital and headed for North Carolina. He eventually reached Johnston's army, but by then it was too late. The war in North Carolina was already drawing to a rapid conclusion. On April 26, Thompson would surrender with the rest of Johnston's army to Sherman. Though he was unable to contribute anything to the war in North Carolina, Private Thompson's unwavering dedication to the cause of the Confederacy was, again, so typical of those men who had served as members of the Jeff Davis Artillery.

The war had ended for those veterans from Reese's battery who had remained with the main army all the way through the Appomattox Campaign. For still others, however, namely those held within the walls of some Yankee prison, the road to freedom was not yet attainable.

Captain Reese, Lieutenant Bates, and some thirty other men from the Jeff Davis Artillery, who had been captured at Spotsylvania, Hupp's Hill and along the road to Appomattox, would have to wait two months or more before receiving their paroles. For some, like Privates J. D. Watson and Benjamin Jackson, however, there would be no day of freedom. Watson, an unwitting victim of the disaster at Hupp's Hill, would die on May 7. Jackson, captured a few days before Appomattox, at Burkeville, was to succumb to illness on June 10.

That same day, and for the next two weeks, the Alabamians who had been imprisoned at Fort Delaware, Elmira, Newport News and Point Lookout were set free. With the releasing of the prisoners came the end, not only of the battle for survival, but also of the war.

The struggle for independence was over for the gallant men from Alabama. The difficult times that men like William J. Reese and Dwight E. Bates had been through, from the company's beginnings, were but a bad dream compared to the feelings of despondency that they must have felt as they undertook their long homeward journey. At the same time, there also must have been a feeling of pride, though, for the way their company had fought for the cause so dear.

From Seven Pines to Appomattox, the Alabamians had never once faltered when called upon to engage the enemy. On numerous occasions, the battery had even received praise from the High Command, including General Lee himself, for the way it had handled itself in the field. Even under the most adverse of conditions, when death seemed the only way out, the Alabamians had kept their composure and gone about their destructive work. At the same time, there had been, "A few, very few,..., skulkers and deserters. No shame need blanch the cheeks of friends and relatives on account of any dishonor."[35] During four years of active campaigning, the Jeff Davis Artillery had made for itself a reputation with which any other battery of the Army of Northern Virginia would have been highly pleased.

Still, for the proud Alabamians, there, at present, could be little consolation gained by the knowledge that their battery had done so well. The shock of defeat would remain with them for some time. Certainly though, in the weeks and months to come, thoughts about the glorious reputation won over the four years of conflict would no doubt help to diminish the painful recollection of how the South's quest for independence had ended.

THE END

APPENDIX A

THE STORY OF "MOLLIE GLASS"

BY MRS. MOLLIE GLASS HOPKINS[1]

...My father raised his own horses of fine pedigree. When new colts were separated, I always went down to the pasture, while they still went around on their first wabbly legs and took my choice. I used to ride the young horses before they were bridle wise, and sometimes one would run away with me, then father would insist that I leave the unbroken colts alone. Thinking to make him more amenable to reason, I would reply, "If I cant ride my own horse I will give him to the Confederacy," and finally when "Di Vernon" my favorite riding mare and a perfect beauty, stood upon her hind legs and fell backwards and rolled with me into a ditch and I got home with a broken arm and a cracked rib, there was much family discussion in which my stern parent was both judge and jury and the case went against me. I gave the beautiful Di Vernon to the Jeff Davis Artillery just then going to Virginia for active service. Her name was changed to Mollie Glass and she was called my substitute. She was killed in the battle of Fredericksburg. An old friend Mr. McKarkle (then pastor of the Talladega church) in writing a letter of condolence to my father said "I cannot get over the shock of seeing dear Mary's name in the official list of killed in the battle of Fredericksburg" – Now this godly old man would have thought a live girl in soldier pants was predestined to perdition, but as she was dead he went on thus: "A dauntless soul has gone to her reward, for I know she can give a good account of herself."

Has any one among you, ever had the pleasure of reading a neater little obituary of yourself, 50 years before shuffling off this mortal coil?

Sometime after the battle of Fredericksburg, four of the sick and wounded of the Jeff Davis Artillery came home on furlough and each one availed himself of the sad privilege of telling me that he was riding my beautiful Di when she received the death wound in her gallant breast – that she was his special mount and the pet of the company. In an old diary, yellow with age is the following comment:

"Poor brave fellows, they have fought so well and endured so much, that I gave each of his mead of thanks and praise; though three of them and perhaps four are telling what mother calls an untruth. For be it from me however, to wound them by searching for the truth."

H. P. Thomas –   Montgomery Weekly Advertiser
Lieut. Jeff. Davis Artillery.   Wednesday January 7, 1863.
                                       Page 1. Col. 2.

Casualties of the Jeff, Davis Artillery,
at Fredericksburg on Saturday the 13th:

Killed – John Crosby; Wounded – William Dennis, left foot shot off; E. D. Nabors, in his foot. In no fight since the 14th.

One caison was disabled, and two horses, the pony Mollie Glass was killed.

H. P. Thomas
Lieut. Jeff Davis Artillery[2]

****

APPENDIX B

CORRESPONDENCE OF THE REPORTER

LETTER FROM CAPT. W. J. REESE, OF THE JEFF DAVIS ARTILLERY.

OFF FORTRESS MONROE, }

MAY 15, 1864

Editor Selma Reporter: Please publish the following names of members of my company who were captured in the late battle:

1st Lieut. D. E. Bates, Segts. J. J. Barlow, J. F. Maull; Corps. G. Y. Higgins, G. G. Jackson; Privates D. J. Alford, J. P. Putegnat, J. N. Cowan, James Bulger, R. W. Barlow, T. W. Barlow, J. M. Nolen, W. J. Melton, W. B. Trawick, J. W. Johnson, F. M. Callihan, O. S. Teague, M. M. Teague, James Spencer, A. M. Blackman, W. D. Parnall, Wm. Reese, A. H. Patton, A. B. Patton, J. D. Stewart, W. H. Templin, P. G. Crawford, J. DeFriese, N. Sheffield, M. S. Freeman, Daniel Cosden.
The following were slightly wounded:

Sergt. R. E. Cobb; Privates E. Miner and J. V. F. Walker.

I do not our destination,

Very respectfully,
Wm. J. Reese, Capt.

Selma Morning Reporter, June 22, 1864.[1]

320

APPENDIX C

ROSTER OF THE JEFF DAVIS ALABAMA ARTILLERY

(In a number of cases, the initials and spelling of the names that follow were found to vary in the different sources. The information provided was determined to be the most accurate available. Additionally, in many instances, two or more different enlistment dates appear in an individual's service records. Where that occurs, the first or earliest date that appears on the rolls has been indicated.)

COMMISSIONED AND NON-COMMISSIONED OFFICERS

Beckham, Robert F. - 1st Lieutenant/Captain
Virginian, graduate of West Point; October 14, 1861, assigned to company as lst Lieutenant; ordered to take command of the company by Special Order #423; was in command during latter half of December of 1861 and most of January of 1862; refused to accept the rank of Captain of the company; later transferred to Col. Pendleton's Corps Reserve Artillery.

Bondurant, James W. - Sergeant/Captain
Enlisted July 23, 1861 at Selma, Ala.; mustered in July 27, 1861; elected lst Lieutenant from Sergeant on January 25, 1862; became Captain upon Lt. Beckham's refusal to accept that position; didn't actually command the company until the Peninsula Campaign; left company during spring of 1863; promoted to Major of Artillery on May 8, 1863 and became Chief of Artillery for General D. H. Hill; later Colonel of Company A, lst Regiment Mobile Volunteers, Ala., acted as Inspector and Mustering Officer.

Fry, Charles W. - Captain
Commanded the Orange County Artillery from Virginia; after the battle of Spotsylvania, a portion of the Jeff Davis Artillery was attached to his company.

Montgomery, Joseph T. - Captain
Organized the company in Selma and was its first Captain; sent on recruiting service by Special Order #423, October 14, 1861; cashiered by court martial on December 13, 1861; dismissed from the service, reinstated by President Davis; soon thereafter he resigned; was commissioned Lieutenant-Colonel and authorized to organize a battalion of artillery.

Reese, William J. - 2nd Lieutenant/Captain (fr. Dallas County)
Enlisted July 26, 1861 at Selma, Ala.; mustered in July 27, 1861; left sick at LaGrange, Ga., August 24, 1861; resigned January 16, 1862; served in the lst Regiment Alabama Partisan Rangers; was discharged from Co. H of the 51st Regiment Alabama Partisan Rangers on March 4, 1863 though on February 28, 1863 he took command of the Jeff Davis Artillery; wounded during engagement at Bealton Station, October 26, 1863; taken prisoner at Spotsylvania Court House on May 12, 1864; sent to Fort Delaware on May 17, 1864 and remained there until June 16, 1865 when he was released.

Jones, Hilary P. - Lieutenant
After resignation of Captain Montgomery, he was assigned to the temporary command of the company; held that position from February to early April of 1862 when J. W. Bondurant assumed command of the battery.

Bates, Dwight E. - Engineer/1st Lieutenant (fr. Perry County)
Enlisted at Selma, Ala. on July 15, 1861; mustered in July 27, 1861; appointed acting 2nd Lieutenant on January 20, 1863; taken prisoner at Spotsylvania Court House on May 12, 1864; received at Ft. Delaware on May 17, 1864; sent to Hilton Head, S.C. for retaliation on August 20, 1864, then to Fort Pulaski, then back to Hilton Head; returned to Fort Delaware on March 12, 1865; released on June 16, 1865.

Christian, Richard H. - Junior 2nd Lieutenant/2nd Lieutenant
Enlisted April 19, 1861 at Petersburg, Virginia; assigned to duty as Jr. 2nd Lieutenant with company on October 28, 1863; remained with command until mid-January of 1864; surrendered with General Lee at Appomattox Court House-April 9, 1865.

Fitts, William A. - 4th Lieutenant
Enlisted July 1, 1861; mustered in July 27, 1861; resigned on January 27, 1862-too many officers when battery was reduced from eight to six guns; possibly also resigned as a result of Capt. Montgomery being reinstated to his former rank.

Knight, Edward G. - Private/2nd Lieutenant
Enlisted July 2, 1861 at Selma, Ala.; mustered in July 27, 1861; resigned on December 19, 1862 (action taken as a result of Capt. Bondurant's demand that he be examined by a military board as to his qualifications to fill the position of 2nd Lieutenant).

Lovelace, Charles W. - 2nd Lieutenant/1st Lieutenant
Enlisted July 1, 1861; mustered in July 27, 1861; he resigned on January 16, 1862 (resigned due to the reinstating of Capt. Montgomery to his former rank).

Mitchell, John - Private/2nd Lieutenant
Enlisted July 20, 1861 at Selma, Ala.; mustered in on July 27, 1861; promoted to corporal on December 5, 1861; elected by company to fill a vacancy caused by

resignations of December 19, 1862 but was never permitted to receive a commission or to serve as 2nd Lieutenant; he participated in the battle of Chancellorsville (though he was under arrest at the time) and was severely wounded, having an arm amputated; after having been in the hospital since the battle, he returned to duty on September 22, 1863; he unsuccessfully tried to receive a commission; was discharged in August of 1864.

Shepard, Alexander K. - 1st Lieutenant
Enlisted on July 5, 1861; mustered in on July 27, 1861; resigned on February 1, 1862 (resigned due to the reinstating of Capt. Montgomery to his former rank).

Thomas, Hugh P. - Sergeant/1st Lieutenant
Enlisted July 23, 1861 at Selma, Ala.; mustered in on July 27, 1861; on December 19, 1862 he tendered his resignation as 1st Lieutenant (action taken as a result of Capt. Bondurant's demand that he be examined by a military board as to his qualifications to fill the position of 1st Lieutenant).

Walker, Robert S. - Sergeant/1st Lieutenant
Enlisted July 1, 1861 at Selma, Ala.; mustered in July 27, 1861; elected a lieutenant on September 20, 1861; resigned on January 16, 1862 (due to the reinstating of Capt. Montgomery to his former rank); later a 2nd Lieutenant with Co. I of the 43rd Regiment Alabama Volunteers.

Yeldell, Robert A. - Private/1st Lieutenant
Enlisted July 10, 1861 at Selma, Ala.; mustered in July 27, 1861; promoted from a Corporal to a Sergeant on September 20, 1861; elected a 2nd Lieutenant on January 28, 1862; resigned in December of 1862 (action taken as a result of Capt. Bondurant's demand that he be examined by a military board as to his qualifications to fill the position of 1st Lieutenant).

Barlow, Joseph J. - Private/Sergeant (fr. Lowndes Co.)
Enlisted July 1, 1861 at Selma, Ala.; mustered in July 27, 1861; after October 15 was on sick leave at home in Alabama; promoted to Sergeant on May 1, 1863; captured at the battle of Spotsylvania Court House on May 12, 1864; transferred to Elmira, N.Y. on August 15, 1864; released on June 14, 1865.

Billingslea, John – Private/Sergeant/Private (fr. Perry Co.)
Enlisted on July 15, 1861 at Selma, Ala.; mustered in July 27, 1861; August 10, 1861 - appointed Sergeant in place of William L. Callihan; Sept. 24, 1861 shown as sick at LaGrange, Ga.; left camp on October 26, 1861 on the grounds of not having been mustered into service and not having received pay, making him a deserter; enlisted February 28, 1862 at Bull Run, Va.; substituted for by John Hartigan on March 29, 1863; later with the cavalry in the Tennessee Army.

Callihan, William L. - Sergeant
Mustered in July 27, 1861; courtmartialed and cashiered on August 10, 1861.

Carter, Euphroneus - Sergeant/Stable Guard/Private (fr. Wilcox Co.)
Enlisted July 21, 1861 at Selma, Ala.; mustered in July 27, 1861; admitted to Chimbarazo Hospital in Richmond on November 22, 1861 suffering from intermittent fever; Jan. 3, 1862 still sick in hospital; surrendered with General Lee at Appomattox Court House-April 9, 1865.

Cobb, Robert E. - Corporal/Sergeant (fr. Dallas Co.)
Enlisted July 22, 1861 at Selma, Ala.; mustered in July 27, 1861; Dec. 31, 1862 -
Feb. 28, 1863 shown as on detached service in Alabama; reduced to ranks on
December 27, 1863; restored to Sergeant on January 27, 1864 by Capt. W. J. Reese;
wounded and taken prisoner at battle of Spotsylvania Court House on May 12,
1864; arrived at Elmira, N.Y. on August 12, 1864; exchanged on October 29, 1864;
Oct. 31, 1864 - March 1, 1865 shown as sick at hospital in Macon, Georgia.

Harper, Robert T. - Private/1st Sergeant (fr. Dallas Co.)
Enlisted August 13, 1862 at Selma, Ala.; Dec. 31, 1862 - Feb. 28, 1863 on detached
service at Headquarters; appointed Sergeant on March 1, 1863; promoted to the
rank of lst Lieutenant of the Engineer Corps on May 24, 1863.

Maull, John Fox - Corporal/2nd Sergeant (fr. Lowndes Co.)
Enlisted July 1, 1861 at Selma, Ala.; mustered in July 27, 1861; promoted to
Sergeant on September 20, 1861; from Oct. 31, 1862 - Feb. 28, 1863 on a sick
furlough; taken prisoner at Spotsylvania Court House on May 12, 1864; es-
caped from Elmira Prison on October 7, 1864 by tunneling; from Oct. 31, 1864
- March 1, 1865 assigned to Hardaway's Battalion; paroled at Selma, Ala. in
June of 1865.

McCrary, Columbus W. - Sergeant/Sergeant-Major (fr. Dallas Co.)
Enlisted July 1, 1861 at Selma, Ala.; mustered in July 27, 1861; appointed Ser-
geant-Major on May 22, 1863; assigned to Griffin's Salem Flying Artillery on
May 24, 1864; served with Lamkin's Virginia Light Artillery from Oct. 1864 -
March 1865; surrendered with General Lee at Appomattox Court House - April
9, 1865.

Moore, James L. - 1st Sergeant (fr. Dallas Co.)
Enlisted July 1, 1861 at Selma, Ala.; mustered in July 27, 1861; through the efforts of Capt. Montgomery was discharged on June 10, 1862, promoted to the
rank of Captain and transferred to the Army of Tennessee.

Norwood, James E.- Sergeant (fr. Dallas Co.)
Enlisted June 26, 1861 at Selma, Ala.; mustered in July 27, 1861; severely wounded
at the battle of Chancellorsville on May 2, 1863; severely wounded at Strasburg
on October 13, 1864; shown at hospital until March 1, 1865; paroled some time in
May or June of 1865.

Patton, Augustus B. - Corporal/Sergeant (fr. Dallas Co.)
Enlisted June 27, 1861 at Selma, Ala.; mustered in July 27, 1861; promoted from
a Corporal to a Sergeant on September 20, 1861; taken prisoner at Spotsylvania
Court House on May 12, 1864; transferred to Elmira, N.Y. from Point Lookout,
Md. on August 15, 1864; released on June 14, 1865.

Robinson, Thaddeus P. - Private/Sergeant/Hospital Steward (fr. Autauga Co.)
Enlisted August 1, 1861 at Montgomery, Ala.; mustered in July 27, 1861; Aug. 31 -
Oct 31, 1861 shown as sick in camp; promoted to Sergeant on January 28, 1862;
Oct. 31 - Dec. 31, 1862 shown on detached service in Richmond, Va.; Dec. 31, 1862
- Feb. 28, 1863 shown on detached service in Montgomery, Ala.; Apr. 30 - June 30,
1863 shown as having been reduced to ranks in consequence of being perma-
nently detailed (unfit for full service, thus became a hospital steward); on de-
tached service in Montgomery, Ala., as shown in records, through March 1, 1865.

Snediker, John G. - Quartermaster Sergeant (fr. Dallas Co.)
Enlisted July 1, 1861 at Selma, Ala.; mustered in July 27, 1861; on register of Chimbarazo Hospital #3 on May 14, 1862 suffering from Typhoid and on July 29, 1862 suffering from Dysentery; Oct. 31, 1864 - March 1, 1865 in Battalion Q. M. Department; paroled at Selma, Ala. in June of 1865.

Sears, John W. - Surgeon
Enlisted July 1, 1861 at Selma, Ala.; mustered in July 27, 1861; from July 1 to August 31, 1861 he is shown attending the sick at Charlottesville Hospital.

Burroughs, Thomas A. – Private/Corporal/Private
Enlisted July 1, 1861 at Montgomery, Ala.; mustered in July 27, 1861; promoted to Corporal on January 28, 1862; Feb. 28, 1863 - Nov. 1, 1864 shown as being on detached service with ordnance train; captured at Jetersville, Va. on April 6, 1865; released on June 10, 1865.

DuBose, Christopher P. - Private/Corporal
Enlisted July 18, 1861 at Selma, Ala.; mustered in July 27, 1861; from Dec. 31, 1862 - Feb. 28, 1863 sent to Alabama on detached service; surrendered with General Lee at Appomattox Court House - April 9, 1865.

Gregory, John C. - Private/Corporal (fr. Dallas Co.)
Enlisted July 8, 1861 at Selma, Ala.; mustered in July 27, 1861; promoted to Corporal on December 5, 1861; killed at the battle of Cold Harbor - June 27, 1862.

Herndon, Thomas L. - Private/Corporal
Enlisted September 1, 1861 at Richmond, Va.; was transferred to Capt. Blodgh's (sp?) Company on October 15, 1861.

Higgins, George Y. - Private/Corporal (fr. Dallas Co.)
Enlisted July 1, 1861 at Selma, Ala.; mustered in July 27, 1861; Aug. 31 - Oct. 31, 1861 shown as sick in camp; reduced to ranks on December 27, 1863; restored to Corporal on Jan. 1, 1864 by Capt. W. J. Reese; taken prisoner at Spotsylvania Court House on May 12, 1864; transferred from Pt. Lookout, Md. to Elmira, N.Y. on August 15, 1864; released June 16, 1865; (while in prison, he refused all inducements to take the oath of allegiance and be freed).

Hunter, Alexander - Corporal (fr. Lowndes Co.)
Enlisted July 10, 1861 at Selma, Ala.; mustered in July 27, 1861; Aug. 31 - Oct. 31, 1861 shown as sick in camp; died in Centreville, Va. on November 21, 1861.

Jackson, George G. - Private/Corporal (fr. Montgomery Co.)
Enlisted July 15, 1861 at Selma, Ala.; mustered in July 27, 1861; promoted to Corporal on February 1, 1863; taken prisoner at Spotsylvania Court House on May 12, 1864; escaped from Elmira Prison on October 7, 1864 by tunneling; made his way back to the Confederate lines, then absent on a furlough of indulgence; later rejoined his old command.

Jones, James M. - Private/Corporal (fr. Butler Co.)
Enlisted March 31, 1862 at Greenville, Ala.; wounded at the battle of Cold Harbor - June 27, 1862 (right leg); from Oct. 31 - Dec. 31, 1862 shown as on furlough; promoted to Corporal on February 1, 1863; assigned to Griffin's Salem Flying Artillery on May 24, 1864; served with Lamkin's Virginia Light Artillery from Oct. 1864 - March 1865; surrendered with General Lee at Appomattox Court House - April 9, 1865.

Lee, Brittan C. - Corporal (fr. Lowndes Co.)
Enlisted July 8, 1861 at Selma, Ala.; mustered in July 27, 1861; July 1 - August 31, 1861 shown as sick at private house in Richmond, Va.; Aug. 31 - Oct. 26, 1861 shown as sick at hospital in Richmond; discharged from hospital on October 26, 1861.

Mundy, James J. - Corporal
Enlisted July 1, 1861 at Selma, Ala.; mustered in July 27, 1861; discharged from camp on Surgeon's Certificate on January 13, 1862; was age 46 1/2 and was suffering from a physical disability.

Nobles, Edward W. - Corporal (fr. Lowndes Co.)
Enlisted July 4, 1861 at Selma, Ala.; mustered in July 27, 1861; was severely wounded at the battle of Fredericksburg on December 13, 1862 (shell wound in left foot); shown at hospital from Dec. - February 28, 1863; at home on furlough for the remainder of the war.

Purifoy, John P. - Private/Corporal
Enlisted July 20, 1861 at Selma, Ala.; mustered in July 27, 1861; Aug. 31 - Oct. 31, 1861 shown as sick in camp; Dec. 31, 1861 - Feb. 28, 1862 shown as sick at hospital; was with the company for the remainder of the war.

Soles, Joseph M. - Corporal (fr. Lowndes Co.)
Enlisted July 15, 1861 at Selma, Ala.; mustered in July 27, 1861; January 3, 1862 shown as absent on sick furlough; discharged from hospital in Richmond on January 20, 1862 (officially discharged Jan. 28, 1862).

Stewart, William L. - Private/Corporal
Enlisted July 27, 1861 at Selma, Ala.; mustered in July 27, 1861; Dec. 31, 1862 - Feb. 28, 1863 shown as absent without leave; Feb. 28 - June 30, 1863 shown as sick at hospital; reduced to ranks by General Court Martial on April 16, 1864; Feb. 29 - Nov. 1, 1864 shown on detached service with Captain Christian; Oct. 31, 1864 - March 1, 1865 shown on detached service with Lamkin's Virginia Artillery.

Traylor, Thomas G. - Corporal/Private (fr. Lowndes Co.)
Enlisted July 1, 1861 at Selma, Ala.; mustered in July 27, 1861; Aug. 31 - Oct. 31, 1861 shown as sick in camp; Jan. 3, 1862 - sick at hospital; Feb. 29, 1864 - March 1, 1865 shown on detached service with Braxton's Battalion; surrendered at Lynchburg (?) - date (?).

Vaughan, Fred B. - Corporal (fr. Dallas Co.)
Enlisted July 25, 1861 at Selma, Ala.; mustered in July 27, 1861; Aug. 31 - Oct. 31, 1861 shown as absent without authority at home in Alabama (actually absent on furlough since August 24); January 3, 1862 shown as having been transferred to an Alabama Regiment by a Special Order.

Wootan, Francis M. - Private/Corporal (fr. Wilcox Co.)
Enlisted July 1, 1861 at Selma, Ala.; mustered in July 27, 1861; July 1 - Aug. 31, 1861 shown as sick at Alabama Hospital; Aug. 31 - Oct 31, 1861 shown as sick in camp; Dec. 31, 1861 - Feb. 28, 1862 shown as sick at hospital; promoted to Corporal on February 1, 1863; surrendered with General Lee at Appomattox Court House - April 9, 1865.

Yeldell, William A. - Corporal/Private (fr. Butler Co.)
Enlisted July 10, 1861 at Selma, Ala.; mustered in July 27, 1861; July 1 - Aug. 31, 1861 shown as sick at private hospital in Richmond; Aug. 31 - Oct. 31, 1861 shown as sick in camp; Dec. 31, 1861 - Feb. 28, 1862 shown as sick at hospital; substituted for by John Kane on April 20, 1863 when Yeldell was discharged.

PRIVATES

Acker, Augustus H. (fr. Dallas Co.)
Enlisted July 1, 1861 at Selma, Ala.; mustered in July 27, 1861 (credited $100 for value of horses he furnished to the cause); admitted to Chimbarazo Hospital on March 21, 1862 suffering from diarrhea - returned to duty on April 1.

Adams, Abraham (fr. Dallas Co.)
Enlisted July 1, 1861 at Selma, Ala.; mustered in July 27, 1861; was Acting Sergeant from Aug. 10, 1861; Aug. 31 - Oct. 31, 1861 shown as sick in camp; absent without leave after February 13, 1865; appears on roll of prisoners of war surrendered by Lt. Gen. R. Taylor to Major Gen. E. R. S. Canby on May 4, 1865; paroled June of 1865.

Adams, A. J.
Enlisted February 13, 1863 at Selma, Ala.; from Feb. 28 - Oct. 31, 1863 shown at home on furlough on surgeons certificate; Oct. 31, 1863 - Nov. 1, 1864 on detached service in Alabama (Purchasing agent for Subsistence Dept. of State of Alabama); paroled at Selma, Ala. - June of 1865.

Alexander, Martin L. (fr. Wilcox Co.)
Enlisted July 1, 1861 at Selma, Ala.; mustered in July 27, 1861; July 1 - Aug. 31, 1861 shown as sick at Alabama Hospital; Aug. 31 - Oct 31 shown as sick at hospital in Richmond, Va.; May 31, 1862 appears on register of Soldier's Home Hospital; returned to duty on July 7, 1862; discharged due to physical disability (chronic diarrhea) on July 16, 1862.

Alford, Daniel J. (fr. Dallas Co.)
Enlisted July 1, 1861 at Selma, Ala.; mustered in July 27, 1861; taken prisoner at battle of Spotsylvania Court House on May 12, 1864; transferred from Pt. Lookout, Md. to Elmira, N.Y. on August 15, 1864; transported for exchange on March 14, 1865.

Alley, T. K.
Enlisted on November 8, 1863; Feb. 29 - April 30, 1864 shown as on detached service; May 1 - July 1, 1864 shown as present for duty; from July 1, 1864 - March 1, 1865 shown as in hands of the enemy, supposed to have deserted and taken the oath.

Anderson, John S.
Enlisted July 20, 1861 at Selma, Ala.; mustered in July 27, 1861; was known as "Palmetto" (had been a member of the noted Palmetto Regiment that had served in the war with Mexico); was discharged from the service on October 27, 1861

by Special Order #468; was discharged because of physical disability caused by age and rheumatism.

Ball, G. H.
Enlisted August 28, 1863 at Livingston, Ala.; Feb. 29 - July 1, 1864 shown as sick at hospital (one cause being a contusion of the right lung suffered in a fall): Oct. 31, 1864 - March 1, 1865 shown as sick at hospital; on roll of prisoners of war that were surrendered by Lt. Gen. R. Taylor to Maj. Gen. E. R. S. Canby on May 4, 1865; was paroled on May 17, 1865.

Barker, J. J.
Enlisted September 23, 1863 at Talladega, Ala; Feb. 29 - Nov. 1, 1864 shown as on detached service at Harrisonburg, Va.; Oct. 31, 1864 - March 1, 1865 shown on detached service with Lamkin's Virginia Light Artillery; was captured at High Bridge, Va. on April 8, 1865; on April 15, 1865 was admitted to Subdepot field hospital in Burkeville, Va. suffering from diarrhea.

Barlow, R. W. (fr. Lowndes Co.)
Enlisted April 16, 1863 at Benton, Ala.; received in exchange for R. W. Woodward on June 2, 1863; taken prisoner at battle of Spotsylvania Court House on May 12, 1864; transferred to Elmira, N.Y. from Pt. Lookout, Md. on August 15, 1864; exchanged on October 29, 1864, then was on furlough; paroled June of 1865.

Barlow, J. W.
Enlisted September 18, 1863 at Pleasant Hill, Ala.; taken prisoner at battle of Spotsylvania Court House on May 12, 1864; transferred to Elmira, N.Y. from Pt. Lookout, Md. on August 15, 1864; exchanged on October 29, 1864.

Batton, William
Enlisted October 8, 1863 at Talladega, Ala.; missing after engagement of Spotsylvania Court House on May 12, 1864; (was actually killed in action at above battle).

Belcher, Obediah
Enlisted August 26, 1863 at Randolph, Ala.; discharged on certificate of disability on January 1, 1864.

Bell, G.
Appears on roll of prisoners captured at Strasburg, Va. on October 19, 1864; paroled at Point Lookout, Maryland and transferred to Aiken's Landing, Va. on March 17, 1865 for exchange.

Bentley, James S. (fr. Wilcox Co.)
Enlisted July 9, 1861 at Selma, Ala.; mustered in July 27, 1861; Aug. 31 - Oct. 31, 1861 shown as sick and in Richmond, Va.; died in hospital in Richmond on November 6, 1861.

Bishop, Herman - Bugler
Enlisted August 4, 1861 at Montgomery, Ala.; mustered in July 27, 1861; left company on October 19, 1861 for reason of not having been mustered in or having received pay.

Blackburn, William S.
Enlisted March 23, 1862 at Rapidan, Va.; assigned to Griffin's Salem Flying Artillery on May 24, 1864; Oct. 31, 1864 - March 1, 1865 shown on detached service with Captain Armstrong.

Blackmon, A. M.
Enlisted August 23, 1863 at Talladega, Ala.; taken prisoner at battle of Spotsylvania Court House on May 12, 1864; transferred from Pt. Lookout, Md. to Elmira, N.Y. on August 15, 1864; released on June 19, 1865.

Blackmon, John W.
Enlisted May 7, 1864 at Selma, Ala.; Feb. 29 - Nov. 1, 1864 shown as sick in hospital; on list of prisoners of war surrendered at Appomattox Court House - April 9, 1865.

Blackstock, A.
Enlisted November 9, 1863 at Talladega, Ala.; assigned to Griffin's Salem Flying Artillery on May 24, 1864; served with Lamkin's Virginia Light Artillery from Oct. 1864 - March 1865.

Blankinship, Joseph (fr. Wilcox Co.)
Enlisted July 14, 1861 at Selma, Ala.; mustered in July 27, 1861; Sept. 20, 1861 shown as sick at Alabama hospital; Aug. 31, 1861 - Jan 3. 1862 shown as sick in camp and at hospital; Aug. 31 - Oct 31, 1863 shown as sick at hospital; on October 17, 1863 was injured from the explosion of a cartridge and was given a forty day furlough; surrendered at Appomattox Court House - April 9, 1865.

Blanks, Andrew J. (fr. Perry Co.)
Enlisted August 10, 1861 at Montgomery, Ala.; March 7, 1864 appears on register of hospital in Richmond, Va.; killed in action at battle of Spotsylvania Court House on May 12, 1864.

Bolton, William A.
Appears on company muster roll of Captain Montgomery's Co. Light Artillery, Ala. Vols. from July 1 - Aug. 31, 1861; mustered in July 27, 1861; arrested by order of Major J. Calhoun as a deserter from Captain B. L. Posey's Company, lst Regiment Alabama Volunteers and sent back to Montgomery on August 9, 1861.

Booth, John (fr. Dallas Co.)
Enlisted July 1, 1861 at Selma, Ala.; mustered in July 27, 1861; captured at Jetersville, Va. on April 7, 1865; held at Point Lookout, Md.; released on June 9, 1865.

Bowen, Zack
Enlisted July 10, 1861 at Selma, Ala.; Aug. 31 - Oct. 31, 1861 shown as sick at hospital in Richmond, Va.; discharged from hospital and service on October 29, 1861.

Bradley, Thomas M. (fr. Choctaw Co.)
Enlisted July 10, 1861 at Selma, Ala.; mustered in July 27, 1861; March 22, 1862 shown suffering from paralysis at hospital in Orange Court House, Va.; May 21, 1862 shown suffering from Dysentery at hospital in Richmond, Va.; killed in action at battle of Spotsylvania Court House on May 12, 1864.

Brazealle, James K. (fr. Lowndes Co.)
Enlisted July 11, 1861 at Selma, Ala.; mustered in July 27, 1861; shown as sick in camp on roll dated January 3, 1862; appears on register of officers and soldiers who were killed in battle, died of wounds or disease; died on May 29, 1862.

Breithaupt, William (fr. Wilcox Co.)
Enlisted July 1, 1861 at Selma, Ala.; mustered in July 27, 1861; Aug. 31 - Oct. 31, 1861 shown as having been discharged while sick in LaGrange, Ga.; reenlisted April 26, 1863 at Selma, Ala.; surrendered with the army at Appomattox Court House - April 9, 1865.

Bryant, Joseph
April 2, 1862 shown suffering from Measles at hospital in Richmond, Va.; died on April 29, 1862.

Bulger, James
Enlisted August 4, 1863 at Talladega, Ala.; taken prisoner at battle of Spotsylvania Court House on May 12, 1864; transferred from Pt. Lookout, Md. to Elmira, N.Y. on August 15, 1864; transferred for exchange on October 11, 1864.

Bullard, James W.
Enlisted November 9, 1863 at Talladega, Ala.; deserted - February 6, 1864 on march from Fredericks Hall to Orange Court House, Va.

Burnett, J. J.
Enlisted November 9, 1863 at Talladega, Ala.; Feb. 29 - April 30, 1864 name appears on company roll and is shown as being a deserter.

Burwell, John (fr. Dallas Co.)
Enlisted July 1, 1861 at Selma, Ala.; mustered in July 27, 1861; June 30 - August 31, 1863 listed as absent without leave (supposedly taken prisoner in Pennsylvania, though is shown as having been captured at Falling Waters, Md. on July 14, 1863); (Pvt. Burwell actually deserted at Williamsport, Md. on July 14, 1863 and was ready to take the oath of allegiance; Sept. 18, 1863 appears on register of prisoners of the Provost Marshal General in Washington, D.C.; released on September 24, 1863 and was sent to Philadelphia, Pa.)

Busby, John R. (fr. Bibb Co.)
Enlisted July 11, 1861 at Selma, Ala.; mustered in July 27, 1861; captured at Gettysburg, Pa. on July 4, 1863; released from Pt. Lookout, Md. on January 26, 1864 when he took the oath and joined the U.S. Army.

Butts, W. R.
Shown as having been admitted to hospital in Richmond, Va. on April 7, 1862; returned to duty April 26, 1862.

Caldwell, C. Y.
Appears on roll of Prisoners of War surrendered by Lt. Gen. Taylor on May 4, 1865; paroled at Selma, Ala. during June of 1865.

Caldwell, J. D.
Appears on roll of soldiers killed, died of wounds or disease at Centreville, Va. during the winter of 1861-62.

Caldwell, William
Enlisted July 1, 1861 at Selma, Ala.; mustered in July 27, 1861; Aug. 31 - Oct. 31, 1861 shown as sick at hospital in Richmond, Va.; died in camp near Centreville, Va. on November 27, 1861. (*Compiled Service Records*)

Callahan, F. M.
   Enlisted September 15, 1863 at Pleasant Hill, Ala.; taken prisoner at battle of
   Spotsylvania Court House on May 12, 1864; transferred from Pt. Lookout, Md.
   to Elmira, N.Y. on August 15, 1864; exchanged on October 29, 1864.

Callihan, George W. (fr. Lowndes Co.)
   Enlisted July 12, 1861 at Selma, Ala.; mustered in July 27, 1861; July 1 - Oct. 31,
   1861 shown as sick in Richmond, Va.; discharged on September 13, 1861.

Callihan, John
   Enlisted July 12, 1861 at Selma, Ala.; mustered in July 27, 1861; died in hospital
   on December 22, 1861.

Callihan, William M. (fr. Lowndes Co.)
   Enlisted July 12, 1861 at Selma, Ala.; December 31, 1861 to February 28, 1862
   shown as absent on sick furlough until January 30, then absent without proper
   authority; Oct. 31 - Dec. 31, 1862 on detached service at Richmond; Dec. 31,
   1862 - Feb. 28, 1863 on detached service at Camp Winder Hospital where he
   served as a nurse; surrendered with General Lee at Appomattox Court House
   – April 9, 1865.

Campbell, James S. (fr. Dallas Co.)
   Enlisted July 2, 1861 at Selma, Ala.; mustered in July 27, 1861; Aug. 31 - Oct. 31,
   1861 shown as sick at hospital in Richmond, Va.; on October 8, 1862 was given
   forty day furlough due to liver problems; was later discharged from the service.

Campbell, John D. (fr. Dallas Co.)
   Enlisted July 2, 1861 at Selma, Ala.; mustered in July 27, 1861; Dec. 31, 1861 - Feb.
   28, 1862 served as a teamster and was entitled to two months extra pay; severely
   wounded at the battle of Cold Harbor on June 27, 1862; Oct. 31 - Dec. 31, 1862
   shown on furlough; Dec. 31, 1862 - Feb. 28, 1863 on sick furlough at home; Feb.
   28, 1863 - Jan 1, 1864 shown as being absent without leave; Feb. 29 - Sept. 1, 1864
   shown as being on detached service at hospital; Oct. 31, 1864 - March 1, 1865
   supposed to be on detached service.

Canterberry, Zenephan C.
   Enlisted October 13, 1863 at Talladega, Ala.; died at Howards Grove Hospital in
   Richmond, Va. on August 29, 1864.

Carter, Joseph W. (fr. Wilcox Co.)
   Enlisted July 5, 1861 at Selma, Ala.; mustered in July 27, 1861; died on July 5,
   1862 as a result of the wounds received at the battle of Cold Harbor on June
   27, 1862.

Carter, S. M. (fr. Dallas Co.)
   Enlisted November 3, 1863 at Selma, Ala.; surrendered with General Lee at Appomattox Court House - April 9, 1865.

Cauley, J. L. (fr. Wilcox Co.)
   Enlisted May 27, 1864 at Selma, Ala.; taken prisoner at Middletown, Va. on
   October 19, 1864; sent to Pt. Lookout Prison in Maryland and was admitted to
   camp hospital on January 9, 1865 suffering from chronic diarrhea; died on
   January 26, 1865.

Champion, George M.
Enlisted May 8, 1863 at Hamilton's Crossing, Va.; accepted as a substitute for D. W. Sanders; taken prisoner at Gettysburg, Pa. on July 4, 1863; paroled at Ft. Delaware on July 30, 1863.

Clarke, Richard G.
Enlisted July 20, 1861 at Selma, Ala.; mustered in July 27, 1861; January 3, 1862 shown as sick in camp; Oct. 31 - Dec. 31, 1862 shown as sick in hospital; Feb. 29, 1864 - March 1, 1865 shown at home on sick furlough; captured at Burkeville, Va. on April 6, 1865.

Claughton, Wilber F. (fr. Dallas Co.)
Enlisted July 1, 1861 at Selma, Ala.; mustered in July 27, 1861; wounded at battle of Cold Harbor on June 27, 1862; Oct. 18, 1862 discharged from service because of wound.

Cobb, C. A. (fr. Dallas Co.)
Enlisted February 13, 1863 at Selma, Ala.; taken prisoner at Middletown, Va. on October 19, 1864; sent from Harpers Ferry, W. Va. to Pt. Lookout, Md. on October 23, 1864; transferred to Aiken's Landing, Va. on March 17, 1865 for exchange.

Cochran, John W. - Artificer (fr. Dallas Co.)
Enlisted July 1, 1861 at Selma, Ala.; mustered in July 27, 1861; on list of prisoners of war paroled from May 8 - June 21, 1865; actually paroled May 10, 1865 at Winchester, Va.

Cosdan, Daniel G. (fr. Dallas Co.)
Enlisted July 7, 1861 at Selma, Ala.; mustered in July 27, 1861; taken prisoner at battle of Spotsylvania Court House on May 12, 1864; transferred from Pt. Lookout, Md. to Elmira, N.Y. on August 15, 1864; took oath of allegiance on May 29, 1865.

Cowan, John N. (fr. Lowndes Co.)
Enlisted July 10, 1861 at Selma, Ala.; mustered in July 27, 1861; July 1 - Aug. 31, 1861 shown as sick in camp; Aug. 31 - Oct. 31, 1861 shown as sick at hospital in Richmond, Va.; taken prisoner at battle of Spotsylvania Court House on May 12, 1864; received at Elmira, N.Y. from Pt. Lookout, Md. on August 17, 1864; transferred for exchange on March 14, 1865.

Cox, James W. (fr. Dallas Co.)
Enlisted July 1, 1861 at Selma, Ala.; mustered in July 27, 1861; wounded at the battle of Cold Harbor on June 27, 1862; taken prisoner at Middletown, Va. on October 19, 1864; sent from Harpers Ferry, W. Va. to Pt. Lookout, Md. on October 23, 1864; exchanged on March 17, 1865.

Crawford, P. G.
Enlisted November 5, 1863 at Talladega, Ala.; Jan. 29 - Feb. 9, 1864 shown at hospital in Richmond, Va. due to debility; taken prisoner at battle of Spotsylvania Court House on May 12, 1864; appears on roll of prisoners at Pt. Lookout, Md.; died on June 10, 1864.

Crosby, John J. S. (fr. Lowndes Co.)
Enlisted July 1, 1861 at Selma, Ala.; mustered in July 27, 1861; July 1 - Aug. 31, 1861 shown as sick in camp suffering from diarrhea; Aug. 31 - Oct. 31, 1861

shown as sick at hospital in Richmond, Va.; admitted to hospital in Richmond, Va. on September 27, 1862 because of shell wound to the face; was released on October 17, 1862; killed at battle of Fredericksburg on December 13, 1862.

Cullen, T. F.
Enlisted November 8, 1863 at Talladega, Ala.; Feb. 29 - April 30, 1864 shown as having deserted.

Davidson, C.
Enlisted November 5, 1864 at Butler, (state?); Oct. 31, 1864 - March 1, 1865 shown as sick at hospital.

Davidson, D. R.
Enlisted October 13, 1863 at Talladega, Ala.; Feb. 29, 1864 - Sept. 1, 1864 shown as in the hands of the enemy and supposed to have taken the oath.

Davidson, G. F.
Enlisted December 31, 1863 at Pleasant Hill, Ala.; listed with the company through March 1, 1865.

Day, Mitchell W. (fr. Dallas Co.)
Enlisted July 1, 1861 at Selma, Ala.; mustered in July 27, 1861; Aug. 31 - Oct. 31, 1861 shown as sick in camp; killed at battle of Sharpsburg on September 17, 1862.

Defreese, Joseph
Enlisted August 20, 1863 at Calhoun, Ala.; taken prisoner at battle of Spotsylvania Court House on May 12, 1864; received at Elmira, N.Y. from Pt. Lookout, Md. on August 17, 1864; was to have been exchanged on October 29, 1864; died on November 4, 1864 at Ft. Monroe, Va.

Dennis, William J. (fr. Dallas Co.)
Enlisted July 4, 1861 at Selma, Ala.; mustered in July 27, 1861; shown as sick at LaGrange, Ga. - Aug. 24, 1861; wounded and had his limb amputated at battle of Fredericksburg on December 13, 1862; died on January 9, 1863.

Denson, O.
Enlisted February 21, 1863 at Talladega, Ala.; May 1 - July 1, 1864 shown as on detached service with the Reserve Ordnance Dept., Army of Northern Virginia; captured at Farmville, Va. on April 6, 1865; took oath on June 24, 1865.

Devall, John
Enlisted August 1, 1861 at Montgomery, Ala.; March 30, 1862 - April 8, 1862 shown at Richmond, Va. hospital suffering from diarrhea; taken prisoner at battle of Spotsylvania Court House on May 12, 1864; transferred to Elmira, N.Y. from Pt. Lookout, Md. on August 15, 1864; took oath on June 16, 1865.

Devall, William
Enlisted August 1, 1861 at Montgomery, Ala.

Dingler, M. M.
Captured at Gettysburg, Pa. on July 4, 1863; received at Ft. Delaware - July 7-12, 1863; died January 4, 1864 of smallpox at Ft. Delaware.

Dohn, Charles - Artificer
Enlisted July 1, 1861 at Selma, Ala.; mustered in July 27, 1861; Aug. 31 - Oct. 31, 1861 shown as absent from company without authority, thus being a deserter.

Dossett, W. M.
Enlisted November 9, 1863 at Talladega, Ala.; December of 1863 shown as ambulance driver with the Second Corps; Feb. 29 - Apr. 30, 1864 shown as having deserted.

DuBose, Kimbrough C.
Enlisted July 18, 1861 at Selma, Ala.; mustered in July 27, 1861; Oct. 31 - Dec. 31, 1862 shown as sick at hospital; Feb. 28, 1863 - Feb. 29, 1864 shown as on sick furlough; reduced to ranks on February 1, 1864; present for duty - Oct. 31, 1864 - March 1, 1865.

Dubose, Ned
March 21 - April 23, 1862 shown as at hospital in Richmond, Va.

Duhig, John (fr. Dallas Co.)
Enlisted July 4, 1861 at Selma, Ala.; mustered in July 27, 1861; captured at Falling Waters, W. Va. on July 14, 1863; shown as being held at Old Capitol Prison, Washington, D.C. on July 18, 1863; sent to Philadelphia, Pa. on Sept. 24, 1863.

Dunn, John A. (fr. Choctaw Co.)
Enlisted July 16, 1861 at Selma, Ala.; mustered in July 27, 1861; July 1 - Aug. 31, 1861 shown as sick at private house in Richmond, Va.; Aug. 31 - Oct. 31, 1861 shown as sick in camp; Dec. 31, 1861 - Feb. 28, 1862 shown as being sick at hospital; surrendered with General Lee at Appomattox Court House - April 9, 1865.

Dunn, William H. (fr. Choctaw Co.)
Enlisted July 16, 1861 at Selma, Ala.; mustered in July 27, 1861; Aug. 31 - Oct. 31, 1861 shown as sick in camp; Dec. 31 - Feb. 28, 1862 shown as sick at hospital; January 8, 1862 at Moore Hospital in Danville, Va. (had been run over by a caisson); Feb. 16 - March 15, 1862 at hospital in Charlottesville, Va. having sustained an injury from a cannon; March 16 - May 3, 1862 at hospital in Richmond, Va. because of injury to the spine; assigned to Griffin's Salem Flying Artillery on May 24, 1864; served with Lamkin's Virginia Light Artillery from Oct. 1864 - March 1865.

Dupriest, Henry A.
Mustered in July 27, 1861; was arrested by order of Major Calhoun as a deserter from Captain Posey's Company lst Alabama Regiment on August 9, 1861; sent back to Montgomery, Ala.

Edmondson, H.
Enlisted June 17, 1863 at Shelby, Ala.; assigned to Griffin's Salem Flying Artillery on May 24, 1864; Oct. 31, 1864 - March 1, 1865 shown as on detached service with Captain Armstrong; captured at Farmville, Va. on April 6, 1865.

Edwards, Samuel
Enlisted September 30, 1863; captured at Farmville, Va. on April 6, 1865; oath was given on June 24, 1865.

Ellis, B. Franklin (fr. Dallas Co.)
Enlisted July 17, 1861 at Selma, Ala.; assigned to Griffin's Salem Flying Artillery on May 24, 1864; served with Lamkin's Virginia Light Artillery from Oct. 1864 - March 1865; captured at Farmville (Burkeville?), Va. on April 6, 1865; oath taken on June 24, 1865.

Ellis, J. P.
Enlisted August 11, 1862 at Selma, Ala.; Feb. 29 - Nov. 1, 1864 shown on detached service with Hardaway's Battalion; Oct. 31, 1864 - March 1, 1865 shown
on detached service with Lamkin's Battery; surrendered with General Lee at
Appomattox Court House - April 9, 1865.

Eubanks, John W. (fr. Montgomery Co.)
Enlisted July 2, 1861 at Selma, Ala.; mustered in July 27, 1861; Oct. 31 - Dec. 31,
1862 shown as sick at hospital; Feb. 28 - Apr. 30, 1863 shown as on detached
service at Milford Station; captured at Farmville, Va. on April 6, 1865.

Faill, Thomas F. (fr. Lowndes Co.)
Enlisted July 2, 1861 at Selma, Ala.; mustered in July 27, 1861; Aug. 31 - Oct. 31,
1861 shown as sick at hospital in Richmond, Va.; records end February 28, 1862
(supposedly he died and was buried in a grave marked "Unknown").

Farrar, William
Enlisted August 28, 1863 at Talladega, Ala.; transferred to the Navy by order of
the Secretary of War - April of 1864.

Ferguson, Robert A.
Enlisted July 1, 1861 at Selma, Ala.; was supposed to have mustered in with the
company on July 27, 1861, but left camp before being mustered into the service
and was not heard of again.

Floyd, Owen R. (fr. Dallas Co.)
Enlisted July 16, 1861 at Selma, Ala.; mustered in July 27, 1861; Aug. 31 - Oct. 31,
1861 shown as sick in camp; discharged from hospital in Richmond, Va. on December 17, 1861.

Freeman, M. F.
Enlisted November 3, 1863 at Talladega, Ala.; taken prisoner at battle of
Spotsylvania Court House on May 12, 1864; held at Pt. Lookout Prison and trans-
ferred to Aiken's Landing, Va. on September 18, 1864 for exchange.

Garner, W. H.
Enlisted August 28, 1862 at Jefferson, Ala.; May 1 - July 1, 1864 shown on de-
tached service with the wagon train of the Second Corps Artillery; Feb. 29, 1864
- March 1, 1865 shown on detached service with the Ordnance Train.

Garrard, J. D. (fr. Montgomery Co.)
Enlisted February 13, 1863; surrendered with General Lee at Appomattox Court
House - April 9, 1865; shown at hospital in Farmville, Va. on April 13, 1865 with
fractured Tibia; sent home June 3, 1865.

Gates, James C. - Artificer (fr. Dallas Co.)
Enlisted July 1, 1861 at Selma, Ala.; mustered in July 27, 1861; captured at Gettysburg, Pa. on July 5, 1863; held at Ft. Delaware; discharged on December 26,
1863 - he took the oath.

Gayle, Henry (fr. Lowndes Co.)
Enlisted July 14, 1861 at Selma, Ala.; mustered in July 27, 1861; taken prisoner at
Middletown, Va. on October 19, 1864; arrived at Harpers Ferry, W. Va. on October 25, 1864; transferred to Pt. Lookout, Md.; released on June 13, 1865 when he
took the oath.

Glaze, Thomas
Enlisted November 7, 1863 at Talladega, Ala.; discharged on July 25, 1864 due to having been illegally enrolled - was 47 years old.

Gorman, Michael
Enlisted November 5, 1863 at Talladega, Ala.; assigned to Griffin's Salem Flying Artillery on May 24, 1864; served with Lamkin's Virginia Light Artillery from Oct. 1864 - March 1865; captured at Burkeville, Va. on April 6, 1865; oath taken June 14, 1865.

Gregory, Phillip L.
Enlisted July 15, 1861 at Selma, Ala.; mustered in July 27, 1861; Sept. 20, 1861 shown as sick in camp; Feb. 28 - Apr. 30, 1863 shown as sick at hospital; Apr. 30, 1863 - June 30, 1863 shown as absent without leave; Aug. 31 - Oct. 31, 1863 shown as sick at hospital; Feb. 29 - Nov. 1, 1864 shown on detached service with the supply train; arrested on April 2, 1865; oath given at Clarksburg, (W. Va.?).

Groom, Henry M.
Enlisted July 20, 1861 at Selma, Ala.; mustered in July 27, 1861; Sept. 20, 1861 shown as sick in camp; Aug. 31 - Oct. 31, 1861 shown as sick at hospital in Richmond, Va.; discharged from hospital in Richmond between Dec. 31, 1861 and Feb. 28, 1862.

Gulbrith, Albert
Enlisted October 19, 1863 at Jefferson, Ala.; Nov. 27, 1863 shown at hospital in Richmond, Va. suffering from asthma; was given a forty day furlough on December 21, 1863; was later discharged.

Harris, W. J.
Enlisted September 15, 1863 at Summerville Ford, Va.; May 1 - July 1, 1864 shown on sick furlough; appears on various sick rolls in Richmond, Va. through Oct. 5, 1864.

Harris, W. R.
Enlisted October 30, 1863 at Talladega, Ala.; killed in action near Spotsylvania Court House on May 12, 1864.

Hartigan, John
Enlisted March 29, 1863 at Milford, Va.; (he was accepted as a substitute for John T. Billingslea on same day) killed at Summerville Ford, Va. on September 14, 1863.

Hasselv[w]ander, Adam (fr. Dallas Co.)
Enlisted July 3, 1861 at Selma, Ala.; mustered in July 27, 1861; surrendered with General Lee at Appomattox Court House - April 9, 1865.

Haynes, Edward H. (fr. Lowndes Co.)
Enlisted July 1, 1861 at Selma, Ala.; mustered in July 27, 1861; Apr. 30, 1863 - Feb. 29, 1864 shown as sick at hospital; some time between Oct. 31, 1864 and March 1, 1865 he supposedly died at the hospital, but no official verification was received; (also supposedly died on June 18, 1863 from disease?); (Purifoy's records indicate that he died from a sabre cut inflicted by the Provost Guard.)

Hickman, M.
Only records show him as being admitted to a hospital in Richmond, Va. on April 7, 1862; returned to duty on April 25, 1862.

Hill, George B.
Enlisted August 6, 1861 at Montgomery, Ala.; Dec. 31, 1861 - Feb. 28, 1862 shown as sick at hospital; Feb. 26 - April 14, 1862 at hospital in Charlottesville, Va. due to Chronic Bronchitis; exchanged for Charles Stewart of the 3rd Alabama Regiment on December 1, 1862.

Hill, John
Enlisted November 7, 1863 at Talladega, Ala.; assigned to Griffin's Salem Flying Artillery on May 24, 1864; Oct. 31, 1864 - March 1, 1865 shown on detached service with Captain Armstrong.

Hobby, Seabron O. (fr. Lowndes Co.)
Enlisted June 29, 1861 at Selma, Ala.; mustered in July 27, 1861; Aug. 31 - Oct. 31, 1861 sick at hospital in Richmond, Va.; discharged from hospital in Richmond on November 15, 1861.

Holliday, Samuel J. (fr. Butler Co.)
Enlisted July 28, 1861 at Montgomery, Ala.; mustered in July 27, 1861; Aug. 31 - Oct. 31, 1861 shown as sick in camp; July 21 - Sept. 30, 1863 he served as a teamster; Oct. 31, 1864 - March 1, 1865 shown as being with the Battalion's Quartermaster Dept.

Hopkins, Thomas
Enlisted November 7, 1863 at Talladega, Ala.; deserted February 6, 1864 on march from Fredericks Hall to Orange Court House, Va.

Horton, Abner
Enlisted October 21, 1863 at Talladega, Ala.; deserted February 6, 1864 on march from Fredericks Hall to Orange Court House, Va.

Howell, John J. - Artificer
Enlisted July 19, 1861 at Selma, Ala.; mustered in July 27, 1861; captured at Gettysburg, Pa. on July 4, 1863 (though it may have actually been Waterloo, Pa. on July 5); paroled at Ft. McHenry, Md. and sent to Ft. Delaware on July 9, 1863; transferred to Aiken's Landing, Va. for exchange on September 30, 1864; October 8, 1864 is shown on a forty day furlough.

Humphries, J. J. (fr. Tallapoosa Co.)
Captured at Waterloo, Pa. on July 5, 1863; paroled at Ft. McHenry, Md. and sent to Ft. Delaware on July 9, 1863; exchanged on September 18, 1864; October 4, 1864 shown at hospital in Richmond, Va. suffering from Diarrhea; died on October 21, 1864.

Jackson, Benjamin (fr. Montgomery Co.)
Assigned to Griffin's Salem Flying Artillery on May 24, 1864; served with Lamkin's Virginia Light Artillery from Oct. 1864 - March 1865; captured at Burkeville, Va. on April 6, 1865; died at Newport News, Va. on June 10, 1865 (due to chronic Diarrhea).

Jackson, John B.
Enlisted July 2, 1861 at Selma, Ala.; mustered in July 27, 1861; Feb. 28 - Aug. 31, 1863 shown as sick at hospital; Aug. 31, 1863 - July 1, 1864 shown at home on

sick furlough; Feb. 29 - Nov. 1, 1864 shown on detached service with Hardaway's Battalion; Oct. 31, 1864 - March 1, 1865 shown on detached service with Lamkin's Battery; captured at Burkeville, Va. on April 6, 1865; held at Newport News, Va. until release.

Jackson, Littleton G. (fr. Montgomery Co.)
Enlisted July 26, 1861 at Selma, Ala.; mustered in July 27, 1861; Jan. 3, 1862 shown as sick in camp; Jan. 4 - Feb. 4, 1863 shown on sick furlough at home; Feb. 28 - Aug. 31, 1863 shown on detached service with ordnance train (supposed to have been captured in July of 1863 during the Pennsylvania Campaign); assigned to Griffin's Salem Flying Artillery on May 24, 1864; served with Lamkin's Virginia Light Artillery from Oct. 1864 - March 1865; captured at Burkeville, Va. on April 6, 1865, then was held at Newport News, Va.

Jarrett, George A. (fr. Autauga Co.)
Enlisted February 2, 1863 at Milford, Va.; was accepted as a substitute for N. B. Merritt by Capt. Bondurant; surrendered with General Lee at Appomattox Court House - April 9, 1865.

Johnson, John T.
Only records show him being admitted to a hospital in Richmond, Va. on April 7, 1862 suffering from Measles.

Johnson, J. W.
Enlisted November 8, 1863 at Talladega, Ala.; captured at battle of Spotsylvania Court House on May 12, 1864; transferred to Elmira, N.Y. from Pt. Lookout, Md. on August 15, 1864; died from General Debility at Elmira Prison on February 13, 1865.

Johnson, William M.
Enlisted November 9, 1863 at Talladega, Ala.; deserted - February 6, 1864 on march from Fredericks Hall to Orange Court House, Va.

Jones, A. W.
Feb. 29, 1864 - March 1, 1865 shown as sick at hospital; (on register of hospital in Richmond, Va. having been admitted on April 21, 1864 suffering from intermittent fever; was furloughed for sixty days on May 28, 1864); surrendered with General Lee at Appomattox Court House - April 9, 1865.

Jones, C. S. V. (fr. Butler Co.)
Enlisted March 31, 1862 at Greenville, Ala.; assigned to Griffin's Salem Flying Artillery on May 24, 1864; killed in action below Richmond, Va. at Fort Harrison.

Jones, Eldridge S.
Enlisted June 27, 1861 at Selma, Ala.; mustered in July 27, 1861; September 20, 1861 shown as sick at Alabama Hospital; discharged Sept. 20, 1861 at Richmond, Va.

Jones J. J.
Enlisted August 13, 1862 at Selma, Ala.; Feb. 28 - April 30, 1863 shown as sick with fever at hospital in Richmond, Va.; Feb. 29 - Sept. 1, 1864 shown at hospital; severely wounded at Middletown, Va. on October 19, 1864; Oct. 31, 1864 - March 1, 1865 shown as present for duty; paroled at Selma, Ala. during month of June, 1865.

Kane, John
Enlisted April 20, 1863 at Milford, Va. Substitute for W. A. Yeldell; deserted -
April 22, 1863.

Kersey, James M.
Records show him on register of hospital in Richmond, Va. sick with Measles
(admitted on April 17, 1862 and returned to duty on April 25, 1862).

Key, William J. (fr. Wilcox Co.)
Enlisted July 17, 1861 at Selma, Ala.; mustered in July 27, 1861; Aug. 31 - Oct. 31,
1861 shown as sick in camp; died in Richmond, Va. in July of 1862 (was cutting
a tree for fire wood and it fell on him).

Kirvin, Calvin J. (fr. Dallas Co.)
Enlisted July 8, 1861 at Selma, Ala.; mustered in July 27, 1861; Aug. 31 - Oct. 31,
1861 shown as sick in camp; Dec. 31, 1861 - Feb. 28, 1862 shown as sick at hospital; severely wounded at the battle of Sharpsburg on September 17, 1862 (gun-
shot wounds in both thighs); was later discharged, captured and paroled by
Union forces.

Knight, Monroe W. (fr. Butler Co.)
Enlisted July 2, 1861 at Selma, Ala.; mustered in July 27, 1861; July 1 - Aug. 31,
1861 shown as sick at Alabama hospital; killed at the battle of Seven Pines on
May 31, 1862.

Knight, Thomas
Enlisted November 8, 1863 at Talladega, Ala.; Oct. 31, 1863 - Jan. 1, 1864 shown
as sick at hospital (on register of hospital in Richmond, Va. and shown as having
been admitted on Jan 2, 1864 suffering from Typhoid Pneumonia; was furloughed
for thirty-five days on Feb. 9, 1864); Feb. 29 - Nov. 1, 1864 shown as sick at home
on furlough; Oct. 31, 1864 - March 1, 1865 shown as sick at hospital.

Kuhne, Charles G. - Artificer (f. Dallas Co.)
Enlisted July 1, 1861 at Selma, Ala.; mustered in July 27, 1861; captured at Waterloo, Pa. on July 5, 1863; received at Ft. Delaware July 7-12, 1863; exchanged
on September 30, 1864; Oct. 31, 1864 - March 1, 1865 on detached service in
Selma, Ala.

Laski, Marcus B. (fr. Lowndes Co.)
Enlisted July 21, 1861 at Selma, Ala.; mustered in July 27, 1861; Aug. 31 - Oct. 31,
1861 shown as sick in camp; Oct. 31, 1861 - Jan. 3, 1862 shown as sick at hospital;
Aug. 31 - Oct. 31, 1863 shown as sick at hospital; Feb. 29 - April 30, 1864 shown
on detached service; May 1, 1864 - March 1, 1865 shown on detached service
with General Long's Artillery of the Second Corps; captured March 12, 1865 and
received at Ft. Monroe, Va. on March 17, 1865; sent to Pt. Lookout Prison and
released on June 14, 1865.

Lee, David M. (fr. Lowndes Co.)
Enlisted July 1, 1861 at Selma, Ala.; mustered in July 27, 1861; Aug. 31 - Oct. 31,
1861 shown as sick at Alabama hospital then sick at hospital in Richmond, Va.;
discharged from hospital on October 29, 1861.

Lee, George W. (fr. Lowndes Co.)
Enlisted July 1, 1861 at Selma, Ala.; mustered in July 27, 1861; surrendered with
General Lee at Appomattox Court House - April 9, 1865.

Lee, Loverd L. (fr. Lowndes Co.)
Enlisted August 24, 1861 at Montgomery, Ala.; Oct. 31 - Dec. 31, 1861 shown as on sick furlough.

Lee, S. J.
Enlisted May 18, 1864 at Camp Watts, Ala.; Oct. 31, 1864 - March 1, 1865 shown on furlough of indulgence; surrendered with General Lee at Appomattox Court house - April 9, 1865.

Lee, J.
Records show him being admitted to General Hospital in Richmond, Va. on Nov. 18, 1864 and being returned to duty on Dec. 3, 1864; died on December 24, 1864 at Military Hospital in Staunton, Va.

Littlehale, John M. (fr. Dallas Co.)
Enlisted October 1, 1861 at Richmond, Va.; Apr. 30 - Aug. 31, 1863 shown as absent without leave; Aug. 31, 1863 - April 30, 1864 shown as on detached service at hospital; May 1, 1864 - March 1, 1865 shown on detached service at the Receiving Hospital of the Army of Northern Virginia; captured at Payneville, Va. on April 6, 1865; released on June 14, 1865.

Logan, John A. (fr. Wilcox Co.)
Enlisted June 27, 1861 at Selma, Ala.; mustered in July 27, 1861; Aug. 31 - Oct. 31, 1861 shown as sick in camp; Jan. 17 - Feb. 2, 1862 shown as sick at hospital with Pneumonia; surrendered with General Lee at Appomattox Court House - April 9, 1865.

Loyed, William
Enlisted November 9, 1863 at Talladega, Ala.; deserted - February 6, 1864 on march from Fredericks Hall to Orange Court House, Va.

Luchow, Louis
Enlisted June 27, 1861 at Selma, Ala.; mustered in July 27, 1861; records show that Private Luchow left camp without permission on July 28, 1861.

Marble, William B. (fr. Dallas Co.)
Enlisted July 12, 1861 at Selma, Ala.; mustered in July 27, 1861; Aug. 31 - Oct. 31, 1861 shown as sick in camp; Feb. 28, 1863 - Nov. 1, 1864 shown as sick at hospital; Oct. 31, 1864 - March 1, 1865 shown on detached service at hospital in Richmond, Va.; surrendered with General Lee at Appomattox Court House - April 9, 1865.

Mathews, John A. (fr. Wilcox Co.)
Enlisted July 1, 1861 at Selma, Ala.; mustered in July 27, 1861; Aug. 31 - Oct. 31, 1861 shown as sick at hospital in Richmond, Va.; discharged from hospital on November 16, 1861.

Mayo, Montgomery M. (fr. Dallas Co.)
Enlisted July 1, 1861 at Selma, Ala.; mustered in July 27, 1861; Aug. 31 - Oct. 31, 1861 shown as sick in camp; Jan. 3, 1862 shown as sick at hospital in Richmond, Va.; died at hospital on February 2, 1862.

Mayo, Sidney W. (fr. Dallas Co.)
Enlisted July 1, 1861 at Selma, Ala.; mustered in July 27, 1861; Aug. 31 - Oct. 31, 1861 shown as sick at hospital in Richmond, Va.; discharged on account of physical disability on December 28, 1861.

McCaa, Eugene
Enlisted July 15, 1861 at Selma, Ala.; mustered in July 27, 1861; later with 43rd Regiment Alabama Volunteers.

McCondichie, Patton (fr. Wilcox Co.)
Enlisted July 17, 1861 at Selma, Ala.; mustered in July 27, 1861; died from wounds received at the battle of Chancellorsville on May 2, 1863.

McCondichi[e], Wiley G.
Enlisted July 17, 1861 at Selma, Ala.; mustered in July 27, 1861; (actually left on furlough before being mustered into service and dismissed from the company for failing to return).

McDonald, Thomas H.
Enlisted July 1, 1861 at Selma, Ala.; mustered in July 27, 1861; killed at the battle of Cold Harbor on June 27, 1862.

Meek, Jacob A.
Enlisted July 1, 1861 at Selma, Ala.; mustered in July 27, 1861; wounded at the battle of Seven Pines on May 31, 1862; died on August 8, 1862 in Richmond, Va.

Melson, Robert K. - Artificer/Bugler (fr. Dallas Co.)
Enlisted August 1, 1861 at Montgomery, Ala.; mustered in July 27, 1861; discharged from hospital in Richmond, Va. because of age (45), Rheumatism and General Disability (discharge written up on July 16, 1862).

Melton, James A. - Bugler (fr. Montgomery Co.)
Enlisted August 10, 1861 at LaGrange, Ga.; July 1 - Aug. 31, 1861 shown as sick in camp; surrendered with General Lee at Appomattox Court House - April 9, 1865.

Melton, William J.
Enlisted February 16, 1861 at Columbus, Ga.; transferred from Milledge's Battery to Capt. Reese's Battery on Apr. 1, 1864; captured at the battle of Spotsylvania Court House on May 12, 1864; escaped from Elmira Prison; paroled on May 7, 1865.

Merritt, Napoleon B. (fr. Autauga Co.)
Enlisted July 26, 1861 at Montgomery, Ala.; mustered in July 27, 1861; discharged on February 2, 1863 - furnished a substitute (George A. Jarrett).

Messer, David M.
Enlisted November 9, 1863 at Talladega, Ala.; deserted - December 28, 1863 at camp near Fredericks Hall, Va.

Metcalf, Albert W. (fr. Butler Co.)
Enlisted July 10, 1861 at Selma, Ala.; mustered in July 27, 1861; July 1 - Oct. 31, 1861 shown as sick in camp; Dec. 31, 1861 - Feb. 28, 1862 shown as sick at hospital; assigned to Griffin's Salem Flying Artillery on May 24, 1864; served with Lamkin's Virginia Light Artillery from Oct. 1864 - March 1865; paroled at Selma, Ala. on May 28, 1865.

Methvin, John F. (fr. Lowndes Co.)
Enlisted February 9, 1864 at Newman, Ga.; assigned to Griffin's Salem Flying Artillery on May 24, 1864; served with Lamkin's Virginia Light Artillery from

Oct. 1864 - March 1865; surrendered with General Lee at Appomattox Court House - April 9, 1865.

Miner, E.
Enlisted October 21, 1863 at Talladega, Ala.; badly wounded at the battle of Spotsylvania Court House on May 12, 1864; May 12, 1864 - March 1, 1865 shown at hospital.

Miner, G. W.
Enlisted October 21, 1863 at Talladega, Ala.; Feb. 29, 1864 - March 1, 1865 shown as sick at hospital.

Montgomery, Charles H. - Bugler
Enlisted July 1, 1861 at Selma, Ala.; mustered in July 27, 1861; discharged on account of physical disability on December 16, 1861.

Montgomery, James S.
Enlisted July 1, 1861 at Selma, Ala.; mustered in July 27, 1861; discharged on March 6, 1862 because of physical disability. (Rheumatism).

Nance, A.
Enlisted November 8, 1863 at Talladega, Ala.; discharged on January 18, 1864 for being a minor.

Nelson, R. K.
Shown on register of CSA Hospital in Danville, Va. dated May 28, 1862 suffering from Pneumonia; returned to duty on June 27, 1862.

Nolan, J. M.
Enlisted June 23, 1863 at Randolph, Ala.; captured at battle of Spotsylvania Court House on May 12, 1864; transferred from Pt. Lookout, Md. to Elmira, N.Y. on August 15, 1864; died on February 25, 1865 from Chronic Rheumatism and Inflammation of the lungs.

Oglesby, J. A.
Enlisted October 28, 1863 at Talladega, Ala.; Feb. 29 - April 30, 1864 shown on detached service with Hardaway's Battalion; Feb. 29 - July 1, 1864 shown as sick at hospital (suffering from Rubeola as indicated on register dated June 3, 1864); Aug. 31 - Nov. 1, 1864 still on detached service with Hardaway's Battalion; Oct. 31, 1864 - March 1, 1865 shown on detached service with Lamkin's Battery; paroled May 1-11, 1865.

Oliver, John A. (fr. Lowndes Co.)
Enlisted July 1, 1861 at Selma, Ala.; mustered in July 27, 1861; Dec. 31, 1861 - Feb. 28, 1862 shown as sick at hospital (Jan. 16, 1862 shown as having Pneumonia); Oct. 31 - Dec. 31, 1862 shown on sick furlough; surrendered with General Lee at Appomattox Court House - April 9, 1865.

Parish, James A. (fr. Perry Co.)
Enlisted July 15, 1861 at Selma, Ala.; mustered in July 27, 1861; taken prisoner at Middletown, Va. on October 19, 1864; sent to Pt. Lookout, Md. from Harpers Ferry, W. Va. on October 23, 1864; released on June 16, 1865.

Parnell, William D. (fr. Dallas Co.)
Enlisted July 15, 1861 at Selma, Ala.; mustered in July 27, 1861; Dec. 31, 1861 - Feb. 28, 1862 shown as being sick at hospital; captured at the battle of Spotsylvania

Court House on May 12, 1864; transferred from Pt. Lookout, Md. to Elmira, N.Y. on August 15, 1864; transferred for exchange on October 11, 1864; died at Pt. Lookout, Md. on October 26, 1864 from Chronic Diarrhea.

Parsons, Samuel R.
Enlisted November 9, 1863 at Talladega, Ala.; deserted - February 6, 1864 on march from Fredericks Hall to Orange Court House, Va.

Patton, A. H.
Enlisted November 3, 1862 at Selma, Ala.; taken prisoner at the battle of Spotsylvania Court House on May 12, 1864; transferred to Elmira, N.Y. from Pt. Lookout, Md. on August 15, 1864; transferred for exchange on October 11, 1864; died from Chronic Diarrhea at Elmira, N.Y. on October 31, 1864.

Payne, Asbury (fr. Montgomery Co.)
Enlisted July 10, 1861 at Selma, Ala.; mustered in July 27, 1861; Dec. 31, 1861 - Feb. 28, 1862 shown as being entitled to two months extra pay as a teamster; taken prisoner at Middletown, Va. on October 19, 1864; sent from Harpers Ferry, W. Va. to Pt. Lookout, Md. on October 23, 1864; released on June 16, 1865.

Peak, Solomon M.
Enlisted May 19, 1863 at Talladega, Ala.; assigned to Griffin's Salem Flying Artillery on May 24, 1864; Feb. 29 - July 1, 1864 shown as sick at hospital; served with Lamkin's Virginia Light Artillery from Oct. 1864 - March 1865.

Peebles, John M. (fr. Lowndes Co.)
Enlisted September 18, 1863 at Pleasant Hill, Ala.; killed in action near Cold Harbor on June 3, 1864.

Pendergast, D .J.
Enlisted September 18, 1863 at Talladega, Ala.; assigned to Griffin's Salem Flying Artillery on May 24, 1864; served with Lamkin's Virginia Light Artillery from Oct. 1864 - March 1865; captured April 5, 1865 at Amelia Court House, Va.; arrived at City Point, Va. on April 13, 1865, then sent to Pt. Lookout Prison; released on June 16, 1865.

Pierce, Henry S.
Enlisted August 4, 1861 at Montgomery, Ala.; mustered in July 27, 1861; Aug. 31 - Oct. 31, 1861 shown as sick at hospital in Richmond, Va.; died (November 15, 1861) in the hospital as shown on register dated January 3, 1862.

Pierce, John F. (fr. Lowndes Co.)
Enlisted July 1, 1861 at Selma, Ala.; mustered in July 27, 1861; Aug. 31 - Oct. 31, 1861 shown as sick at hospital; discharged from hospital in Richmond, Va. on December 17, 1861.

Plunkett, James W.
Enlisted November 9, 1863 at Talladega, Ala.; deserted - February 6, 1864 on march from Fredericks Hall to Orange Court House, Va.

Polk, Wiley J. (fr. Wilcox Co.)
Enlisted July 19, 1861 at Selma, Ala.; mustered in July 27, 1861; Aug. 31 - Oct. 31, 1861 shown as sick at hospital in Richmond, Va.; assigned to Griffin's Salem Flying Artillery on May 24, 1864; served with Lamkin's Virginia Light Artillery from Oct. 1864 - March 1865; surrendered with General Lee at Appomattox Court House - April 9, 1865.

Pollard, William J.
Mustered in July 27, 1861; was arrested on August 9, 1861 by order of Major J. S. Calhoun as a deserter from Capt. Posey's Company of the lst Alabama Regiment and sent to Montgomery.

Powell, James M. (fr. Lowndes Co.)
Enlisted July 19, 1861 at Selma, Ala.; mustered in July 27, 1861; Aug. 31 - Oct. 31, 1861 shown as sick at camp; Jan. 3, 1862 shown as sick at hospital in Richmond, Va.; taken prisoner at Gettysburg, Pa. on July 5, 1863; sent to Elmira Prison from Pt. Lookout, Md. on July 28, 1864; died on February 22, 1865.

Powers, John A.
Enlisted July 1, 1861 at Selma, Ala.; mustered in July 27, 1861; Aug. 31 - Oct. 31, 1861 shown as sick in hospital; discharged on November 22, 1861.

Putegnat, John P. (fr. Texas)
Enlisted July 1, 1861 at Selma, Ala.; mustered in July 27, 1861; taken prisoner at the battle of Spotsylvania Court House on May 12, 1864; transferred from Pt. Lookout, Md. to Elmira, N.Y. on August 15, 1864; escaped from Elmira Prison by tunneling on October 7, 1864.

Quarles, Whitfield S. (fr. Lowndes Co.)
Aug. 31 - Oct. 31, 1861 shown as sick in hospital; discharged from Richmond, Va. hospital on November 15 (16?), 1861.

Reese, William M. (fr. Dallas Co.)
Enlisted October 1, 1863 at Selma, Ala.; captured at battle of Spotsylvania Court House on May 12, 1864; transferred from Pt. Lookout, Md. to Elmira, N.Y. on August 15, 1864; transferred for exchange on March 2, 1865.

Reid, William L.
Enlisted June 26, 1861 at Selma, Ala.; mustered in July 27, 1861; Jan. 3, 1862 shown as sick in camp; died on August 25, 1862 of Chronic Diarrhea.

Roberson, Andrew J. (fr. Lowndes Co.)
Enlisted August 1, 1861 at Montgomery, Ala.; mustered in July 27, 1861; died in hospital in Richmond, Va. in October of 1861.

Ryan, Benjamin
Enlisted July 15, 1861 at Selma, Ala., mustered in July 27, 1861; captured at Frederick, Md. on Sept. 12, 1862; sent for exchange from Ft. Delaware to Aiken's Landing on October 2, 1862; Oct. 31 - Dec. 31, 1862 shown as sick at hospital; Dec. 31, 1862 - Feb. 28, 1863 shown as absent without leave; April 30 - June 30, 1863 shown as sick at hospital; Feb. 29 - Nov 1, 1864 shown as undergoing sentence of court-martial; Oct. 31, 1864 - March 1, 1865 shown on detached service with Lamkin's Battery.

Sanders, David M. (fr. Wilcox Co.)
Enlisted July 15, 1861 at Selma, Ala.; mustered in July 27, 1861; absent on sick furlough from Jan. 15 - Feb. 2, 1862; Oct. 31 - Dec. 31, 1862 shown on sick leave; Dec. 31, 1862 - Feb. 28, 1863 shown as sick in hospital; discharged and substituted for by George M. Champion on May 8, 1863.

Sheffield, N.
Enlisted November 7, 1863 at Talladega, Ala.; taken prisoner at battle of Spotsylvania Court House on May 12, 1864; transferred from Pt. Lookout, Md.

to Elmira, N.Y. on August 15, 1864; transferred for exchange on February 20, 1865.

Sills, Handy
Enlisted June 27, 1861 at Selma, Ala.; mustered in July 27, 1861; Aug. 31 - Oct. 31, 1861 shown as sick at hospital in Richmond, Va.; died in hospital in Richmond, Va. on November 15, 1861.

Skinner, A. W. (fr. Wilcox Co.)
Enlisted April 6, 1864 at Selma, Ala.; surrendered with General Lee at Appomattox Court House - April 9, 1865.

Skinner, B.A. (fr. Wilcox Co.)
Enlisted April 26, 1863 at Selma, Ala.; taken prisoner at Middletown, Va. on October 19, 1864; sent to Pt. Lookout, Md. from Harpers Ferry, W. Va. on October 23, 1864; exchanged on February 13, 1865; paroled at Selma, Ala. in June of 1865.

Skinner, Ira (fr. Wilcox Co.)
Enlisted July 23, 1861 at Selma, Ala.; mustered in July 27, 1861; shown as sick at Alabama hospital on Sept. 20, 1861; died in Richmond, Va. on April 18, 1862 from Measles which led to Pneumonia.

Small, William H. (fr. Dallas Co.)
Enlisted July 21, 1861 at Selma, Ala.; mustered in July 27, 1861; July 1 - August 31, 1861 shown as sick at hospital; discharged from hospital in Richmond, Va. on October 29, 1861.

Smart, G. F. (fr. Lowndes Co.)
Enlisted November 27, 1863 at Pleasant Hill, Ala.; died at hospital in Richmond, Va. on August 30, 1864.

Smith, Henry A.
Enlisted July 20, 1861 at Selma, Ala.; mustered in July 27, 1861; Aug. 31 - Oct. 31, 1861 shown as sick at hospital in Richmond, Va.; Dec. 31, 1861 - Feb. 28, 1862 shown as present for duty; no other records.

Smith, James K.
Enlisted July 30, 1861 at Selma, Ala.; mustered in July 27, 1861; Oct. 31 - Dec. 31, 1862 shown as being on furlough (was wounded at the battle of Mechanicsville on June 26, 1862 - right arm was amputated as a result of the wound caused by the premature discharge of a gun); discharged on surgeons certificate of disability on April 19, 1863.

Smith, L. A. H.
Enlisted August 21, 1861 at Charleston, S.C.; transferred from 5th Regiment Alabama Infantry on April 6, 1864; Feb. 29 - Nov. 1, 1864 said to be on the retired list; September 6, 1864 shown as unfit for duty because of disability (left knee); Oct. 31, 1864 - March 1, 1865 shown on detached service with Lamkin's Battery.

Smith, Pitt M. (fr. Butler Co.)
Enlisted July 20, 1861 at Selma, Ala.; mustered in July 27, 1861; Feb. 29 - Nov. 1, 1864 shown on detached service; Oct. 31, 1864 - March 1, 1865 shown on detached service with Captain Armstrong.

Smith, William H.
  Enlisted July 20, 1861 at Selma, Ala.; mustered in July 27, 1861; Oct. 31 - Dec. 31, 1862 shown as sick at hospital; Dec. 31, 1862 - Feb. 28, 1863 shown as sick at hospital; died in hospital in Staunton, Va. on November 3, 1862.

Smoke, Henry (fr. Wilcox Co.)
  Enlisted May 27, 1864 at Selma, Ala.; May 1 - July 1, 1864 shown as sick at hospital; Aug. 31, 1864 - March 1, 1865 shown as sick at hospital.

Soles, N. Pinckney (fr. Lowndes Co.)
  Enlisted August 27, 1861 at Montgomery, Ala.; discharged by special orders from Headquarters on October 22, 1861 because of Rheumatism.

Spencer, James (fr. Dallas Co.)
  Enlisted July 10, 1861 at Selma, Ala.; mustered in July 27, 1861; taken prisoner at the battle of Spotsylvania Court House on May 12, 1864; transferred from Pt. Lookout, Md. to Elmira, N.Y. on August 15, 1864; released on May 17, 1865.

Stewart, Charles (fr. Lowndes Co.)
  Enlisted December 16, 1862 near Fredericksburg, Va.; Feb. 29 - Apr. 30, 1864 shown as having been discharged by order of the Secretary of War; May 1 - July 1, 1864 shown as having been promoted to lst Lieutenant and transferred to the Army of the West.

Stewart, William R.
  Enlisted July 15, 1861 at Selma, Ala.; mustered in July 27, 1861; Aug. 31, 1861 - Feb. 28, 1862 shown as sick at hospital; Oct. 31 - Dec. 31, 1862 shown as sick at hospital; Feb. 28 - Apr. 30, 1863 shown as absent without leave; taken prisoner at Middletown, Va. on October 19, 1864; severely wounded at Middletown; sent from Harpers Ferry, W. Va. to Point Lookout, Md. on October 23, 1864; released on June 19, 1865.

Stoker, Davidson
  Enlisted February 13, 1863 at Selma, Ala.; Feb. 29 - Nov. 1, 1864 shown on detached service; Oct. 31, 1864 - March 1, 1865 shown on detached service with Captain Armstrong; surrendered with General Lee at Appomattox Court House - April 9, 1865.

Stuart, John B.
  Enlisted July 15, 1861 at Selma, Ala.; mustered in July 27, 1861; Aug. 31 - Oct. 31, 1861 shown as sick in camp; taken prisoner at Middletown, Va. on October 19, 1864; arrived at Harpers Ferry, W. Va. on October 25, 1864; sent to Pt. Lookout, Md. on October 23, 1864; released from Pt. Lookout on June 17, 1865.

Stuart, Joseph D.
  Enlisted July 12, 1861 at Selma, Ala.; mustered in July 27, 1861; taken prisoner at battle of Spotsylvania Court House on May 12, 1864; transferred from Pt. Lookout, Md. to Elmira, N.Y. on August 15, 1864; died on February 7, 1865 of Variola.

Stuart, Rufus P. (fr. Dallas Co.)
  Enlisted May 14, 1864 at Enterprise, Miss.; Oct. 31, 1864 - March 1, 1865 shown as present for duty; was later paroled.

Teague, M. M.
Enlisted December 28, 1862 at Talladega, Ala.; taken prisoner at battle of Spotsylvania Court House on May 12, 1864; transferred to Elmira, N.Y. from Pt. Lookout, Md. on July 23, 1864; released on May 29, 1865.

Teague, O. S.
Enlisted September 20, 1862 at Randolph, Ala.; taken prisoner at battle of Spotsylvania Court House on May 12, 1864; transferred from Pt. Lookout, Md. to Elmira, N.Y. on August 15, 1864; died at Elmira Prison on November 21, 1864 from Chronic Diarrhea.

Templin, William H. (fr. Lowndes Co.)
Enlisted July 23, 1861 at Selma, Ala.; mustered in July 27, 1861; Aug. 31 - Oct. 31, 1861 shown as sick in camp; wounded at battle of Cold Harbor, June 27, 1862; was a teamster from April 1 - May 31, 1863, then was discharged from that duty; taken prisoner at battle of Spotsylvania Court House on May 12, 1864; transferred from Pt. Lookout, Md. to Elmira, N.Y. on August 15, 1864; escaped from Elmira Prison on October 7, 1864 by tunneling; thereafter was on furlough; later rejoined his old command.

Thomas, William M. (fr. Bibb Co.)
Enlisted July 13, 1861 at Selma, Ala.; mustered in July 27, 1861; Oct. 31 - Dec. 31, 1862 shown as sick at hospital in Richmond, Va.; was a teamster from April 1 - May 31, 1863, then was discharged from that duty; Oct. 31, 1864 - March 1, 1865 shown on daily duty in Battalion Quartermaster Dept.; surrendered with General Lee at Appomattox Court House April 9, 1865.

Thompson, John A. (fr. Choctaw Co.)
Enlisted July 16, 1861 at Selma, Ala.; mustered in July 27, 1861; Dec. 31, 1861 - Feb. 28, 1862 shown as absent on sick furlough; captured at Farmville, Va.; was wounded in last charge made by General Gordon; on roll of U.S. Hospital at Farmville from April 7 - June 15, 1865; surrendered with General Johnston at Bennett's House near Durham, North Carolina on April 26, 1865.

Tiner, Jefferson
Enlisted September 21, 1863 at Talladega, Ala.; deserted - December 28, 1863 from camp near Fredericks Hall, Va.

Tomlinson, Jerome (fr. Wilcox Co.)
Enlisted August 2, 1861 at Selma, Ala.; Dec. 31, 1861 - Feb. 28, 1862 shown as sick at hospital; Oct. 31 - Dec. 31, 1862 shown as sick at hospital in Richmond, Va.; Feb. 28 - Oct. 31, 1863 shown on detached service at hospital (was a nurse at the General Hospital at Camp Winder); Feb. 29, 1864 - March 1, 1865 shown as sick at hospital.

Traweek, Ira Y. (fr. Butler Co.)
Enlisted July 10, 1861 at Selma, Ala.; mustered in July 27, 1861; July 1 - Aug. 31, 1861 shown as sick at private house in Richmond, Va.; Aug. 31 - Oct. 31, 1861 shown as sick at camp; Dec. 31, 1861-Feb. 28, 1862 shown as sick at hospital in Richmond, Va.; taken prisoner at Middletown, Va. on October 19, 1864; sent from Harpers Ferry, W. Va. to Pt. Lookout, Md. on October 23, 1864; released from Pt. Lookout on June 21, 1865.

Traweek, Washington B. (fr. Wilcox Co.)
Enlisted July 10, 1861 at Selma, Ala.; mustered in July 27, 1861; Aug. 31 - Oct. 31, 1861 shown as sick at camp; taken prisoner at battle of Spotsylvania Court House

on May 12, 1864; transferred from Pt. Lookout, Md. to Elmira, N.Y. on August 15, 1864; escaped from Elmira Prison by tunneling on October 7, 1864; then shown as on furlough.

Traylor, P. W. (fr. Lowndes Co.)
Enlisted September 1, 1862 at Montgomery, Ala.; Oct. 31 - Dec. 31, 1862 shown on sick leave of absence; Dec. 31, 1862 - Feb. 28, 1863 shown at hospital (injured by gun carriage); Feb. 28, 1863 - March 1, 1865 shown on detached service at hospital (was a nurse); paroled at Selma, Ala. on May 28, 1865.

Tucker, Matthew (fr. Montgomery Co.)
Enlisted July 27, 1861 at Selma, Ala.; mustered in July 27, 1861; surrendered with General Lee at Appomattox Court House - April 9, 1865.

Vaughn, F. B.
Mustered in July 27, 1861 at Montgomery, Ala.; transferred to Capt. F. M. Hopkins' Company of Alabama Volunteers.

Wade, William T. (fr. Dallas Co.)
Enlisted July 15, 1861 at Selma, Ala.; mustered in July 27, 1861; taken prisoner at Waterloo, Pa. on July 5, 1863; received at Ft. Delaware July 7-12, 1863; died on November 18, 1863 of Smallpox.

Waldron, William S. (fr. Dallas Co.)
Enlisted July 1, 1861 at Montgomery, Ala.; Aug. 31 - Oct. 31, 1861 shown as sick in camp; died near Centreville, Va. in winter of 1861-62.

Walker, John V. F. (fr. Dallas Co.)
Enlisted March 18, 1864 at Selma, Ala.; wounded and captured at battle of Spotsylvania Court House, May 12, 1864; escaped from Union field hospital; taken prisoner at Middletown, Va. on October 19, 1864; sent from Harpers Ferry, W. Va. to Pt. Lookout, Md. on October 23, 1864; released on June 21, 1865.

Walker, W. M.
Enlisted August 22, 1863 at Shelby, Ala.; assigned to Griffin's Salem Flying Artillery on May 24, 1864; served with Lamkin's Virginia Light Artillery from Oct. 1864 - March 1865.

Ward, W. F.
Enlisted November 8, 1863 at Talladega, Ala.; assigned to Griffin's Salem Flying Artillery on May 24, 1864; served with Lamkin's Virginia Light Artillery from Oct. 1864 - March 1865; surrendered with General Lee at Appomattox Court House - April 9, 1865.

Watson, J. D. (fr. Wilcox Co.)
Enlisted February 9, 1864 at Notasulga, Ala.; taken prisoner at Middletown, Va. on October 19, 1864; sent from Harpers Ferry, W. Va. to Pt. Lookout, Md. on October 23, 1864; died on May 7, 1865 at Pt. Lookout Prison.

Watts, Charles T.
Enlisted July 1, 1861 at Selma, Ala.; mustered in July 27, 1861; July 1 - Aug. 31, 1861 shown as sick at Alabama hospital; Aug. 31 - Oct. 31, 1861 left sick at hospital in Richmond, Va.; discharged from hospital in Richmond, Va. on October 29, 1861.

Webster, T. P.
Enlisted February 9, 1864 at Talladega, Ala.; assigned to Griffin's Salem Flying Artillery on May 24, 1864; served with Lamkin's Virginia Light Artillery from Oct. 1864 - March 1865.

Woodruff, Cicero (fr. Lowndes Co.)
Enlisted January 1, 1864 at Pleasant Hill, Ala.; Feb. 29 - July 1, 1864 shown as sick at hospital suffering from Diarrhea; furloughed sixty days on May 29, 1864.

Woodward, Robert W.
Enlisted July 25, 1861 Selma, Ala.; mustered in July 27, 1861; Aug. 31 - Oct. 31, 1861 shown as sick in camp; exchanged for R. W. Barlow on June 2, 1863; transferred to Company H of the 3rd Alabama Regiment.

Wootan, Israel (fr. Wilcox Co.)
Enlisted July 10, 1861 at Selma, Ala.; mustered in July 27, 1861; Aug. 31 - Oct. 31, 1861 shown as sick at hospital in Richmond, Va.; discharged from hospital in Richmond, Va. on October 21, 1861.

Wright, Edward D.
Enlisted August 5, 1861 at Montgomery, Ala.; mustered in July 27, 1861; Oct. 31, 1862 - Jan. 1, 1864 shown as sick at hospital; Dec. 31, 1863 - Apr. 30, 1864 shown as absent without leave; May 1 - July 1, 1864 shown as under arrest; captured at Burkeville, Va. on April 6, 1865; sent to Newport News, Va. on April 14, 1865; took oath on June 25, 1865.

Young, A. A.
Enlisted November 15, 1862 at Randolph, Ala.; surrendered with General Lee at Appomattox Court House - April 9, 1865.

ADDENDUM TO ROSTER

Garrett, J. W.
In June of 1861 was elected to hold rank of Senior 2nd Lieutenant, but did not accept that position or ever serve with the battery.

Holloway, E. M.
In June of 1861 was elected to hold rank of Senior 1st Lieutenant, but did not keep that position or ever serve with the battery.

Sprott, Dr.
In June of 1861 was elected to hold rank of Junior 1st Lieutenant, but did not accept that position or ever serve with the battery.

NDNOTES

NOTES for CHAPTER I

1. At that time, there was a greater need for artillery commands than for cavalry units in the Confederate service. Qualified cannoneers were at a premium while good horsemen were common in the South.
2. The reason(s) for their refusal is not known.
3. Oddly enough, the names of the other three gentlemen never appeared on the company roster, nor is there any record of their ever enlisting in the company.
4. John Purifoy, *Jeff Davis Artillery, History of*, filed with the Alabama Department of Archives and History (Montgomery, Alabama) on July 27, 1904, p. 15.
5. Ibid., (first page of introduction – not numbered).
6. Taken from a letter received from Mr. Maurice B. Andrews (the grandson of Matthew Tucker), of Chickasaw, Alabama, during June of 1987.
7. Purifoy, p. 16.
8. Ibid.
9. *Captions and Record of Events*, Jeff Davis Artillery Alabama Volunteers. National Archives, M311, Microfilm Roll #76, p. 1.
10. Purifoy, p. 16.
11. No records or photographs have been found which indicate that there was any strict adherence to regulations.
12. Wilber F. Claughton, letter appearing under "Buttons Made In The Confederacy," *Confederate Veteran*, V (June 1897), pp. 246-247.
13. Purifoy, p. 16.
14. The reasons for this action are not known.
15. The reason for this action is not known.
16. Columbus W. McCrary, *Historical Memoranda of "Jeff Davis" Artillery Ala. Vol.*, (exact date when written is unknown) National Archives, Record Group #109, p. 1.
17. The date of the War Department directive (Special Order #423) was October 14, 1861. It is believed that Captain Montgomery left the command before it departed for Centreville on October the 15th. National Archives, *Compiled Ser-*

vice Records of Confederate Soldiers Who Served in Organizations from the State of Alabama, M311, Microfilm Roll #77.
18. Captions and Record of Events, p. 1.
19. The exact nature of the charges is not known.
20. The War of the Rebellion: A Compilation of the Official Records of the Union and Confederate Armies, Series I, Vol. 5, p. 926. Hereafter, this work will be cited as The Official Records. All references are to Series I, and IV. (Washington, D.C.: Government Printing Office, 1880-1902.)
(Note: This correspondence, dated October 29, was the second of the Secretary of War Judah P. Benjamin's responses sent General Joseph E. Johnston regarding the Montgomery case.)

NOTES for CHAPTER II

1. William J. Reese, letter to Margaret E. Walker, his future wife and sister of Lieutenant Robert Walker, written on November 26, 1861 (from encampment of the Army of the Potomac), p. 3. Sturdivant Hall Museum Association, Selma, Alabama.
2. Ibid., pp. 1-2.
3. Ibid., p. 3.
4. Purifoy, p. 18.
5. Ibid.
6. Robert S. Walker, letter to Margaret E. Walker on January 19, 1862 (from camp of Jeff Davis Artillery), pp. 1-2. Sturdivant Hall Museum Association, Selma, Alabama.
7. Ibid., p. 2.
8. Ibid., pp. 2-3.
9. Ibid., p. 3.
10. William J. Reese, letter to Secretary of War Judah P. Benjamin from camp of Jeff Davis Artillery on January 8, 1862. National Archives, Compiled Service Records of Confederate Soldiers Who Served in Organizations from the State of Alabama, M311, Microfilm Roll #77.
11. Lieutenant Fitts requested a transfer siting that the battery had too many officers for its present complement of guns. The company had been reduced from eight to six guns.
12. Robert S. Walker, Letter to Secretary of War Judah P. Benjamin from camp of Jeff Davis Artillery on January 9, 1862. National Archives, Compiled Service Records of Confederate Soldiers Who Served in Organizations from the State of Alabama, M311, Microfilm Roll #77.
13. McCrary, p. 1.
14. Purifoy, pp. 17-18.

NOTES for CHAPTER III

1. E. A. Pollard, The Lost Cause (New York: E. B. Treat & Co., 1867), p. 264.
2. Federal forces would eventually swell to about 100,000 men.
3. The Official Records, Vol. 11, Part III, p. 482. Organization of the Army of Northern Virginia about April 30, 1862.
4. Ultimately, the Confederate army would occupy a position less than ten miles from Richmond.
5. Purifoy, p. 19.
6. Ibid.
7. Ibid.

8. Joseph E. Johnston, "Manassas to Seven Pines," *Battles and Leaders of the Civil War*, Vol. II (New York: Thomas Yoseloff, Inc., 1956), p. 211.
9. McCrary, p. 3.
10. *The Official Records*, Vol. 11, Part I, p. 966. (General Garland had taken over for General Early, who had been wounded at Williamsburg.)
11. Ibid., p. 901.
12. Ibid., p. 966.
13. *The Official Records*, Vol. 11, Part I, p. 966. (Private James Spinner, for reasons yet to be determined, does not appear in the *Compiled Service Records*)
14. Ibid. (From report of Brigadier General Samuel Garland, Jr., Commanding 3rd Brigade, D. H. Hill's Division, June 3, 1862.).
15. This was probably near dusk.
16. Purifoy, pp. 21-22.
17. Ibid., p. 22, (Colonel Tennent Lomax).

NOTES for CHAPTER IV

1. This was arranged by Captain Montgomery, though for reasons that remain unclear.
2. Purifoy, p. 23.
3. It should be noted that the commands belonging to Major Generals Benjamin Huger and John B. Magruder were being held in position opposite the bulk of McClellan's army, south of the Chickahominy River.
4. Purifoy, p. 23.
5. *The Official Records*, Vol. 11, Part II, p. 623. (From report of Major General Daniel H. Hill, July 3, 1862.)
6. Purifoy, p. 23.
7. Ibid., p. 24.
8. Ibid.
9. *The Official Records*, Vol. 11, Part II, p. 353.
10. Purifoy, p. 25.
11. Ibid.
12. Ibid., p. 26.
13. *The Official Records*, Vol. 11, Part II, p. 641.

NOTES for CHAPTER V - PART I

1. Purifoy, pp. 27-28.
2. Ibid., p. 28.
3. Ibid.
4. Ibid., p. 29.
5. Ibid.
6. Ibid., p. 30.
7. John Purifoy, letter to Ezra A. Carman, July 15, 1899. Ezra Ayers Carman Collection, Manuscript Division, Library of Congress, p. 2.
8. Purifoy, p. 30
9. John Purifoy, letter to Ezra A. Carman, July 15, 1899, p. 2.
10. John Purifoy, letter to Ezra A. Carman, August 7, 1900. Ezra Ayers Carman Collection, Manuscript Division, Library of Congress, p. 1.
11. Purifoy, p. 77.
12. John Purifoy, letter to Ezra A. Carman, August 7, 1900, p. 1.
13. This was Captain John Lane's Georgia Battery, "E", Sumter Battalion.

14. *The Official Records*, Vol. 19, Part I, p. 434. Report of Captain Asa M. Cook, Eighth Massachusetts Battery, September 21, 1862.
15. Ibid., p. 428. Report of Brigadier General Orlando B. Willcox, Commander First Division, IX Corps, September 21, 1862.
16. Ibid.
17. Ibid.
18. Ibid. (Note: Major General Jesse Reno was commander of the IX Corps.)
19. Following the Peninsula Campaign, the Jeff Davis Artillery's armament had been reduced from six to four guns.
20. *The Official Records*, Vol. 19, Part I, p. 155. Journal of Lieutenant Colonel Edward Porter Alexander, Chief of Ordnance, October 1-November 15.
21. Purifoy, p. 32.
22. Ibid., p. 33.

NOTES for CHAPTER V - PART II

1. In approximately an hour and a half, one-fourth of Hooker's 12,000 man force had been killed or wounded.
2. *The Official Records*, Vol. 19, Part I, p. 291.
3. Private Kirvin would later be captured by the enemy and then paroled.
4. John Purifoy, letter to Ezra A. Carman, August 7, 1900, p. 2.
5. Following the capture of Harpers Ferry, Hill had been left behind by Jackson (who had begun the march to Sharpsburg) in order to dispose of any prisoners and property that had fallen into Confederate hands.
6. *The Official Records*, Vol. 19, Part I, p. 1024. Report of Major General Daniel H. Hill, December 24, 1862.
7. Purifoy, p. 34.
8. Ibid.
9. Ibid.

NOTES for CHAPTER VI

1. *The Official Records*, Vol. 19, Part II, p. 652.
2. Ibid.
3. Purifoy, p. 35.
4. Ibid.
5. Ibid., p. 37.
6. Ibid.
7. Purifoy, p. 36.
8. Ibid.
9. Ibid., p. 38.
10. Ibid.
11. *The Official Records*, Vol. 21, p. 643. Report of Major General Daniel H. Hill, December 24, 1862.
12. Ibid.
13. Purifoy, p. 38.
14. Ibid.
15. Ibid.
16. Ibid.
17. Ibid.
18. *The Official Records*, Vol. 21, p. 638. Report of Colonel Stapleton Crutchfield, Chief of Artillery, Second Corps, January 1, 1863.

19. Purifoy, p. 39.
20. Ibid.
21. Ibid.
22. John Purifoy, letter appearing under "Was This A Coincidence?", *Confederate Veteran*, IX (April 1901), p. 167.
23. *The Official Records*, Vol. 21, p. 634. Report of Lieutenant General Thomas J. Jackson, Commander Second Corps, January 3, 1863.
24. Ibid.
25. John Purifoy, "Was This A Coincidence?", p. 167.
26. Ibid.
27. Ibid.
28. *The Official Records*, Vol. 21, p. 566.
29. Ibid., Series IV, Vol. 2, p. 153.
30. Ibid., p. 205.
31. Ibid.

NOTES for CHAPTER VII

1. Douglas Southall Freeman, *Lee's Lieutenants*, Vol. II (New York: Charles Scribner's Sons, 1943), p. 421.
2. James W. Bondurant, letter written to Brigadier General William N. Pendleton from the camp of the Jeff Davis Artillery on January 15, 1863. National Archives, *Compiled Service Records of Confederate Soldiers Who Served in Organizations from the State of Alabama*, Microfilm Roll #76.
3. John Purifoy, "Lieut. Dwight E. Bates, Jeff Davis Artillery, C.S.A.," *Confederate Veteran*, XXXIII (May 1925), p. 175.
4. Ibid.
5. Darius N. Couch, "Oh great God! See how our men are falling!" *Battles and Leaders of the Civil War* (ed. Ned Bradford) (New York: Hawthorn Books Inc., 1956), p. 314.
6. *The Official Records*, Vol. 11, Part I, p. 973. Report of Brigadier General Robert E. Rodes, June 7, 1862.
7. Jennings Cropper Wise, *The Long Arm of Lee*, Vol. I (Richmond, Virginia: Owens Publishing Co., 1988), p. 414.
8. Ibid., pp. 413-414.
9. Freeman, Vol. II, pp. 447-448.
10. *The Official Records*, Vol. 25, Part II, p. 637.
11. Purifoy, p. 42.
12. As shown in the *Compiled Service Records*.
13. The new recruits were: C. A. Cobb, O. Denson, J. D. Garrard, George A. Jarrett and Davidson Stoker.
14. Private Merritt's reason for having to leave the command is not known, and one can only speculate why he asked Jarrett to take his place.
15. Purifoy, pp. 40-41.
16. Ibid., pp. 41-42.
17. McCrary, p. 4.
18. William J. Reese, letter written to Margaret E. Walker on March 2, 1863 from Milford, Virginia, p. 2. Sturdivant Hall Museum Association, Selma, Alabama.
19. Ibid.
20. Ibid., p. 3.

21. Handwritten copy of General Order No. 2 from Hd. Qrs. Artillery 2nd Corps, March 19, 1863, to Captain C. Thompson commanding Louisiana Guard Artillery. (From author's collection).
22. The reason why William A. Yeldell was discharged has not yet been discovered.

NOTES for CHAPTER VIII - PART I

1. During his reorganization of the Army of the Potomac, General Joseph Hooker had abolished the grand divisions which had been utilized by his predecessor during the Fredericksburg campaign.
2. At that time, this was not considered to be a permanent change in command. Major General Edward Johnson, D. H. Hill's chosen successor, had been prevented from taking command because of a slow healing wound he had received at the battle of McDowell in May of 1862.
3. Brigadier General Cadmus Wilcox's brigade was guarding Banks' Ford, while both Brigadier General William Mahone's and Brigadier General Carnot Posey's brigades were stationed farther upriver at U.S. Ford.

NOTES for CHAPTER VIII - PART II

1. William J. Reese, letter written to Margaret Walker from a camp near Fredericksburg on May 15, 1863, p. 1. Sturdivant Hall Museum Association, Selma, Alabama.
2. Ibid.
3. Purifoy, p. 43.
4. William J. Reese, letter from Fredericksburg on May 15, 1863, p. 1.
5. John Purifoy, "Jackson's Last Battle," *Confederate Veteran*, XXVIII (March 1920), p. 93.
6. William J. Reese, letter of May 15, 1863, p. 2.
7. In the December battle, one section of the battery was positioned near Hamilton's Crossing.
8. Purifoy, p. 43. He refers to Major John Pelham of Stuart's Horse Artillery.
9. Ibid.
10. *The Official Records*, Vol. 25, Part I, p. 254. Report of Major General John F. Reynolds, May 1863.
11. Ibid., p. 258.
12. William J. Reese, letter of May 15, 1863, p. 2.
13. The terrain surrounding Anderson's original position invited ambush, so the decision was made to move to a safer post nearer to Fredericksburg.
14. Stuart's cavalry was still operating on the flank but had not yet formed a junction with Anderson.
15. William J. Reese, letter of May 15, 1863, p. 2.
16. Purifoy, p. 43.
17. Ibid.

NOTES for CHAPTER VIII - PART III

1. Purifoy, p. 43.
2. *The Official Records*, Vol. 25, Part I, p. 940. Report of Major General Robert E. Rodes, commanding D. H. Hill's division, [May] 1863.
3. Purifoy, pp. 43-44.
4. Ibid., p. 44.
5. John Purifoy, "Jackson's Last Battle," p. 94.

6. The marching route was not marked by many streams, wells, etc.
7. John Purifoy, "Jackson's Last Battle," p. 94.
8. William J. Reese, letter of May 15, 1863, pp. 3-4.
9. John Purifoy, "Jackson's Last Battle," p. 94.
10. Ibid.
11. Ibid.
12. Shelby Foote, *The Civil War - A Narrative,* Vol. II (New York: Random House, 1974), p. 292.
13. Purifoy, p. 44.
14. John Purifoy, "Jackson's Last Battle," p. 95.
15. Ibid.
16. Ibid.
17. *The Official Records,* Vol. 25, Part I, p. 999. Report of Lieutenant Colonel Thomas H. Carter, March 12, 1864.
18. Ibid.
19. John Purifoy, "Jackson's Last Battle," p. 95.
20. Ibid.
21. Private John Mitchell was "under arrest" at the time of his wounding. The reason(s) for this is not known.
22. Such a description appears in the *Compiled Service Records.*
23. The situation around Chancellorsville demanded that, regardless of what battalion to which they were originally assigned, batteries with certain types of ordnance be used where they would be most effective against the enemy. Hence, depending upon their armament, batteries, or sections thereof, could and would be switched to different positions on the field.
24. Purifoy, p. 46.
25. Major David Gregg McIntosh.
26. William J. Reese, letter of May 15, 1863, p. 4.
27. Purifoy, p. 46.
28. Ibid.
29. William J. Reese, letter of May 15, 1863, p. 5.
30. Some time since February 20, 1863, when the battery had undergone a thorough inspection, its twelve pound brass howitzer had been replaced by a twenty-four pounder. The reason for this had not yet been determined.
31. This does not include General Hooker and his staff. They had crossed the river on the morning of the 5th.
32. If one will recall, it was during February of 1863, that the Army of Northern Virginia's artillery was reorganized into battalions. "Chancellorsville" was the first test of the new command system in action.
33. *The Official Records,* Vol. 25, Part I, pp. 887-888, May 6, 1863.
34. William J. Reese, letter of May 15, 1863, p. 6. (The "Robert" referred to is Robert Walker who had not yet accepted the position of lieutenant with the company.)

NOTES for CHAPTER IX - PART I

1. To fill out the command, two brigades were also brought up from Richmond and North Carolina.
2. Major General Edward Johnson had returned to the army after recuperating from an injury sustained earlier in the war. He subsequently replaced Brigadier General Raleigh Colston, who had been removed from command because of a questionable performance at Chancellorsville.

3. Sergeant Robert T. Harper had been on detached service at Headquarters during most of the previous winter, and whether this had anything at all to do with his departure from the company is not known.
4. Purifoy, p. 47.
5. *The Official Records*, Vol. 27, Part II, p. 547. Report of Major General Robert E. Rodes, Division Commander - Second Corps, (1863).
6. During the advance at Berryville, there had been poor cooperation between the cavalry and infantry.
7. John Purifoy, "With Jackson In The Valley," *Confederate Veteran*, XXX (No. 10) (October 1922), p. 383.
8. Purifoy, p. 47.
9. *The Official Records*, Vol. 27, Part II, p. 548.
10. Ibid., pp. 548-549.
11. Purifoy, p. 47.
12. John Purifoy, "With Jackson In The Valley," p. 384.
13. *The Official Records*, Vol. 27, Part II, p. 549.
14. During the Maryland Campaign, the difficulties of this arrangement had been most apparent.
15. John Purifoy, "With Jackson In The Valley," p. 384. (Note: After the battle of Chancellorsville, Captain William J. Reese wrote that his battery had contained a twenty-four pound howitzer included in its armament. That was either a mistake on Reese's part, or an indication that a temporary change had been made with regard to the type of howitzer used at that particular battle.)
16. *The Official Records*, Vol. 27, Part II, p. 550.
17. From June 24-27, Hooker had conducted a crossing of the Potomac at Edwards' Ferry.
18. Purifoy, p. 48.
19. Freeman, III, p. 36.
20. The Union army, made up of seven corps, had been divided into five separate columns for the advance against Lee. One column contained three corps under the overall command of Major General John Reynolds, and it was that particular force whose movements were being protected, as it turned out, by mounted troops being led by Brigadier General John Buford.
21. On July 1, six of the seven Federal corps had received marching orders. Only the VI Corps was held at its present position at Manchester, Maryland, pending the arrival of further orders.

NOTES for CHAPTER IX - PART II

1. Purifoy, p. 48.
2. Ibid.
3. Ibid.
4. *The Official Records*, Vol. 27, Part II, p. 552.
5. Though the Federal command had been apprised of Ewell's approach from the north, no countermove had yet been made. Consequently, the barrage from Carter's artillery caught it off guard.
6. *The Official Records*, Vol. 27, Part II, p. 602. (Dated August 5, 1863.)
7. Ibid., p. 552-553. Report of Major General Robert E. Rodes.
8. Ibid., p. 553.
9. Ibid., p. 552.

10. John Purifoy, "The Battle Of Gettysburg, July 1, 1863," *Confederate Veteran*, XXXI (January 1923), p. 23.
11. Ibid.
12. *The Official Records*, Vol. 27, Part II, p. 603. Report of Lieutenant Colonel Thomas H. Carter.
13. Purifoy, p. 49.
14. *The Official Records*, Vol. 27, Part II, p. 603.
15. John Purifoy, "The Battle Of Gettysburg, July 1, 1863," p. 24.
16. *The Official Records*, Vol. 27, Part II, p. 342. (According to a notation on the aforementioned page, the casualties of Carter's battalion were "not reported in detail.")

NOTES for CHAPTER IX - PART III

1. Freeman, Part III, p. 178.
2. In addition, Major William Nelson's Battalion had been left awaiting orders north of Gettysburg.
3. *The Official Records*, Vol. 27, Part II, p. 448. Report of Lieutenant General Richard S. Ewell (1863).
4. Ibid., p. 603. Report of Lieutenant Colonel Thomas H. Carter.
5. Ibid., p. 320. Report of General Robert E. Lee, January 1864.
6. Colonel Thomas W. Osborn, "The Artillery At Gettysburg," *Philadelphia Weekly Times*, May 31, 1879, Vol. III, No. 14, p. 1. The Free Library of Philadelphia. Philadelphia, Pennsylvania.
7. "Tribute of Respect - To the memory of Dr. W. J. Reese, Who Was a Veteran of Two Wars," (newspaper unknown). Sturdivant Hall Museum Association, Selma, Alabama. Reese died on August 9, 1887.
8. Foote, II, p. 547.
9. Wise, II, pp. 689-690.
10. James Longstreet, *From Manassas to Appomattox, Memoirs of the Civil War in America* (Philadelphia: J. P. Lippincott, 1896), p. 395.

NOTES for CHAPTER IX - PART IV

1. John Purifoy, "The Retreat From Gettysburg," *Confederate Veteran*, XXXIII (September 1925), p. 338.
2. Ibid., p. 339.
3. Ibid.
4. John Purifoy, "The Horror Of War," *Confederate Veteran*, XXXIII (June 1925), p. 237.
5. Francis Trevelyan Miller, ed., *The Photographic History of The Civil War*, Vol. VII (New York: Castle Books, 1957), p. 58.
6. W. Emerson Wilson, *Fort Delaware* (Delaware: University of Delaware Press, 1957), p. 16.
7. The circumstances surrounding the capture of Private M. M. Dingler are unclear.
8. John Purifoy, "The Retreat From Gettysburg," p. 340.
9. Ibid.
10. Ibid., p. 339.
11. Ibid.
12. Ibid.
13. Ibid., pp. 339-340.

14. *The Official Records*, Vol. 27, Part II, p. 353. Report of Brigadier General William N. Pendleton, September 12, 1863.
15. *The Official Records*, Vol. 27, Part III, p. 991. Correspondence from General Robert E. Lee to Major General Jeb Stuart, July 10, 1863; 5:30 a.m.
16. Purifoy, p. 50.
17. Ibid., p. 51
18. Ibid.
19. Ibid.
20. Ibid.
21. Ibid., pp. 51-52.
22. Ibid., p. 52.
23. Ewell was without Early's division which had been detached at Winchester and was now moving south along a different route.
24. *The Official Records*, Vol. 27, Part II, p. 449. Report of Lieutenant General Richard S. Ewell. According to Lieutenant Colonel Thomas H. Carter, the enemy force had 12 or 15,000 infantry and one battery. (*The Official Records*, Vol. 27, Part II, p. 604.)
25. *The Official Records*, Vol. 27, Part II, p. 560-561. Report of Major General Robert E. Rodes, ...1863.
26. Lee had started out with 75,000 men. He came back with less than 50,000. Losses at Gettysburg were: 3,903 killed, 18,735 wounded and 5,425 missing (Prisoners of war), which included an unusually high percentage (20%) of his general officers. Such losses could not be easily retrieved.
27. Captain William P. Carter's command had 4 men killed and 7 wounded. Captain Richard C. M. Page's command had 2 men killed and 26 wounded.

NOTES for CHAPTER X

1. *The Official Records*, Vol. 27, Part II, p. 355 (undated).
2. Pickett's Division still had not recovered from the losses suffered at Gettysburg, and was left at the Richmond defenses. At the same time though, Brigadier General Micah Jenkins' brigade was added to Longstreet's command.
3. *The Official Records*, Vol. 29, Part II, p. 694. Lieutenant General James Longstreet to General Robert E. Lee, September 2, 1863.
4. Purifoy, pp. 52-53.
5. Freeman, III, p. 233.
6. Jones and Andrews were posted on the south side of the river in order to guard the crossing. The reserve artillery was placed nearby to render assistance should the advance on the morrow be obstructed once again.
7. Foote, II, p. 789.
8. *The Official Records*, Vol. 29, Part I, p. 418. Report dated January 30, 1864.
9. Ibid., p. 243. Report dated October 25, 1863.
10. Whether or not the battery from Jones' battalion, which had been engaged earlier, took part in that action, is not known.
11. *The Official Records*, Vol. 29, Part I, p. 408. Correspondence from General Lee to President Jefferson Davis dated October 17, 1863.
12. It is not known whether the Jeff Davis Artillery was among those selected for that assignment.
13. Purifoy, p. 53.
14. Ibid.
15. Ibid.

16. *The Official Records*, Vol. 29, Part II, p. 392.
17. *The Official Records*, Vol. 29, Part I, p. 338. Report dated November 3, 1863.
18. Ibid., p. 828. Report of General Robert E. Lee, April 27, 1864. (Also, p. 877; Report of Major General Robert E. Rodes, February 25, 1864.)
19. Ibid., p. 423. Report of Lieutenant Colonel Thomas H. Carter, January 28, 1864.
20. Ibid., p. 829. Report of General Robert E. Lee.ⱼ
21. Purifoy, pp. 54-55.

NOTES for CHAPTER XI

1. The exact date of the arrival of the new recruits has not as yet been verified. In his work, Purifoy mentions both November (p. 13) and early winter (p. 55) as the time of their arrival.
2. Purifoy, p. 55.
3. Ibid.
4. McCrary, p. 5. [The date that event took place is not noted, however. Thus, there is still some question as to when the actions described actually occurred. (i.e., November-December 1863)].
5. Purifoy, p. 55.
6. *Compiled Service Records of Confederate Soldiers Who Served in Organizations from the State of Alabama*, National Archives, Microfilm Roll #76, 77. (Private Belcher was discharged on a certificate of disability on January 1, 1864. His exact ailment is not known.)
7. Purifoy, p. 56.
8. Ibid.
9. William J. Reese, letter written by him from Frederick[s] Hall, Virginia, January 14, 1864, to Margaret E. Walker, p. 4. Sturdivant Hall Museum Association, Selma, Alabama.
10. *The Official Records*, Vol. 33, p. 516. Circular from Seth Williams, Assistant Adjutant General, February 5, 1864.
11. Ibid., p. 524.
12. George H. Steuart's brigade which had, by happy circumstance, been relieving two regiments each of S. Dodson Ramseur's and George Doles' brigades, was on hand.
13. Privates James W. Bullard, Thomas Hopkins, Abner Horton, William N. Johnson, William Loyed, Samuel K. Parsons and James W. Plunkett.
14. Purifoy, p. 56.
15. William J. Reese, letter written to General Samuel Cooper from Fredericks Hall, Virginia, dated February 2, 1864. National Archives, Records Group No. 109, M474, Microfilm Roll #149. "Letters received by Adjutant and Inspector General's Office-Confederate."
16. Walker did not want to transfer to the Jeff Davis Artillery, as he wrote his mother from Chattanooga the previous November:
I am doing as well here perhaps as I would in the Jeff Davis Artillery + as I have always felt + said I do not wish to force myself upon any company that has the right to elect its officers although I disapprove of elections. But as long as the system is allowed by our government I think the men ought all to fare alike + enjoy the privilege throughout the service.
From what is written, Walker seemed content enough where he was. (Robert S. Walker, letter of November 11, 1863, p. 4. Sturdivant Hall Museum Association, Selma, Alabama.)

17. After February 29, 1864, Mitchell is shown as discharged and on retired list. National Archives, *Compiled Service Records of Confederate Soldiers Who Served in Organizations From the State of Alabama,* Microfilm Roll #77.
18. Documents found on one officer's body killed during the raid called for the destruction of the city and the killing of Jefferson Davis and his Cabinet.
19 *The Official Records,* Vol. 33, p. 194. Report of Captain John F. B. Mitchell, Second New York Cavalry, March 15, 1864.
20. Ibid.
21. Ibid., pp. 210-211. Report made March 1, 1864.
22. Ibid., p. 211.
23. Ibid., p. 1267.
24. Robert A. Hardaway took over the spot vacated by Colonel Brown.

NOTES for CHAPTER XII - PART I
1. Foote, III, p. 144.
2. Ibid., p. 135.
3. Over the winter, the Federal forces had been consolidated into three corps: Major General Winfield S. Hancock's II, Major General Gouverneur Warren's V, and Major General John Sedgwick's VI.
4. Freeman, III, p. 350.
5. *The Official Records,* Vol. 36, Part I, p. 1085. Report of Brigadier General Armistead L. Long, November 25, 1864.
6. Edward Porter Alexander, *Fighting for the Confederacy,* ed. Gary W. Gallagher (Chapel Hill: The University of North Carolina Press, 1989), p. 354.
7. Wise, II, p. 767.
8. *The Official Records,* Vol. 36, Part I, p. 1085. Report of Brigadier General Armistead L. Long, November 25, 1864.
9. Ibid.
10. Ibid.

NOTES for CHAPTER XII - PART II
1. *The Official Records,* Vol. 36, Part I, p. 1041. Report of Brigadier General William N. Pendleton, February 28, 1865.
2. Ibid., p. 1071. Report made by Lieutenant General Richard S. Ewell, March 20, 1865.
3. Ibid., p. 1086. Report made by Lieutenant General Armistead L. Long, November 25, 1864.
4. Ibid., p. 1072. Report of Lieutenant General Richard S. Ewell.
5. Ibid., p. 1086. Report of Brigadier General Armistead L. Long.
6. Major Richard C. M. Page, "The Captured Guns at Spotsylvania Courthouse - Correction of General Ewell's Report, "*Southern Historical Society Papers,* VII, p. 535.
7. Freeman, III, p. 399.
8. *The Official Records,* Vol. 36, Part I, pp. 1079-1080. Report of Major General Edward Johnson, August 16, 1864.
9. Foote, III, p. 215.
10. Wright was the new commander of the VI Corps. On May 9, Major General John Sedgewick, its former commander, had been killed by a sharpshooter.
11. Foote, III, pp. 210-211.

12. *The Official Records*, Vol. 36, Part I, p. 1086.
13. Purifoy had been promoted to the rank of corporal during the winter of 1863-1864.
14. John Purifoy, "Jeff Davis Artillery At The Bloody Angle," *Confederate Veteran*, XXXI (September 1923), p. 331.
15. Major Richard C. M. Page, pp. 535-536.
16. *The Official Records*, Vol. 36, Part II, p. 656.
17. John Purifoy, "Jeff Davis Artillery At The Bloody Angle," p. 331.
18. Ibid.
19. Ibid.
20. Upon the promotion of Richard C. M. Page, Charles B. Montgomery took over command of the Louisa "Morris" battery.
21. John Purifoy, "Jeff Davis Artillery At The Bloody Angle," p. 331.
22. Major Richard C. M. Page, p. 536.
23. John Purifoy, "Jeff Davis Artillery At The Bloody Angle," p. 331.
24. John Purifoy, "The Jeff Davis Artillery At Bloody Angle," *Confederate Veteran*, XXIV (May 1916), p. 223.
25. Ibid.
26. Purifoy, p. 58.
27. Ibid.
28. Ibid., pp. 58-59.
29. John Purifoy, "Jeff Davis Artillery At The Bloody Angle," p. 332.
30. Purifoy, p. 60.
31. John Purifoy, "Jeff Davis Artillery At The Bloody Angle," p. 332.
32. Ibid.
33. Purifoy, p. 59.
34. John Purifoy, "The Jeff Davis Artillery At Bloody Angle," p. 224.
35. Purifoy, p. 60.
36. Foote, III, p. 221.
37. Twelve from Page's battalion. Eight from Cutshaw's battalion.
38. *Captions and Record of Events*, p. 6.
39. Purifoy, p. 60.

NOTES for CHAPTER XIII

1. *Captions and Record of Events*, p. 6.
2. *The Official Records*, Vol. 36, Part I, p. 1087. Report made November 25, 1864.
3. Ibid., p. 1088
4. It is not known whether those men from the Jeff Davis Artillery who were without a command travelled with Fry's battery.
5. Foote, III, p. 271.
6. Purifoy, p. 61.
7. Wise, II, p. 812.
8. *The Official Records*, Vol. 36, Part I, p. 1090. Report made by (?) From the Itinerary of Hardaway's Light Artillery Battalion. From Record of Events on muster-roll of field and staff for June 30.
9. *The Official Records*, Vol. 40, Part II, p. 710. Special Order #35, Headquarters Department of North Carolina and Southern Virginia, July 2, 1864.
10. Wise, II, p. 821.

NOTES for CHAPTER XIV - PART I

1. Abraham Adams, letter written by him from a camp near Richmond, Virginia on June 22, 1864, to Governor Thomas H. Watts. (author's collection).
2. Governor Thomas H. Watts, from comments written by him on the back of the letter written by Private Abraham Adams, dated June 22, 1864.
3. *The Official Records*, Vol. 40, Part III, p. 745.
4. Ibid., p. 756. Report made by Lieutenant General Richard S. Ewell on July 9, 1864.
5. *The Official Records*, Vol. 40, Part I, p. 806. Report of Colonel Thomas H. Carter made on July 16, 1864.
6. Ibid., P. 807
7. This according to John Purifoy, (Purifoy, p. 61.), but it is not substantiated elsewhere.
8. Purifoy, p. 62.
9. *The Official Records*, Vol. 40, Part I, p. 321. Report made by Major W. G. Mitchell, Aide-de-camp to Major General Hancock. (Copy of daily memoranda taken at headquarters of Second Corps).
10. Ibid., p. 322.
11. Bruce Catton, *Grant Takes Command* (Boston: Little, Brown and Company, 1969), p. 321.
12. The exact date of their arrival is not known. It is possible that the new recruits joined Fry's battery before the Southern army's shift to the Northside.
13. He reentered the hospital near the end of August. (Shown as sick in hospital from August 31, 1864 - March 1, 1865.) National Archives, *Compiled Service Records of Confederate Soldiers Who Served in Organizations from the State of Alabama*, M311, Microfilm Roll #76.

NOTES for CHAPTER XIV - PART II

1. *The Official Records*, Vol. 42, Part I, p. 873. Report of (?) Diary of First Corps, Army of Northern Virginia, of operations of August 1 - October 18.
2. McCrary, p. 6.
3. The reason for this action on the part of the War Department is not known.

NOTES for CHAPTER XIV - PART III

1. Major General Edward O. C. Ord had taken the place of William F. Smith as commander of the XVIII Corps. Major General David B. Birney had taken the place of Winfield S. Hancock, whose Gettysburg wound had worsened.
2. John F. Methvin, from a newspaper clipping in Georgia Archives. (Jeff Davis Artillery, Drawer, Box 34). Georgia Department of Archives and History, Atlanta, Georgia.
3. Ibid.,
4. *The Official Records*, Vol. 42, Part I, p. 935. From Itinerary of Hardaway's Light Artillery Battalion, August 13 - December 31.
5. Ibid., p. 794. Report of Major General Edward O. C. Ord, June 15, 1865.
6. The exact date of the transfer is not known.
7. Wise, II, p. 898.
8. *The Official Records*, Vol. 42, Part I, p. 859. Report of Brigadier General William N. Pendleton, February 28, 1865.
9. *The Official Records*, Vol. 43, Part I, p. 556. Report of Lieutenant General Jubal A. Early, October 9, 1864.

10. Wesley Merritt, "Destroying, burning..." in *Battles and Leaders of the Civil War,* ed. Ned Bradford, p. 543.
11. *The Official Records,* Vol. 43, Part I, p. 431. Report of Brevet Major General A.T.A. Torbert, November 1864.
12. Purifoy, p. 62.
13. Ibid.

NOTES for CHAPTER XV - PART I

1. Purifoy, p. 62.
2. Jeffrey D. Wert, *From Winchester to Cedar Creek: The Shenandoah Campaign of 1864* (New York: Simon and Schuster Inc., 1987), p. 211.
3. Freeman, III, 603-604.
4. Ibid.
5. Purifoy, p. 63.
6. Thomas A. Lewis, *The Guns of Cedar Creek* (New York: Harper & Row, Publishers, 1988), p. 257.
7. *The Official Records,* Vol. 42, Part I, p. 864. Report of Brigadier General William N. Pendleton made on February 28, 1865.
8. Purifoy, p. 63.
9. Ibid.
10. Ibid.
11. *The Official Records,* Vol. 42, Part I, p. 865. Report made February 28, 1865.
12. *The Official Records,* Vol. 43, Part I, p. 581. Report made by Captain Jedediah Hotchkiss, journal - Wednesday, October 19.
13. Purifoy, p. 64.
14. *The Official Records,* Vol. 43, Part I, p. 563. Report made by Lieutenant General Jubal A. Early, October 21, 1864.
15. *The Official Records,* Vol. 42, Part I, p. 865.
16. *The Official Records,* Vol. 43, Part I, p. 563.
17. Purifoy, p. 64.

NOTES for CHAPTER XV - PART II

1. Clay W. Holmes, A. M., *The Elmira Prison Camp* (New York and London: G. P. Putnam's Sons, 1912), p. 173.
2. Scruggs had the job of carrying rations from the cook house to those who were sick in their quarters, because the hospital was too full to receive them. (Holmes, p. 173).
3. Holmes, pp. 170-186.
4. Ibid., p. 179.
5. Ibid., p. 180.
6. Ibid., p. 182
7. Ibid.
8. Ibid., p. 184.
9. Ibid., p. 193.
10. Ibid., p. 186.
11. Ibid., p. 197.
12. Ibid.
13. Ibid., p. 198.
14. Ibid., p. 203.

NOTES for CHAPTER XVI - PART I

1. Purifoy, p. 65.
2. Ibid.
3. Ibid.
4. As reported by John Purifoy. The exact number of days on the march is not known. (page 65.)

NOTES for CHAPTER XVI - PART II

1. *The Official Records*, Vol. 46, Part II, p. 1083.
2. Ibid.
3. Purifoy, p. 66.
4. Columbus W. McCrary, letter written by him to William P. Chilton on January 21, 1865, pp. 1-2. National Archives, M-474, Microfilm Roll #154.
5. Ibid., p. 2.
6. Ibid., p. 1.
7. William P. Chilton, letter written by him to Secretary of War James A. Seddon on January 24, 1865. National Archives, M-474, Microfilm Roll #154.
8. Freeman, III, p. 621.
9. Purifoy, p. 66. Reprinted with the permission of Scribner, an imprint of Simon and Schuster.
10. *The Official Records*, Vol. 46, Part II, p. 1284.
11. Ibid.
12. Purifoy, p. 66.
13. *The Official Records*, Vol. 46, Part III, pp. 1316-1317.
14. Ibid., pp. 1319-1320.
15. Ibid., p. 1329.
16. Ibid., p. 1364.

NOTES for CHAPTER XVII

1. Foote, III, p. 864.
2. Ibid., p. 883.
3. Carlton McCarthy, *Detailed Minutiae of Soldier Life in the Army of Northern Virginia 1861-1865* (Richmond: J. W. Randolph & English, 1888), p. 123.
4. Purifoy, p. 66.
5. William C. Davis, "The Campaign to Appomattox," *Civil War Times Illustrated,* Gettysburg, Pa.: Historical Times Inc. (April, 1975), Vol. XIV, No. 1, p. 11.
6. Freeman, III, 689.
7. Major General Charles Griffin had replaced Warren, who had been relieved of command by Sheridan at Five Forks, as commander of the V Corps.
8. Purifoy, p. 67.
9. Freeman, III, p. 694. Reprinted with the permission of Scribner, an imprint of Simon and Schuster.
10. William C. Davis, "The Campaign to Appomattox," p. 17.
11. *Compiled Service Records of Confederate Soldiers Who Served in Organizations From the State of Alabama*, National Archives, M311, Microfilm Roll #76, 77.
12. Purifoy, p. 67.
13. Ibid.
14. Foote, III, p. 932.
15. Ibid.
16. *The Official Records*, Vol. 46, Part I, p. 1282. Report dated April 10, 1865.

17. Ibid.
18. Ibid., p. 1132. Report made on April 15, 1865.
19. Purifoy, p. 75.
20. Ibid., p. 76.
21. Ibid.
22. Ibid.
23. Ibid., p. 68.
24. Ibid., p. 77.
25. Wise, II, p. 945.
26. Purifoy, p. 77.
27. Ibid., pp. 68-69.
28. Ibid., p. 73.
29. Ibid., pp. 73-74.
30. Based on a list which appears under "Paroles of the Army of Northern Virginia" in the *Southern Historical Society Papers*, Vol. XV, p. 26. Writer believes the name G. A. Jant should read G. A. Jarrett.
31. The total number of men encompassed by the surrender was 28,231. Lee's own force numbered about 10,000 effectives, in addition to the artillery, at the time of the surrender.
32. Purifoy, p. 74.
33. Ibid., p. 69.
34. Ibid., p. 70.
35. Ibid., p. 69.

NOTES for APPENDIX A

1. "She Learned First Sewing On Uniforms." *The Selma Journal*, October 16, 1912, Vol. 22, No. 77, p. 3, Selma/Dallas County Public Library. Selma, Alabama.
2. Alabama Department of Archives and History, Military History – Jeff Davis Artillery files. Montgomery, Alabama.

NOTES for APPENDIX B

1. Alabama Department of Archives and History, Military History – Jeff Davis Artillery files. Montgomery, Alabama.

B IBLIOGRAPHY

MANUSCRIPT AND MISCELLANEOUS SOURCES

Adams, Abraham. Letter (dated June 22, 1864) to Gov. Thomas H. Watts of Alabama. Author's collection.

Captions and Record of Events, Jeff Davis Artillery Alabama Volunteers. National Archives. M-311, Roll #76. (See also below: *Compiled Service Records.*)

Compiled Service Records of Confederate Soldiers Who Served in Organizations from the State of Alabama, Jeff Davis Artillery Alabama Volunteers. National Archives. M-311, Rolls #76-77.

Chilton, William P. Letter (dated January 24, 1865) to Secretary of War James A. Seddon. National Archives. M-474, Roll #154, 147C, 1865.

Claughton, Wilber F. Letter under "Buttons Made In The Confederacy": in *Confederate Veteran,* V (June 1897), 246-247.

Crutchfield, Col. Stapleton. General Order #2 from Artillery Headquarters - 2nd Corps. (dated March 19, 1863) a handwritten copy to Capt. C. Thompson. Author's collection.

Hopkins, Mrs. Mollie Glass, "She Learned First Sewing On Uniforms." *The Selma Journal,* October 16, 1912, Vol. 22, No. 77, p. 3, Selma/Dallas County Public Library. Selma, Alabama.

McCrary, Columbus W. Letter (dated January 21, 1865) to W. P. Chilton. National Archives. M-474, Roll #154, 147C, 1865.

——, "Historical Memoranda of 'Jeff Davis' Artillery Ala. Vol." National Archives. Record Group #109.

Methvin, John F. From a newspaper clipping; an account of the battles around Richmond in September of 1864. Jeff Davis Artillery, Drawer 283, Box 34. Georgia Department of Archives and History. Atlanta, Georgia.

Osborn, Col. Thomas W. under "The Artillery At Gettysburg." *Philadelphia Weekly Times*, May 31, 1879, Vol. III, No. 14, p. 1. The Free Library of Philadelphia. Philadelphia, Pennsylvania.

Page, Maj. Richard C. M. Letter under "The Captured Guns at Spotsylvania Courthouse --Correction of General Ewell's Report" in *Southern Historical Society Papers*, VII (November 1879), 535-538.

Purifoy, John. "Jeff Davis Artillery, History of." Filed in Montgomery, Alabama - July 27, 1904. Alabama Department of Archives and History. Montgomery, Alabama.

——, "Concerning Battle Of Gettysburg," in *Confederate Veteran*, XIX (February 1911), 77.

——, "Jackson's Last Battle," in *Confederate Veteran*, XXVIII (March 1920), 93-96.

——, "Jeff Davis Artillery At The Bloody Angle," in *Confederate Veteran*, XXXI (September 1923), 331-333.

——, Letter to Ezra A. Carman, July 15, 1899. Ezra Ayers Carman Collection. Manuscript Division. Library of Congress.

——, Letter to Ezra A. Carman, August 7, 1900. Ezra Ayers Carman Collection. Manuscript Division. Library of Congress.

——, "Lieut. Dwight E. Bates, Jeff Davis Artillery, C.S.A.," in *Confederate Veteran*, XXXIII (May 1925), 174-176.

——, "The Battle Of Gettysburg, July 1, 1863," in *Confederate* Veteran, XXXI (January 1923), 22-25.

"The Horror of War," in *Confederate Veteran*, XXXIII (June 1925), 224-225, 237.

——, "The Jeff Davis Artillery At Bloody Angle," in *Confederate Veteran*, XXIV (May 1916), 222-224.

"The Retreat From Gettysburg," in *Confederate Veteran* XXXIII (September 1925), 338-340.

——, "Was This A Coincidence?," in *Confederate Veteran*, IX (April 1901), 167.

——, "With Jackson In The Valley," in *Confederate Veteran*, XXX (October 1922), 383-385.

Reese, William J. Letter (dated November 26, 1861) to Margaret E. Walker. Sturdivant Hall Museum Association. Selma, Alabama.

——, Letter (dated March 2, 1863) to Margaret E. Walker. Sturdivant Hall Museum Association. Selma, Alabama.

——, Letter (dated May 15, 1863) to Margaret E. Walker. Sturdivant Hall Museum Association. Selma, Alabama.

——, Letter (dated January 14, 1864) to Margaret E. Walker. Sturdivant Hall Museum Association. Selma, Alabama.

——, Letter (dated February 2, 1864) to General Samuel Cooper. National Archives. Record Group No. 109, M-474, Roll #149.

"To The Memory of Dr. W. J. Reese, Who Was a Veteran of Two Wars," (Tribute of Respect), source unknown. 1887?. Sturdivant Hall Museum Association. Selma, Alabama.

Walker, Robert S. Letter (dated January 19, 1862) to his sister. Sturdivant Hall Museum Association. Selma, Alabama.

——, Letter (dated November 11, 1863) to his mother. Sturdivant Hall Museum Association. Selma, Alabama.

BOOKS AND ARTICLES

Alexander, Edward Porter. *Fighting for the Confederacy.* Gary W. Gallagher, ed. Chapel Hill: The University of North Carolina Press, 1989.

Battles and Leaders of the Civil War. 4 vols. New York: Thomas Yoseloff, Inc., 1956.

Bowman, John S., Exec. ed. *The Civil War Almanac. New York:* World Almanac Publications, 1983.

Bradford, Ned, ed. *Battles and Leaders of the Civil War.* New York: Hawthorn Books, Inc., 1956.

Calkins, Christopher M. *Thirty-Six Hours Before Appomattox.* C. M. Calkins, 1980.

Catton, Bruce. *Grant Takes Command.* Boston: Little, Brown and Company, 1969.

Cullen, Joseph P. *The Battle of Chancellorsville. Civil War Times Illustrated.* Robert H. Fowler, ed. Gettysburg, Pa., Historical Times Inc., 1968.

——, *The Peninsula Campaign 1862.* New York: Bonanza Books, 1973.

Davis, Major George B. *The Official Military Atlas of the Civil War.* New York: Arno Press, Inc./Crown Publishers, Inc., 1978. (Originally published-Washington: Government Printing Office, 1891-95).

Davis, William C. *The Campaign to Appomattox. Civil War Times Illustrated.* XIV (April 1975). Gettysburg, Pa., Historical Times Inc., 1975.

Davis, William C., ed. *The Image of War: 1861-1865.* 6 vols. New York: Doubleday & Company, Inc., 1981.

Foote, Shelby. *The Civil War-A Narrative.* 3 vols. New York: Random House, 1974.

Fowler, Robert H., ed. *Gettysburg!. Civil War Times Illustrated.* II (July 1963). Gettysburg, Pa.: Historical Times Inc., 1963.

Freeman, Douglas Southall. *Lee's Lieutenants.* 3 vols. New York: Charles Scribner's Sons, 1942-44.

Holmes, Clay W. *The Elmira Prison Camp.* New York: G.P. Putnam's Sons, 1912.

Jaynes, Gregory. *The Killing Ground-Wilderness to Cold Harbor. The Civil War.* Alexandria, Va.: Time-Life Books, Inc., 1986.

Lewis, Thomas A. *The Guns of Cedar Creek.* New York: Harper & Row, Publishers, 1988.

Longstreet, James. *From Manassas to Appomattox, Memoirs of the Civil War in America.* Philadelphia: J. P. Lippincott, 1896.

McCarthy, Carlton. *Detailed Minutiae of Soldier Life in the Army of Northern Virginia 1861-1865.* Richmond, Va.: J. W. Randolph & English, 1888.

Miller, Francis Trevelyan, ed. *The Photographic History of the Civil War.* 10 vols. New York: Castle Books, 1957.

Pollard, E. A. *The Lost Cause.* New York: E. B. Treat & Company, 1867.

Priest, John Michael. *Before Antietam – The Battle for South Mountain.* Shippensburg, Pa.: White Mane Publishing Company, Inc. 1992.

Sommers, Richard J. *Richmond Redeemed-The Siege at Petersburg.* New York: Doubleday & Company, Inc., 1981.

Stackpole, Edward J. *Drama on the Rappahannock-The Fredericksburg Campaign.* New York: Bonanza Books, 1957.

U.S. War Department. *The War of the Rebellion: A Compilation of the Official Records of the Union and Confederate Armies;* Washington, D.C.: Government Printing Office, 1880-1901. 128 bks. (incl. Index) Series I, IV.

Wellman, Manly Wade. *Rebel Boast.* New York: Henry Holt and Company, 1956.

Wert, Jeffrey D. *From Winchester to Cedar Creek: The Shenandoah Campaign of 1864.* New York: Simon and Schuster Inc., 1987.

Wise, Jennings Cropper. *The Long Arm of Lee.* 2 vols. Richmond, Va.: Owens Publishing Company, 1988.

Wilson, W. Emerson. *Fort Delaware.* Newark, Del.: University of Delaware Press, (Pamphlet) 1957.

INDEX

(Note: A search was made for the first names of every battery member, but as shown in the listing that follows, an individual's initials often represented the best information that could be found.)

A

Acker, Pvt. Augustus H., 138
Adams, Pvt. Abraham, 6, 172, 238, 241
Adams, Col. Julius W., 25
Alabama troops;
    1st Inf. (Gladden's Brigade, Army of Pensacola), 5-6
    3rd Inf. (Mahone's Brigade, Huger's Division), 27, 123, 266
    9th Inf. (Perrin's Brigade, Anderson's Division, Third Corps), 272
    13th Inf. (Colquitt's Brigade, D. H. Hill's Division), 61
    43rd Inf. (Gracie's Brigade, Preston's Division), 187
    Alabama Mounted Rifles, 5
    51st Cav. (Partisan Rangers, Wheeler's Cavalry), 90-91
Alexander, Brig. Gen. Edward Porter, 206, 253
Alexander, Pvt. Martin L., 29
Alrich Tavern, Va., 106
Alfred, 116
Amelia Court House, Va., 295-99, 303, 306
Anderson, Brig. Gen. George B., 35, 47, 50

Anderson, Brig. Gen. George T. "Tige", 50
Anderson, Pvt. John S. "Palmetto", 2
Anderson, Lt. Gen. Richard H., 56, 97, 100, 102-7, 110, 119, 141, 143, 168, 199-200, 202-7, 224, 228-32, 236, 243, 245-48, 252, 288, 294, 296, 299, 301-2
    R. H. Anderson's Corps, 220, 224, 228, 242, 292-93
    R. H. Anderson's Division, 97, 99, 110, 118, 141, 143, 145, 160, 168, 195, 197
Anderson, 1st Lt. Robert M. (Richard Howitzers, Cabell's Battalion, First Corps), 185
Anderson Station, 228
Andrews, Lt. Col. R. Snowden (Artillery-Second Corps), 166-67, 171
Antietam, battle of, 53-62
Antietam Creek, 53, 56-8
Appomattox Court House, Va., 305-6, 310-12, 314-16
Appomattox River, 281, 288, 294-96, 299, 302-3, 308
Appomattox Station, 305-7

371

Archer, Brig. Gen. James J., 110
Armament, Jeff Davis Artillery, 7, 15-16, 118, 127, 217, 253, 264-65
Armistead, Brig. Gen. Lewis A., 150
Artillery, Second Corps, 77, 84, 96, 99-100, 141, 165, 189-90, 195, 197, 200, 206, 222, 226, 264, 280, 284, 286-87, 290
Atlanta, Ga., 6
Atlee Station, Va., 231
Auburn, N.Y., 273
Auburn, Va., 167, 169, 171

B

Bailey's Creek, Va., 243
Ball, Pvt. G. H., 163
Banks' Ford, Va., 82, 96-97, 100, 102
Barksdale, Brig. Gen. William, 103, 143
Barlow, Maj. Gen. Francis C., 56, 136, 304
Barlow, Sgt. Joseph J., 221
Barlow, Pvt. J. W., 163
Barlow, Pvt. R. W., 123
Barrett's Ford, Va., 165
Bates, 1st Lt. Dwight E., 6, 82-83, 90, 94, 120, 123, 148, 172-73, 183, 187, 217, 221-22, 316
Battle, Brig. Gen. Cullen A., 197, 205
Batton, Pvt. William, 221
Bealeton, Va., (See Bealeton Station)
Bealeton Station, Va., 172-73
  battle of, 172-73
Beauregard, Gen. Pierre G. T., 227-28, 232-36, 248
Beaver Dam Creek, Va., 29, 31-33
Beaver Dam Station, 187
Beckham, 1st Lt. Robert F. (Jeff Davis Artillery, Early's Brigade, First Division-Van Dorn), 7, 9, 12, 14
Beech Creek, Ala., 2
Belcher, Pvt. Obediah, 163, 183
Belle Grove, Va., 256-57
Belle Island, Richmond, Va., 187-88
Belle Plain, Va., 222
Benjamin, Judah P. (Secretary of War-C.S.A.), 7-8
Bentley, Pvt. James S., 12
Bentonville, N.C., 288
Berryville, Va., 125, 160, 247
  1st engagement at, 125-26
  2nd engagement at, 160

Bethesda Church, 35
Betts, Lt. Col. W. H. (13th Ala. Inf.), 61
Bevill's Bridge, Va., 294
Big Round Top, Gettysburg, 143
Billingslea, Sgt. John T., 6, 93, 164
Birney, Maj. Gen. David B., 110, 251
Blackburn, Pvt. William S., 230
Blackmon, Pvt. A. M., 163
Blackmon, Pvt. John W., 244-5, 313
Blackstock, Pvt. A., 230
Blankinship, Pvt. Joseph, 22, 43, 46-7, 171, 214, 218, 261, 313
Blanks, Pvt. Andrew J., 89-90, 221
Bloody Angle, Spotsylvania, 90, 220
Blue Ridge Mountains, Va., 125, 160-61, 247, 253
Bolton, Pvt. William A., 5
Bondurant, Maj. James W. (Jeff Davis Artillery, D.H. Hill's Division, Second Corps), 6, 14-15, 19, 22-23, 25-26, 29, 31-33, 35, 37-38, 40, 43, 45-46, 49, 51, 56, 61, 63, 65, 67, 71, 74, 76-78, 80, 82-83, 86, 90-91, 93-94, 123
Bondurant's Battery (See Jeff Davis Artillery), 20, 22-23, 40, 47, 49-50, 52, 56-57, 61, 71, 83, 86
Boonsboro, Md., 44, 46, 51
Boonsboro Pike, 61
Bottom's Bridge, Va., 186
Bowman's Ford, Va., 256-57
Bowman's Mill, 256
Boydton Plank Road, Va., 252, 275, 285
Bradley, Pvt. Thomas M., 221
Bragg, Gen. Braxton, 5, 164-65
Branch, Brig. Gen. L. O'Brien, 30
Brandy Station, Va., 124-25, 166
Braxton, Lt. Col. Carter M. (Artillery-Second Corps), 114, 188, 202, 226
Braxton's Battalion, 188, 190, 200, 205, 226, 235, 281, 287, 290
Breckinridge, Maj. Gen. John C., 227-28, 235-36, 249-50
Breithaupt, Pvt. William, 5, 94, 313
Bristoe Station, Va., 167-71
  battle of, 168-69
Broad Run, Bristoe Station, 168-69
Brock Road, Va., 109, 198, 200, 204
Brook Turnpike, 189
Brown, Col. John Thompson (Artillery-Second Corps), 67, 84, 145, 167, 188, 190, 195, 200

Brown's Battalion, 67, 84, 188, 190
Brown's Gap, Va., 254
Bryant, Pvt. Joseph, 16
Buford, Maj. Gen. John, 132, 172-73
Bulger, Pvt. James, 163
Bumpass Station, Va., 189
Burgess's Mill, Va., 275, 294
Burkeville, Va., 295, 297-98, 303, 316
Burnside, Maj. Gen. Ambrose E., 57-58, 65-68, 73-74, 76, 79-80, 82-83, 191, 196, 207, 219, 225, 229, 244, 252
Burroughs, Pvt. Thomas A., 303
Burwell, Pvt. John, 159
Busby, Pvt. John R., 154
Butler, Major Gen. Benjamin F., 185-86, 232, 236, 251, 275-76

C

Cabell, Col. Henry C. (Artillery-First Corps), 185-86
Caldwell, Pvt. William, 12
Calhoun, Maj. James L., 3,5
Callahan, Pvt. F.M., 163,
Callihan, Pvt. John, 13
Callihan, Sgt. William L., 6
Callihan, Pvt. William M., 313
Campbell, Pvt. John D., 39
Canterberry, Pvt. Zenephan C., 249
Carlisle, Pa., 128-30, 269
Carlisle Barracks, 129
Carlisle Road, 134, 141, 146
Carter, Sgt. Euphroneus (Stable Guard), 6, 116
Carter, Pvt. Joseph W., 39
Carter, Pvt. S.M., 313
Carter, Col. Thomas H. (Artillery-Second Corps), 25, 84, 99, 110, 112, 122, 126, 133-34, 136-37, 141, 160, 173, 177-78, 188, 190, 195, 200, 209, 224, 226, 231, 236, 241-43, 249-50, 254, 257, 259-61, 263-64, 280-81, 284, 286-87
Carter's Battalion, 83-84, 100, 107, 110, 112, 115, 122, 125, 133, 136-37, 139, 141, 144-45, 152, 154, 156, 158-61, 163, 165-67, 170-71, 173, 175-78, 185, 190
Carter, Capt. William P. (King William Artillery, Carter's Battalion, Second Corps), 74, 83, 112, 122, 133, 164, 209-11

Carter's Battery (Thomas H.), 25
Carter's Battery (William P.), 161, 176, 209, 211
Cashtown, Pa., 129-30, 132, 137
Catharine Furnace, Chancellorsville, 108, 110
Catharpin Road, 195
Cauley, Pvt. J.L., 244, 284
Cedar Creek, Va., 254-57, 259, 263-64, 278
  battle of, 257-64
Cedar Mountain, Va., 173, 175
Cedarville, Va., 247
Cemetery Hill, Gettysburg, 138-39, 141, 144, 146, 148
Cemetery Ridge, Gettysburg, 141, 146, 148-50, 152
Centreville, Va., 7, 9, 13-14, 16-17, 19, 170, 191
Chaffin's Bluff, Va., 242, 251
Chambersburg, Pa., 128-29, 132, 245, 269
Chambersburg Pike, Gettysburg, 132, 137
Champion, Pvt. George M., 154
Chancellor, Melzi (House), 112
Chancellorsville, Va., 96, 100, 102-4, 106, 112, 116, 118, 120-21, 123, 173, 179, 196, 255
  battle of, 105-119
Charlestown, W. Va., 247
Chattanooga, Tenn., 164
Chemung River, 271
Chester Gap, Va., 125, 161
Chesterfield Bridge, Va., 228-29
Chew, Lt. Col. Robert P. (Horse Artillery), 281
Chickahominy Bluff, 31
Chickahominy River, Va., 22-23, 29-32, 233
Chickamauga, battle of, 164
Chilton, William P., 283-84
Christian, 2nd Lt. Richard H., 173, 183-84
City Point, Va., 242, 245
Clark's Mountain, Va., 193
Clarke, Capt. P. H. (Long Island Battery, Reserve Battalion, D. H. Hill's Division), 37
Clarke, Pvt. Richard G., 303

Claughton, Pvt. Wilber F., 4, 39
Clutter, Capt. Valentine C. (Richmond Battery, Johnson's Battalion, First Corps), 311
Coal Harbor, Va., 82 (See Cold Harbor, 1862)
Cobb, Pvt. C.A., 88-89, 264
Cobb, Sgt. Robert E., 6, 184, 214, 217, 221
Cobean, Samuel, 133-4, 136
Cochran, John W. (Artificer), 154
Cold Harbor, Va., 39, 232, 235, 278 (See Old Cold Harbor/Gaines' Mill)
    (1862) battle of, 35-39
    (1864) battle of, 234
Colquitt, Brig. Gen. Alfred H., 45, 107
Colston, Brig. Gen. Raleigh E., 97, 107, 112
Colston's Division, 97, 103, 110
Confederate States' Armies;
    Army of Northern Virginia, 28-29, 32, 39, 42-45, 57, 61-63, 65, 74, 78, 80, 83-84, 95, 98, 103, 119, 121, 123, 130, 132, 138, 159, 163, 190-92, 220, 223, 287, 305, 311, 313-14, 317
    Army of the Potomac, 6, 9, 16-17, 27
    Army of Tennessee, 29, 93, 164, 287
    Army of the Valley, 245, 247, 250, 253-54, 259, 263-66, 276, 278, 281, 285
Conner, Brig. Gen. James, 255
Cook, Capt. Asa M. (8th Mass. Battery), 49
Cooley, J., (House), 256
Cooper, Gen. Samuel, 77, 80, 187, 285-86
Corps, Army of Northern Virginia, (C.S.A.);
    First, 65, 97, 100, 104-5, 122, 128, 141, 146, 157, 160, 164-65, 191, 195, 199-200, 202-4, 206, 219, 232, 243, 247, 276
    Second, 65-66, 70, 73, 97, 103-4, 107, 112-14, 121-22, 124, 127-29, 132, 135, 137-39, 141, 145, 150, 152, 155, 160, 165-66, 168-69, 176, 180, 185, 190-91, 197-99, 203-5, 226-27, 231-32, 235-36, 238, 256, 288, 295-96, 302
    Third, 122-24, 128, 132-33, 141, 150, 152, 157-58, 160, 165-69, 191, 195, 198-99, 204, 228-29, 243

Corps, Army of the Potomac (U.S.A.);
    I, 44, 53, 69, 96, 101, 132, 134, 137
    II, 54, 73, 96, 102, 139, 167-69, 185, 198, 207, 225, 227-28, 242, 244, 251, 297-98, 302-5
    III, 96, 102, 110, 143, 172, 177
    V, 29, 95, 99, 168, 197, 203, 220, 224, 226-28, 293, 297-98
    VI, 71, 96, 141, 155, 198, 204-5, 219, 224-25, 229, 232, 254, 257, 259, 294, 297, 301
    VIII, 257
    IX, 44, 49, 57-58, 196, 244, 297
    X, 232
    XI, 95, 99, 110, 112, 132, 134-38, 146
    XII, 54, 95, 99
    XVIII, 232, 235, 251
    XIX, 257
    XXIV, 294
Couch, Maj. Gen. Darius N., 73, 96, 102
Cowan, Pvt. John N., 5
Cox, Pvt. James W., 39, 264
Crampton's Gap, Md., 45, 50
Crawford, John S., 141
Crawford, J. W., 271-72
Crook, Bvt. Maj. Gen. George, 257
Crosby, Pvt. John J. S., 5, 71, 74-75
Crutchfield, Col. Stapleton (Chief of Artillery, Second Corps), 77, 86, 93-95, 112-13, 165
Culp's Hill, Gettysburg, 138-39, 141, 143-45
Culpeper, Va., 65
Culpeper Court House, Va., 124, 160, 165-66, 175
Cumberland Church, Va., 304-5
Cumberland Valley, 128
Custer, Bvt. Major Gen. George A., 276, 306
Cutshaw, Lt. Col. Wilfred E. (Artillery, Second Corps), 188, 202, 206, 222, 233-35, 241-42, 247-48, 250, 260, 281, 285-87, 290, 295, 299, 302, 304
Cutshaw's Battalion, 188, 190, 195, 200, 206, 222, 236, 241, 245, 247, 249, 254, 281, 286-87, 290, 295-96, 298, 302, 304, 314

Cutts, Col. Allen S. (Artillery, Third Corps), 12, 51

D

Dahlgren, Col. Ulric (Third Division, Cavalry Corps), 187-90
Dallas County, Ala., 1, 2, 148
Dandridge, Lt. Edmund P., 86-87
Daniel, Brig. Gen. Junius, 136, 155, 206
Danville, Va., 291, 295, 297-98
Darkesville, Va., 160
Davidson, Pvt. G. F., 184
Davis, Jefferson, 8, 13, 15, 22, 28, 31, 170, 187
Day, Pvt. Mitchell W., 57
Deas, Lt. William A. (Fry's Battery), 209, 211, 314
Deep Bottom, Va., 241-43
Defreese, Pvt. Joseph, 163
Dennis, Pvt. William J., 5, 71, 75
Denson, Pvt. O., 303
Department of Virginia and North Carolina, 98
Devil's Den, Gettysburg, 143
Dingler, Pvt. M. M., 154
Dinwiddie Court House, Va., 293
Doles, Brig. Gen. George, 135-36, 155, 197, 205-6
Dowdall House, Chancellorsville, 114
Dranesville, Va., 12
Drayton, Brig. Gen. Thomas F., 50
Drewry's Bluff, Va., 227, 280
DuBose, Cpl. Christopher P., 313
Duhig, Pvt. John, 159-60
Dunker Church, Antietam, 54
Dunn, Pvt. John, 312, 315
Dunn, Pvt. William H., 230
DuPriest, Pvt. Henry A., 5

E

Early, Lt. Gen. Jubal A., 18, 20, 70, 97, 103, 118, 123, 127-30, 132, 135, 137-38, 143-45, 175-77, 201, 204, 222, 224, 231-36, 245-51, 253-56, 259-61, 263-65, 268, 271, 276, 278-81, 285, 288
Early's Division, 70, 97, 123, 125, 165, 167, 170, 204
East Cemetery Hill, Gettysburg, 138, 143-44
Edmondson, Pvt. H., 230, 303

Edwards' Ferry, 272
Edwards, Pvt. Samuel, 303
Elliott's Salient, Petersburg, 244
Ellis, Pvt. B. Franklin, 230, 303
Ellis, Pvt. J.P., 230, 313
Elmira Prison, N.Y., 154, 222, 266, 268, 271, 273, 284, 316
Ely's Ford, Va., 99, 193, 196
Emmitsburg Road, Gettysburg, 149
Emory, Bvt. Maj. Gen. William H., 257
Eubanks, Pvt. John W., 303
Ewell, Lt. Gen. Richard S., 65, 122-25, 127-30, 132-133, 138, 141, 143-45, 152, 160-61, 166-69, 176, 185-86, 193, 195-201, 203-5, 207, 225-31, 235, 241, 296, 298-99, 301
Ewell's Corps, 125, 127-28, 132, 137, 150, 152, 156-57, 165, 169, 172, 186, 195, 197, 225, 227-28

F

Fair Oaks, Va., 275
Fairfax Court House Va., 6
Fairfield, Pa., 152
Fairfield Road, 152
Fairview, Chancellorsville, 114-15
Falling Waters, W. Va., 156-61, 270
Falmouth, Va., 66, 76, 80, 83, 119
Farmville, Va., 299, 303-4, 306, 308, 316
Farrar, Pvt. William, 163
Ferguson, Pvt. Robert A., 5
Field, Maj. Gen. Charles W., 243, 293-95, 299
Fisher's Hill, Va., 250, 253-54, 263, 265
Fishersville, Va., 276-8
Fitts, 4th Lt. William A., 2, 5-6, 14
Five Forks, Va., 292-93
  battle of, 292-93
Flag, Alabama Battery, 92
Forrest, Brig. Gen. Nathan B., 91
Fort Clifton, Va., 281, 283, 285-88, 290, 293, 295, 297
Fort Delaware Prison, Del., 47, 154, 222, 316
Fort Fields, Va., 251
Fort Gilmer, Va., 251-52, 278
Fort Gregg, Va., 294
Fort Harrison, Va., 251-53
Fort Monroe, Va., 18
Fort Stedman, Va., 288-90

Fort Sumter, S.C., 1
Fort Varina, Va., 251
Fort Whitworth, Va., 294
Fox's Gap, Md., 45-46, 50
    battle of, 45-50
Franklin, Maj. Gen. William B., 65, 82
Frederick, Md., 42-44, 47, 129-30, 157
Fredericksburg, Va., 66-68, 73, 76-77, 82-
    83, 96-97, 99-103, 106, 118-20, 124
    battle of, 69-76
Fredericks Hall, Va., 183-91
French, Maj. Gen. William H., 54, 176
Front Royal, Va., 160, 247
Fry, Capt. Charles W. (Richmond Or-
    ange Artillery, Carter's Battalion,
    Second Corps), 37, 83, 122, 133, 136,
    176, 206, 209, 211, 222-24, 233, 244-
    45, 261, 264-65, 302
Fry's Battery, 37, 161, 210, 227-28, 234,
    238, 242, 248, 254-56, 259, 261, 264-
    65, 276-78, 302, 312
Furnace Road, 108

G

Gaines' Mill, Va., 32-33, 39-40
    battle of, 35-39 (*See* Cold Harbor,
    1862/Old Cold Harbor)
Garland, Brig. Gen. Samuel Jr., 25, 31,
    35, 40, 45-47, 82
Garrard, Pvt. J. D., 313
Garnett, Brig. Gen. Richard B., 150
Garrett, Senior 2nd Lt. J. W., 2
Gates, James C. (Artificer), 154
Gayle, Pvt. Henry, 264
Georgia troops, 23rd Inf. (Colquitt's Bri-
    gade, Rodes' Division, Jackson's
    Corps), 110
Germanna Ford, Va., 99-100, 193, 196,
    201
Germanna Ford (Plank) Road, 197, 201
Getty, Brig. Gen. George W., 198, 257,
    259
Gettysburg, Pa., 128, 130, 132-35, 137-39,
    141, 144, 152, 161, 163, 179, 246, 269-
    70, 284
    battle of, 132-49
Gibbon, Maj. Gen. John, 69-70, 294
Glaze, Pvt. Thomas, 245, 277
Globe Tavern, Va., 248, 252

Goode's Bridge, Va., 296, 298
Gordon, Maj. Gen. John B., 137, 197, 200-
    1, 204, 217-19, 221, 249, 256-57, 259-
    60, 270, 279, 288-89, 294, 298-99,
    301-7, 310-11
Gordon's Corps, 295-96, 298
Gordon's Division, 205, 217, 219, 255-
    57, 260, 278
Gordonsville, Va., 40-41, 191, 195, 279
Gorman, Pvt. Michael, 230, 303
Gracie, Brig. Gen. Archibald Jr., 187, 308
Grant, Lt. Gen. Ulysses S., 191-192, 195,
    197, 201-2, 204, 206-7, 224-27, 229-
    32, 234-35, 237, 242, 244, 247, 249,
    251, 255, 273, 275, 285, 287, 292, 294,
    297, 305, 307, 311
Greene, Brig. Gen. George S., 54
Greensboro, N.C., 291
Greenville, Pa., 132
Greenwich, Va., 167-68
Gregg, Maj. Gen. David M., 285
Gregory, Cpl. John C., 39
Gregory, Pvt. Philip L., 88
Griffin, Bvt. Maj. Gen. Charles, 297-98
Griffin, Capt. Charles B. (Salem Flying
    Artillery, Hardaway's Battalion,
    First Corps), 230, 234, 252
Griffin's Battery, 231, 233-234, 251, 253,
    278
Grimes, Maj. Gen. Bryan, 278
Guard Hill, 247
Guiney Station, Va., 227
Gulbrith, Pvt. Albert, 183
Gunter's Warehouse, 3

H

Hagerstown, Md., 44, 127, 156, 160, 269
Hagerstown Pike, Antietam, 53-54
Halltown, W. Va., 247
Hamilton's Crossing, Fredericksburg,
    69, 96, 104
Hampton, Maj. Gen. Wade, 226-27, 235,
    252, 275, 279
Hancock, Maj. Gen. Winfield S., 139,
    196, 198-200, 207, 209, 219-21, 225,
    227-29, 235-36, 242-44, 248, 275
Hanover Junction, Va., 227-28
Hanovertown, Va., 231-32
Hardaway, Lt. Col. Robert A. (Artillery-
    Second Corps), 31, 78, 84, 190, 202,
    205-6, 222, 232-35

Hardaway's Alabama Battery, 31, 84
Hardaway's Battalion, 167, 190, 200, 205, 222, 225, 230, 233, 236, 241, 271, 278
Harper, 1st Sgt. Robert T., 123
Harpers Ferry, W. Va., 44, 50-51, 53, 58, 249
Harris, Brig. Gen. Nathaniel H., 294
Harris, Pvt. W. J., 163-64
Harris, Pvt. W. R., 221
Harrisburg, Pa., 128-29, 269
Harrison's Landing, Va., 32-33, 40-41
Harrisonburg, Va., 254
Hartigan, Pvt. John, 93, 164
Haskell, Col. John C. (Artillery-First Corps), 204, 253, 276, 278
Hasselvander, Pvt. Adam, 313
Hatcher's Run, Va., 275, 285, 290, 292
Haw's Shop, Va., 232
Hays, Maj. Gen. Harry T., 177
Hazard, Capt. John G. (1st Rhode Island Light Artillery, Commanding Artillery Brigade, II Corps), 167
Hazel Grove, Chancellorsville, 114
Heidlersburg, Pa., 130, 132
Heidlersburg Road, 132
Heth, Maj. Gen. Henry, 132-33, 137, 145, 158-59, 168, 198-99, 243, 296, 298-99
Higgins, Cpl. George Y., 184, 221
High Bridge, Va., 302-3
Hill, Lt. Gen. Ambrose P., 30-33, 58, 65, 97, 106-7, 110, 112-13, 122, 124, 127-28, 130, 132, 141, 158, 160, 166-69, 178, 195, 197-201, 203-4, 228-31, 248, 275, 279, 288-89, 294
  A. P. Hill's Corps, 124, 127, 132, 135, 141, 150, 160, 167-68, 176, 195-96, 198, 228, 236, 252, 296
  A. P. Hill's Division, 31, 39, 58, 97, 103, — 110, 122-23
Hill, Lt. Gen. Daniel H., 18-19, 29, 33, 35, 39, 42, 44-45, 47, 50, 54, 56-57, 65-67, 69, 80, 82, 85, 90, 284
  D. H. Hill's Division, 18-20, 23, 29-31, 33, 35, 37, 39, 41-42, 44, 54, 66-69, 74, 78, 83-84, 96
Hill, Pvt. John, 230
Hobby, Pvt. Seabron O., 9
Hogan, Meredith, 312-13

Hoke, Maj. Gen. Robert F., 232, 235-36
Holloway, E. M., 2
Hood, Maj. Gen. John B., 50, 54, 98
Hood's Division, 98, 141, 164
Hooker, Maj. Gen. Joseph, 53-54, 65, 82-83, 95-97, 102-10, 114, 118-19, 124, 127-28, 130, 164
Hotchkiss, Maj. Jedediah, 107
Howard, Maj. Gen. Oliver Otis, 95, 99, 110-12, 132, 134-35, 137-38
Howell, John J. (Artificer), 154
Howlett Line, Va., 236, 280, 296
Humphreys, Maj. Gen. Andrew A., 209, 285, 297-98, 302-5
Humphries, Pvt. John J. (Artificer), 154
Hunter, Cpl. Alexander, 6
Hunter, Maj. Gen. David, 234-37
Hupp's Hill, Va., 254, 256-57, 263-64, 284, 316
Hurt, Capt. William P. (Hardaway's Alabama Battery, McIntosh's Battalion, Third Corps), 84

I

Imboden, Brig. Gen. John D., 270
Ithaca, N.Y., 272
Iverson, Brig. Gen. Alfred, 136

J

Jack's Shop, Va., 165
Jackson, Pvt. Benjamin, 230, 303, 316
Jackson, Cpl. George G., 43, 213, 215, 221, 266, 270-1
Jackson, Pvt. John B., 303
Jackson, Pvt. Littleton G., 230, 303
Jackson, Lt. Gen. Thomas J. "Stonewall", 28, 30-33, 35, 39, 41, 44, 50-51, 53, 65-66, 68-71, 73-74, 77, 97, 100, 104-10, 112-14, 121-22, 171, 179
Jackson's Corps, 65-66, 97
James River, 32-33, 39, 41, 47, 190, 235-38, 241-42, 244-45, 248, 251, 275-78, 280, 283, 290, 295
Jamestown Road, 302
Jant, G. A. (See George A. Jarrett?), 313
Jarrett, Pvt. George A., 88-90
Jeff Davis Alabama Artillery, first encampment, 2; stay at Montgomery, Ala., 3-4; stopover at LaGrange,

Ga., 5; camp near Centreville, Va., 6-7; Lieutenant Beckham steps in, 7, 9, 12, 14; Capt. Montgomery is ousted, 12-15; Yorktown and a new commander, 18-20; withdrawal to New Bridge, 20-22; movement on Seven Pines, 22-23; Seven Pines, 23-27; at Mechanicsville Bridge, 29-31; Mechanicsville, 29-32; the road to Old Cold Harbor, 33-35; Old Cold Harbor, 35-38; explosion in Maryland, 43; South Mountain, 45-50; race to Sharpsburg, Md., 51-52; Antietam, 56-62; the Shenandoah Valley, 63-65; Port Royal, Va., 67-68; Fredericksburg, 70-74; reorganization, 83-86; part of a battalion, 83; an inspection, 86; arrival of Lt. Reese, 90-92; called up from Milford, Va., 94-95, 99; promotion of Capt. Bondurant, 90, 93, 123; Fredericksburg again, 101-2; the flank march, 107-10; Chancellorsville, 105-19; Berryville, Va., 125-26; Martins-burg, W. Va., 126-27; Carlisle, Pa., 128-29; Gettysburg, first day, 133-40; Gettysburg, Cemetery Hill, 146-48; the retreat, 152-61; Falling Waters, 157-59; commended by Gen. Lee, 159; Bristoe Campaign, 165-71; Bealeton, 172; Mine Run Campaign, 176-79; defense of Fredericks Hall camp, 188-89; the Wilderness, 195, 197-98, 200, 202; Spotsylvania, 205-17; near destruction of the battery, 210-17; combined with Capt. Fry's Battery, 222-23; transfer to Capt. Griffin's Battery, 230; Cold Harbor, 234; James River operations, 236-38, 241-42; Fort Varina, 251-52; as part of Capt. Lamkin's Mortar Battery, 253; Cedar Creek, 257-64; disaster at Hupp's Hill, 263-64; the retreat, 261, 263-65; Fort Clifton, 281, 283, 285, 288-90; evacuation of Petersburg lines, 295; Sailor's Creek, 302; first charge as infantry, 304; the last charge, 310-11; capitulation and the receiving of paroles, 313;

Jeff Davis Mounted Artillery, 1, 4, 6, 18
Jenkins, Brig. Gen. Albert G., 125-27, 129
Jericho Mills, Va., 228-29
Jetersville, Va., 297-98, 303
Johnson, Maj. Gen. Edward, 123, 128, 137, 143-45, 172, 177, 205, 207, 209, 211, 221
Johnson's Division, 123, 125, 127-29, 132, 137, 139, 141, 143, 167, 172, 175, 177, 196, 204-7, 211, 218, 221
Johnson, Pvt. J.W., 284
Johnson, Maj. Marmaduke (Artillery-First Corps), 311
Johnston, Gen. Joseph E., 6-8, 17-20, 22-23, 26, 28, 287-88, 290, 295, 297, 307, 312, 316
Johnston, Brig. Gen. Robert D., 206, 217
Jones, Pvt. A. W., 313
Jones, Pvt. C.S.V., 230, 251
Jones, Maj. Gen. David R., 58
Jones, Col. Hilary P. (Artillery-Anderson's Corps), 15, 19, 37, 114, 260
Jones' Battalion, 114-15, 166-67, 169
Jones, Pvt. J. J., 264
Jones, Jake, 312
Jones, Cpl. James M., 39, 83, 230, 313
Jones, Brig. Gen. John M., 196-98, 211
Jones, J. William (Chaplain), 129
Jones' Neck, Va., 241-42

K

Kane, Pvt. James, 94
Kautz, Brig. Gen. August V., 251
Kelly's Ford, Va., 173, 175, 178
Kemper, Maj. Gen. James L., 150
Kershaw, Maj. Gen. Joseph B., 204, 242-43, 245, 247-48, 250, 254-57
Kershaw's Division, 204, 242-43, 245, 247, 250, 254, 256-57, 260, 276
Kilpatrick, Brig. Gen. Judson, 152, 187-89
King, Col. J. Floyd (Artillery-Second Corps), 286-87
King William Artillery (Carter's), 25, 74, 83-84, 112, 133, 164
Kirvin, Pvt. Calvin J., 43, 57
Knight, 2nd Lt. Edward G., 15, 76-77, 82, 125
Knight, Pvt. Monroe W., 23, 27
Knight, Pvt. Thomas, 183
Kuhne, Charles G., (Artificer), 154

L

LaGrange, Ga., 4-6
Lamkin, Capt. James N. (Nelson Battery, Haskell's Battalion, First Corps), 253
Lamkin's Battery, 253, 276, 278, 283, 286
Lang, Col. David (Perry's Brigade, Anderson's Division, Third Corps), 145, 150
Law, Brig. Gen. Evander M., 73
Lee, Cpl. Brittan C., 6
Lee, Maj. Gen. Fitzhugh, 51, 107, 109, 203, 232, 245, 247, 292-93, 307, 310, 312
Lee, Pvt. G. W., 313
Lee, Gen. Robert E., 22, 28-31, 33, 39-42, 44-45, 50-51, 53-54, 57-58, 61-66, 68-69, 74, 77, 82, 84-85, 95-100, 102-3, 105, 107-8, 110-11, 118-19, 121-25, 127-31, 137-38, 141, 145, 148-52, 156-57, 159-61, 163-66, 169-70, 175-79, 185, 191-93, 195-98, 201-2, 204, 206, 218, 220-22, 224-37, 241-43, 245-46, 248, 250, 252, 270, 273, 276, 278, 280, 286-99, 303-7, 311-16
Lee, Pvt. S. J., 244, 313
Lee, Maj. Gen. William H. F., 243, 292
Leesburg, Va., 42
Lewis's Creek, Chancellorsville, 107, 110
Liberty Mills, Va., 121
Lincoln, Abraham, 130
Little Round Top, Gettysburg, 143, 146
Little Sailor's Creek, Va., 301
    battle of, 301
Little Sayler's Creek, Va., (See Little Sailor's Creek)
Little Washington, Va., 166
Lloyd, Capt. W.P. (North Carolina Battery, Jones' Battalion, Reserve Artillery), 51
Lockett's Hill, Va., 302
Locust Grove, Va., 176-77, 195, 197-98, 200, 202
Logan, Pvt. John A., 313-14
Lomax, Maj. Gen. Lunsford L., 254, 257
Lomax, Col. Tennent (3rd Alabama Inf.), 27
Long, Brig. Gen. Armistead L., 165, 167, 169, 188-89, 201-2, 205-7, 225-26, 228, 231, 234-35, 249, 281, 285, 311

Longstreet, Lt. Gen. James, 19, 23, 33, 44, 50, 53, 62, 65-66, 97-98, 122, 128, 132, 137, 141, 145-46, 149, 152, 164-65, 191, 193, 195, 197, 199-200, 202, 276, 290, 296-97, 299, 303, 305, 307, 311
Longstreet's Corps, 66, 73, 122, 124, 127, 137, 141, 150, 160, 187, 191, 199, 288, 293
Longstreet's Division, 19, 30, 39, 45, 50
Louisa Morris Artillery (Page's), 83
Lovelace, 1st Lt. Charles W., 2, 5-6, 14
Lowndes County, Ala., 2, 314
Luchow, Pvt. Louis, 5
Luray, Va., 161
Luray Valley, Va., 247
Lynchburg, Va., 234, 236-37, 299, 304, 307
Lynchburg Road, 310

M

Madison Court House, Va., 161, 165
Magruder, Maj. Gen. John B., 18-19
Mahone, Maj. Gen. William, 100, 118, 219, 296, 298-99, 301-5
Malone, Cecrops, 272-73
Malvern Hill, Va., 39-40, 235, 242
Manassas, Va., 6, 16-17, 19, 170
Manassas Gap, Va., 160
Manassas Junction, Va., 169-70
Manchester, Md., 130
Mansfield, Maj. Gen. Joseph, 54
Marble, Pvt. William B., 88
Martinsburg, W. Va., 44, 126-27, 246, 270
    engagement at, 126-27
Massachusetts troops, 8th Massachusetts Battery (Willcox's Division, IX Corps), 49
Matadequin Creek, Va., 234
Mathews, Pvt. John A., 9
Maull, 2nd Sgt. John Fox, 6, 38, 88, 221, 266, 268-71
Maulsby, Capt. Thomas A. (Third Brigade, First Division, VIII Corps), 126
McCall, Brig. Gen. George A., 29
McClellan, Maj. Gen. George B., 17-19, 22-23, 28-30, 32-33, 39-42, 44-45, 50-51, 53, 57, 62-63, 65

McCondichie, Pvt. Patton, 112-13
McCoull house, Spotsylvania, 206
McCrary, Sgt. Maj. Columbus W., 6, 123, 209, 230-31, 248, 283-86, 313
McDonald, Pvt. Thomas H., 39
McGibony, August, (Detective), 6
McIntosh, Col. David Gregg (Artillery-Third Corps), 84, 115
McLaughlin, Maj. William (King's Artillery Battalion-Second Corps), 286-87
McLaws, Maj. Gen. Lafayette, 44, 47, 50, 54, 97, 100, 104-5, 107, 118-19, 124, 143
McLaws' Division, 44-45, 50, 97, 103, 124, 164
McPherson Ridge, Gettysburg, 133
Meade, Maj. Gen. George G., 69-70, 95, 99, 130-32, 139, 141, 145-46, 149-50, 152, 157, 163-64, 166, 169-71, 173, 176-77, 185, 192-93, 197, 201, 225, 228-29, 232, 234-36, 245-46, 248, 278, 285, 288, 290
Meadow Bridges, 30-31
Mechanicsville, Va., 29, 31-32, 85, 191, 231
engagement at, 31-32
Mechanicsville Road, 31, 231
Mechanicsville Road Bridge, 29-31, 85
Meek, Pvt. Jacob A., 25, 27
Melton, Pvt. James A. (Bugler), 5, 313
Melton, Pvt. William J., 138, 213
Merritt, Pvt. Napoleon B., 88-9
Merritt, Bvt. Maj. Gen. Wesley, 203
Messer, Pvt. David M., 183
Metcalf, Pvt. Albert W., 230
Methvin, Pvt. John F., 186, 230, 251, 312, 315
Middleburg, Md., 130
Middletown, Pa., 132
Middletown, Va., 259-60
Middletown Road, Gettysburg, 132, 136
Miles, Lt. Col. Nelson A., 56
Milford, Va., 84, 88, 90, 93
Milford Station, Va., 78, 80, 96, 99
Military Road, 104
Milledge, Capt. John Jr. (Georgia Regular Battery, Nelson's Battalion, Second Corps), 198
Miller, Capt. M.B. (3rd Co. Washington

Artillery, Eshleman's Battalion, First Corps), 146
Mine Run, Va., 176-77, 181
Miner, Pvt. E., 221
Mitchell, 2nd Lt. John, 90, 113, 173, 187, 248, 277
Mitchell Station, 247
Mollie Glass, 75
Monocacy Junction, 246
Monocacy River, Md., 43, 245
Monterey, Pa., 152
Montgomery, Ala., 2-5
Montgomery, Pvt. Charles H. (Bugler), 13
Montgomery, Capt. Charles R. (Louisa Morris Artillery, Carter's Battalion, Second Corps), 209-11, 222
Montgomery, Pvt. James S., 16
Montgomery, Capt. Joseph T. (Jeff Davis Artillery, Early's Brigade, First Division-Van Dorn), 1-9, 12-15, 78, 91
Montgomery's Battery (See Jeff Davis Artillery), 5-6
Montgomery's Independent Company of Alabama Cavalry, 1
Moore, Gov. Andrew B., 4-5
Moore, 1st Sgt. James L., 6, 28
Moore's Church, Va., 298
Morris Artillery (Page's), 74, 83, 134, 136, 190
Morton's Ford, Va., 165, 176, 179, 181, 185-87
Mosby, Col. John S. (43rd Virginia Cavalry Battalion), 272
Moseley, Lt. Col. Edgar F. (Artillery-Anderson's Corps), 233
Moss Neck, 97
Mount Crawford, Va., 253
Mule Shoe Salient, Spotsylvania, 205-6, 218, 220-21
Mundy, Cpl. James J., 6, 15

N

Nance, Pvt. A., 184
Nelson, Col. William N. (Artillery-Second Corps), 190, 202, 205, 249-50, 254
Nelson's Battalion, 167, 190, 195-6, 198, 200, 235, 281, 287, 290
Nelson Light Artillery (Lamkin's), 253

New Baltimore, Va., 166
New Bridge, Va., 22
New Cold Harbor, Va., 35
New Kent Court House, Va., 20
New Market, Va., 66, 227, 265-66, 276
New Market and Malvern Hill Road, 243
New Store, Va., 305
Newport News, Va., 316
New York troops, 1st Light Artillery, 101
61st Inf. (Caldwell's Brigade, First Division, II Corps), 56
67th Inf. (Abercrombie's Brigade, First Division, IV Corps), 25
Ni River, Va., 226-27
Nobles, Cpl. Edward W., 6, 71, 75
Noel's Ferry, 42
North Anna River, Va., 195, 227-29, 231
Northside, 242-44, 248-49, 251-53, 275, 278, 286, 296
North Woods, Antietam, 53
Norwood, Sgt. James E., 6, 113, 214, 254-55

O

Oak Hill, Gettysburg, 133-34, 136
Oak Ridge, Gettysburg, 133, 136
Ohio troops, 126th Inf. (Third Brigade, Carr's Division, III Corps), 172 (See Smith, Col. Benjamin F.)
Old Capitol Prison, Washington, D.C., 160
Old Church Road, 35, 231
Old Cold Harbor, Va., 33, 35
battle of, 35-39 (See Cold Harbor, 1862/Gaines' Mill)
Old Fair Grounds, Montgomery, Ala., 3
Old Turnpike, Va., 105-6, 109-12
Oliver, Pvt. John A., 215, 313
O'Neal, Col. Edward A. (Rodes' Division, Second Corps), 125, 136, 160
Orange Artillery (Fry's), 133, 136, 223-24, 242, 259, 264
Orange Court House, Va., 66, 161, 185-87
Orange Plank Road, 104-10, 114, 118, 120, 195, 197-200, 205
Orange Turnpike, 195-98, 200
Ord, Maj. Gen. Edward O. C., 251, 297

Osborn, Col. Thomas W., 146
Ox Ford, Va., 228-29
Ox Hill, Va., 42

P

Page, Maj. Richard C.M. (Carter's Battalion, Second Corps), 83, 122, 134, 136, 190, 195, 202, 206-7, 209-11, 215, 222, 224, 233, 284
Page's Battalion, 190, 195, 197-98, 200, 205-7, 210, 221, 225, 227, 232
Page's Battery, 136, 159, 161
Pamunkey River, Va., 30, 231-32
Parish, Pvt. James A., 264
Parke, Maj. Gen. John G., 252, 275, 297
Parker's Store, Va., 196
Patton, Sgt. Augustus B., 6, 221
Payne, Pvt. Asbury, 264
Peebles, Pvt. John M., 163, 234
Peak, Pvt. Solomon M., 230
Pegram, Brig. Gen. John, 256, 260-1, 278-79
Pegram, Capt. Richard G. (Petersburg Battery, Branch's Battalion, Anderson's Corps), 244
Pelham, Maj. John, 101
Pender, Maj. Gen. W. Dorsey, 137, 145
Pendergast, Pvt. D. J., 230
Pendleton, Capt. S. H. (Louisa Morris Artillery, Carter's Battalion, Second Corps), 74, 190
Pendleton, Brig. Gen. William N., 9, 12, 15, 63, 75, 82, 84-85, 95, 97, 163, 187, 190, 263, 280-81, 295, 306-7
Penick, Capt. Nathan (Pittsylvania Battery, Poague's Battalion, Third Corps), 243
Peninsula, The, 18-19, 29, 35
Peninsula Campaign, 18-41, 44, 100
Pensacola, Fla., 5
Perry, Brig. Gen. E. A., 100
Petersburg, Va., 234-36, 244, 248, 252-54, 273, 275, 281, 283, 288, 290, 294-96, 298
Petersburg Battery (Pegram's), 244
Peyton's Ford, Va., 165
Pickett, Maj. Gen. George, 98, 132, 146, 148, 292-94, 296

Pickett's Division, 98, 132, 145, 150, 228, 288, 292

Pierce, Pvt. John F., 13

Pierson, Maj. S. F. (D. H. Hill's Division, Second Corps), 40

Pipe Creek, 130-31

Piper, Henry, (farm) Antietam, 56-58, 61

Pisgah Church, Va., 165, 195

Pittsylvania Battery (Penick's), 243

Po River, Va., 225, 227

Poague, Col. William T. (Artillery-Third Corps), 168, 199, 233, 243

Point Lookout Prison, Md., 154, 222, 264, 266, 284, 316

Pole Green Church, Va., 231, 233

Polk, Pvt. Wiley J., 230, 313

Pollard, Pvt. William J., 5

Pony Mountain, Va., 175

Pope, Maj. Gen. John, 41-42, 44

Porter, Brig. Gen. Fitz-John, 29-33, 35, 39

Port Royal Va., 66-68

Port Tobacco, Va., 67

Posey, Capt. Benjamin Lane (1st Alabama Inf.), 5

Posey, Brig. Gen. Carnot, 100, 105

Potomac River, 17, 42, 58, 62, 65, 124-25, 127-28, 150, 156-60, 222, 270, 272

Powell, Pt. James M., 154, 284

Powers, Pvt. John A., 9

Powhite Swamp, 35

Purifoy, Cpl. John, 2-5, 12, 22, 26, 29, 33, 38, 43, 45-47, 51-52, 66-69, 75, 82, 89, 101, 104-9, 111-12, 114, 116, 125, 129, 133, 152, 154-55, 157-59, 171, 181, 183, 186, 207, 209, 211, 214-15, 217-18, 230-31, 242, 255, 259, 261, 265, 276-77, 283, 285, 289, 297, 304, 310-13, 315

Putegnat, Pvt. John P., 266, 272-3

Q

Quarles, Pvt. Whitfield S., 9

R

Raccoon Ford, Va., 195

railroad cut, Gettysburg, 134, 136

railroads, Baltimore and Ohio Railroad, 43, 160

Erie Railroad, 272

Montgomery and West Point Railroad, 3

Orange and Alexandria Railroad, 165-66, 170

Petersburg and Weldon Railroad, 279

Piedmont Railroad, 291

Richmond and Danville Railroad, 291, 295, 297

Richmond and Fredericksburg Railroad, 228

Southside Railroad, 252, 275, 291-94, 304-5

Virginia Central Railroad, 41, 183, 187-90, 228, 242, 244, 276, 279

Weldon Railroad, 248

Williamsport and Elmira Railroad, 271

Ramseur, Maj. Gen. Stephen Dodson, 105, 218, 249, 256, 260-61

Rapidan River, Va., 99-100, 161, 163-65, 171, 175-79, 181, 183, 185-87, 191-93, 196

Rappahannock River, Va., 17-19, 66-68, 76-77, 82, 84, 95-96, 100-1, 104-5, 118-20, 124, 127, 164, 166, 170-73, 175

Rappahannock River Bridge, 171-73

Rappahannock Station, Va., 173

Reese, Capt. William J. (Jeff Davis Artillery, Carter's Battalion, Second Corps), 4-6, 9, 14, 90-93, 95, 100-1, 103, 108, 113-14, 116, 120, 122-23, 125-26, 134, 136, 140, 145-46, 148, 155, 158-60, 162, 172-73, 179, 181, 184, 186-87, 203, 205, 209-11, 213, 217, 219, 221-22, 227, 246, 266, 290, 295, 315-16

Reese's Battery (See Jeff Davis Artillery), 96, 127, 136, 138, 141, 144, 152, 155-56, 166, 222-23, 237-38, 286, 302-3, 311, 313-14, 316

Reid, Pvt. William L., 42

Reno, Maj. Gen. Jesse L., 50

Reynolds, Maj. Gen. John F., 69, 96, 101, 132

Rhett, Capt. A. Burnett (South Carolina Battery, Reserve Battalion, D. H. Hill's Division), 37

Rice's Station, Va., 299
Richardson, Maj. Gen. Israel, 54, 56-57
Richmond, Va., 6, 15-18, 20, 22-23, 28, 33, 41, 66, 78, 80, 82, 85, 98, 119, 123, 127, 154, 164, 185, 187, 189-90, 202, 227, 231, 234-36, 241-43, 248, 251, 278, 281, 288, 290, 296-97
Richmond Battery (Clutter's), 311
Richmond Howitzers (Anderson's), 185
Richmond Orange Artillery (Fry's), 83
Richmond Road, 295
Ripley, Brig. Gen. Roswell S., 31-32, 50
River Road, 295
Rockbridge Artillery (Capt. Archibald Graham's), 242-43
Rockfish Gap, Va., 253
Rodes, Maj. Gen. Robert E., 54, 56, 84, 96-97, 105-7, 109-10, 112-13, 122, 126-29, 132-37, 144-45, 167, 175-77, 204-5, 219, 234, 249-50
  Rodes' Division, 100, 103-4, 106-7, 109-11, 122, 124-30, 132, 137, 144, 155-56, 160, 165-67, 175-76, 204-5, 218, 278
Rosecrans, Maj. Gen. William S., 164
Rosser, Maj. Gen. Thomas L., 254, 257, 260, 263, 279, 292
Ryan, Pvt. Benjamin, 47

S

Sailor's Creek, Va., 302-3, 308
Salem Flying Artillery (Griffin's), 230
Sanders, Pvt. Davis M., 88
Saurine, Frank, 266
Sayler's Creek, Va., (See Sailor's Creek)
Schurz, Maj. Gen. Carl, 112
Scruggs, J. P., 267
Second Bull Run, Va., 42
Seddon, James A. (Secretary of War-C.S.A.), 284
Sedgwick, Maj. Gen. John, 54, 96, 118-19, 141, 155, 185, 196, 198, 204
Selma, Ala., 1, 2, 9, 94, 154, 238
Seminary Ridge, Gettysburg, 133, 137, 141, 149, 152
Seven Pines, Va., 22-23, 27-28, 80-82, 84, 231, 316
  battle of, 23-27
Shady Grove Church, Va., 196

Shady Grove Church Road, 205
Sharpsburg, Md., 51-53, 57-58, 62
Shenandoah River, 161, 247, 256, 263
Shenandoah Valley, Va., 28, 41, 63-65, 125, 160-61, 227, 234, 246-47, 249, 252-53, 265, 273, 276-79, 281, 292
Shepard, 1st Lt. Alexander K., 2, 5-7, 14
Shepard, Pvt. Seth, 5
Shepherdstown, W. Va., 127
Sheridan, Maj. Gen. Philip H., 234-35, 242-43, 246-47, 249-51, 253-56, 259-60, 263, 265, 276-79, 285, 292-93, 297, 301
Sherman, Maj. Gen. William T., 288, 290, 316
Shippensburg, Pa., 128
Sickles, Maj. Gen. Daniel, 96, 102, 110
Sills, Pvt. Handy, 12
Skinker's Neck, 97
Skinner, Pvt. A. W., 313
Skinner, Pvt. Ira, 16
Slocum, Maj. Gen. Henry, 95, 99
Smart, Pvt. G. F., 249
Smith, Col. Benjamin F., 172 (See Ohio troops)
Smith, Lt. Col. C. Ross (Chief of Staff, Cavalry Corps), 173
Smith, Maj. Gen. Gustavus W., 19, 26-28
Smith, Halsey, 312, 315
Smith, Pvt. James K., 32
Smith, Maj. Gen. William F., 71, 232, 235-36
Smith, Pvt. William H., 64
Smoke, Pvt. Henry, 244-45
Snediker, QM Sgt. John G., 2, 6
Snell's Bridge, Va., 225, 227
Soles, Cpl. Joseph M., 6, 15
South Mountain, Md., 44-45, 47, 50-1, 83
  battle of, 45-50
South Mountain, Pa., 152, 155
Southside, 236, 252-53, 288, 292-93
Southworth, Pvt. A. F., 159
Spangler's Mill, Cedar Creek, 263
Spinner, James, 25, 27
Spotsylvania Court House, Va., 90, 187-88, 201-5, 224, 226-28, 230, 233, 248, 264, 266, 277, 281, 284, 316
  battle of, 203-26

Sprott, Dr., 2
Stansbury Hill, Fredericksburg, 100
Staunton, Va., 64, 234, 276
Steuart, Brig. Gen. George H., 143-44,
　177, 207, 211, 213, 221
Stevensburg, Va., 175
Stewart, Pvt. William R., 264
St. John, Brig. Gen. Isaac, 299
Stoker, Pvt. Davidson, 313
Stone-House Mountain, Va., 166
Stony Creek, Va., 279
Strasburg, Va., 254, 256, 263
Stuart, Maj. Gen. James E. B. "Jeb", 12,
　44, 96, 100, 113-15, 118-19, 124, 127-
　28, 171-72, 204
Stuart, Pvt. John B., 264
Stuart, Pvt. Joseph D., 284
Stuart, Pvt. Rufus P., 244
Suffolk, Va., 98
Summerfield, Ala., 1
Summerville Ford, Va., 164
Summit Point, W. Va., 247
Sumner, Maj. Gen. Edwin V., 54, 65, 83
Sunken Road, Antietam, 54, 56-57
Susquehanna River, 128, 269, 271
Sykes, Maj. Gen. George, 168

T

Taylor, Col. Walter H., 290
Telegraph Road, 227
Templin, Pvt. William H., 39, 266, 270-1
Thomas, Brig. Gen. Edward L., 110
Thomas, 1st Lt. Hugh P., 6, 15, 76-77, 82
Thomas, Pvt. W. M., 313
Thompson, Pvt. John A., 310, 316
Thoroughfare Gap, Va., 42
Tilghman's Gate, Va., 242
Tiner, Pvt. Jefferson, 183
Toombs, Brig. Gen. Robert, 57-58
Torbert, Brig. Gen. Alfred T. A., 73, 254
Totopotomoy River, Va., 231, 233
Traweek, Pvt. Ira Y., 264
Traweek, Pvt. Washington B., 138, 266-
　67, 271-73
Traylor, Cpl. Thomas G., 6, 312
Trevilian Station, Va., 235
Tucker, Pvt. Matthew, 2, 87, 213, 313
Turkey Island House, Va., 242
Turner's Gap, Md., 44-45, 50

U

Upton, Col. Emory, 205-6
United States Armies;
　Army of the Cumberland, 164
　Army of the James, 297
　Army of the Potomac, 17, 29, 39-41,
　44, 53, 65-66, 76, 83, 127, 130, 132,
　139, 163-64, 168, 177, 185, 191-93
　Army of Virginia, 41-42, 44
U.S. Ford, Va., 97, 100, 102
United States Regulars, 5th Artillery,
　Battery I (Sykes' Division, V
　Corps), 35

V

Valley Pike, 257, 259-61, 263
Varna, N.Y., 272
Vaughan, Cpl. Fred B., 6
Verdiersville, Va., 195, 202
Virginia troops, 6th Cav. (Col. John S.
　Green, Lomax's Brigade, Fitzhugh
　Lee's Division), 271

W

Wade, Pvt. William T., 154
Wainwright, Col. Charles F. (1st N.Y. Ar-
　tillery, acting Chief of Artillery), 101
Walker, Brig. Gen. James A., 206, 211,
　298, 304
Walker, Brig. Gen. John, 53
Walker, Pvt. John V. F., 221, 225, 264
Walker, Margaret, 92
Walker, Brig. Gen. R. Lindsay, 306
Walker, 1st Lt. Robert S., 6, 13-14, 91-92,
　120, 187, 225
Walker, Pvt. W. M., 163, 230
Walker's Farm, Va., 241
Wall, Conrad, 308, 310
Walton, Col. James B. (Chief of Artillery,
　First Corps), 146
Ward, Pvt. W. F., 230, 313
Warren, Maj. Gen. Gouverneur K., 167-
　70, 185-86, 196-98, 203, 207, 220, 224,
　226-29, 248, 252, 275, 279, 285, 293
Warrenton, Va., 65-66, 166
Warrenton Junction, 166
Warrenton Pike, 6, 13

Warrenton Springs, Va., 166, 169, 171
Warwick River, 18
Washington, D.C., 41-42, 65, 127-28, 131,
    160, 170, 235, 245, 255
Watson, Pvt. J. D., 186, 264, 316
Watts, Pvt. Charles T., 5
Watts, Gov. Thomas H., 238, 241
Waynesboro, Pa., 128, 156
Waynesboro, Va., 253, 285
Webster, Pvt. T. P., 186, 230
Weed, Capt. Stephen H. (5th Artillery),
    35 (*See* United States Regulars)
West Words, Antietam, 54
Wharton, Brig. Gen. Gabriel C., 257, 260-
    61, 279
White House, Va., 30, 32
White House Landing, 235
Wigfall, Brig. Gen. Louis T., 8
Wilcox, Maj. Gen. Cadmus M., 100, 105,
    118, 145, 150, 198-99, 228-29, 294,
    296, 298-99
Wilcox County, Ala., 2
Wilderness, Va., 195-96, 201-5, 244
    battle of, 197-201
Wilderness Tavern, 196
Willcox, Brig. Gen. Orlando B., 49-50
Williamsburg, Va., 20
    Alabama Battery's withdrawal after,
    20-22
Williamsburg Road, 22-23, 25, 27-28
Williamsport, Md., 127, 156-57, 159, 270
Williamsport, Pa., 269, 271
Winchester, Va., 65-66, 125, 127, 157, 247,
    249-50, 253, 257, 272
    battle of, 249-50
Winchester Pike, 247, 270
Wise, Daniel, 46, 49-50
Wise, Brig. Gen. Henry A., 301
Woodruff, Pvt. Cicero, 184
Woodstock, Va., 265
Woodward, Pvt. Robert W., 123
Wootan, Cpl. Francis M., 5, 46, 83, 184,
    214-15, 218, 222, 308, 310-11, 313
Wright, Maj. Gen. Ambrose R. "Rans",
    97, 100, 143, 160
Wright, Pvt. Edward D., 303
Wright, Maj. Gen. Horatio G., 155, 207,
    219, 224-25, 229, 235, 254-55, 257,
    278, 297, 301

Y

Yeldell, 1st Lt. Robert A., 6, 15, 76-77, 82
Yeldell, Cpl. William A., 6, 94
York, Pa., 128-29
Yorktown, Va., 18-20
Young, Pvt. A. A., 313